D00085287

CRITICAL INSIGHTS

Flannery O'Connor

CRITICAL INSIGHTS

Flannery O'Connor

Editor
Charles E. May
California State University, Long Beach

Salem Press
Pasadena, California Hackensack, New Jersey

Cover photo: AP/Wide World Photos

∞ The paper used in these volumes conforms to the American National Standard for Permanence of Paper for Printed Library Materials, Z39.48-1992 (R1997).

Library of Congress Cataloging-in-Publication Data

Flannery O'Connor / editor, Charles E. May.
p. cm. — (Critical insights)
Includes bibliographical references and index.
ISBN 978-1-58765-831-0 (alk. paper)
1. O'Connor, Flannery—Criticism and interpretation. 2. Women and literature—Southern States—History—20th century. I. May, Charles E. (Charles Edward), 1941-
PS3565.C57Z667845 2012
813'.54—dc22

2011019111

PRINTED IN CANADA

Contents

Career, Life, and Influence

Critical Contexts

Critical Readings

Resources

About This Volume

Charles E. May

The fiction of Flannery O'Connor has always posed unique challenges to modern readers. Her narrative style is symbolically unrealistic, her characters confront complex religious trials beyond their understanding, and her themes are often dependent on paradoxical concepts of Christian theology.

O'Connor knew from the beginning of her career that both her method and her message would be bewildering to many readers. When editor John Selby, expecting a traditional novel, balked at the manuscript of *Wise Blood*, O'Connor, convinced that the quality of her fiction would derive precisely from the peculiarities to which he objected, cancelled her contract, declaring that she had no intention of writing a conventional novel.

Several years later, fully aware that she was often trying to communicate with many who did not share her religious beliefs, O'Connor justified her shocking characters and their outrageous actions by insisting that, to the hard of hearing, one had to shout, and to the almost blind, one had to draw "large and startling figures." She made no apologies that the subject of her fiction was always "the action of grace in territory largely held by the devil."

As a result of her tenacious adherence to an unfamiliar narrative genre and an esoteric complex of theological themes, few twentieth-century fiction writers seem more in need of interpretation and analysis than Flannery O'Connor. And indeed, as Irwin H. Streight's comprehensive survey amply shows, the critics have responded to the challenge of O'Connor in staggering numbers. Outlining the dichotomy of O'Connor critics as between co-religionists who have the ears to hear and eyes to see the "intrusion of grace" in her stories and skeptics who think her fictional world is brutal and grotesque, Streight provides a comprehensive overview of critics who have analyzed her Southern regional roots, her use of the tradition of the grotesque, and her philosophic and literary sources, as well as summarizing such contemporary critical approaches to her work as postmodern critical theory, psychoanalysis, and feminism.

This volume is an effort to introduce O'Connor to a new generation of readers by including twelve previously published essays that clarify her religious ideas, her narrative technique, her use of humor, and the regional and social context of her fiction, and five original essays commissioned especially for this volume that make significant new contributions to the understanding and appreciation of her work.

The Religious Context

The religious issue is always first in any consideration of O'Connor, for religion was foremost in her own mind as she wrote. In his essay "Flannery O'Connor and the Art of the Holy," Arthur F. Kinney establishes the basic dichotomy in O'Connor's fiction between what Mircea Eliade calls the "sacred and the profane." He clarifies O'Connor's central articulation of her subject—"the action of grace in territory largely held by the devil"—and explains why she felt she had to use shock and awe to make this vision apparent to her readers. Tracing her literary and theological sources to Poe, Hawthorne, Conrad, Aquinas, Augustine, and Teilhard de Chardin, Kinney cites examples in O'Connor's fiction of the embodiment of the "holy" and the violent "leap of grace," explaining how O'Connor is an "incarnational writer," who constantly transforms the ordinary world into something sacred.

T. W. Hendricks discusses O'Connor's most famous and most disturbing story, "A Good Man Is Hard to Find," from a Catholic point of view in order to make clear exactly what constitutes the "duel" between the Misfit and the Grandmother at the conclusion of the story. Hendricks delineates the story's characters and defends the Misfit's role as a prophet critical of the fallen secular society represented by Bailey, his wife, and his two children. In answer to the nagging question, why the Misfit kills the grandmother when she calls him one of her children, Hendricks cites the central Catholic concept that grace must originate in the common and material. Although the Misfit may be right to reject the grandmother's notion that one can be saved by good family, good manners, and respect for one's heritage, he is mistaken when he fails to understand that grace can come from the touch and sympathetic identification of a misguided old woman.

John Desmond's explanation for the shocking conclusion of "A Good Man is Hard to Find" focuses on the Misfit's sense of the mystery of evil, arguing that the Misfit's flaw is that he cannot admit the need for a power beyond logic and human justice, the power that O'Connor calls divine grace. The Misfit, says Desmond, knows that good actions and behavior are not enough for salvation, but resents the doctrine of the resurrection because it undermines the code of logic and human behavior he wishes to affirm. Desmond explains the controversial final scene in the story by arguing that the Misfit is determined to hold on to his isolated role as a misfit, for without it he must admit his error and failure. When the grandmother reaches out to touch him, he recoils because he recognizes it as the touch of sympathy for his suffering.

Henry T. Edmondson III uses O'Connor's second most famous story, "Good Country People," to clarify her objections to rationalism. He suggests that O'Connor's conviction that this story would not rouse the religious reader but rather the rationalists means that the story is central to understanding her quarrel with rationalism and her warnings against the dangers of nihilism. Joy/Hulga thinks she is a true believer in rationalism and thus nihilism, but her belief is merely academic. It is only when she encounters someone whose nihilism is an intrinsic part of his life that she realizes she is but a naïve child who has not foreseen the implications of nihilism. Central to Edmondson's analysis is O'Connor's conviction that Cartesian rationalism oversimplifies the complex reality of the human soul's longing and thus drains the mystery out of life.

Flannery O'Connor has been compared to many other American

writers, from Nathanael West to Cormac McCarthy. However, as unlikely as the surface comparison may seem, perhaps no other writer matches her for exploring issues of Christian faith and life than John Updike. As Avis Hewitt makes clear, if Flannery O'Connor is the American Catholic novelist par excellence, then John Updike is the classic American Protestant novelist. Regardless of their doctrinal differences, Hewitt illustrates how both O'Connor and Updike are profoundly interested in the spiritual poverty of their characters. Both, she argues, know that good deeds and tenderness are not enough to stand up to evil and horror, for both know that Christian belief is more powerful than conventional morality.

The Comic Context

For many readers, one of the most puzzling of O'Connor's techniques is her humor, which is often thought to be inappropriate, or at least incompatible, with her religious ideas and the violence in her stories. J. P. Steed argues that Henri Bergson's theories of humor help us understand how the three elements of violence, religion, and humor blend so effectively in O'Connor's fiction by showing how laughter serves a corrective social function. Steed explains how O'Connor's humor supports her primary purpose to be persuasive about her religious convictions. The inflexibility of her characters is their most crucial flaw, for Christian redemption can only occur with a change of heart, and change can only occur within a flexible process of becoming.

In her essay on O'Connor's "Temple of the Holy Ghost," Denise T. Askin clarifies what several other critics have noted about the relationship between O'Connor's comic vision and Mikhail Bakhtin's theory of the Carnivalesque and the Dialogic. Arguing that "Temple of the Holy Ghost" is a portrait of the Catholic comedic artist as a young Carnivalesque, Askin claims the story is O'Connor's own sly endorsement of herself as an artist whose vocation is based on the "inherent connection between the comic and the holy, between the carnival and the temple." By placing O'Connor in the medieval carnival tradition, Askin shows how the action in "Temple of the Holy Ghost" echoes the medieval "Feast of Fools." Pointing out the similarity between Bakhtin's distrust of the monologic as a leap over concrete reality and O'Connor's Catholic conviction that the spiritual can only be reached through the concrete and the profane, Askin persuasively reads "Temple of the Holy Ghost" as a validation of O'Connor's "comic/satiric voice and vocation."

The Social Context

As John Hayes points out, in addition to some understanding of the religious context out of which Flannery O'Connor wrote, some knowledge of the social context is also essential to fully appreciate and understand her fiction. O'Connor's life as a Catholic intellectual in Southern Bible Belt Protestantism makes it necessary, as Hayes claims, to be familiar with the well defined color lines and class lines of O'Connor's childhood, as well as the transformations that took place in the South during her adulthood. Although O'Connor was staunchly Catholic, many of her characters spring from the various forms of Protestantism, as Hayes outlines, from the religion of the propertied class to the folk religion of the lower class, both black and white.

Peter A. Smith's essay on O'Connor's "empowered women" also makes an important contribution to understanding the social world of her fiction by defining her female characters squarely within Southern society, arguing that O'Connor's women devise strategies by which they can survive in what is essentially a man's world. Analyzing the motivation and behavior of Mrs. Cope in "The Circle in the Fire," Mrs. McIntyre in "The Displaced Person," Mrs. Turpin in "Revelation," Mrs. Hopewell in "Good Country People," and Mrs. May in "Greenleaf," Smith accounts for both the successes and the failures of these women within the context of the rigid social world and class distinctions of the American South.

In her final volume of short stories, *Everything That Rises Must Converge*, as Bryant N. Wyatt makes clear, O'Connor focuses more on social reality and domestic relations than ever before, often subsuming the religious themes that overpowered family relations in her first collection. Analyzing the relationships within families in all the stories in O'Connor's final collection, Wyatt provides a balance to discussion of her religious themes. However, he is quick to warn readers that in spite of the fact that O'Connor's final stories are more oriented toward the social than her earlier ones, the domestic themes in these stories serve as a catalyst for her religious concerns. The predominant use of realism and social class-consciousness "minimizes starkly moral concerns" in these stories, says Wyatt, and renders the spiritual in a domestic context.

Richard Giannone, who has written two well-respected books on O'Connor, issues a similar warning by tackling the issue of social significance in the O'Connor story most likely to inspire such a reading, "The Artificial Nigger." O'Connor was never reluctant to voice her disdain for stories that espoused social messages, he reminds us. In 1963, she wrote in a letter that the "topical" was poison to her and that she was not interested in writing about the "race business." Giannone says if we are looking for a political interpretation to "The Artificial nigger," then we will be frustrated, and we will miss the story's depth, which has its source in Dante. Old Mr. Head passes through the hell of Atlanta, the purgatorial fire of his encounter with the lawn statue and his denial of his grandson to an acknowledgement of original sin in the Garden and hope of redemption in Gethsemane.

The Genre Context

Ronald Emerick's essay makes clear why one cannot read O'Connor's *Wise Blood* as a conventional realistic novel but must approach it as a symbolic romance. Emerick lays out the characteristics of the romance form as Hawthorne defined them in his critical prefaces, clarifying how Hawthorne and O'Connor saw the romance form as a genre that deals with the borderland between the natural and the supernatural. Important to both Hawthorne and O'Connor is the fact that their characters' obsession or monomania transforms them into allegorical figures. If Haze Motes in *Wise Blood* is not understood as symbolic of his spiritual quest, and if Enoch Emery is not understood as a comically grotesque result of his own compulsions, then they cannot be understood at all.

In my own discussion of the question as to why Flannery O'Connor abjured the conventional realistic novel for the symbolic short story and novella, I try to show that O'Connor was well aware that, given her allegorical and anagogical vision, short fiction was, by its traditional origins in the romance and its generic characteristics as a poetic form, more apt to fulfill her thematic and narrative needs than the novel. Building on a theory of short fiction that derives from the theories of philosophical anthropologists Ernst Cassirer and Mircea Eliade about the distinction between the everyday and the mythical, the profane and the sacred, I try to illustrate that the short story was the inevitable form to which O'Connor would devote her creative life.

Marie Lienard argues that O'Connor chose the short story because of its origin in the parable form, which lends itself to anagogic interpretation that perceives different levels of reality in a single image or situation, and because its usual movement is toward a revelation or epiphany. Focusing on the titles of O'Connor's two short-story collections, *A Good Man is Hard to Find, and Other Stories* and *Everything that Rises Must Converge*, as well as the most famous stories from each, Lienard says O'Connor uses titles as clues to understanding the movement from the literal (manners) to the figurative (mystery).

Christina Bieber Lake's essay on *The Violent Bear It Away* shows how O'Connor's final novel moves from Hawthorne's nineteenth-century romance form to a modernist self-reflexive romance by revealing the relationship between the role of the prophet and the role of the artist. Reminding us that O'Connor's vision is a poetic, symbolic one, not a realistic depiction of ordinary reality, Lake shows how Mason Tarwater is an image of the prophet artist, Rayber a representation of the modern rationalist, and the child Bishop a symbol of the work of art itself. In her efforts to use fiction as a means by which one penetrates into the heart of mystery, as Conrad and Hawthorne did before her, O'Connor scorned the modern fiction writer's insistence on realism and avoidance of mystery.

In her essay on O'Connor and the "Art of Story," Susan Srigley places O'Connor solidly within a storytelling tradition as old as the Old Testament. By looking at how three different O'Connor stories—"Parker's Back," "Revelation," and "Greenleaf"—owe much of their power and significance to allusions to the Bible, works of literature, and theological ideas, Srigley builds on O'Connor's conviction of the relationship between religion and literature and shows how the interpretative process is part of the reader's overall experience of her stories. Asserting a dictum that O'Connor and many other modern writers would accept—that stories come from stories—Srigley shows how ancient texts, the fiction of other writers, and theological ideas from religious writers provide important sources to allow O'Connor to bring to life complex human questions.

Post Scriptum

Flannery O'Connor's career as a writer lasted only twelve years. As Paul Elie points out, although she only published two short novels, two dozen short stories, ten essays, and several hundred letters, this small corpus is "as distinctive a body of work as any in modern writing. . . . It is work that demands our full attention but eludes our full understanding." The 2009 MLA International Bibliography lists Flannery O'Connor as the subject of 1,427 entries of critical books and articles. In 2009, more than ten thousand people cast ballots for what they considered to be the best book of fiction among all the National Book Award winners in its history. Flannery O'Connor's *Complete Stories* was the winner. Although these numbers do not speak louder than words, especially the words of Flannery O'Connor, they would surely make that wise and wonderful writer shake her head in wry amusement.

CAREER, LIFE, AND INFLUENCE

On Flannery O'Connor and the Short Story/Romance Tradition

Charles E. May

In 2009, the judges of the National Book Award chose a shortlist of six books as the best of the seventy-seven winners in the fiction category since the beginning of the award in 1950. For the first time in its history, the NBA then polled the public to vote for the one book as the "Best of the National Book Awards in Fiction." More than ten thousand people cast ballots. What was surprising—given the fact that novels sell better than short story collections—was that four of the six books—*The Stories of John Cheever*, *Eudora Welty's Collected Stories, Collected Stories of William Faulkner*, and *The Complete Stories of Flannery O'Connor*—were short story collections. The only two novels to make the shortlist were Ralph Ellison's *Invisible Man* and Thomas Pynchon's *Gravity's Rainbow.* It is a remarkable testimony to the public's abiding admiration and enthusiasm for Flannery O'Connor, who wrote nothing but short fiction—publishing two short story collections and two short novels in a relatively short career—that her *Complete Stories* was chosen as the Best of the Best.

Although the public was puzzled when O'Connor's first book, *Wise Blood*, appeared in 1952 and shocked when her second, *A Good Man Is Hard to Find, and Other Stories*, was published in 1955, academic critics embraced her work immediately—in spite of the fact that she specialized in short fiction rather than the more academically respectable novel. In his introduction to the first of many collections of critical responses to her work, Melvin Friedman noted what many other critics have said since: O'Connor is "essentially a story writer who twice strayed into the novel form," adding that even when she was providing an installment from a novel in progress, "the pieces fall neatly into place as they do in the well-made short story" (Friedman 14). Regardless of this early recognition that short fiction was O'Connor's forte, and despite the fact that thousands of pages have been written analyzing her religion and explicating her stories from many different critical perspectives, no one has examined the correlation between her narrative method and view of reality and the short story as a literary genre. This essay is an attempt to provide an historical and theoretical context for O'Connor's short fiction to explain why the short story was the inevitable form to which she devoted her literary career.

From the very beginning of her writing life, O'Connor faced misunderstandings about the short fiction genre within which she had chosen to work. After reading nine chapters of her first book, *Wise Blood*, John Selby, an editor at Holt Rinehart, expecting a traditional novel, was baffled by the kind of story O'Connor had sent him and requested many changes. Committed to her narrative vision, O'Connor asked for a release from her contract, making it clear that Selby obviously did not understand the tradition within which she was writing: "I feel that whatever virtues the novel may have are very much connected with the limitations you mention. I am not writing a conventional novel, and I think that the quality of the novel I write will derive precisely from the peculiarity or aloneness, if you will, of the experience I write from" (*HB* 10). Indeed, neither of O'Connor's two long stories, *Wise Blood* and*The Violent Bear It Away*, are, as she well knew, conventional novels, but rather novellas, in the tradition of Herman Melville's *Billy Budd*, Joseph Conrad's *Heart of Darkness*, and Thomas Mann's *Death in Venice*. In a description O'Connor would have recognized as applicable to her two longer works, Howard Nemerov has argued that the short novel, like the short story, has a symbolic structure of constellation and patterning, fashioned like a musical composition with clusters of imagery. The form has an analogical style of composition, says Nemerov, and is often a philosophic parable or myth, a sacred book of a "symbolic universe of whose truth we can be persuaded only by fictions" (235).

Although O'Connor struggled with her two short novels and was never quite satisfied with them, spending five difficult years on *Wise Blood* and referring to *The Violent Bear It Away* as her "Opus Nauseous" (*HB* 284), she was inordinately fond of many of her short stories. Just before *A Good Man Is Hard to Find, and Other Stories* came out in 1955, she wrote Ben Griffith that there was one long story in the collection ("The Displaced Person") that she wanted him to see, and another called "Good Country People" that pleased her to "no end." "You will observe," she said, "that I admire my own work as much if not more than anybody else does. I have read 'The Artificial Nigger' several times since it was printed, enjoying it each time as if I had nothing to do with it" (*HB* 78). At about the same time, she told Robie Macauley that she liked her stories "better than anybody. I read them over and over and laugh and laugh, then get embarrassed when I remember I was the one wrote them" (*HB* 81). However, when she was working on *The Violent Bear It Away*, she wrote J. F. Powers that she was writing herself "ragged on a novel that died a natural death after the first chapter when it ceased to be a short story" (*HB* 185).

O'Connor always liked short stories. The author she cites as the earliest influence on her desire to write was the first theorist and self-conscious practitioner of the form in America, Edgar Allan Poe. In a letter to Betty Hester in 1955, she said that as a child she read a lot of slop, but following the "Slop Period" was the Edgar Allan Poe period, which lasted for years (*HB* 98). Later in her career, however, she recognized that her true precursor was Nathaniel Hawthorne. In 1961, she told John Hawkes, "I think I would admit to writing what Hawthorne called 'romances'. . . . Hawthorne interests me considerably. I feel more of a kinship with him than with any other American" (*HB* 457). In her essays and talks, her many reviews, and her letters, O'Connor often affirmed her commitment to the short story and to the romance form out of which it developed and with which it has always been aligned. She knew that the style and narrative technique demanded by the short story was quite different than that expected in the novel. She once said, "I believe that it takes a rather different type of disposition to write novels than to write short stories, granted that both require fundamentally fictional talents" (*MM* 76). In a good short story, she argued, "certain of the details will tend to accumulate meaning from the story itself, and when this happens, they become symbolic in their action." (*MM* 70) In response to the question, "What is a short story?" she insisted that it is not a joke, an anecdote, a lyrical rhapsody in prose, a case history, or a reported incident, for it has an "extra dimension" that occurs when the writer puts us in the middle of some "human action and shows it as it is illuminated and outlined by mystery." In every story, O'Connor insisted, there is some "minor revelation which, no matter how funny the story may be, gives us a hint of the unknown, of death" (*Symposium* 18).

In 1960, O'Connor wrote Betty Hester that she had come upon the 1957 book by Richard Chase, *The American Novel and Its Tradition*, which reaffirmed her conviction that she was writing in the tradition of the romance. By contrast to the novel, which Chase noted renders reality closely and in comprehensive detail, the romance "feels free to render reality in less volume and detail. It tends to prefer action to character, and action will be freer in a romance than in a novel, encountering, as it were less resistance from reality" (13). Noting that characters in the romance may not be complexly related to society or the past and that when they are involved the involvement is deep, narrow, and obsessive, Chase argued that the romance, more freely than the novel, veers toward "mythic, allegorical, and symbolistic forms" (13). O'Connor was aware of Hawthorne's famous description of the realm of romance in the Custom House Sketch of *The Scarlet Letter*: Describing how objects in a room become spiritualized by the imagination even as they remain concrete, Hawthorne notes how ordinary objects can become "invested with a quality of strangeness and remoteness, though still almost as vividly present as by daylight," making a familiar room "a neutral territory, somewhere between the real world and fairy-land, where the Actual and Imaginary may meet, and each imbue itself with the nature of the other." This transformation of the trivial has often been remarked by short story writers. Raymond Carver once said: "It's possible in a . . . short story to write about commonplace things and objects using commonplace but precise language, and to endow those things—a chair, a window curtain, a fork, a stone, a woman's earring—with immense, even startling power" (15). Similarly, O'Connor argued that "the peculiar problem of the short-story writer is how to make the action he describes reveal as much of the mystery of existence as possible. . . . [H]is problem is really how to make the concrete work double time for him" (*MM* 98).

In a review of William Lynch's *Christ and Apollo* (1960), O'Connor made clear that this process of the actual becoming the symbolic is best exemplified in medieval scriptural exegesis, in which three kinds of meaning were found in the literal level of the sacred text: "the moral, the allegorical, and the anagogical. This is the Catholic way of reading nature as well as scripture, and it is a way which leaves open the most possibilities to be found in the actual" (*Presence of Grace* 4) This is the kind of vision, she said, by which the artist is able to see different levels of reality in one image or situation" (*MM* 72). In a letter to Betty Hester in 1956, she tried to explain that her commitment to the concrete world had a moral basis:

> I suppose when I say that the moral basis of Poetry is the accurate naming of the things of God, I mean about the same thing that Conrad meant when he said that his aim as an artist was to render the highest possible justice to the visible universe. For me the visible universe is a reflection of the invisible universe. (*HB* 128)

Erich Auerbach's famous distinction between the Hebraic and Homeric narrative styles reflects the basic difference O'Connor perceived between the short story/romance tradition within which she was working and the conventional novel tradition. The Homeric, Auerbach notes, presents "externalized, uniformly illuminated phenomena, at a definite time and place, connected together without lacunae in a perpetual foreground." The Hebraic, on the other hand, he says, externalizes only so much of the "phenomena as is necessary for the narrative, all else left in obscurity." Both time and place in the Hebraic style, argues Auerbach, are undefined and call for interpretation. Moreover, thoughts and feeling remain unexpressed, and are only "suggested by the silence and the fragmentary speeches; the whole, permeated with the most unrelieved suspense and directed toward a single goal (and to that extent far more of a unity), remains mysterious and 'fraught with background'" (11-12). O'Connor would surely have agreed that the Homeric style has given rise to the novel, while the Hebraic has primarily influenced the romance form and the short story. She would also probably have agreed with Northrop Frye that the romance is the "structural core of all fiction; being directly descended from folktales, it brings us closer than any other aspect of literature to the sense of fiction, considered as a whole, as the epic of the creature, man's vision of his own life as a quest" (15).

Writers have always acknowledged this connection between the short story and the romance. For example, in the middle of the famous battle between the Howells school of realism and the proponents of romance during the latter half of the nineteenth century in America, Ambrose Bierce, linking the romance with the short story form for which he was famous, says that the capable writer does not give probability a moment's attention, except to make the fiction seem probable or true in the reading process. Nothing is as improbable as what is true, says Bierce; the unexpected does occur, "but that is not saying enough; it is also the unlikely—one might almost say the impossible (246). Similarly, Flannery O'Connor says, "Much of my fiction takes its character from a reasonable use of the unreasonable, though the reasonableness of my use may not always be apparent" (*MM* 109). She argued that the writer in the romance tradition makes "alive some experience which we are not accustomed to observe everyday or which the ordinary man may never experience in his ordinary life" (*MM* 40). She recognized that although the characters in the romance may not demonstrate a coherence to their social framework, they have an inner coherence. "Their fictional qualities lean away from typical social patterns, towards mystery and the unexpected" (*MM* 40).

O'Connor was also aware of the short story/romance tradition's focus on seemingly unmotivated behavior, claiming that a short story always involves, in a dramatic way, the "mystery of personality." She relates an anecdote about lending some stories to a woman who lived down the road from her. When the woman returned the book, she said, "Well, them stories just gone and shown you how some folks *would* do" (*MM* 90). O'Connor reports that she thought to herself that that was right; "when you write stories, you have to be content to start exactly there—showing how some specific folks *will* do, *will* do in spite of everything" (*MM* 90). The short story's focus on mysteriously motivated behavior is at least as old as Poe's exploration of the perverse. Whereas the novel may focus on cause and effect in time, the short story accepts the fact that what makes characters behave the way they do is not so simple. For example, Peter Bitsilli says the complexity of Chekhov's characters leads us to feel there is something about them we do not understand, a something hidden from us, a something that is part of Chekhov's appeal (125). According to Ambrose Bierce, the problem with realistic novelists is:

> It is not known to them that all men and women sometimes, many men and women frequently, and some men and women habitually, act from impenetrable motives and in a way that is consonant with nothing in their lives, characters and conditions. (243-44)

Mary Rohrberger, a well-known short story theorist, has made the most emphatic statement about the relationship between the romance and the short story as a genre, arguing, in terms with which O'Connor would have surely agreed, that the metaphysical view that there is more to the world than that which can be apprehended through the senses provides the rationale for the short story.

> As in the metaphysical view, reality lies beyond the ordinary world of appearances, so in the short story, meaning lies beneath the surface of the narrative. The framework of the narrative embodies symbols which function to question the world of appearances and to point to a reality beyond the facts of the extensional world. (141)

Flannery O'Connor objected to the novelistic orthodoxy that demanded "a realism of fact," which she felt was limiting. She also objected to the novelistic insistence that fiction deal with the "movement of social forces" and with the "typical," with fidelity to the way things look and happen in "normal times" (*MM* 38-39). This recognition of short fiction's detachment from a social context dates back to Friedrich von Schlegel's 1801 characterization of short fiction as a story striking enough to arouse interest in and of itself, without regard to any connection with society, the times, or culture (7). Short fiction's disengagement from a contemporary cultural background has, much to the chagrin of social critics, always been a perceived characteristic of the form. Frank O'Connor has famously argued: "The novel can still adhere to the classical concept of civilized society, of man as an animal who lives in a community . . . but the short story remains by its very nature remote from the community—romantic, individualistic, and intransigent" (21). The short story's refusal to embrace the limiting realism of fact associated with social forces has also been emphasized by Terry Eagleton, who has noted that whereas realism, the most common modal perspective of the novel, is primarily a form concerned to "map the causal processes underlying events and resolve them into some intelligible pattern, the short story, by contrast, can yield us some single bizarre occurrence of epiphany of terror whose impact would merely be blunted by lengthy realist elaboration." As Eagleton suggests, "since realism is a chronically naturalizing mode, it is hard for it to cope with the ineffable or unfathomable, given those built-in mechanisms which offer to transmute all of this into the assuringly familiar" (150).

Flannery O'Connor declared her commitment to a kind of "realism" with qualities that "lean away from typical social patterns, toward mystery and the unexpected," focusing on "experiences which we are not accustomed to observe every day, or which the ordinary man may never experience in his ordinary life" (*MM* 40-41). The kind of fiction O'Connor admired, while it did not slight the concrete, is interested in the surface only so far as it can be gone through into an experience of mystery itself. For her, the meaning of a story did not begin except at "a depth where adequate motivation and adequate psychology and the various determinations have been exhausted" (*MM* 41). Some of the most important critics of the twentieth century have suggested that the short story as a genre has always focused on the kind of experience that O'Connor felt most drawn to in her fiction. For example, Georg Lukács has said that the short story has always been concerned with the strangeness and ambiguity of life, "concealing its lyricism behind the hard outlines of the event" (52-53).

The short story has been, from its beginnings, primarily a literary mode that has remained closest to the primal narrative form that embodies and recapitulates mythic perception and thought as Ernst Cassirer and others have described it. Cassirer says that when one is under the spell of mythic thinking, it is as though the whole world were simply annihilated; the immediate content, whatever it be, that commands one's "religious interest so completely fills his consciousness that nothing else can exist beside and apart from it." The characteristic of such an experience, says Cassirer, is not expansion, but an impulse toward concentration; "instead of extensive distribution, intensive compression. This focusing of all forces on a single point is the prerequisite for all mythical thinking and mythical formulation" (32). The short story form manifests this impulse toward compression and demands this intense focusing for the totality of the narrative experience primarily because it takes for its essential subject the mysterious and dreamlike manifestation of what Cassirer calls the "momentary deity," which, Cassirer says, "is something purely instantaneous, a fleeting, emerging, and vanishing mental content. . . . Every impression that man receives, every wish that stirs in him, every hope that lures him, every danger that threatens him can affect him thus religiously" (18).

C. S. Lewis once lamented that the problem for the storywriter was that "In real life, as in a story, something must happen. That is just the trouble. We grasp at a state and find only a succession of events in which the state is never quite embodied" (91). For Lewis, life and art reflect each other, in that both embody the tension between our desire for a state and our despair of ever catching that state in our everyday net of time and event. This definition of a tension-filled life and art is of course a religious one, regardless of whether we use William James's basic definition of the religious impulse as stemming from a feeling that there is something wrong about us as we naturally stand (*Varieties of Religious Experience*), or Mircea Eliade's definition of *homo religiosus* as one whose desire is to live in the sacred represents the desire to live in objective reality (*The Sacred and the Profane*).

The important distinction that O'Connor felt must be made is between narratives that strive to make the realm of value seem temporal and graspable by experience and reason and narratives that strive to transform the temporal into the spiritual. The first requires development in the temporal sense, a slow process of "as if" lived experience in a world of objects, social relationships, and conceptual frameworks. The second, on the other hand, requires only the moment, an instantaneous single experience that in its immediacy challenges social and conceptual frameworks. Outside the stories of Flannery O'Connor, the most emphatic and succinct statement and illustration of how story escapes the naked worm of time can be found in Isak Dinesen's story "The First Cardinal's Tale." In telling his female penitent a story to answer her question, "Who are You?" Cardinal Salviati explains to her how the story has answered her question. "Stories," the Cardinal says, "have been told as long as speech has existed, and *sans* stories the human race would have perished, as it would have perished *sans* water." The new novelistic "literature of the individual" is a noble art, says the

Cardinal, but it is only a human product. "The divine art is the story. In the beginning was the story," concluding that those "who hold our high office as keepers and watchmen to the story, may tell you, verily, that to its human characters there is salvation in nothing else in the universe. . . . For within our whole universe the story only has authority to answer that cry of heart of its characters, that one cry of heart of each of them: 'Who am I?'" (26)

Neither short fiction in general nor Flannery O'Connor's short fiction in particular, focuses on time in the profane sense as the novel does; rather it focuses on that very tension between the profane and the sacred wherein the world is hierophantically transformed; it does so not by focusing on characters "as if" they existed in the real world but by transforming them into functions of the primitive and recurring fable itself. Thus, in the short story, the formal demands of the tale outweigh the realistic demands of verisimilitude, both because the story's shortness requires an aesthetic rather than a natural form, and because the short story remains closer to its ancestry in myth and folklore than the novel does. In the short story, a fictional character may seem to act according to the conventions of verisimilitude and plausibility. However, since the very shortness of the form prohibits the realistic presentation of character by extensive detail, and since the history of the short story is one in which a character suddenly confronts a crucial event or crisis rather than slowly developing over time, the very form and tradition of short fiction militates against the central conventions of realism.

As Flannery O'Connor says, the problem of the short-story writer is how to make the action he or she describes "reveal as much of the mystery of existence as possible" (*MM* 98). If the mystery is solved by placing the phenomenon described within the framework of the natural, the psychological, or the social, then the Homeric or realistic impulse has succeeded. If the knowledge arrived at is inchoate, metaphysical, inexplicable, then we know we arc in the revelatory Hebraic realm of the short story. There is a different "rhythm of reality" and a different "realm of reality" embodied in the short story than in the novel form, a realm from which shines that mysterious radiance Eudora Welty refers to when she says the first thing you notice about a story is that you "can't really see the solid outlines of it—it seems bathed in something of its own. It is wrapped in an atmosphere. This is what makes it shine, perhaps, as well as what initially obscures its plain, real shape" (163). For Conrad's Marlowe, sitting Buddha-like on the deck telling the story of Kurtz, the "meaning of an episode was not inside like a kernel but outside, enveloping the tale which brought it out only as a glow brings out a haze, in the likeness of one of those misty halos that, sometimes, are made visible by the spectral illumination of moonshine" (9). O'Connor, who admired the work of Conrad, knew that "The type of mind that can understand good fiction is not necessarily the educated mind, but it is at all times the kind of mind that is willing to have its sense of reality deepened by contact with mystery. Fiction should be both canny and uncanny" (*MM* 79).

Flannery O'Connor knew that there are two basic modes of experience in prose fiction: one that involves the development and acceptance of the everyday world of phenomenon, sensate, and logical relation—a realm that the novel has always taken for its own—and the other that involves an experience that challenge the acceptance of the real world as simply sensate and reasonable—an experience that has dominated the short story since its beginnings. The novel involves an active quest for reality, a search for identity that is actually a reconciliation of the self with the social and experiential world—a reconciliation that is finally conceptually accepted, based on the experience one has undergone. The short story in general, and Flannery O'Connor's short stories in particular, more often focus on a character who is confronted with the world of spirit, which then challenges his or her conceptual framework of reason and social experience.

As Flannery O'Connor knew well, the short story has always remained close to the folk tale, the ballad, the romance, and the mythic forms that constitute the very source of narrative. If the novel creates the illusion of reality by presenting a literal authenticity to the material world, then the short story creates a similitude of a different realm of reality, that reality of the sacred which Mircea Eliade says primitive man saw as true reality. Flannery O'Connor's short stories attempt to be authentic to the immaterial reality of the inner world of the self in its relation to eternal rather than temporal reality. The short story form is, as Flannery O'Connor knew throughout her short life, closer to the nature of "reality" as we experience it in those moments when we are made aware of the inauthenticity of the everyday life, those moments when we sense the inadequacy of our ordinary categories of perception.

Given the brevity of her career and the small amount of work she produced, Flannery O'Connor's significant position in twentieth-century literature is extraordinary. Beloved by popular readers, revered by academic critics, and honored by her fellow authors, she ranks near the top of the most important modern fiction writers. In addition to the spiritual vision and scrupulous style that characterizes her individual talent, her success is also due to her devotion to the narrative tradition she chose early and maintained throughout her life. Although friends, editors, and critics urged her to write more conventional realistic novels, she stayed true to the symbolic romance form that has always aligned itself with short fiction. The thousands of readers who voted her *Complete Stories* the "Best of the Best" of the National Book Awards are glad she did.

Works Cited

Auerbach, Erich. *Mimesis*. Princeton, NJ: Princeton UP, 1953.

Bierce, Ambrose. "The Short Story." *The Collected Works of Ambrose Bierce*. Vol. X. 1911. New York: Gordian Press, 1966. 234-48.

Carver, Raymond, "On Writing." *Fires*. New York: Vintage, 1983.

Cassirer, Ernst. *Language and Myth*. Trans. Susanne K. Langer. New York: Dover, 1946.

Chase, Richard. *The American Novel and its Tradition*. New York: Vintage, 1957.

Conrad, Joseph. *Heart of Darkness*. 3d ed. New York: W. W. Norton, 1963.

Dinesen, Isak. "The Cardinal's First Tale." *Last Tales*. New York: Random House, 1957. 3-27.

Eagleton, Terry. *Heathcliff and the Great Hunger: Studies in Irish Culture*. London: Verso, 1995.

Eliade, Mircea. *The Sacred and the Profane*. Trans. Willard R. Trask. New York: Harper & Row, 1961.

Friedman, Melvin J., and Beverly Lyon Clark, eds. *Critical Essays on Flannery O'Connor*. Boston: G. K. Hall, 1985.

Frye, Northrop. *The Secular Scripture: A Study of the Structure of Romance*. Cambridge, MA: Harvard UP, 1976.

Lewis, C. S. *Essays Presented to Charles Williams*. Grand Rapids, MI.: William B. Eerdmans, 1966. 90-105.

Lukács, Georg. *The Theory of the Novel*. Trans. Anna Bostock. Cambridge, MA: MIT Press, 1971.

Nemerov, Howard. "Composition and Fate In the Short Novel." *The Graduate Journal* 5.2 (Fall 1963).

O'Connor, Flannery. *The Habit of Being: Letters of Flannery O'Connor*. Ed. Sally Fitzgerald. New York: Farrar, Straus and Giroux, 1979. (Cited in text as *HB*).

____________. *Mystery and Manners: Occasional Prose*. Eds. Sally and Robert Fitzgerald. New York: Farrar, Straus and Giroux, 1961. (Cited in text as *MM*).

____________. *The Presence of Grace and Other Book Reviews by Flannery O'Connor*. Comp. Leo J. Zuber. Ed. Carter W. Martin. Athens: U of Georgia P, 1983.

O'Connor, Frank. *The Lonely Voice: A Study of the Short Story*. Cleveland, OH: World, 1963.

Rohrberger, Mary. *Hawthorne and the Modern Short Story: A Study in Genre*. The Hague, Netherlands: Mouton and Co., 1966.

Schlegel, Friedrich von. *Nachrichten von den poetischen Werken des G. Boccaccio*, 1801. Cited by E. K. Bennett. *A History of the German Novelle*. Revised by H. M. Waidson. New York: Cambridge UP, 1965.

"Symposium on the Short Story." *Conversations with Flannery O'Connor*. Ed. Rosemary M. Magee. Jackson: UP of Mississippi, 1987.

Welty, Eudora. "The Reading and Writing of Short Stories." *Short Story Theories*. Ed. Charles E. May. Athens: Ohio UP, 1976, pp. 159-77.

Biography of Flannery O'Connor

Charles E. May

Two of the most important influences on Flannery O'Connor's life and art were passed on to her at birth. First, although the lupus that dominated most of her adult life and led to her death is not directly inherited from a parent, a predisposition to developing the disease, which caused the death of her father, is. Second, her Catholic roots date back to immigrant great-grandparents in the mid-nineteenth century—a religious heritage that influenced her fiction throughout her life. In a 1955 letter to John Lynch, she said emphatically, "I am a born Catholic, went to Catholic schools in my early years, and have never left or wanted to leave the Church. I have never had the sense that being a Catholic is a limit to the freedom of the writer, but just the reverse" (*HB* 114).

Because O'Connor spent most of her adult life on a farm near Milledgeville, Georgia, she did not expect to receive much public attention. She wrote to her friend Betty Hester in 1958: "There won't be any biographies of me because, for only one reason, lives spent between the house and chicken yard to not make exciting copy" (*HB* 290-91). And indeed, because O'Connor's mother Regina, who outlived her by over three decades, guarded her privacy so carefully, there were no biographies for several years after her death, even though her fiction generated a great deal of public and critical interest. Moreover, it was understood that if there was going to be a biography it would be by her friend Sally Fitzgerald, who is supposed to have left an unfinished manuscript when she died in 2000. Since Fitzgerald's death, two biographies have appeared: *Flannery O'Connor: A Life* by Jean Cash in 2002, and *Flannery* by Brad Gooch in 2009, both of which reveal that O'Connor's life was far from that of a rural recluse.

It is not surprising, given her self-deprecating attitude and religious commitment to avoid self-assertion, that O'Connor would not be tempted to write an autobiography. In a 1957 letter, she said: "Autobiography sounds very grand but I don't think grand folks are the ones to write it. I think no one should write one unless he's called on by the Lord to do so." (*HB* 242). When asked by her first editor Robert Giroux for a biographical sketch for *Wise Blood*, she provided only her birth, education, and publishing information, concluding that she was living in Milledgeville, Georgia, "raising ducks and game birds, and writing. . . . If you need any more, I will have to make it up" (*HB* 29).

O'Connor's maternal great-grandfather, Hugh DonnellyTreanor, and his wife, Johannah Harty Treanor, emigrated to America from Ireland in the mid-nineteenth century and settled in Milledgeville, Georgia where Treanor set up a grist mill. Her maternal grandfather, Peter James Cline, was Milledgeville's mayor for a number of years. Peter Cline married Kate Treanor, and when she died, he married her sister Margaret Ida Treanor. With these two daughters of Hugh and Johannah Treanor, Cline had sixteen children; Flannery O'Connor's mother, Regina, was born of his second marriage.

O'Connor's paternal great grandfather, Patrick O'Connor, came to Savannah, Georgia, in the mid-nineteenth century where he set up a wagon manufacturing company. Edward Francis O'Connor, Sr., one of his eleven children, a banker, was O'Connor's grandfather. His son, Edward O'Connor, Jr., married Regina Cline in 1922, after serving in France in World War I. He went into the real estate business as owner and operator of the Dixie Realty Company and the Dixie Construction Company.

Flannery O'Connor, born March 25, 1925, in Savannah, Georgia, and baptized Mary Flannery, was the only child of Edward and Regina O'Connor. She attended St. Vincent's Grammar School and Sacred Heart Parochial School for Girls in Savannah. The closest thing to autobiography we have from her, in addition to the invaluable collection of letters, *The Habit of Being* (1979), is the essay she published in *Holiday* magazine in 1961, which she titled "The King of the Birds," but which the editors renamed "Living With a Peacock." O'Connor opens the essay with tongue firmly in cheek: "When I was five, I had an experience that marked me for life," recounting how a photographer from Pathé News was sent down from New York to film her and her famous Cochin Bantam chicken that could walk backward. O'Connor says from that day she began to collect chickens, a quest that ended with peacocks, when, as an adult, she ordered four seven-week-old peabiddies (*MM* 5).

Her father took a job with the Federal Housing Administration in Atlanta. O'Connor and her mother stayed there with him for a short time and then moved to the family home in Milledgeville, a white-columned house purchased by Peter James Cline in 1886 that was once the governor's mansion. O'Connor's father was diagnosed with the incurable disease of lupus in 1940, and he moved to Milledgeville, where he died in 1941 and where he is buried.

O'Connor attended Peabody High School, and, having a talent for drawing, served as art editor of the school newspaper, *The Peabody Palladia*. When she graduated in 1942, she attended Georgia State College for Women in Milledgeville, located about a block from her home. She was art editor of the college newspaper, *The Colonnade*, as well as editor of the college literary magazine, *The Corinthian*, for which she wrote parodies and comic pieces. She also drew satiric cartoons, which she sent to *The New Yorker* (None were accepted.).

O'Connor's philosophy professor, George W. Beiswanger, encouraged her to apply for graduate school at his alma mater, the University of Iowa. When she graduated in 1945, with a major in social science, she enrolled in Iowa's journalism department. However, her real interest was in writing fiction, so she dropped her first name (explaining, "Who was likely to buy the stories of an Irish washerwoman?") and went to see Paul Engle, director of the university's fledgling Writers' Workshop. Engle once told Robert Giroux, O'Connor's editor, that at his first meeting with O'Connor in his office, he could not understand a word of her Georgia accent and, embarrassed, asked her to write down what she had just said. She wrote: "My name is

Flannery O'Connor. I am not a journalist. Can I come to the Writer's Workshop?" (Giroux vii)

Engle has said that O'Connor sat in the back of the room in his class and seldom spoke. She fulfilled the requirements for an M.F.A. in 1947 with her creative thesis, *The Geranium: A Collection of Short Stories*, containing six stories. She published her first story, "The Geranium," in *Accent* in 1946, and, with Engle's recommendation, won the Rinehart-Iowa Fiction Award the following year. The award came with a $750 honorarium and an option from Rinehart to publish her first novel. After receiving her M.F.A., O'Connor was invited to Yaddo, the writers' colony in Saratoga Springs, New York, where she lived for seven months while she worked on her first book, *Wise Blood*. During this period, she met several people who were to play important roles in her life: the poet Robert Lowell, her future editor, Robert Giroux, and the translator Robert Fitzgerald and his wife, Sally. She said the Fitzgeralds became her "adopted kin." She lived in a garage apartment at their home in Connecticut during the summer of 1949, still working on *Wise Blood*, while babysitting the Fitzgerald children. Fitzgerald describes his and his wife's first meeting with O'Connor: "We saw a shy Georgia girl, her face heart-shaped and pale and glum, with fine eyes that could stop frowning and open brilliantly upon everything" (Fitzgerald 10).

O'Connor was unhappy with the kind of editorial response she received from Holt Rinehart for *Wise Blood* and asked to be released from her contract, complaining that a letter to her from the editor John Selby "was addressed to a slightly dim-witted Camp Fire Girl" (*HB* 9). She wrote Selby: "I feel that whatever virtues the novel may have are very much connected with the limitations you mention. I am not writing a conventional novel, and I think that the quality of the novel I write will derive precisely from the peculiarity or aloneness, if you will, of the experience I write from." She concluded: "The question is: is Rinehart interested in publishing this kind of novel?" (*HB* 10).

On a train trip from the Fitzgeralds to Atlanta in December, 1950,

O'Connor became ill with what was later diagnosed as lupus; she was hospitalized at Emory University Hospital in Atlanta and given shots of the experimental cortisone drug ACTH. Because the medicine left her too weak to live in New York alone as she had planned, she and her mother, Regina, moved to a dairy farm that her mother had inherited called Andalusia, a few miles from Milledgeville, where O'Connor lived for the rest of her life.

O'Connor was restricted to working a few hours in the morning before recuperating, she said, the rest of the day. Andalusia was a working farm, which her mother, a competent woman, ran. The ACTH hormone with which O'Connor injected herself was so debilitating that by the mid 1950s she had to use crutches, for her hips were failing rapidly. Although her movements were somewhat restricted, O'Connor was by no means a recluse. She wrote hundreds of letters to friends and acquaintances, entertained many visitors who came to see her, and gave guest lectures and readings at many colleges and universities. She described her life at Andalusia in her usual wry and witty way: "My mother and I live on a large place and I have bought me some peafowl and sit on the back steps a good deal studying them. I am going to be the World Authority on Peafowl, and I hope to be offered a chair some day at the Chicken College" (*HB* 57).

On one of her most famous sojourns away from Milledgeville, at the urging of a cousin, she and her mother went on a diocesan pilgrimage to Lourdes in 1959. She wrote Betty Hester: "I am going as a pilgrim, not a patient. I will not be taking any bath. I am one of those people who could die for his religion easier than take a bath for it" (*HB* 258). She and her mother went to Rome for the general audience with the Pope and sat on the front row. She wrote: "When it was over the Pope came down, shook our hands & the ArchB asked him to give me a special blessing [on acct. the crutches] which he did. There is a wonderful radiance and liveliness about the old man" (*HB* 280).

O'Connor's first book, *Wise Blood*, appeared in 1952. Some of the several stories she was publishing during this time in journals and literary quarterlies were chosen for *Best American Short Stories* and *O. Henry Award Stories*. Her first volume of stories, *A Good Man Is Hard to Find, and Other Stories* was published in 1955. O'Connor won a Kenyon Review Fellowship in 1953 and a Ford Foundation Grant in 1959. Her second novel, *The Violent Bear It Away*, appeared in 1960. Afterward, she published several more stories in journals and quarterlies, which appeared in the posthumous collection *Everything That Rises Must Converge* in 1965.

In 1963, O'Connor became anemic because of a benign fibroid tumor. Although her doctor feared surgery would reactivate her lupus, the tumor was removed in 1964, after which she developed a kidney infection. She requested and received Extreme Unction, now called the Sacrament of the Sick, in July, 1964. While in the hospital, she continued to work, telling her friend Maryat Lee in one of her final letters, dated July 21, that she was still "puttering" on "Parker's Back," but not much, for "I go across the room & I'm exhausted" (*HB* 594).

Flannery O'Connor died on August 3, 1964, from kidney failure. She is buried in Milledgeville, Georgia. In 2009, more than 10,000 people voted her *Complete Stories* as the Best of the National Book Awards in Fiction

Works Cited

Fitzgerald, Robert. "Introduction." *Everything That Rises Must Converge*. New York: Farrar, Straus and Giroux, 1965.

Giroux, Robert. "Introduction." *Flannery O'Connor: The Complete Stories*. New York: Farrar, Straus and Giroux, 1971.

O'Connor, Flannery. *The Habit of Being: Letters of Flannery O'Connor*. Ed. Sally Fitzgerald. New York: Farrar, Straus and Giroux, 1979. (Cited in text as *HB*).

____________. *Mystery and Manners: Occasional Prose*. Ed. Sally and Robert Fitzgerald. New York: Farrar, Straus and Giroux, 1961. (Cited in text as *MM*).

The *Paris Review* Perspective

Paul Elie for *The Paris Review*

"I wish they could be written and deposited in a slot for the next century myself," Flannery O'Connor told the writer John Hawkes in a letter after her novel *The Violent Bear It Away* was panned in *Time* and the *New York Times*. "I never know where the next word is coming from, and now I don't know where the next 60,000 are coming from." Commiseration over, she went back to her desk, and in the few months to follow before she died of lupus in 1964, at age thirty-nine, continued writing.

Now it *is* the next century, and no one is panning O'Connor's work any more. The imaginative writer dismissive of "interleckshuls" has been subjected to a vast scholarly commentary. The gradualist on black civil rights is thought to have gone deeper into the paradoxes of "that issue" than her progressive counterparts. The daughter of the South who worried that her "horse and buggy" would get stuck on the tracks that Faulkner was roaring down has a cult as ardent as his, and her house outside Milledgeville, like his outside Oxford, is a bus stop on the air-conditioned pilgrimage through the literary South.

Why do we readers of the next century still study what she wrote?

Because she was good at it: that was her own conversation-stopping answer to the "why I write" question, and that is the simple answer to the question half a century on. Her two novels, two dozen stories, ten essays, and several hundred letters are as distinctive a body of work as any in modern writing: eloquent, unexpected, often nutty, always funny, grave in its preoccupations, inimitably her own. It is work that demands our full attention but eludes our full understanding, a combination that allows new readers to come to it fresh, and makes it possible for the work itself to be refreshed in the encounter.

My own first encounter with her work came in freshman English. The professor, a Jesuit priest, Father Boyd, was teaching Christian humanism as it appears in the poetry of Housman, Eliot, Frost, and Hopkins, but he kept referring to Flannery O'Connor. The name alone made me curious. After Christmas I exchanged a crisp twenty for *The Complete Stories*, a thick white paperback with hand-drawn peacocks on the cover but no photograph of the author. I thought that Flannery O'Connor was a man, like Tennessee Williams and Erskine Caldwell, to be found in a general store or a whorehouse at the dark end of a tobacco road.

Robert Giroux's introduction to the book set me straight. He sketched her precocity at the Iowa Writers' Workshop and at Yaddo, the fierce protectiveness she felt for her first novel, and her will to make a writer's life for herself in spite of her illness. Giroux derided readers who "recognized her power but missed her point." I was such a reader and I knew it. It wasn't until I found myself writing a book about O'Connor and her associates—Catholic writers on pilgrimage in twentieth-century America—that I began to understand her work and not just admire it. The independence of her protagonists, from the dissident preacher Hazel Motes onward, became a key to O'Connor herself, isolated by her father's early death and her mother's incomprehension of her work. The title "The Life You Save May Be Your Own" suggested a pattern whereby writer and believer alike reckon with an inheritance and make it their own without violating or shrinking it to the size of the self.

The South African novelist J. M. Coetzee defined a classic as a work of art that survives the interrogation of subsequent eras with its character intact. In those terms, O'Connor's work is classic. But there is more to it than that. Her books interrogate us—they prompt us to reconsider our own story in light of our encounter with another's. Hazel Motes cannot banish the "ragged figure" of Christ from the back of his mind. The handyman Mr. Shiftlet ambles up the road toward the house convinced that "the world is almost rotten." The Misfit administers rough justice on an old lady at the roadside. Ruby Turpin at the hog pen vents grandiloquently about her station in life. O. E. Parker tries to prove himself to his pious wife by having the face of Christ in all its resplendent detail tattooed into his back. These are figures that stay with us, and the work in which they are found is wisdom literature: stories that we measure our lives against, in such a way that our lives are at once enriched and found wanting.

Bibliography

Coetzee, J. M. *Stranger Shores: Literary Essays*. New York: Penguin, 2002.

O'Connor, Flannery. *The Complete Stories*. New York: Farrar, Straus and Giroux, 1972.

____________. *The Habit of Being: Letters*. New York: Farrar, Straus and Giroux, 1979.

____________. *Mystery and Manners*. New York: Farrar, Straus and Giroux, 1969.

____________. *Wise Blood*. New York: Farrar, Straus and Giroux, 1962.

CRITICAL CONTEXTS

Flannery O'Connor and the Art of the Story

Susan Srigley

In a posthumous collection of Flannery O'Connor's essays and public lectures titled *Mystery and Manners*, we read her observation that "it takes a story to make a story" (202). The idea sounds simple enough; O'Connor is drawing attention to the way stories generate and live in other stories, yet the idea can also provide an approach for the interpretation of her fiction. How do the stories *within* O'Connor's stories help us to understand her fiction in more nuanced ways, and how can looking at the different levels of a story teach us something about reading generally? This essay will use the "story within a story" approach to read O'Connor as a writer who understood herself to be writing from within a storytelling religious tradition, and as such, an author whose work reveals multiple layers of meaning available to the discerning reader.

Rather than assuming one way of reading or interpreting O'Connor, I will argue that O'Connor's use of biblical narratives and allusions, as well as literary and theological texts, in fact *expands* the possibilities for the interpretation of her stories. Stories not only make stories, they make the story larger and open to further exploration. O'Connor laments that in the teaching of literature, and in this case the short story, interpretation often leans toward narrowing what the story can yield, with more focus on *the* (i.e., one) meaning: "In most English classes the short story has become a kind of literary specimen to be dissected" (*MM* 108). She resists this type of reduction of meaning in a story to a statement or an idea, and instead she suggests that "a story isn't any good unless it successfully resists paraphrase, unless it hangs on and expands in the mind" (108).

For this discussion I will draw on O'Connor's essays in *Mystery and Manners*, not as a template for how to read her work but in order to explore O'Connor's ideas about interpretation itself, including the interpretation of both fiction and the biblical texts. We will look at three different stories by O'Connor to find examples of biblical allusions, references to other works of literature, and theological ideas. These examples will inform our discussion by demonstrating how such allusions can reveal a more expansive reading of O'Connor's art.

Interpretation and Levels of Meaning

O'Connor affirmed the significance of region for any writer, and as Ralph Wood and others have carefully traced, the South undeniably influenced her writing. When she talks about the stories that have shaped her own, she is referring specifically to the biblical stories as the ones that "make" hers. She says, "The Hebrew genius for making the absolute concrete has conditioned the Southerner's way of looking at things. That is one of the reasons why the South is a storytelling region" (*MM* 202). Not only the drama of the stories themselves but also the biblical insistence on portraying the concrete action of the human/divine encounter is what she has learned. And this can be seen in much of what she says about fiction writing. O'Connor recalls us to the fact that the stories that live in her fiction do not appear out of nowhere—they are part of her region and her life as a writer. However, this does not necessarily imply that their meaning is already determined, since stories have lives of their own, full of paradox and tension. In this regard, O'Connor recognized the limitations of literalism when reading both literature and the biblical texts.

In her essay on "The Nature and Aim of Fiction" O'Connor explains how the medieval commentators on scripture interpreted the text according to its different levels of meaning. The *literal* level of the text covered the details of the narrative, and within that literal rendering one could also discern other voices of the text: "one they called *allegorical*, in which one fact pointed to another; one they called *tropological*, or *moral*, which had to do with what should be done; and one they called *anagogical*, which had to do with the Divine life and our participation in it" (72). What she describes here is what Origen (c.

185-254 C.E.), one of the first systematic theologians of the Christian faith, also wrote about the different levels of meaning in the biblical texts. He argues in *On First Principles*:

> Now what man of intelligence will believe that the first and the second and the third day, and the evening and the morning existed without the sun and the moon and stars? And that the first day, if we may so call it, was even without a heaven (Gen. 1:5-13)? And who is so silly as to believe that God, after the manner of a farmer, 'planted a paradise eastward of Eden,' and set in it a visible and palpable 'tree of life,' of such a sort that anyone who tasted of its fruit with his bodily teeth would gain life; and again that one could partake of 'good and evil' by masticating the fruit taken from the tree of that name (Gen 2:8,9)? And when God is said to 'walk in the paradise in the cool of the day' and Adam to hide himself behind a tree, I do not think anyone will doubt that these are figurative expressions which indicate certain mysteries through a semblance of history and not through actual events (Gen. 3:8). (qtd in Kerr, 47)

The purpose in referencing this passage from Origen is to further emphasize the point that O'Connor is making about interpreting scripture, and also literature. She attests to the fact that the earliest Christian thinkers were not biblical literalists, and the different types of meaning to be found in scripture were connected to a larger, multivalent view of life itself. O'Connor continues her point, suggesting that "although this was a method applied to biblical exegesis, it was also an attitude toward all of creation, and a way of reading nature which included most possibilities, and I think it is this *enlarged view* of the human scene that the fiction writer has to cultivate." (*MM* 73) (emphasis mine). Different levels of meaning imply this expansion of vision, rather than a narrowing of vision often evident in literal-only readings of texts.

Even though Flannery O'Connor identified herself as a Catholic, and there is considerable discussion in the scholarship about how her religious faith is evident, or not, in her fiction, the point to be made here is that O'Connor did not see her religious views as having a limiting effect on what she expressed in her fiction. In fact, as her comments in "The Nature and Aim of Fiction" illustrate, she witnessed a more expansive and open approach to interpretation in the ancient commentators on scripture than one might find in a modern reader of the bible. O'Connor explicitly links this approach to biblical exegesis with fiction in her essay, and it offers a method of interpretation for reading O'Connor's own work. This is especially evident when she employs the biblical stories in her writing in order to increase the symbolic landscape even further.

Before turning to particular examples of stories and literary/theological allusions in O'Connor's fiction, some brief remarks on the relationship between religion and literature are worth exploring for this discussion. There are clearly parallels that O'Connor notes between the interpretation of fiction and the interpretation of biblical texts. In both instances, she argues for a multilayered approach to the different voices of the text, and in her fiction it is often biblical stories that provide the interpretive opening into larger vistas. Interestingly, O'Connor's Catholic faith is more often thought of as something which potentially limits her creativity, whereas she countered this idea as a mistaken assumption, especially the opposition between creativity and dogma: "I have found that people outside the Church like to suppose that the Church acts as a restraint on the creativity of the Catholic writer and that she keeps him from reaching his full development" (*MM* 177). Dogma, she says, should not "fix anything that the writer sees in the world"; instead, O'Connor argues that "the Catholic fiction writer is entirely free to observe. He feels no call to take on the duties of God or to create a new universe" (178). If one thinks about the biblical stories in O'Connor's fiction as stories open to multiple meanings and interpretation rather than interpretively fixed dogma, the possibilities for interpreting her fiction increase.

It is not surprising, therefore, that literature sometimes offers access to moral and religious questions in unconventional ways. In the case of O'Connor's storytelling, one can read a story about a character from the American South of the 1950s and be drawn into the theology of a fifteenth-century Italian mystic. And because her fiction is open to different levels of interpretation, without being explicitly religious, there is a wider appeal and a wider audience who can appreciate her work. Essentially, the genius of O'Connor's fiction, seen from within the richness of a storytelling tradition that deals with questions of meaning, is the way the reader is ultimately invited *into* the interpretation. Stories have lives of their own, and the interpretive process itself is part of the experience of those stories. To say there is one method, or a set formula or meaning to O'Connor's use of biblical stories and theological texts is to reduce the potential for myriad openings into her art. One of O'Connor's comments to Dr. Ted Spivey in a letter (dated 25 May 1959) reflects her resistance to formulaic readings of symbols/imagery:

> Week before last I went to Wesleyan and read 'A Good Man is Hard to Find.' After it I went to one of the classes where I was asked questions . . . 'Miss O'Connor,' he said, 'why was the Misfit's hat *black*?' I said most countrymen in Georgia wore black hats. He looked pretty disappointed. Then he said, 'Miss O'Connor, the Misfit represents Christ, does he not?' 'He does not,' I said. He looked crushed. 'Well, Miss O'Connor,' he said, 'what is the significance of the Misfit's hat?' I said it was to cover his head; and after that he left me alone. Anyway, that's what's happening to the teaching of literature. (*HB* 334)

In this humorous episode, Flannery O'Connor is serious about articulating her mistrust of interpretations that make a particular symbol *equivalent* to a particular meaning. The prevalence of "Christ figures" in discussions of literature, rarely with any conscious analysis of what that means beyond the phrase itself, is one type of obstacle O'Connor describes in her letter. These cautions about symbolic interpretations that determine meaning in advance reveal O'Connor's penchant for images and stories that invite further questioning. She says that what makes a story "work" is an action or a gesture "that transcended any neat allegory that might have been intended or any pat moral categories a reader could make" (*MM* 111).

Stories Within Stories

Probably the best way to explore how Flannery O'Connor uses stories within her stories is to look at some examples of them in the fiction. To illustrate this I will refer to her use of an episode from the biblical narrative about Moses in "Parker's Back," a theological idea about purgatory from the mystic St. Catherine of Genoa in her story "Revelation," and finally an allusion to another work of literature by Fyodor Dostoevsky in her story "Greenleaf." The purpose of drawing attention to these stories is not to offer up set interpretations, but rather to demonstrate how carefully O'Connor worked with literature, scripture, and theological ideas in the creation of her fiction. She did this neither to appear erudite, nor to propose a symbolic key to the meaning of a story, but in order to allow the reverberations of other ancient and modern stories to give depth and complexity to the characters and lives in her stories.

"Parker's Back"

"Parker's Back" is a story that overflows with biblical and theological allusions on questions of beauty, idolatry, sacramentalism and incarnation, but for the purpose of this discussion I will refer to one episode in which Parker encounters God in a theophanic vision. In her essay "Novelist and Believer," O'Connor describes the specificity required when writing out of the conviction that God reveals Godself and is known and experienced through relationship. She says, "it is the experience of an encounter, of a kind of knowledge which affects the believer's every action" (*MM* 160). She cannot avoid that she is a writer who believes in the "God of Abraham, Isaac, and Jacob" (161). In "Parker's Back," the main character is searching for a "religious" tattoo to appease his wife who is not particularly thrilled with Parker's tattoos covering most of his body. He wants to get a tattoo on his one remaining blank canvas, his back, and he cannot decide what kind of religious motif to choose. As he is out baling hay one morning, the vision of what the tattoo needs to be comes to him. O'Connor uses imagery reminiscent of the scene in Exodus 3: 2-7 where Moses encounters God in the burning bush.

In Exodus 3, Moses has been tending flocks for his father-in-law when he comes across a bush engulfed in flames that is not being consumed. Moses turns away and God says to Moses, "'Come no closer! Remove the sandals from your feet, for the place on which you are standing is holy ground.' He said further, 'I am the God of our father, the God of Abraham, the God of Isaac, and the God of Jacob'" (Exodus 3:5-7 *NRSV*). What O'Connor manages to convey in "Parker's Back," by a few noticeable allusions to this biblical story, is the idea of an encounter, not with some vague spiritual feeling but a real beckoning that speaks to Parker. In the story, Parker circles a tree on the tractor, which for him is only an inconvenience, and sees suddenly "the tree reaching out to grasp him. A ferocious thud propelled him into the air, and he heard himself yelling in an unbelievably loud voice, 'GOD ABOVE!'" (*CW* 665). While the tree and the tractor burst into flame, Parker notices that his shoes have been thrown off his feet. Unwittingly, Parker *encounters* God in the burning tree, which had reached out to him and which now left him with the clear impression he was on holy ground: "if he had known how to cross himself he would have done it" (665). On the heels of this experience, Parker understands that the only possible religious tattoo would be an image of God. O'Connor's use of the Exodus story to frame that of Parker's evokes O'Connor's idea of the *encounter* with God, lived and felt in the flesh and experienced as holy. The reverberations from Exodus that continue in "Parker's Back," including the Israelites' struggles with idolatry and Parker's struggle with his wife's accusations of idolatry, only deepen the possibilities for interpretation.

"Revelation"

Another example of how O'Connor layers ideas in her fiction is through her extensive reading in philosophy and theology. A reference to something she has read can sometimes yield a clue about a deeper idea she wants to explore. For example, in the story "Revelation," Ruby Turpin has a revelatory experience that O'Connor, in a letter to Betty Hester, describes as a "purgatorial vision" (*HB* 577). In a letter written much earlier to Hester (25 November 1955), O'Connor discusses the idea of purgatory according to the mystic St. Catherine of Genoa (1447-1510) who wrote a *Treatise on Purgatory* that O'Connor had read. O'Connor laments to Hester that she did not fully bring out the idea of Purgatory as the beginning of suffering for Mrs. McIntyre in her story "The Displaced Person." She then explains that St. Catherine conceived of Purgatory as self-realization (118). O'Connor notes the challenges associated with writing about internal spiritual reorientations for her characters. In the case of "The Displaced Person," she adds, "Understatement was not enough. However there is certainly no reason why the effects of redemption must be plain to us and I think they usually are not" (118). O'Connor's comment *could* allow the possibility that she may have stumbled across an idea for a story in which she would represent a purgatorial transformation of self-realization according to St. Catherine of Genoa.

The story "Revelation" chronicles the spiritual movement of Ruby Turpin's soul from being judged a "wart hog" through her purgatorial ascent to a proper vision and understanding of herself in relation to God. In her efforts to make sense of being called a "wart hog from hell," Ruby must descend into herself and grapple with the meaning of the judgment. The struggle is fierce as she seeks alongside Job and other biblical characters to find a response that will justify herself to God. However, what she discovers in the process, which has its culmination in her final vision, is that it is precisely her self-justification that hinders her ascent. Ruby needs to be purged of the idea of her own righteousness and to seek the source of righteousness outside of the shallow category of a "good disposition." She takes it for granted that her religious beliefs keep her in right relation to God, but she lacks a proper relation to herself; she does not understand who or what she is. In a sense, Ruby needs to be confronted with herself from a perspective different than her own. Her self-love distorts her vision of others: religious self-satisfaction makes her a harsh critic. As the story unfolds, Ruby's self-righteous attitude is revealed as irresponsible and harmful to others: her love of her Christian virtue is a disordered form of love. Instead of loving God and others, she loves herself more than everything by priding herself on her goodness. The point of the purgatorial experience, therefore, is not to punish the rebel or the hypocrite, but to bring them to a realization of the order of love.

What O'Connor's reference to St. Catherine of Genoa and her *Treatise on Purgatory* brings to an interpretation of this story is the theological question of who the self is before God (a question central to O'Connor's thought) and the ethical implications for this in Ruby Turpin's experience. This is *the* question of the story, shouted out to God, then returned and asked of Ruby also: "Who do you think you are?"(*CW* 653). Purgatory, or a purgatorial vision as Ruby experiences it and St. Catherine describes it, is the cleansing of the soul from self-love in order to know who the self is more truly in relation to God. In Ruby's case, self-love inflates her image of herself and her Christian virtue, in turn making her love her own goodness more than God. What she learns from her purgatorial vision is that her virtue is only a false moral superiority when it is divorced from a love of God and others. It takes her virtues being "burned away" for Ruby to begin to see how love is the ordering force of morality in her vision.

"Greenleaf"

In her essay that appeared as the introduction to *A Memoir of Mary Ann*, O'Connor makes reference to one of Dostoevsky's characters from his novel *The Brothers Karamazov*. The topic pervading the essay is the problem of suffering. O'Connor was asked by the Sisters of

Our Lady of Perpetual Help Free Cancer Home in Atlanta to write about a young patient who had suffered and died from a tumor that had disfigured her face since birth. O'Connor declined the invitation to write the memoir, leaving that up to the nuns who knew Mary Ann, but she did agree to write the introduction. O'Connor concludes the essay with a description of one particular reaction to suffering: "One of the tendencies of our age is to use the suffering of children to discredit the goodness of God, and once you have discredited his goodness, you are done with him" (*MM* 227). Foremost in her mind is Ivan Karamazov's heated conversation with his younger brother Alyosha in the chapter called "Rebellion," where Ivan makes his argument against God. As O'Connor notes, "Ivan Karamazov cannot believe, as long as one child is in torment" (227). The problem is a serious one. How does one respond theologically to the question of human suffering, and in particular children's, who seem even less likely to have done anything to warrant their suffering?

While O'Connor engages the question of suffering and Ivan Karamazov's response directly in this essay, she presents another kind of response in her story "Greenleaf." In something of a side story, the character of Mrs. Greenleaf presents herself as another irritation to the more pressing concerns of the protagonist Mrs. May. Mrs. Greenleaf provides a counterbalance to the "efficient" Mrs. May. Her housework, gardening and mothering skills were all lacking, but more significantly, her own preoccupation was something that Mrs. May considered completely useless: Mrs. Greenleaf prayed. The episode where Mrs. May confronts Mrs. Greenleaf is preceded by a description of her strange habit of what she called prayer healing:

> Every day she cut all the morbid stories out of the newspaper—the accounts of women who had been raped and criminals who had escaped and children who had been burned and of train wrecks and plane crashes and the divorces of movie stars. She took these to the woods and dug a hole and buried them and then she fell on the ground over them and mumbled and

groaned for an hour or so, moving her huge arms back and forth under her and out again and finally just lying down flat and, Mrs. May suspected, going to sleep in the dirt. (*CW* 505)

In this story, O'Connor's connects her art to Dostoevsky's story through the newspaper clippings, a key part of Ivan's speech in "Rebellion." In Dostoevsky's account, Ivan Karamazov is so outraged by the suffering of 'innocent' children that he gathers the newspaper records of the terrible suffering of children in order to mount his case against God. He says to Alyosha: "You see, I'm an amateur and collector of certain little facts; I copy them down from newspapers and stories, from wherever, and save them—would you believe it?—certain kinds of little anecdotes. I already have a nice collection of them" (239).

When Mrs. Greenleaf prays over newspaper clippings in O'Connor's story, thus invoking Ivan's rebellion, the story expands, the prayer healing becomes a response and part of a larger conversation about God and the meaning of suffering. How is Mrs. May's reaction like or unlike Alyosha's? In what way does Mrs. Greenleaf's use of the clippings differ from Ivan's? These are differences worth noting, where O'Connor gestures to possibilities beyond Ivan's questioning. Ivan focuses on the suffering of children; for him, children are the only "innocents," and therefore no justifiable reason can be argued for their suffering. His newspaper collection is part of a legally inspired case that he makes against God; his engagement with actual children is minimal. Mrs. Greenleaf, on the other hand, has no intellectual use for the clippings; she takes them into the earth and throws her whole body over them, taking on the sufferings in those words as if they were her own: "Oh Jesus, stab me in the heart!" (*CW* 506). Also interestingly, the clippings that Mrs. Greenleaf collects are not just the sufferings of children. Ivan is trying to make a rational argument, and so his concern is to show the logical problem of reconciling a good God with innocent suffering. He does not intend to alleviate suffering; he wants to make a point. Mrs. Greenleaf's response is felt in body and soul, and she takes on *all kinds* of suffering: women, criminals, children, large-scale disasters such as train wrecks and plane crashes and even the sufferings of divorcing movies stars. The opening into further speculations about the question of suffering, theodicy and the meaning and efficacy of prayer over rational argument are all initiated by O'Connor's use of Dostoevsky's trope of the newspaper clippings.

The Moral of the Story?

One might still ask: To what end does Flannery O'Connor employ these biblical, literary and theological references in her stories? The simplest answer once again is her claim that it takes a story to make a story, and all of these have fueled her imaginative art. But surely there are reasons to account for *which* particular stories she uses? I have argued elsewhere (*Flannery O'Connor's Sacramental Art*) that O'Connor's moral universe is framed by an ethic of responsibility, an ethic that she draws from the Hebrew and Christian scriptures. In her essay "The Catholic Novelist in the Protestant South," she makes the claim that what the shared sacred history of the South allows is "the meaning of their every action to be heightened and seen under the aspect of eternity" (203). The moral of the story is not so much prescriptive about a particular code of living as it is an invitation to think about how human choices have both visible and invisible consequences and effects. Human beings do not live entirely unto themselves, and so every action affects oneself and others in ways that are not always apparent outwardly. O'Connor is not interested in simply reiterating some kind of moral message in her fiction; she wants to bring the questions to life by engaging the ancient sources, and other writers, who are trying to understand the meaning of suffering, the problem of evil, the absence or presence of God. Above all, her moral framework can be best summed up as encompassing rather than restricting. As she says in "The Teaching of Literature,"

> So far as I am concerned as a novelist, a bomb on Hiroshima affects my judgment of life in rural Georgia, and this is not the result of taking a relative view and judging one thing by another, but of taking an absolute view and judging all things together; for a view taken in the light of the absolute will include a good deal more than one taken merely in the light provided by a house-to-house survey (*MM* 134).

From a brief overview of some of the sources that feed her fiction, one can situate O'Connor's stories within a larger tradition of thinking about meaning in human life. What can we gather from an approach to her fiction that makes room for multiple voices in the text and that recognizes different levels of meaning in a story? Certainly there is hope for the richness that comes when there is diversity of thought and interpretation. Some may enjoy O'Connor's stories on the simplest level of the literal text; some may appreciate her use of allegory or the moral symbolism that provokes the reader to think existentially about the meaning of a story. Others still may be transformed by the experience, or encounter with the text, invisible threads weaving their way into the mind or heart of the reader. All of these are part of reading O'Connor's fiction. Both her stories and those she evokes offer the possibility of the enjoyment of good fiction and keep moral wondering alive.

Works Cited

Dostoevsky, Fyodor. *The Brothers Karamazov*. Trans. Richard Pevear and Larissa Volokhonsky. New York: Random House, 1991.

Kerr, Hugh T., ed. *Readings in Christian Thought*. Nashville, TN: Abingdon Press, 1966.

O'Connor, Flannery. *Collected Works*. Ed. Sally Fitzgerald. New York: Library of America, 1988.

__________. *The Habit of Being: Letters of Flannery O'Connor*. Ed. Sally Fitzgerald. New York: Farrar, Straus and Giroux, 1979. (Cited in the text as *HB*).

__________. *Mystery and Manners: Occasional Prose*. Eds. Sally and Robert Fitzgerald. New York: Farrar, Straus and Giroux, 1961. (Cited in the text as *MM*).

Srigley, Susan. *Flannery O'Connor's Sacramental Art*. Notre Dame, IN: U of Notre Dame P, 2004.
St. Catherine of Genoa. "Purgation and Purgatory." *Classics of Western Spirituality: Purgation and Purgatory and the Spiritual Dialogue*. Trans. Serge Hughes. Mahwah, NJ: Paulist Press, 1979: 71-87.
Wood, Ralph. *Flannery O'Connor and the Christ-Haunted South*. Grand Rapids, MI: William B. Eerdmans, 2004.

The "Christ-Haunted" South: Contextualizing Flannery O'Connor

John Hayes

Flannery O'Connor's work has a wide, constantly growing international audience, both academic and popular, composed of readers occupying all sorts of positions on a philosophical and ideological spectrum. Yet fully appreciating O'Connor's fictional world requires some basic knowledge of two quite distinct, specific forces in the context from which she wrote: a particular region, the U.S. South; and a particular religion, Christianity. These left an indelible imprint not only on O'Connor herself but also on the remarkable literature she created.

"It's great to be at home in a region, even this one," O'Connor quipped in a 1959 letter, but beneath the humorous satire was profound attachment (Coles 50). Except for five years in her early twenties (1945-1950), O'Connor spent her entire life in the South, in her native Georgia. In O'Connor's youth the family lived in Savannah (1925-1938), Atlanta (1938), and Milledgeville (1938-1945). In the most active years of her writing life (1951-1964), O'Connor lived with her mother on the family farm, Andalusia, four miles out from Milledgeville. Like fellow writers of her generation William Faulkner and Eudora Welty, O'Connor was deeply informed by her regional home and used the complicated milieu of the South as the setting for her fiction: both of her novels, and all but one of her stories, are set in the region. Her extensive correspondence, published posthumously in 1979 as *The Habit of Being*, resounds with her acutely self-conscious southern identity (and her ever-ingenious sense of humor, even in the face of a fatal disease, lupus, that took her life at age thirty-nine). Of a family pilgrimage to Rome in 1958, during which she met Pope Pius XII, O'Connor wrote that her standard was, "when in Rome, do as you done in Milledgeville" (*CW* 1032). In a series of essays and lectures (collected and published posthumously, in 1969, as *Mystery and Manners*), O'Connor ruminated on regional identity, the changing South of the 1950s and 1960s, and her place as a writer living in, and drawing inspiration from, a distinct region. In a 1962 speech, she argued that "the best American fiction has always been regional," that it has germinated in fertile soil "wherever there has been a shared past, a sense of alikeness, and the possibility of reading a small history in a universal light" (*MM* 58).

O'Connor was born into a Catholic family who, on both mother's and father's side, traced their lineage back to Irish Catholics who had immigrated to Georgia in the early-to-mid nineteenth century. Her childhood home was on the same city square in Savannah as the elegant, imposing Cathedral of St. John the Baptist (where she also attended grammar school). As a young woman in graduate school in Iowa, O'Connor began attending Mass daily, and she came to realize, as she later put it in an essay and a letter, that she was "no vague believer," that she "was a Catholic not like someone else would be a Baptist or a Methodist but like someone else would be an atheist" (*MM* 32). O'Connor's fervent adult Catholicism marked the rest of her life, informing the advice and critique in her letters, shaping the imaginative framing of her fiction, and displaying itself in everyday practices. She reviewed some 120 books for Catholic periodicals, read widely in Catholic theology (from medieval Thomas Aquinas to contemporary Pierre Teilhard de Chardin), and, with her mother, was an active member of Milledgeville's small Catholic church.

Yet as a Catholic, O'Connor was very much part of a marginalized, minority group in her native region. Protestants—overwhelmingly Baptist and Methodist—dominated religious life in the South, and their cultural power manifested itself in all sorts of ways, from urban geography, to political rhetoric, to ideas of morality, to mundane conversation. Paradoxically, O'Connor the Catholic came to feel a profound appreciation for this Protestant imprint on the South. As a writer with a theological vision, she stated in a 1963 lecture that she struggled against the grain of a national context, one where "it becomes more and more difficult in America to make belief believable" (*MM* 201).

But in the South, by contrast, matters of religious belief and unbelief were part and parcel of daily life. "In this," O'Connor went on to say, "the Southern writer has the greatest possible advantage. He lives in the Bible Belt" (201). Thus she claimed that a writer like herself enjoyed, not only a regional audience for whom struggles of faith were intelligible, but even more importantly a Christianity-infused culture that was a conducive jumping-off point for fictional creativity. The South, she famously said in a 1960 lecture, was "Christ-haunted," and "the Southerner, who isn't convinced of it, is very much afraid that he may have been formed in the image and likeness of God" (*MM* 44-45). Through a creative synthesis of her Catholic vision and the cultural material of southern society itself, then, she could readily imagine and explore characters who were "forced out to meet evil and grace and who act on a trust beyond themselves" (*MM* 42) in a fictional world infused with "mystery and the unexpected" (40).

Some basic acquaintance with the South, and with the specific types of Protestantism that shaped it, is therefore crucial for interpreting her work. The South of O'Connor's adulthood was a region undergoing major structural transformation after a long era of relative stagnancy, one that began in the late nineteenth century and continued into the early 1940s. Prominent regional politicians, journalists, and preachers had optimistically proclaimed a "New South" in the 1880s, but this New South in fact materialized as the poor, peripheral stepchild in an increasingly prosperous, powerful nation. As the majority of Americans left the countryside for the exploding cities, found jobs in the expanding industrial, corporate economy, and saw millions of European immigrants pour into this fast-developing matrix, the South stumbled into the twentieth century as a peculiar backwater. The population remained heavily rural, agriculture continued to be the backbone of the regional economy, and the region attracted but a trickle of incoming immigrants. Towns and cities did sprout and blossom, scattered industrialization did happen (especially textile mills, coal mines, and timber camps), but the region paid the lowest wages in the nation, and most of the industrial stock fell ultimately into the hands of capitalists outside the region. Emblematic of what did and did not change in the New South, more cotton was planted in the New South era (the 1910s being all-time peak years) than ever had been the case in the pre-Civil War South.

This society that spoke of expansive change yet saw little of it, that chased modern prosperity yet came to experience absentee control, put a very heavy emphasis on social place, especially in matters of race and class. A new feature of the New South was the code of segregation (or, as it was colloquially known, "Jim Crow"). Through state and municipal laws, in everyday etiquette and manners, by cultural articulation in word and image, whites sought to display "white supremacy" over blacks, circumscribing where African Americans could be and what they could do. Segregation was codified in all sorts of ways, from the mundane—whites refusing to address black people with the titles of "Mr." or "Mrs.," and calling even elderly African Americans by their first name—to the egregiously theatrical—dramatically violent lynchings of alleged black criminals in very public places, like courthouse squares or railroad bridges. O'Connor's fiction indirectly displayed the power of this regional code of segregation: Although her home county, Baldwin, had a large black population (40 percent in the years she was at Andalusia) and although black characters do populate her stories, all of O'Connor's main characters are white, and she never tried to narrate the interiority of her black characters. In her personal life, she lived in a largely segregated world; to give one example, she refused to meet with the black writer James Baldwin when he was in Georgia because, she wrote in a letter, "I observe the traditions of the society I feed on—it's only fair" (*CW* 1094-95). The "color line" was a regional inheritance that O'Connor, as a white southerner, did not venture to challenge or cross.

The same was not true, however, of another carefully drawn regional line, the line of class. Less dramatic and much less remembered than the color line, sharp divisions of class were also a signal feature of the New South. As the New South society began to coalesce in the

1880s and 1890s, some did benefit from its agricultural intensification, its new or expanding towns and cities, and its full incorporation into a national market economy. This prospering minority—an elite class of industrialists, planters, large-scale businesspeople, and a middling class of landowning small farmers, salespeople, small businesspeople, and foremen—sought, in conscious and unconscious ways, to differentiate themselves from the impoverished masses. They became town-oriented (either moving their residence there, or focusing their social life there) and, in league with national cultural currents, looked down on country-dwellers, ridiculing them with new terms like "hayseed," "hillbilly," and "peckerwood." They came to view poverty not just as a sign of failure, but as a badge of a deeper deficiency and immorality. Poor whites and poor blacks—landless tenants and sharecroppers, marginal farmers, and industrial workers—heard themselves dehumanized with denigrations like "poor white trash" and "shiftless niggers." So powerful was the disdain of propertied whites for impoverished whites that the propertied used the machinery of state government to establish programs, beginning in the 1920s, that sterilized some seventy thousand poor white men and women across the South. As the home of Georgia's State Hospital, Milledgeville became a regional site of sterilization.

O'Connor's regional peers, such as William Faulkner and Eudora Welty, participated in this culture of class condescension, as did fellow Georgian Erskine Caldwell, who created lasting imagery of poor whites in his 1932 novel *Tobacco Road*. Yet in striking contrast, O'Connor (though of propertied, landowning, "respectable" status) made poor whites central to her fiction, exploring the depths and intricacies of the human soul through her poor white characters. The leading figures in her two novels, Hazel Motes and Francis Marion Tarwater, are impoverished rural whites, as are many (though not all) of the main characters in her stories, such as the Misfit, Manley Pointer, O. E. Parker, and T. C. Tanner. A later section of this essay will explore the religious rationale of O'Connor's crossing the class line, but for now it is sufficient to say that it made her, and her fiction, stand out. "Tell that girl to quit writing about poor folks," one local man (and would-be critic) told O'Connor's uncle after the publication of her first book, *Wise Blood* (*MM* 131), and another queried why she didn't write about "some nice people" (*CW* 906). These were admonitions O'Connor ignored, but certainly felt the force of, in the place-conscious, status-conscious society of the South.

But the New South, the South of O'Connor's birth and youth (the 1920s and 1930s), was coming unraveled and being transformed in the years of her active writing (the late 1940s to early 1960s). Federal agricultural programs infused capital into the region, enabling mechanization of farming, diversification of crops, and the consolidation of landholdings. Emergent "agribusiness" was capital, not labor, intensive, and the pressing need for human labor (a need that had marked the South back to the seventeenth century) began to drastically shrink. The millions of tenants and sharecroppers, once so basic to the economy, began to find that their labor capacity was economically superfluous. Masses of people began to leave the southern countryside, heading for the cities and towns, or outside the region altogether. At the same time, southern state and municipal governments began to aggressively recruit both national corporations and government facilities. Offering low corporate taxes and a labor force with minimal history of unionization, using the considerable clout of southern politicians in the Democratic party, such recruitment was highly successful, and the industrialization of the region—light and scattered in the New South era—materialized in earnest in the post-World War II years. A New South city such as Atlanta could boast, in 1940, that it was home to the *world's* largest mule market. Some ten years later, such ties to rural life were barely visible, and the city could instead note its Ford and General Motors factories, the headquarters of Delta Air Lines, and a Lockheed plant manufacturing aircraft for the U.S. military.

These changes in the economy made the South a more prosperous place, and, with the development of inexpensive air-conditioning window-units by General Electric, the region became a more appealing magnet for outsiders. In increasing numbers, people began to migrate to the South, especially the expanding towns and cities. O'Connor told an emblematic anecdote in 1962 about a female friend from Wisconsin who moved to Atlanta. Her realtor was himself a newcomer, from Massachusetts, and he commended the for-sale property by saying, "You'll like this neighborhood. There's not a southerner for two miles" (*MM* 57). Through such movements, and the movement of rural southerners outside the region, the South became a less isolated, less distinct place. In a similar way, the spread of a national popular culture, especially through television and radio, chipped away at the old barriers between region and nation.

In these same midcentury decades of economic, demographic, and cultural change, black southerners organized a collective challenge to another distinguishing mark of the New South—its code of segregation. The first major public instance of this challenge was the 1955-1956 black boycott of the bus system in Montgomery, Alabama. The ensuing decade witnessed other dramatic displays of African American activism, in such places as Little Rock, Greensboro, Birmingham, and Selma. National and international media covered these civil rights struggles, but collective black activism and protest was a regionwide, and nationwide, phenomenon, waged in innumerable local settings—in obscure counties and in minor towns, in ways both dramatic and deceptively everyday. This Civil Rights movement catapulted O'Connor's fellow Georgian Martin Luther King, Jr., to a very public place as *the* voice of black activism.

These transformative changes occurred at different paces in different parts of the South. A place such as O'Connor's Baldwin County was slower to display such change, but even there, only a few miles up the road from O'Connor's Andalusia, the Georgia Power Company in 1953 constructed a massive plant and dam to supply hydroelectric power for an expanding, electrified consumer base. Indeed, at Andalusia itself, O'Connor's mother Regina switched the century-old cotton plantation to a dairy operation in the 1950s, with greater capital investment, lessened labor requirements, and a herd of cattle in place of the old king, cotton.

O'Connor wrote against the backdrop of all of these changes, as the New South transitioned to the "Sun Belt." The massive changes in agriculture are basic to the plotline of "The Displaced Person," as the tenant-farming Shortleys find their labor rendered superfluous in the face of a tractor and an industrious immigrant family from Poland. A bulldozer—a new force in the South in the 1950s—is central to the climax of "A View of the Woods," and cows (having replaced cotton) are critical to the plots of "Greenleaf" and "The Enduring Chill." The new excitements of the city, with its movie theaters, neatly cut suburban lawns, and cruising automobiles, shape the mood and drama of *Wise Blood*, "The Artificial Nigger," "The Comforts of Home," and *The Violent Bear It Away.* Scattered references to the sit-in movement and to integrated bus systems appear, and the contentious, changing race relations of the region are basic to the plots of "Everything That Rises Must Converge" and "Judgement Day." Currents in twentieth-century thought, neither unique to the South nor alien to its people, shape rationalist, scientific psychologists like Sheppard in "The Lame Shall Enter First" and Rayber in *The Violent Bear It Away*, while Hazel Motes in *Wise Blood* and Hulga Hopewell and Manley Pointer in "Good Country Peopl"e are nihilists who reject the idea of any morality or meaning in the world.

O'Connor's fictional South was thus very much a place displaying signs of change. Yet unlike fellow southerner and Catholic Walker Percy, whose fiction took place in a thoroughly Sun Belt world of suburbs and interstate highways, amnesia and anomie, O'Connor's South still bore the strong imprint of its impoverished, rural, isolated, peripheral New South past. Like her character Hazel Motes—an ex-farm boy fresh out of the U.S. Army, haunted by memories of his preacher grandfather and the vanished rural community of Eastrod where he grew up—O'Connor's fictionalized South did not shake off its past easily. An elaborate code of manners, characters who dream of old ancestral plantations, characters who eke out a living from the soil or in low-paying industrial work, the everyday rhythms of agriculture, a public pattern of assumed white supremacy and dissimulating black deference, routine travel by train, mass river baptisms, traveling Bible salesmen, and carnival freak shows—all of these elements of O'Connor's stories bespeak an older South, one that to many readers today will feel considerably further back in time than the mid-twentieth century.

Nowhere is this older, distinct regional imprint more evident than in the Protestant religion informing O'Connor's fiction. The post-World War II decades were a time of heightened religious consciousness in the United States: the phrase "under God" was added to the pledge of allegiance, and "In God We Trust" became the official national motto, imprinted on every coin of the U.S. Treasury. As Jewish theologian Will Herberg noted in his 1955 book *Protestant, Catholic, Jew*, the real object of worship here was the U.S. nation. "Americans, by and large, do have their 'common religion,'" Herberg wrote critically, and "that 'religion' is the system familiarly known as the American Way of Life. . . . It is the American Way of Life about which Americans are admittedly and unashamedly 'intolerant'" (75).

This religious nationalism, so evident in the U.S. mainstream, was not the religion behind O'Connor's fiction. In a letter she described herself as a "hillbilly Thomist," and this is a revealing clue as to exactly where her regional religious affinities lay (*CW* 934). O'Connor the devoted Catholic was a distinct minority in the nation's most heavily Protestant region, but she deeply appreciated the power of Protestantism in the South because it had shaped the culture in theological, Christian ways. Within this overarching sensibility, though, O'Connor (and a number of historians and religious scholars) discerned different forms of Protestantism in a seemingly homogenous region. Clarifying these forms is essential to making sense of O'Connor's fictional world.

One form might be called "uptown religion." It was the religion of the propertied, white classes of the New South, people who put a premium on upstanding, moral behavior, on self-control, propriety, and respectability. This form was embodied in "First" and "Second" churches in the towns and cities, imposing brick and stone buildings that manifested both the wealth and established security of their congregants. Uptown Protestants had the political clout to pass laws articulating their vision for the South, most notably in late nineteenth-early twentieth century prohibitions on alcohol consumption, trade, and manufacture. They developed theological justifications for the race and class hierarchies of the New South, and they came to view the South as an outpost of the true faith in a nation that in the early twentieth century was experiencing decline in the old Protestant groups, incoming waves of Catholic, Eastern Orthodox, and Jewish immigrants, and an increasing secular sensibility. In O'Connor's critical judgment, uptown religion became too easily a benediction on the southern status quo, its potential Christian injunctions muted by its commanding cultural dominance.

A number of O'Connor characters—the Grandmother in "A Good Man is Hard to Find," Mrs. Hitchcock in *Wise Blood*, Mrs. Hopewell in "Good Country People," Julian's mother in "Everything That Rises Must Converge," Mrs. May in "Greenleaf"—embody this comfortable, respectable, accommodated uptown religion, but none more so than Ruby Turpin in "Revelation." In the waiting room of a doctor's office, Mrs. Turpin sizes up the strangers around her, carefully noting details of dress and speech so as to clarify everyone's social position. The Turpins are hardly elite, rather of middling status, but Mrs. Turpin believes herself "a respectable, hard-working, church-going woman," and she is proud of her position above others. In a moment of reflection, she exults that Jesus "had not made her a nigger or white-trash or ugly! He had made her herself and given her a little of everything. Jesus, thank you! She said. Thank you thank you thank you!" (*CS* 502). Whenever she counted her blessings she felt as buoyant as if she weighed one hundred and twenty-five pounds instead of one hundred and eighty" (*CS* 497). In a letter, O'Connor wrote critically that characters like Ruby Turpin had, unknowingly, merely a "superficial" relation to Christianity, one that needed moments of unsettling crisis or violence to become more profound (*CW* 1148).

It was with a different form of regional religion—what we might call "folk religion"—that O'Connor's personal and literary sympathies lay. Folk religion was found among the impoverished masses of the South, both white and black, and it was institutionalized in rural churches and small working-class churches in urban areas. Rather than upright propriety, folk religion demanded passionate devotion to the point of complete abnegation and loss of self-control. It listened for the voice of God in dreams and visions, and it struggled with evil not in moral admonitions but rather in the form of a visceral, irrational, destructive Devil. It drew sharp distinctions between God's order and the order of the world; in the Misfit's words, "Jesus thown everything off balance" (*CS* 131). At the same time, though, it displayed a marked tendency toward tangible, physical expressions of the holy, or what might be called a "Protestant sacramentalism." O. E. Parker in "Parker's Back," with his full-back tattoo of a stern Byzantine Christ, and Mason Tarwater in *The Violent Bear It Away*, with his obsession about the necessity of baptism, are but two O'Connor characters who display this sacramental drive in folk religion.

O'Connor in her fiction crossed the class, but not the color, line of the South, and religion was critical to this dynamic. She saw in the folk religion of the South a religious form to which she felt herself a kindred spirit. Folk religion was the religion of a marginalized group—the poor—and as a Catholic, O'Connor may have felt some kinship in marginality, but much more importantly, it was in folk religion that O'Connor saw a Christianity as devout, passionate, and uncompromising as her own. As she explained in a 1963 lecture, "The Catholic Novelist in the Protestant South":

> I think he [the Catholic novelist] will feel a good deal more kinship with backwoods prophets and shouting fundamentalists than he will with those politer elements for whom the supernatural is an embarrassment and for whom religion has become a department of sociology or culture or personality development. His interest and sympathy may very well go—as I know my own does—directly to those aspects of Southern life where the religious feeling is most intense and where its outward forms are farthest from the Catholic. (207)

The real-world presence of Southern folk religion became, then, fertile imaginative soil from which O'Connor crafted many of her major characters, characters who allowed her to explore struggles of belief and unbelief, evil and grace.

Speech, clothing, place of residence, occupation, and various other details signify that characters like Hazel Motes in *Wise Blood*, the Misfit in "A Good Man is Hard to Find," Bevel Summers in "The River," Tom T. Shiftlet in "The Life You Save May Be Your Own," Mr. Head and Nelson in "The Artificial Nigger," Manley Pointer in "Good Country People," Rufus Johnson in "The Lame Shall Enter First," O. E. Parker in "Parker's Back," and Mason and Francis Marion Tarwater in *The Violent Bear It Away* are, or come from the ranks of, impoverished rural whites. The shape and content of their religious struggles—involving passionate extremes of belief or unbelief, a ready ear for the mysterious and the mystical, a predilection toward tangible manifestations of unseen truth—demonstrate that O'Connor was not just a brilliant creator of literature, but also a keen observer of the Southern scene, especially in its religious intricacies.

O'Connor's sense of kinship with Southern folk religion and her distinct emphasis on impoverished and working-class characters baffled some of her contemporaneous audience, and it may confuse the present-day reader. In the early 1960s a reviewer for *Time* noted condescendingly that she wrote of "God-intoxicated hillbillies," and another in *Library Journal* wrote with a sniff of her "band of poor God-driven

Southern whites" (*Time*, *CW* 1121). Occasionally in the criticism one finds O'Connor lumped together with Erskine Caldwell, who both peopled his fiction with poor whites drawn with egregious ridicule and portrayed their religion as little more than an inspiration for flagrant sexual activity and wishful dreaming. Such ridicule, distance, and stereotyping was far from O'Connor's purpose.

Rather, in crafting mid-twentieth-century literature from her Catholic theological vision, O'Connor felt herself writing very much against the grain. She found national popular culture to be dominated by a comfortable materialism that took its cues from the twin poles of Hollywood and Madison Avenue. In her more discrete circle of peers, that of her fellow professional writers and intellectuals, she encountered cultured disdain for traditional religious commitment, such as a dinner party where one writer remarked that the Eucharist, while a quaint timepiece, nevertheless had utility as an interesting literary symbol. Much closer to home, in the social circles of propertied southern whites like herself, O'Connor thought that uptown religion was too closely entwined with the social order, with the world of the country club and the Kiwanis Club. It was in southern folk religion, then, that O'Connor found a larger imaginative home, and real-world types from whom she could craft believable fictions.

But as noted, the South of O'Connor's era was undergoing major transformation, and this touched not only the economy and social order, but religion too. Most pertinently for O'Connor's fiction, the folk religion that had developed in the New South among the impoverished rural masses was facing a radically different context, as regional poverty, rural life, and cultural isolation were becoming things of the past. Materialist consumer culture had a not inconsiderable allure for "folk" off the farm, and scientific, rationalist thinking made inroads into the region that had once prohibited Darwinian theory from its public schools. A character like Enoch Emery in *Wise Blood*, a once-poor country boy comes to the city, lives and moves in a world of movies, ice cream, and soda pop. Meanwhile, an old-style member of the folk—the backwoods prophet Mason Tarwater, who lives in a rickety shack in a small forest clearing called Powderhead—finds himself utterly dismissed by his scientific, rationalist nephew Rayber. Rayber lived with Tarwater for a time, asking him all sorts of questions and carefully noting his answers. Tarwater thought that this was because Rayber wanted to understand his own Christian redemption, but then to his astonishment and horror, he learned that Rayber's queries had the ultimate goal of reducing faith to psychological explanations. Tarwater fumes as Rayber mockingly says, "Uncle, you're a type that's almost extinct!" (*The Violent Bear It Away* 29).

While evoking such religious change, O'Connor's stories display, in religion as in society more generally, the heavy imprint of the past. The religious forms of the older South, especially its folk religion, cast an unmistakable aura across the new, emergent Sun Belt. Although he tries to thoroughly revoke his rural past, Hazel Motes cannot do it. Comically to the reader, unconsciously for Hazel, his founding of the "Church Without Christ" bespeaks, by way of negative repudiation, the force of Christianity in his—and the South's—past. Indeed, *Wise Blood*'s narrator tells us that Hazel is a haunted man, troubled by a vision where "he saw Jesus move from tree to tree in the back of his mind, a wild ragged figure motioning him to turn around and come off into the dark" (*Wise Blood* 22). For O'Connor, this religious tradition that couldn't be shaken off was a good thing, one of the genuine merits of the South. "Ghosts can be very fierce and instructive," she argued in a lecture. "They cast strange shadows." (*MM* 45).

In an early twenty-first century context, with an ongoing process of globalization, an international awareness of considerable religious difference, and a more aggressive, more materialist national culture of consumption, O'Connor's fiction, with its transparent regionalism and particularist religious allegiance, may seem too foreign to be relevant or pertinent. O'Connor's characters may strike us, as they did some of her contemporary readers, as unintelligible "freaks." Yet despite—or maybe, precisely because of—her limited, distinct context, O'Connor's fiction enjoys a wide, ever-growing, international audience.

Although billed as a new chapter of progress and a new epoch of information, globalization is bringing rapid, unsettling change, insecurity, declining purchasing power, and falling social status to many people, undermining some of their most basic assumptions about how the world works. In that sense, some of the staples of an older era are "going South." Indeed, some of the staple features of the older South (the "New South") are reappearing in a new guise: absentee control, extractive use of resources, low wages. Meanwhile, in open contradiction to what sociologists and religion scholars call the "secularization hypothesis," many different places in our global world are witnessing an increased devotion to, and interest in, religion. Some of this interest, especially in the United States, takes a noninstitutional direction, as people pursue "spirituality" outside older religious groups. In such a context, where some of the older verities no longer hold up, where human lives face strain and uncertainty, O'Connor's fiction resonates. Her theological portrait of human beings as essentially *spiritual* animals—not just *social*, or *economic*, or *political* ones—may especially speak to those who have found the old gods of nation or market to be insufficient. Punctuated as her stories are with violent crisis moments, they may come across not as off-putting, but rather as appropriately unsettling, as people feel their own lives upset and uncertain. In such a context of anomie and alienation, readers may find in O'Connor's anxious, haunted, mysterious South an all-too-pertinent imaginative home.

Works Cited

Coles, Robert. *Flannery O'Connor's South*. Athens: U of Georgia P, 1980.

Herberg, Will. *Protestant, Catholic, Jew*. Garden City, N.Y.: Doubleday, 1955.

O'Connor, Flannery. *Collected Works*. Athens: U of Georgia P, 1980. (Cited in text as *CW*).

____________. *The Complete Stories*. New York: Farrar, Straus and Giroux, 1971. (Cited in text as *CS*).

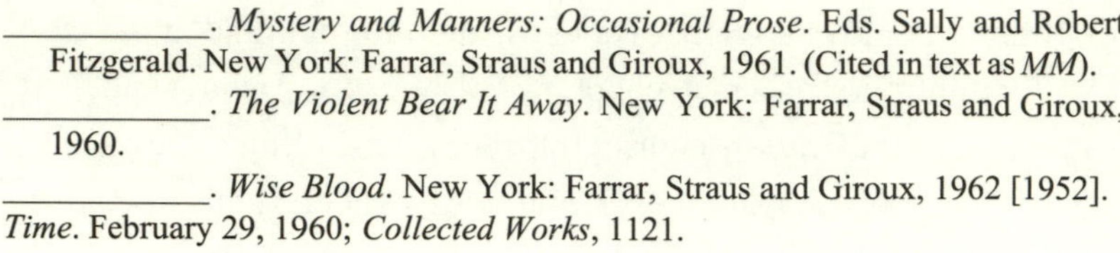

___________. *Mystery and Manners: Occasional Prose*. Eds. Sally and Robert Fitzgerald. New York: Farrar, Straus and Giroux, 1961. (Cited in text as *MM*).

___________. *The Violent Bear It Away*. New York: Farrar, Straus and Giroux, 1960.

___________. *Wise Blood*. New York: Farrar, Straus and Giroux, 1962 [1952].

Time. February 29, 1960; *Collected Works*, 1121.

Flannery O'Connor, John Updike, and the Writer's "True Country"

Avis Hewitt

John Updike—tall, tan, and tony—is generally pictured on his dust jackets against a backdrop of the sea or the golf course. Wind ruffles his hair that never thinned but was to the end of his life boyishly thick and just a tad longish and a bit out of control. A genial toothy grin conveys a non-elitist welcome to his readers and belies the aristocratic breadth of knowledge, the level of erudition that goes into painting the quotidian realities his books dramatized for more than half a century. Flannery O'Connor wielded a public image that privileged her life with peacocks, crutches bearing her up, as, on the porch steps of Andalusia, she shoots one of her straight looks at the camera or as, seated on the farmhouse sofa, she attempts to match the dour countenance of the self-portrait on the wall above her. The sharp contrast of their public images notwithstanding, what they have in common as contemporary American writers is Christian conviction.

Updike observed, "When you moved toward Christianity it disappeared, as fog solidly opaque in the distance thins to transparency when you walk into it. I decided I nevertheless *would* believe" (*SC* 230). By contrast, O'Connor omits the fog. In "The Fiction Writer and His Country," she offers clear witness: "I am no disbeliever in spiritual purpose and no vague believer. I see from the standpoint of Christian orthodoxy. This means that for me the meaning of life is centered in our Redemption by Christ and that what I see in the world I see in its relation to that" (*MM* 32). In fact, Michael M. Jordan has argued that "O'Connor (in her letters, essays, and fiction—all three) is the most significant and perceptive Christian writer America has produced and that as Christian witness, apologist, prophet, and literary and cultural critic, she even rivals Chesterton and Lewis, though certainly not in terms of influence, at least not yet" (1). She seems the top-ranking Catholic novelist in American literary history. As for Updike, David

Lodge noted, when reviewing *Roger's Version* in 1986, that Updike's erudition makes him

> well able to evoke the ethos of an academic theology department [because he] has manifested an interest in religion and theology in previous books. If there was ever such a species as the Protestant novelist, comparable to that much discussed animal, the Catholic novelist, Mr. Updike may be its last surviving example. (1)

In *Mystery and Manners* (1969), a collection of O'Connor's occasional prose that Sally Fitzgerald compiled from O'Connor's talks on the college lecture circuit and other public speaking venues, the author makes an impressively persuasive bid to control her own reception by detailing the frame of reference by which readers should engage her work. Using a structure offered by St. Thomas Aquinas, she sees fiction as functioning simultaneously on at least three levels. The first, of course, is

> everything from the actual countryside that the novelist describes, on, to, and through the peculiar characteristics of his region and his nation, and on, through, and under all of these to his true country, which the writer with Christian concerns will consider to be what is eternal and absolute. (27)

That "true country," and the way in which O'Connor and John Updike as professing Christians each engage it, makes them—even with all their binaries of male/female, Northern/Southern, Protestant/Catholic—not an obvious match, but an apt one.

Updike and O'Connor shared the rare contemporary coupling of deep intellect with a will to belief. Writing of his boyhood moment of religious decision, Updike testifies in the last of six essays in his *Self-Consciousness: Memoirs*, titled "On Being a Self Forever": "What I felt in that basement Sunday school of Grace Lutheran Church in Shillington, was a clumsy attempt to extend a Yes, a blessing, and I accepted that blessing, offering in return only a nickel a week and my art, my poor little art" (231). A cradle Catholic, O'Connor does not write of "the hour she first believed." But her work attests to the steady testing of faith that the contemporary world exacts: "If you live today you breathe in nihilism. In or out of the Church, it's the gas you breathe. If I hadn't had the Church to fight it with or to tell me the necessity of fighting it, I would be the stinkingest logical positivist you ever saw right now" (HB 97). In 1994 Updike wrote, "My impression is that orthodox religion scarcely figures at all, even as a force to be reacted against, in contemporary American writing" ("Remarks" 77). What is worse is that "lives seem to have little meaning beyond the immediate emotional need"; yet "the very lack of meaning is scarcely felt," and characters would "no more look within themselves for significance than they look into the flickering dramas of television or the flickering affective lives of their friends and kin" (79). O'Connor wrote Betty Hester, "I am a Catholic peculiarly possessed of the modern consciousness, that thing Jung described as unhistorical, solitary, and guilty" and admitted that it was a burden (*HB* 90). For her part, O'Connor decided that "the Church is the only thing that is going to make the terrible world we are coming to endurable; the only thing that makes the Church endurable is that it is somehow the body of Christ and that on that we are fed" (*HB* 90).

O'Connor and Updike—two seemingly quite disparate authors—lived lives replete with uncanny commonalities. If we focus only on superfluities, few contemporary American authors seem less alike than John Updike (1932-2009) of Pennsylvania, New York, and finally New England, and Flannery O'Connor (1925-1964), who, although she lived in the North for five of her thirty-nine years, is associated almost completely with the Deep South, particularly Georgia. Born only seven years later than O'Connor, Updike was, like her, an only child. His parents, Wesley and Linda Hoyer Updike, struggled for some dubious place near the bottom of that devastation the Depression had wracked upon the middle class, even though their cherished "Chonnie" was surprised to learn as an adult that his father had actually considered them always to have been poor. Having had his Schwinn bike, Flexible Flyer sled, and Jimmy Foxx fielder's glove, Updike had felt no deprivation (*SC* 29). His achieving upper middle class status seemed as much a cause as an effect of Updike's writerly success, and in fact, the two remain inextricably entangled. Updike told Jane Howard in 1966, "My subject is the American Protestant middle class. I like middles. It is in the middle that extremes clash, where ambiguity restlessly rules. Something quite intricate and fierce occurs in homes, and it seems to me without doubt worthwhile to examine what it is" (11).

In contrast to Updike's affluent subjects, O'Connor focused on the overtly disadvantaged:

> when I look at the stories I have written I find that they are, for the most part, about people who are poor, who are afflicted in both mind and body, who have little—or at best a distorted—sense of spiritual purpose, and whose actions do not apparently give the reader a great assurance of the joy of life. (*MM*, 32)

But overweening pride and hardness of heart observe no economic boundaries. Spiritual poverty—in life and in fiction—abounds. O'Connor and Updike both interest themselves in the spiritual poverty that ensnares their characters, but the worldly wealth of Updike's characters disguises it from modern eyes, including generally their own. O'Connor, however, draws her characters' shortcomings in "large and startling figures" since most of us are made "almost blind" by egotism, and she also recognizes that "to the hard of hearing you shout" (*MM* 34). Her stories are noted for their violence because she sees it as "strangely capable of returning my characters to reality and preparing them to accept their moment of grace"; most of us are so hard-headed that "almost nothing else will do the work," but we need reality, even though it is something "to which we must be returned at considerable cost" (*MM* 112). Updike too recognizes the primacy of reality. He has “felt free to describe life as accurately” as he could, especially its “human erosions and betrayals” (*SC*, 231). He ascribes to his “small faith” whatever courage he has had as an artist on the “theory that God already knows everything and cannot be shocked [and that] only truth is useful” because it “can be built upon so that finally only truth is holy” (*SC* 231).

This said, we must acknowledge that O’Connor and Updike’s affinities are not apparent in appearances. Lorraine Murray labeled O’Connor in her 2009 monograph on O’Connor’s spiritual life “the abbess of Andalusia,” and in 1986 David Lodge accused Updike of having written in such dubious detail about sexuality that he has “taken a leading part in the tendency of contemporary art to blur” the sometimes difficult distinction between “the discourse of eroticism” and that of “pornography” (1). Updike’s fiction speaks to those with a readerly penchant for sexuality; O’Connor’s to those with a similar penchant for violence. Between them, they are literary big box-office. Updike characters deal in angst, but O’Connor’s characters deal in abjection. In O’Connor’s work we suffer *in extremis*. She writes regarding the grandmother’s confrontation with the Misfit and his lethal intentions for her that the granny “is in the most significant position life offers the Christian. She is facing death. And to all appearances she, like the rest of us, is not too well prepared for it. She would like to see the event postponed. Indefinitely” (*MM* 110).

But in Updike’s world, suffering has the mild middle-class vexation-unto-death that we are left to endure after money and status and education and myriad other privileges and perks have done their best to assuage all of life’s negatives. Denis Donoghue ends his *New York Times* book review of Updike’s 1989 *Self-Consciousness: Memoirs* with the topic of aging, accusing Updike at fifty-seven of having adapted the attitude of “nothing to look forward to but sunset and the western porch” (7) because Updike writes, “Between now and the grave lies a long slide of forestallment, a slew of dutiful, dutifully paid-for maintenance routines in which dermatological makeshift joins periodontal work and prostate examinations on the crowded appointment calendar of dwindling days" (*SC* 78). Donoghue's response: "Meanwhile, I note that he is four years younger than I am" (7). And so it is with much that Updike writes. We measure our lives against what he describes because he has found the words to delineate our subjectivity by cataloging lyrically the quotidian particulars that mark our era. Updike's *in extremis* occurs in the dentist's chair, not in a dirt-road ditch.

David Foster Wallace sheds light upon the Updikean middleness. To Wallace, Updike, along with Philip Roth and Norman Mailer, is one of "the Great Male Narcissists" of American letters, one "whose rise in the 1960s and '70s established him as both the chronicler and the voice of probably the single-most self-absorbed generation since Louis XIV" (51). Wallace thinks that the "subforty"-year-old literati dislike Updike most of all the group because his protagonists "are basically all the same guy," and "they always live in either Pennsylvania or New England, are either unhappily married or divorced, are roughly Updike's age," and while they share Updike's "effortlessly lush, synesthetic" gifts in thinking and speaking, they unfortunately share as well his "incorrigibly narcissistic, philandering, self-contemptuous, self-pitying . . . deeply alone" nature (53). Wallace's final blow: these Updike protagonists "never really love anybody" (53). Updike's offense is to have drawn painfully accurately the generation that made the mess that Wallace and his peers had to face while growing up. He charges that the young adults of the 1990s were

> the children of all the impassioned infidelities and divorces Updike wrote about so beautifully, [the offspring] who got to watch all this brave new individualism and sexual freedom deteriorate into the joyless and anomic self-indulgence of the Me Generation. (54)

Indeed one clear message that *Self-Consciousness* narrates is that Updike's leap resembles Ben Franklin's in his *Autobiography*, given his "having emerged from the Poverty & Obscurity in which [he] was born & bred, to a State of Affluence & some degree of Reputation in the World" (3). Updike's good fortune took him from Shillington to Harvard and Manhattan and Ipswich. But having "it" and fitting in, he is both attracted to and at odds with the trendy, clubby crowd populating Ipswich. He finds himself thrilled by "a surge of belonging" that now permeates his life—from the "committees and societies," from the "recorder group and poker group," from "play[ing] volleyball and touch football in season, [and] read[ing] plays aloud," as well as the "Greek-dancing, dinner parties, clambakes, concerts, and costume balls" (52). He loved what he calls the "clubbiness" (*SC* 55). He confesses, "in Ipswich my impersonation of a normal person became as good as I could make it" (54). Yet his stance on Vietnam, "On Not Being a Dove," was not normal among his left-leaning crowd. He secretly enjoyed an obstinate alignment against his mainly liberal friends. To him, the Harvard-Radcliffe Democrats, "secure in the upper middle class, were Democrats out of human sympathy and humanitarian largesse, because this was the party that helped the poor. Our family had simply *been* poor, and voted Democrat out of crude self-interest" (119). And as such, he sympathized with Lyndon Johnson, that "lugubrious bohunk from Texas," who was snobbishly dismissed by the Eastern establishment: "These privileged members of a privileged nation believed that their enviable position could be maintained without anything visibly ugly happening in the world" (120). Updike was not at one with their sense of dismissive privilege. He perennially re-cast himself as a spy in their midst: "a literary spy [from] average, public school, supermarket America" who had infiltrated the tony "North Shore upper class" (53). And eventually this reasoning regarding his hawkish political position becomes a theological tenet:

> A dark Augustinian idea lurked within my tangled position: a plea that Vietnam—this wretched unfashionable war led by clumsy Presidents from the West and fought by nineteen-year-old sons of the poor—could not be

disowned by a favored enlightened few hiding behind college deferments, fleeing to chaste cool countries, snootily pouring pig blood into draft files, writing deeply offended Notes and Comments, and otherwise pretending that our great nation hadn't had bloody hands from the start, that every generation didn't have its war, that bloody hands didn't go with having hands at all. (135-36)

Such bloody hands smack of original sin and suggest a meeting ground between O'Connor's orthodoxy and Updike's vague sense of the transcendent. Lupus intensified O'Connor's religious questing, preparing her spiritually as her intense study in theology prepared her intellectually for her role as epistolary Christian apologist in her relationship with Betty Hester[1]—and to a lesser extent, Cecil Dawkins, Alfred Corn, and others. Their seeker stance provided her a chance to articulate the Christian witness as her belief evolved depth upon depth. Updike, deciding in boyhood that he *would* believe, entangled himself in religious struggle mainly, it seems, from his unhappiness in his first marriage, the ethical costs of deserting the wife of his youth and, at some level, his children and choosing to love other women and eventually a wife who was not their mother. This clash of duty and desire became the engine driving his religious quest. In some ways, we must suspect O'Connor's bodily afflictions to have been the lighter cross to bear than Updike's divorce and desertions because hers were not accompanied by a tortured conscience.

Among Updike and O'Connor's characters, the salient actions that drive plots are frequently strikingly unethical. Her characters swindle, shoot, drown, and gore people, not to mention running over them with tractors and cars, but for only one of them is the answer to most of what ails us in life the decision to commit adultery. Updike sees a disconnect between belief in God and ethics. The first, he writes, in the introduction to *Soundings in Satanism*, is creedal: "I call myself 'a Christian' by defining a Christian as 'a person willing to profess the Apostle's Creed'" (xi). As to the second, Updike takes his cue from Karl Barth:

"Ethics is the attempt to give a human answer to the question of dignity, correctness, and excellence of human activity" (86). In fact, Barth, in his signature work, *Church Dogmatics*, writes that both Christians and non-Christians stay enmeshed in and participate "fully and very concretely in the perversity and futility of all human efforts" (50). And Updike told Jane Howard in 1966, "I believe that all problems are basically insoluble and that faith is a leap out of total despair" (14).

Updike's commitment to the Barthian premise that God is Wholly Other, thereby unknowable and His ways unknowable, has caused Bernard Schopen to argue that "since Updike's Christianity is determined only by his profession of the Apostle's Creed, it contains no inherent moral system" (525). In Barth's *The Word of God and the Word of Man*, this lack is underscored: "Man cannot begin to answer the ethical questions in actual life. He can only recognize that he is wholly incapable of commanding an answer" (166). With God as Wholly Other and human beings as "wholly incapable," we should not be surprised that the fictional world of Updike's prose invites despair. In "Separating," a story from *Problems and Other Stories* (1979), which Donald Greiner believes will eventually be seen as "one of the major collections of short stories published in the twentieth century" (269), the protagonist is separating from his wife, who wants him to break the news to each of their four children separately. In the concluding moment, his older son and namesake Dickie asks him, after what is described as a "passionate" good night kiss, "Why?" And the narrator tells us, "Richard had forgotten why" (130-31). Yet we know from life and from the later placement of "Separating" in the short story cycle *Too Far to Go* (1979), that with or without a clear reason, separate he did. In the blurred zone between life and fiction and in novels like *Couples* (1968) and *Marry Me* (1976), readers spot that he fought the ethical battles inherent in not loving his wife as passionately or in the same way that he loved his mistresses and that one of them at last became so crucial for his psychic survival that he broke with his family.

In *Self-Consciousness* Updike tells us that finally he could not get his breath in his own home. He reports that when his wife returned from her Monday night singing group, "I lay gasping on the floor . . . had many bad nights . . . my breath traveling in and out of me through a very small aperture" (99) because "I had tried to break out of my marriage on behalf of another, and failed, and began to have trouble breathing" (98). Finally, the symptom was traced to cat dander (100), and since the cats were "too old and stubborn to change habits" and stay outdoors or in the cellar, "it seemed easier to get rid of me" (101). We need not read that excuse as a dodge. But since a part of staying "out of harm's way" (*SC* 33)—the guiding Updike tenet—is the artful dodge, he lets the cats take the fall: "In the end, rather than discomfit the cats, I discomfited the human beings in my family and moved to Boston" (101). Updike has relentlessly conflated sex and religion, making this moving to Boston his overarching but necessary sin: "to give myself brightness and air I read Karl Barth and fell in love with other men's wives" (98). He sees his study of Barth, Kierkegaard, Chesterton, Maritain, and C. S. Lewis as having created for him a "pinhole of light" by which his spirit could survive" (98). The other half of the survival tactic, the wives, was more problematic: "I would see them in bright party dresses or in bathing suits down at the beach, and in my head they would have their season of budding, of flamboyant bloom, and of wilt, all while my aging, emphysematous body remained uxorious and dutiful" (98).

Frederick Crews, in his "Mr. Updike's Planet" from *The Critics Bear It Away*, confirms that "as his career progressed, Updike radically divorced his notion of Christian theology from that of Christian ethics" and refused to "feel bound by standard notions of sin. Instead, he would seek in sheer experience, and above all in sexual experience, continual reassurance against the terror of nothingness" (171). Crews finds that Updike's novels after the mid-1970s have an "anaesthetic tone and moral inconclusiveness" as they dramatize "disintegrating marriages"; in fact, the books "stew in a pervasive yet unacknowledged atmosphere of self-reproach" (172). Just as lupus might be seen as a sea change in O'Connor's development as a writer, marital discontent and the attenuated act of divorce was likely Updike's: his "whole project of mooting ethical injunctions looks like an overreaction to self-judgment on the single point of adultery" (173). He joins Karl Barth in an anti-works path to salvation since it allows him to relish further his private hostilities toward the tony North Shore set with whom at the same time he delights in feeling "clubby": "Updike's wandering husbands ardently champion . . . Barth, heaping abuse on the Christian liberals' retreat from the Cross to charitable works and kindly feelings—the values invariably associated with the deserted or soon-to-be-deserted wives" (173). In her "Introduction" to *A Memoir of Mary Ann*, O'Connor takes a similar dim view of "kindly feelings":

> If other ages felt less, they saw more, even though they saw with the blind, prophetical, unsentimental eye of acceptance, which is to say, faith. In the absence of this faith now, we govern by tenderness. It is a tenderness which, long since cut off from the person of Christ, is wrapped in theory. When tenderness is detached from the source of tenderness, its logical outcome is terror. It ends in forced labor camps and in the fumes of the gas chamber. (*MM*, 227)

Neither Updike nor O'Connor traffics much in good deeds. Hothouse "tenderness" does not stand up to horror. Conventional morality is secondary to belief in the central dynamics of Christianity: our sinful natures redeemed by sacrificial love. Both authors concern themselves with sanctification, not justification—with the numinous epiphany.

One means of comparing O'Connor and Updike's theological understanding is their use of a particular sort of "tenderness"—the intense desiring known as eros. In the late 1950s Updike reviewed the then recently translated work of Denis de Rougemont, *Love in the Western World* and its sequel *Love Declared*. What evidently resonated most with Updike is de Rougemont's notion that "only in being loved do we find external corroboration of the supremely high valuation each ego secretly assigns itself"; moreover, we want "to choose that other being in whose existence our own being is confirmed and amplified" (*Assorted Prose*, 180). And choose Updike did, over and over in his autobiographical protagonists. In his own life, his position as seducer was "improved [and] enhanced by a touch of wealth and celebrity," making him "a stag of sorts in our herd of housewife does" (*SC*, 222). Ralph Wood, in *The Comedy of Redemption*, traces Updike's uneasy peace with adultery to his reading of Søren Kierkegaard, "who first taught us that sensuousness is not a pagan but a Christian phenomenon" in its "render[ing] sensuousness self-conscious for the first time" and according flesh "a certain desperate power" in the very act of denying and suppressing it (179-180). In this seeming standoff between the needs of the ego as it supremely values itself and the violent intervention into human history of Christ's fulsome sacrifice as the embodied element of the Triune God, Father M. C. D'Arcy, a Jesuit leader of the mid-century Catholic intellectual revival, mediates an integration of our notion of love.

Father D'Arcy's 1947 work, *The Mind and Heart of Love: A Study in Eros and Agape*, traces love from Plato's *Symposium* forward and smartly summarizes the dichotomized definition to which de Rougemont ascribed: for him,

> Eros consisted of a dark passion which was lawless and infinitely discontented with the earthly and temporal existence of the soul. Agape, on the other hand, made the best of time and of the present and wore the bonds of marriage, for instance, as a freeman, as belonging to a new covenant with God made man. (73)

D'Arcy's prescient delineation of Updike's issues becomes apparent in almost all of Updike's domestic fiction. He certainly yearned, as we have seen, toward "validating his existence through immersion in the tangible" and in particular in intimate encounters with women, but not the encounters available in the marriage bed. As Frederick Crews has aptly observed, Updike relentlessly implies that

> the seeker's wife [is] almost by definition a death bearer who would clip his metaphysical wings and, by entrapping him in bland and benign routine, allow the doomsday clock to tick irreversibly away. Somebody else's wife, on the other hand, would be another story. (172)

In O'Connor's most direct dramatization of domestic dissonance, her last story, "Parker's Back," O. E. Parker, its protagonist, seeks succor in a tattoo parlor, even if not in other people's bedrooms, because his wife is not his type: she is "plain" and refuses to "paint her face [even though] God knew some paint would have improved it"; she is suspicious and "forever sniffing up sin" and sanctimonious in that she does "not smoke or dip, drink whiskey, [or] use bad language"(*CW* 655). Moreover, she is a bad cook: "Sarah Ruth just threw food in the pot and let it boil" (664), and she beats poor Parker's back with a broom both beginning and end. What is clear, however, is that he desires her deeply, all superfluities disregarded. He married her because "he couldn't have got her any other way" (655), and in the climactic episode, he lies in "the long dormitory of cots" at the Haven of Light Mission "long[ing] miserably for Sarah Ruth" and recognizing her "sharp tongue and ice pick eyes" to be "the only comfort he could bring to mind" (669).

Parker desires Sarah Ruth against his own "reason"—or, as Father D'Arcy would put it, his heart works against his mind. This is the affliction, the grotesque response to God's offer of loving wholeness that pride causes us to suffer. Grace, on the other hand, embodies the interface of eros and agape that Pope Benedict XI illuminated in his 2005 initial papal encyclical, *Deus Caritas Est*. He sees human beings as only truly themselves when "body and soul are intimately united" (18). Eros initiates human desire, and at some point the egocentric element of it that Updike cites stands to be overcome by a selfless yearning for the good of the beloved. While the Greeks saw it as an intoxicant, they acknowledged that "in the very process of being overwhelmed by divine power, [we] experience supreme happiness" (16). But Pope Benedict, as Ralph C. Wood points out, "wants to reclaim eros for the Church, regarding it as an authentic sign of the human hunger for and expression of the Holy" ("Flannery" 6). Beyond the moment of intoxication lies the conduit between our full humanness and God's transcendent divinity. That conduit is desire. Leon Kass reminds us that in Plato's *Symposium*, Socrates names eros as "the heart of the human soul, an animating power born of lack but pointing upward" (27). This pointing upward appears early in Updike's work. He sees himself as having been branded with a Cross from boyhood, as believing that "at the core of the core, there is a right-angled clash to which, of all verbal combinations we can invent, the Apostles' Creed offers the most adequate correspondence and response" ("Dogwood Tree," 143).

Our horizontal relationships to humankind and our vertical reaching toward God are captured for Updike in the image of the cross. Leon Kass takes this emblem of seemingly "crossed" purposes into the realm of human flourishing:

> Eros emerges as both self-seeking and over-flowingly generative—at bottom the fruit of the peculiar conjunction of, and conjunction between, two conflicting aspirations born in a single living body, both tied to our finitude: the impulse of self-preservation and the urge to reproduce. The former is a self-regarding concern for our own personal permanence and satisfaction; the latter is a self-forgetting aspiration for something that transcends our own finite existence, and for the sake of which we spend and even give our lives. (27)

Pope Benedict names the Song of Songs as representing the eros relationship between God and His people: "a source of mystical knowledge and experience"; yet it is "no mere fusion, a sinking into the nameless ocean of the Divine; it is a unity which creates love, a unity in which both God and man remain themselves and yet become fully one" (32). Ralph Wood's recent application of Pope Benedict's conception of divine eros to the fiction of Flannery O'Connor insists on readers seeing that divine grace "erupts from within the very nature and existence of things, bursting outward, so as to transform them" (8). This dynamic resonates with readers' own experience of intense and transformative desire, but as a powerful undercurrent in O'Connor's evolving fiction, it has gone largely unnoticed. In a November 1955 letter to Betty Hester, only a few months after their correspondence began, O'Connor addresses the issue by confirming her friend's "uncanny" observation of what O'Connor calls "the lacking category" (*HB* 117). By this we know she means eros, for she paraphrases Chekhov's having said that "he-and-she is the machine that makes fiction work" but asserts that his is "too exclusive a view"; yet Hester must have "accused" O'Connor of failing to associate eros with "the virtuous emotions," causing O'Connor to protest that she indeed does "associate it a good deal beyond the simply virtuous emotions; I identify it plainly with the sacred. My inability to handle it so far in fiction may be purely personal, as my upbringing has smacked a little of Jansenism even if my convictions do not" (117). Her work between 1955 and 1964 relentlessly gained ground over her "inability" to deal with eros and culminated in a masterpiece of its exploration: "Parker's Back."

Yet like Updike, O'Connor's convictions lean one way, but her proclivities somehow another. By noting an unwilling tendency to Jansenist notions, she identifies herself as feeling that man is too fallen to choose toward the sacred. Jansenism was a Counter-Reformation debate/heresy of the early seventeenth century that disavowed moral agency in the acceptance or rejection of God's grace. If the grace is irresistible, then no mere human creature can, of course, resist it. Agape and eros in this seem similar. Irresistible, inexplicable desire draws Parker to Sarah Ruth and Updike's protagonists to their various forbidden women. And while Crews may argue that Updike's infidelities divorced his Christian theology from his Christian ethics, he yet concedes that the writer spent much of his subsequent prose worrying after that scandal of his spirit. O'Connor, who is notable for taking characters to the moment when their hardhearted pride is violently shattered so that grace has an entry, does not usually take them any farther. With Parker, she does. Post-shatter, Parker owns his full name and "lean[s] against [a] tree, crying like a baby" (*CW* 675). He must be born again, and he is. For both Updike and O'Connor, the artful dodge of bourgeois morality is subsumed by their overarching need to depict the violent and passionate encounters of their yearning characters with the transcendent—with that which offers a fulfillment beyond the earthly, yet relentlessly increases the mystery that lies beyond our quotidian manners.

Note

1. Elizabeth Hester (1923-1998) was a native of Rome, Georgia, with a troubled past (a parental suicide and a dishonorable discharge from the Air Force because of a lesbian incident that met with vehement official disapproval in the Cold War era). She lived with a female relative on Peachtree Road in Atlanta, working by day at an office job and late into the night as a self-styled intellectual: "Each night the reclusive clerk returned to her aunt's apartment and took up her station on the living room couch, where she slept, as well as read and wrote, surrounded by stacks of books, ashtray—she was a heavy smoker—and a menagerie of cats" (Gooch 268). She first wrote O'Connor after *A Good Man Is Hard to Find, and Other Stories* was published in June 1955. The young author was elated to find a correspondent of her own intellectual caliber, and the timing was especially felicitous, given the fact that O'Connor's illness had taken a turn and she found herself having to begin the use of crutches (Gooch 268-283). Connie Ann Kirk reminds us that O'Connor wrote more letters to Hester than to any other correspondent, unless to Regina—all of which are unpublished and consequently uncounted (225). As Brad Gooch points out, Hester was O'Connor's "happiest connection" (278). In January 1956 Hester decided to be baptized in the Catholic Church, even though the conversion away from agnosticism lasted not quite three years before she lapsed. It was the intense theological quest of Hester during those 1950s exchanges that provided O'Connor an opportunity to articulate and clarify her own intense reading and thinking with regard to religious issues. To the extent that *The Habit of Being* is a theological text, a work of powerful Christian apologetics, it is Hester's friendship that evoked those arguments on orthodoxy and belief.

Works Cited

Barth, Karl. *Church Dogmatics: A Selection*. Ed. and trans. G. W. Bromiley. New York: Harper, 1962.

____________. *God Here and Now*. Trans. Paul M. Van Buren. New York: Harper, 1964.

____________. *The Word of God and the Word of Man*. Trans. Douglas Horton. New York: Harper, 1964.

Benedict XVI. *Deus Caritas Est: Encyclical Letter of the Supreme Pontiff*. San Francisco, CA: Ignatius Press, 2006.

Crews, Frederick. *The Critics Bear It Away: American Fiction and the Academy*. New York: Random House, 1992.

D'Arcy, Father Martin Cyril, S.J. *The Mind and Heart of Love: Lion and Unicorn, A Study in Eros and Agape*. New York: Henry Holt, 1947.

De Bellis, Jack. *The John Updike Encyclopedia*. Westport, CT: Greenwood Press, 2000.

Detweiler, Robert. *Breaking the Fall: Religious Readings of Contemporary Fiction*. Louisville, KY: Westminster John Knox Press, 1989.

Donoghue, Denis. "I Have Preened, I Have Lived." *The New York Times Book Review* 5 Mar. 1989: 7.

Franklin, Benjamin. *The Autobiography and Other Writings*. Ed. Kenneth Silverman. New York: Penguin, 1986.

Gooch, Brad. *Flannery: A Life of Flannery O'Connor*. New York: Little, Brown, 2009.

Greiner, Donald J. "John Updike." *Dictionary of Literary Biography*. Vol 143. *American Novelists since World War II*. Ed. James R. Giles and Wanda H. Giles. Detroit: Gale, 1994.

Gross, Terry. "'Fresh Air with Terry Gross': John Updike." WHYY Philadelphia. National Public Radio. 1988. Rpt. in *Conversations with John Updike*. Ed. James Plath. Jackson: UP of Mississippi, 1994.

Howard, Jane. "Can a Nice Novelist Finish First? Interview with John Updike." *Life* 61 (4 Nov. 1966): 74-82. Rpt. in *Conversations with John Updike*. Ed. James Plath. Jackson: UP of Mississippi, 1994. 9-17.

Jordan, Michael M. "A Closer Look: An Interview with Marion Montgomery." *Cheers! The Flannery O'Connor Society Newsletter*. 17.1 (Spring 2010): 1-4.

Kass, Leon. "Defending Human Dignity: What It Is and Why It Matters." *Criterion* 47.1 (Spring/Summer 2009): 18-27, 34.

Kirk, Connie Ann. *Critical Companion to Flannery O'Connor: A Literary Reference to Her Life and Work*. New York: Facts On File-Infobase, 2008.

Lodge, David. "Chasing after God and Sex." *New York Times Book Review* 31 Aug. 1986: 1, 15.

Murray, Lorraine V. *The Abbess of Andalusia: Flannery O'Connor's Spiritual Journey*. Charlotte, NC: St. Benedict Press, 2009.

O'Connor, Flannery. *Collected Works*. Ed. Sally Fitzgerald. New York: Library of America, 1988.

____________. *The Habit of Being*. Ed. Sally Fitzgerald. New York: Farrar, Straus and Giroux, 1979. (Cited in the text as *HB*).

____________. *Mystery and Manners: Occasional Prose*. Ed. Sally and Robert Fitzgerald. New York: Farrar-Noonday, 1969. (Cited in the text as *MM*).

Plath, James, ed. *Conversations with John Updike*. Jackson: UP of Mississippi, 1994.

Schopen, Bernard A. "Faith, Morality, and the Novels of John Updike. *Twentieth Century Literature* 24.4 (Winter 1978): 523-35.

Updike, John. "The Dogwood Tree: A Boyhood." *Assorted Prose*. New York: Knopf-Fawcett, 1962. 220-33.

____________. "Introduction." *Soundings in Satanism*. Ed. F. J. Sheed. New York: Sheed & Ward, 1972.

____________. "More Love in the Western World." Review of *Love Declared*. Denis de Rougemont. *Assorted Prose*. New York: Knopf-Fawcett, 1962. 220-33.

____________. *Problems and Other Stories*. New York: Knopf, 1979.

____________. "Remarks on Religion and Contemporary American Literature." *New Letters*. Special Edition: "The Writer and Religion." 60.4 (1994). 77-80.

____________. *Self-Consciousness: Memoirs*. New York: Knopf, 1989. (Cited in the text as *SC*).

Wallace, David Foster. *Consider the Lobster and Other Essays*. New York: Little, Brown, 2006.

Wood, Ralph C. *The Comedy of Redemption: Christian Faith and Comic Vision in Four American Novelists*. Notre Dame, IN: U of Notre Dame P, 1989.

____________. "Flannery O'Connor, Pope Benedict XVI, and Divine Eros." *Christianity and Literature*. 60.1 (Fall 2010).

Flannery O'Connor: Critical Reception

Irwin H. Streight

> I see from the standpoint of Christian orthodoxy. This means that for me the meaning of life is centered in our Redemption by Christ and what I see in the world I see in relation to that. I don't think that this is a position that can be taken halfway or one that is particularly easy in these times to make transparent in fiction.
>
> —Flannery O'Connor

Reviewers of Flannery O'Connor's first novel, *Wise Blood*, published in 1952, thought she was being ironic and satirical. How could a modern author seriously engage with religious fanaticism, with a backwoods Southern redneck who would maim and blind himself for the sake of getting religion? Snake oil, certainly, and more medieval than modern. While the modern reader might rightly be sceptical about matters of religion, and regard all religious fanatics as freaks, O'Connor was on the side of her Christ-haunted characters. Of her moonshiner backwoods prophet Mason Tarwater, in her second novel *The Violent Bear It Away*, she once remarked in an interview, "I'm right behind him 100 per cent" (Magee 83). O'Connor's vision, grounded in her Catholic beliefs—as expressed in the epigraph—was not easy to make apparent to the common reader, for whom the meaningfulness of the Christian doctrines of sin and redemption and the prospect of revelation was more missing than mystery. Thus Flannery O'Connor's work has met with polar responses from critics: her co-religionists reading her fiction with eyes to see and ears to hear "the almost imperceptible intrusions of grace" that she says are operative in her often violent stories (*MM* 112); and those critics resistant to or sceptical of her Christian worldview and who thus find the world of her fiction brutal, uncharitable, and disturbingly grotesque.

The writer of *Wise Blood*, a twenty-five-year-old, privileged young woman descended from two leading families in the state of Georgia, would not be persuaded by a respected editor, her mother, a priest, or anyone else who tried to tell her what kinds of stories she should write or what words she should use. Right from the start, Flannery O'Connor staked the territory and tenor of her fiction, what one critic calls the "tormented, uproarious, red-clay world" of her native Georgia (Butler 101). As Joyce Carol Oates would reflect in a generous and wise review essay published in 1973, "the amazing thing about O'Connor is that she seems to have known exactly what she was doing and how she might best accomplish it" (*Reviews* 339).

Contemporary Book Reviews

Flannery O'Connor's elderly cousin Katie, a well-to-do dowager who had been supportive of the O'Connor family in the midst of some years of financial misfortune, is reported to have gone to bed for a week upon reading *Wise Blood*. She sent Flannery a note with this curt critical response: "I do not like your book" (*HB* 139). Most book reviewers, though not given to the same brevity, were of the same mind. O'Connor's "Christian realism" as she called it strikes one contrary reviewer as "deliberate unreality," her repugnant characters being so far removed from normal human experience as to "not seem real" (*Reviews* 10). An unnamed reviewer for *Time* magazine makes the same judgement, slightly commending the novel for its "arty" structure but remarking that O'Connor's fanatical characters are "far from humanity" (*Reviews* 12). A reviewer in the influential *Saturday Review* finds O'Connor's protagonist, Hazel Motes, "so repulsive that one cannot become interested in him" and the novel as a whole, "savage" and "sheer monotony" (*Reviews* 10).

While most of the reviews of O'Connor's first novel called it dreadful, reviewers in the mainstream, such as *The New York Times Book Review*, *Newsweek*, and, across the Atlantic, *The Times Literary Supplement* agreed, in the words of book critic William Goyen, that she was "a writer of power," possessed of an intense imagination and with a remarkable gift for writing fiction (*Reviews* 6). Ten years after the publication of *Wise Blood*, when her literary stock was riding high, O'Connor requested that her publisher re-release her first novel, with the implication that she had by then attracted a readership that would now better understand the serio-comic substance of her first novel. *Wise Blood* was reissued in a hardcover second edition in 1962 with O'Connor's brief and reluctantly added Preface describing the book as "a comic novel about a Christian *malgré lui*, and as such, very serious."

O'Connor's second book, a collection of short fiction titled *A Good Man Is Hard to Find, and Other Stories*, published in 1955, is perhaps her most successful and familiar work. Its title story and two other stories—"Good Country People" and "The Artificial Nigger"—the latter, O'Connor's own favorite—have been the most frequently anthologized of her short fiction. However, initial critical responses to the stories in this collection registered some shock at their often-violent content. An unnamed reviewer in *Time* accuses O'Connor of being "highly unladylike" in her subject matter (*Reviews* 36), and the review in the nearby *Atlanta Journal and Constitution* treats the stories as gothic horror fiction in the manner of Edgar Allan Poe. In a letter to her friend Ben Griffith, O'Connor vents her indignation at inept reviewers, remarking, "The review in *Time* was terrible, nearly gave me apoplexy. The one in the *Atlanta Journal* was so stupid it was painful" (*HB* 89). More perceptive book reviewers, such as Orville Prescott in *The New York Times*, recognized O'Connor as "an extraordinarily accomplished short story writer" (*Reviews* 37). Her first collection of short fiction is likewise highly praised in such respected literary journals as *The Virginia Quarterly Review*, *Kenyon Review*, and *Sewanee Review*, the latter two of which had published several of O'Connor's stories as they were written. With the publication of the stories in *A Good Man Is Hard to Find*, Flannery O'Connor emerged as a significant new author in America.

O'Connor's second novel, *The Violent Bear It Away* (1960), which, over a seven-year labor to write, she came to call her "Opus Nauseous," she describes as "about a boy who has been raised up in the backwoods by his great uncle to be a prophet. The book is about his struggle not to be a prophet—which he loses" (*HB* 344). O'Connor's irreligiously religious rednecks, old and young Tarwater, and plot matter, as she recognized, are not the stuff that contemporary readers would find overly interesting or even believable. Indeed, apart from a few favorable and insightful reviews, including a few in Catholic periodicals, reviewers of *The Violent Bear It Away* are almost equally divided between those who are mystified by or resistant to her Christian worldview, what she called "the added dimension" (*MM* 150) in her art, yet find her writerly gifts remarkable, and those who find her fictional world far removed from modern reality, her religious outlook untenable or intolerable, and the tormented characters within her fiction freaks and madmen. While at the time of its publication O'Connor remarks characteristically that she would likely be "the book's greatest admirer" (*HB* 344), literary critics since that time have come to regard *The Violent Bear It Away* as a remarkably crafted narrative offering profound theological insight, its structure and symbolic elements reminiscent of Hawthorne's methods in *The Scarlet Letter.* Despite its novelistic shortcomings in continuity, and critical concern over the credibility of her secular humanist character, George Rayber, *The Violent Bear It Away* continues to be of literary interest because of its visionary intensity. *Über*-critic Harold Bloom considers O'Connor's second novel her "masterwork" and a story "of preternatural power" (*Modern* 1-2). Young Tarwater's final prophetic vision in the closing pages of the novel is certainly unlike anything else previously attempted in fiction.

At the time of her death in August 1964, O'Connor was working to complete a final story for a second collection, literally scratching out revisions to "Parker's Back" on her deathbed. The posthumously published collection of nine stories in *Everything That Rises Must Converge* appeared in 1965 and met with mixed responses from contemporary book reviewers. Some, such as Irving Howe in *The New York*

Review of Books, found the stories too limited in range and with predictable ironic reversals and denouements. O'Connor, Howe observes, in a remark echoed by other reviewers, bears a subtle "hostility" toward her liberal-minded, unrepentant characters that he finds personally objectionable and detrimental to her art (*Reviews* 292). However, most reviewers of O'Connor's final offering of fiction took the occasion to praise her literary accomplishments, concurring with Granville Hicks's assessment in *Saturday Review* that "she was one of the best writers of short stories this era has seen" (*Reviews* 224).

Many contemporary reviewers and later O'Connor scholars, including myself, consider *Everything That Rises Must Converge* to be her greatest book. A number of stories from this collection are included in recent anthologies of literature for the college and university market, most notably her comic gem about hypocrisy and grace, "Revelation," and the complex title story about the cultural forces surrounding racial integration in the South. Critics agree that the last three stories O'Connor wrote before her untimely death—"Revelation," "Parker's Back," and "Judgement Day"—indicate that she was headed in a new direction in her storytelling, with an interest in the post-epiphany lives of her characters and the transforming effect of the invariable shock of grace they have experienced. The common eulogizing phrase in reviews of her last collection of stories is that Flannery O'Connor died "at the height of her powers."

After O'Connor's death, her friends and literary executors Robert and Sally Fitzgerald collected and compiled a number of talks that O'Connor had given to writers' groups and at universities and colleges, along with an article about her passion for raising peacocks that she had published in a popular magazine, *Holiday*, a piece of literary theory she had published in Granville Hicks's *The Living Novel* (1957), and the introduction to a book she had edited about a disfigured child who died young, titled *A Memoir of Mary Ann* (1961), written by a group of Dominican nuns who cared for the child. This collection of O'Connor's essays and occasional pieces, *Mystery and Manners*

(1969), is considered by many O'Connor scholars as indispensable to reading and understanding her fiction. Frequently cited essays outlining her literary theory are "The Fiction Writer and His Country," "Some Aspects of the Grotesque in Southern Fiction," and "The Nature and Aim of Fiction." O'Connor discusses her challenges as a writer with a Catholic worldview in several of the collected pieces, notably in "The Church and the Fiction Writer" and "The Catholic Novelist in the Protestant South." Casebooks on O'Connor in undergraduate anthologies include excerpts from these and other essays, in which the author discusses her approaches to writing fiction and offers critical readings of her own stories, most helpfully her most famous story, "A Good Man Is Hard to Find."

Sally Fitzgerald selected and edited a collection of letters from O'Connor's voluminous correspondence and published them in 1979 as *The Habit of Being: Letters*. O'Connor's collected letters offer insights into her habits and concerns as a writer and reveal the depth of her religious convictions. She emerges from the letters as witty and wise and with a gift for aphorism, as a devout Catholic who is profoundly conscious of the spirit of her age, generous to her many correspondents, a writer and thinker of strong opinions who at times could be revealingly personal. In his review article on her letters, Robert Coles regards O'Connor's collected correspondence as a kind of autobiographical narrative in which the reader discovers, in all senses of the word, the *character* of O'Connor in what Coles describes as "a long, absorbing, entertaining, edifying story" ("Letters" 6). *The Habit of Being* is considered by many literary critics as the most valuable collection of letters by any twentieth-century American writer. There has been, however, some concern amongst critics regarding Fitzgerald's alleged sanitizing and biased selection of the letters.

The occasional pieces collected and edited in *Mystery and Manners* along with O'Connor's collected letters in *The Habit of Being* have been invaluable resources for scholars, many of whom, rightly or wrongly, read O'Connor on her own terms based on the theological ideas and theories of fiction she expresses in her essays and talks and in her carefully crafted letters.

O'Connor's corpus of short fiction was published as *The Complete Stories of Flannery O'Connor* in 1971 and won the National Book Award, the only time that the award has been granted to a non-living author. In an online poll in 2010, O'Connor's *Complete Stories* was voted *the* book most deserving of that award over its sixty-year history. O'Connor's thirty-one stories are here arranged in chronological order, including the six stories that constitute her previously unpublished master's thesis, composed while attending the Writer's Workshop at the University of Iowa in 1945-1947.

O'Connor's *Collected Works* were published in 1988 in a definitive single volume in the prestigious Library of America series. The fact that her works were added to the series before such canonical modern authors as Ernest Hemingway, F. Scott Fitzgerald, and Sherwood Anderson speaks to her stature in American letters and to her unmoveable canonicity. Along with her published fiction and a number of her most cited essays, the Library of America volume, once more edited by Sally Fitzgerald, includes among other key correspondence twenty-two refreshingly uncensored letters that were omitted from *The Habit of Being* and that reveal more of O'Connor's wit and unblinkered observations about faith and art.

Bibliographies

In spite of her small corpus and the fact that most modern readers do not share her religious viewpoint, Flannery O'Connor's writings have certainly received an enormous amount of critical attention. Scholars are indebted to several bibliographic works that have collected and described O'Connor criticism. Robert E. Golden and Mary C. Sullivan's *Flannery O'Connor and Caroline Gordon: A Reference Guide* (1977) offers year-by-year, briefly annotated entries for books, articles, reviews, and dissertations on O'Connor published before 1976. Of the

799 items listed, eighteen are scholarly monographs. R. Neil Scott's magisterial 1,083-page *Flannery O'Connor: An Annotated Reference Guide to Criticism* (2002) picks up where Golden left off in an exhaustive collection and description of 3,297 scholarly publications on O'Connor, including a section describing publications in eleven languages other than English. Scott's *Reference Guide* lists and describes eighty-one books on O'Connor, including monographs and essay collections, 1,643 scholarly articles or book chapters on her work, and over three hundred doctoral dissertations and more than five hundred master's theses concerned to some extent with O'Connor's works. Since Scott's bibliography, to date no fewer than 37 book-length titles have been added to the expanding shelf of O'Connor scholarship, including the first full-length biography, Brad Gooch's *Flannery: A Life of Flannery O'Connor* (2009). The *MLA International Bibliography* lists Flannery O'Connor as the subject of 1,427 entries at the time of this printing. The website for the Flannery O'Connor Collection at Georgia State University and College (GSUC) offers a select list of 117 books titles on, or with chapters dedicated to, the author. An annual journal edited at GSUC, originally titled *The Flannery O'Connor Bulletin* (1972-2000) and now called *Flannery O'Connor Review*, is the major forum for scholarly work on the author, and boasts the distinction of being the longest running journal devoted to a single woman writer. Added to a list of scholarly resources is Cambridge University Press's *Flannery O'Connor: The Contemporary Reviews* (2009), edited by R. Neil Scott and Irwin Streight, which contains largely whole texts of the over 430 book reviews and review essays published on O'Connor's works during her lifetime and shortly following her death.

A Catholic Writer?

O'Connor scholarship began in earnest with two pamphlets published in 1966, Robert Drake's *Flannery O'Connor: A Critical Essay* and Stanley Edgar Hyman's enduring *Flannery O'Connor* issue for the Pamphlets on American Writers series published by the University of Minnesota (No. 54). Both of these early critics affirm the centrality of O'Connor's Catholic beliefs to the making and understanding of her art. The first full-length book study of O'Connor's fiction is Carter Martin's *The True Country: Themes in the Fiction of Flannery O'Connor* (1969). Martin offers an "orthodox Christian" reading of O'Connor, insisting that in order to understand the meaning of O'Connor's fiction the critic must first "know the meaning of the sacramental view of life" (9). It is therefore most ironic that the second full-length book study of O'Connor, Josephine Hendin's *The World of Flannery O'Connor* (1970) is predicated on reading O'Connor psychoanalytically, dismissing her Catholic religious convictions as irrelevant to understanding her fictional world. O'Connor criticism since has been working the territory between these two early polar readings of her art and vision. A glance through the indexes to *The Contemporary Reviews* and the *Annotated Reference Guide* shows that the literary categorical terms that most often appear in scholarly responses to O'Connor's works are *Catholic writer*, *Southern writer*, and *grotesque*.

One of many paradoxes about Flannery O'Connor is that while she did not want to be labeled as a Catholic writer she surely wanted to be recognized as one. O'Connor was wary of the implications of being considered a "Catholic" writer. She acknowledged to her friend and fellow writer Elizabeth Bishop, "Although I am a Catholic writer, I don't care to be labeled as such in the popular sense of it, as it is then assumed that you have some religious axe to grind" (*HB* 391). O'Connor did not write stories that are expressly Catholic in the manner of her contemporaries Evelyn Waugh, Graham Greene, and J. F. Powers. Indeed, apart from two old priests who make albeit significant brief appearances in her stories "The Displaced Person" and "The Enduring Chill," and a moment with the bustling Sister Perpetua at the comically named convent school Mount St. Scholastica in "A Temple of the Holy Ghost," her fiction is almost devoid of identifiably Catholic elements.

(Prevalent Eucharistic images and the sacramental urgency of baptism in her fiction are not exclusive to Catholic practices and doctrines but are more broadly Christian and often equally Protestant.) Religious axe grinding was left to contemporary Catholic reviewers and critics, a number of whom questioned her orthodoxy and even judged her work as anti-Catholic.

O'Connor was often stung by criticism from her co-religionists, and in her letters she frequently vents both her impatience and despair over frequently uncharitable, imperceptive, and oftentimes harsh critical responses to her work by reviewers in Catholic periodicals. Her first novel was largely ignored by reviewers in leading Catholic journals. With the publication of her first collection of short fiction, she was met with mixed responses from reviewers in the leading Catholic periodicals *Commonweal* and *Catholic World*, but ignored by the influential Jesuit-run weekly *America*. "The silence of the Catholic critic is so often preferable to his attention. I always look in the Catholic magazines my mother reads to see if my book has been reviewed, and when I find it hasn't, I say an act of thanksgiving," O'Connor remarks in typical style in a letter to Father John Lynch, a young priest teaching at Notre Dame who had championed her fiction to fellow Catholics (*HB* 114). By the end of her life, however, the Catholic literati were mostly reconciled to O'Connor's art and vision, and perhaps somewhat uneasily to her unorthodox orthodoxy. Nonetheless, reviews in leading Catholic periodicals of her final collection of stories, *Everything That Rises Must Converge*, indicate an abiding ambivalence toward her work by some contemporary Catholic critics. A reviewer in the monthly *Catholic World*, for example, refers to her last collection of stories as a "disturbing volume" that completes O'Connor's "unusual legacy" (*Reviews* 277). If tensions between O'Connor's art and the literati in the Catholic Church yet abide, there was little evidence of such at "Reason, Faith and Fiction: An International Flannery O'Connor Conference" in April 2009, hosted by the Pontifical University of the Holy Cross in Rome—a stone's throw from The Vatican. The conference brought scholars from around the globe into the heart of the Catholic Church to celebrate O'Connor's life and legacy.

Theological Readings

To date the majority of critical responses to O'Connor have focused, by far, on ways in which her Catholic faith informs her fiction. And despite a growing aversion by a number of current O'Connor scholars to further religious readings of her stories, O'Connor's brand of "Christian realism," with its infusion of mystery in the manners and materials of our daily living, continues to elicit new and insightful critical responses. Most of the luminous O'Connor scholars over the last fifty years have been her co-religionists, critics whom one dissenting contemporary critic calls the "True Believers" (Timothy P. Caron).

Many noteworthy scholarly books on Flannery O'Connor respond to her art and life from a range of theological positions. Driskel and Brittain's *The Eternal Crossroads: The Art of Flannery O'Connor* (1971) briefly traces the literary and theological influences on O'Connor, including Nathanael West, Hawthorne, and French Catholic novelist François Mauriac. Their book is in large part a religious thematic study of O'Connor that examines literary themes, symbols, and biblical references in her stories and novels. Sister Kathleen Feeley's early monograph *Flannery O'Connor: Voice of the Peacock* (1972) offers a highly spiritualized view of O'Connor through examination of her readings in theology, philosophy, and church history. Feeley's application of these "sources" to illuminate readings of O'Connor's stories lacks scholarly rigour, but the book has value as an early arraying of religious thinkers who influenced O'Connor—St. Augustine, John Cardinal Newman, Teilhard de Chardin, and Voegelin. Miles Orvell's *Invisible Parade: The Fiction of Flannery O'Connor* (1972) is a careful study of O'Connor's use of symbolism to import religious meaning into her stories in the tradition of the American Romance. Dorothy Walters's *Flannery O'Connor* volume for the Twayne United States

Authors series (1973) and Preston Browning Jr.'s monograph of the same name published a year later (1974) are largely thematic studies of her fiction that cover already familiar ground in recognizing how O'Connor's religious vision informs her art. Both books nonetheless serve as good introductions to her fiction.

John R. May in *The Pruning Word: The Parables of Flannery O'Connor* (1976) concurs with Martin in asserting that ascent to, or understanding of, O'Connor's Christian worldview is essential to assessing her achievement. May offers close readings of O'Connor's stories, comparing them to the parables of Jesus as likewise "dramatic narratives involving conflicts between human beings that symbolize rather than describe man's relationship to ultimate reality" (14). John Desmond's *Risen Sons: Flannery O'Connor's Vision of History* (1987) argues that her belief in the Incarnation of Christ both informs and unites her "vision of history" and her technique as a writer (3), an argument that ties directly to the epigraph for this chapter. O'Connor's analogical imagination, her sense of the divine nature of life, becomes manifest in what Desmond calls "the incarnational image" in her fiction (46)—as in the statue of an artificial Negro in one of her most contentious stories—which bears at the same time both physical and metaphysical significance. In *The Comedy of Redemption: Christian Faith and Comic Vision in Four American Novelists* (1988), Ralph C. Wood turns a fundamentalist Baptist's eye to reading O'Connor's fiction for evidence of "the grace of God" (117), and offers similar responses to the works of Walker Percy, John Updike, and Peter DeVries.

Flannery O'Connor: A Proper Scaring (1988, revised edition issued in 1998), by Jill Peláez Baumgaertner, engages in detailed religious readings of O'Connor's fiction, strongly supported by Baumgaertner's biblical knowledge. She links O'Connor's strong visual metaphors to the sixteenth-seventeenth century "emblem book" with its exaggerated, literal "pictorial representations of scriptural truths" (20). Likewise, Baumgaertner considers O'Connor's novels as akin to medieval morality plays or as somewhere in the realm of

"Christian myth" (142). Richard Giannone's two books, *Flannery O'Connor and the Mystery of Love* (1989) and *Flannery O'Connor, Hermit Novelist* (2000), offer erudite Catholic readings of her fiction and the facts of her life. *Mystery of Love* looks beneath the violent surfaces of O'Connor's stories to find the Charity within—the God whose own anguished suffering brought a holy, saving love and ultimately redemption to the world. *Hermit Novelist* assesses O'Connor in light of the practices of the ascetic Catholic spirituality of the third- and fourth-century desert fathers and mothers—practices that Giannone traces in the author's life and art. Giannone casts O'Connor in the role of a prophet speaking to her age as well as a kind of spiritual adviser for followers of the Way. Father George Kilcourse shows how O'Connor's reading of Catholic theology—particularly that of her contemporaries Romano Guardini and William F. Lynch—influenced her art in *Flannery O'Connor's Religious Imagination: A World with Everything Off Balance* (2001). Both Giannone and Kilcourse suggest that O'Connor might be considered a latter-day Doctor of the Church.

One of the most highly regarded recent works of O'Connor scholarship is Susan Srigley's study of O'Connor's "ethic of responsibility" in *Flannery O'Connor's Sacramental Art* (2004). Srigley, a professor of Religions and Cultures at a small Canadian university, explores the implications of O'Connor's remark, via Thomistic philosopher Jacques Maritain, that "In the greatest fiction, the writer's moral sense coincides with his dramatic sense, and I see no way for it to do this unless his moral judgment is part of the very act of seeing" (*MM* 31). O'Connor's stories reveal her "sacramental vision of reality" (7), Srigley argues, and reading them will lead to a deeper understanding of the transcendent nature of our experience. Further exploration of the influence of Thomistic thought on O'Connor's art can be found at length in Marion Montgomery's two-volume study, *Hillbilly Thomist: Flannery O'Connor, St. Thomas and the Limits of Art* (2006). Also widely well received is Christina Bieber Lake's *The Incarnational Art of Flannery O'Connor* (2005). Lake shows how O'Connor's grounding in the

Christian doctrine of the Incarnation bears on the embodied nature of her characters, who, despite their often distorted or grotesque appearances, are consummately presented as whole and complete fictional selves.

Southern Writer

Flannery O'Connor resisted being labeled a Southern writer because on the one hand she felt limited by any label (Catholic, Southern, the grotesque) and on the other, she was particularly wary of the narrow assumptions of regionalism, of local-color writer, that the label "Southern writer" implied (*MM* 37-38). Yet, however "vertical" the range of her stories, to use Robert Fitzgerald's term, or of her "true country," in O'Connor's own phrase, her horizontal world was the red clay roads, the dark lines of pine trees, the sharecroppers' shacks, and the stereotypical backwoods yokels, religious fanatics, and black farmhands found in her home state of Georgia and in nearby Tennessee. The world of the American South in the 1950s-1960s, its places, people, and manners, forms the concrete stuff of O'Connor's fiction.

Several essays collected in Friedman and Lawson gather some of the early scholarship that explores O'Connor's connections with the traditions of Southern literature and her affinities with the Southern Agrarians, in particular essays by C. Hugh Holman, Louis D. Rubin, Jr., and P. Albert Duhamel. A number of significant scholarly monographs situate O'Connor as definably a Southern writer. In *The World of Flannery O'Connor* (1970) Josephine Hendin argues that whatever her artistic view of the South, O'Connor in her personal life followed "quite rigidly" the repressive Southern codes of social compliance, emotional detachment, and noblesse oblige. The tensions in O'Connor's fiction, she claims, are rooted in her identity as a Southerner of high social standing subject to the "rigorous code of Southern, genteel womanhood" under which she silently suffered in her writing years at Andalusia, yet with evident fury assailed in her fiction (12). While her book is largely a thematic study of O'Connor's fiction, Hendin sees O'Connor's work as being less about religious transcendence and more concerned with transcending the contradictions and conflicts of Southern life and culture (41). Robert Coles's semi-autobiographical *Flannery O'Connor's South* (1980) attempts to situate O'Connor's fiction in the social conflicts of the American South during the period in which she wrote: the 1950s and 1960s. Drawing on a personal encounter with O'Connor, interviews with her acquaintances, and supplemented by liberal references to her essays and talks collected in *Mystery and Manners* and her collected letters, Coles discusses the ways in which O'Connor's "distinctly historical view" of familiar Southern society and personality informs her fiction (xxvi).

Sarah Gordon, who began reading O'Connor's fiction in 1966, taught it for more than thirty years, and was associate editor and then editor of the *Flannery O'Connor Bulletin/Review* for a combined twenty-seven years, has distilled a scholarly lifetime of rereading O'Connor and rethinking her own critical positions in a dense and far-ranging study of the author's life, beliefs, and art, *Flannery O'Connor: The Obedient Imagination* (2000). Like Hendin, Gordon sees O'Connor's life and art as fraught with complexity and unsettling tensions as a woman and a Catholic writing from the white, patriarchal social and religious culture of the South in the 1950-1960s, and likewise argues that O'Connor writes paradoxically both within and against Southern literary traditions and sensibilities. Pervasively a feminist reading of O'Connor, Gordon's book nonetheless adopts the critical purview that O'Connor's mind and art were borne along by the powerful undercurrents of conservative white Southern culture and the equally conservative and patriarchal constraints of pre-Vatican II Catholicism. Ralph C. Wood's highly regarded *Flannery O'Connor and the Christ-Haunted South* (2004) examines O'Connor's art and beliefs in the context of Southern Bible Beltism. O'Connor's visionary fiction, writes Wood, affirms the "sweated and hard-edged Christianity" of old-fashioned Southern fundamentalism, despite the anomaly of its doctrinal dissonance with her own Catholic sacramentalism (3). The beliefs and practices of the Southern Church are here expounded alongside and within the mystery and manners of O'Connor's fiction, with a healthy dose of Wood's own biography interwoven.

The Grotesque

In her published talk "Some Aspects of the Grotesque in Southern Fiction," O'Connor makes the following well-traveled wry remark: "I have found that anything that comes out of the South is going to be called grotesque by the Northern reader, unless it is grotesque, in which case is it going to be called realistic" (*MM* 40). Indeed, along with being labeled a Catholic or Southern writer, the most frequent label used by early reviewers of O'Connor's fiction and later critics is the term *grotesque*. Those few appreciative reviewers of her first novel *Wise Blood* recognized that O'Connor employed the grotesque, like G. K. Chesterton, as a means to "stand the world on end that we might look at it" (*Reviews* 19). As O'Connor once commented on Kafka's story "The Metamorphosis," in her own work "a certain distortion is used to get at the truth" (*MM* 97-98). As well, it must be granted that the culture and forms of religious extremism in the American South about which O'Connor often writes may appear grotesque to the outsider.

Some of the most respected scholarly monographs on O'Connor regard her ultimately as a writer in the traditions of the grotesque. Indeed, the very first article published in *The Flannery O'Connor Bulletin*, "Freaks in a Circus Tent: Flannery O'Connor's Christ-Haunted Characters," by Stuart Burns (1972) is a defense of O'Connor's use of the grotesque to compel a deeper understanding of her religious themes. Contrastingly, Irving Malin's essay "Flannery O'Connor and the Grotesque," collected in *The Added Dimension*, regards the grotesque in her fiction as more in service of psychological realism than of her Christian beliefs—in order to show "the grotesquerie of existence"

(121). Just what O'Connor's grotesques reveal about our human nature is the question several critics have attempted to answer at book length. Gilbert H. Muller in *Nightmares and Visions: Flannery O'Connor and the Catholic Grotesque* (1972) discusses O'Connor's use of the grotesque as a means of disengaging her characters from the world of her stories and highlighting their need for grace. He argues that O'Connor presents the terrifying truths of a "Catholic grotesque" as a kind of back door to her religious concerns (18). Frederick Asals's *Flannery O'Connor: The Imagination of Extremity* (1982) examines her "passion for extremes" in what is effectively a study of O'Connor's art of the grotesque—the most frequently used critical term in Asals's book and fittingly its last word.

The first critic to draw on Mikhail Bakhtin's theory of the grotesque, Marshall Bruce Gentry, in *Flannery O'Connor's Religion of the Grotesque* (1986), distinguishes between two kinds of grotesqueness in O'Connor's stories: "the positive grotesque," wherein characters "bring about their own redemption," and stories that involve "negative grotesquerie" in which a character's transformation "comes from outside" through some other agent (14, 18). Gentry provocatively views the grotesque elements in O'Connor's fiction as conflicting with the Catholic notion of redemption that runs through her works. In *American Gargoyles: Flannery O'Connor and the Medieval Grotesque* (1993), Anthony Di Renzo finds analogues between the grotesques in O'Connor's fiction and the sacred uses of the grotesque in medieval paintings, woodcuts, sculpture, and architecture. Di Renzo argues that O'Connor employs the "demonic topsy-turviness" of the grotesque in her efforts to subvert the secularism and spiritual complacency of her age through a kind of "comic shock treatment" (4-5). The grotesque distortions of action and person in her stories, says O'Connor, are of the kind "that reveals or should reveal" a meaningfulness and point to a mystery (*MM* 162). Although somewhat shopworn, the nature of the grotesque in O'Connor's art is still a matter for critical inquiry. Her stories are darkly comic and often screamingly funny, and there is room for more scholarship that looks at O'Connor as a writer of the comic grotesque.

The Demonic School of O'Connor Criticism

In a damning, vituperative book review of O'Connor's final collection of stories, Webster Schott contends that her vision of humanity is unremittingly dark and sinister and concludes that in her stories "evil is man's inevitable fate" (*Reviews* 290). More virulently, Rene Jordan, writing what appears to be more of a rant than a book review in the *British Association for American Studies Bulletin* (1966), suggests that O'Connor's final collection of stories "is a book conceived by a dying woman who is not afraid of going to hell: she's been in it too long and has begun to find it cozy and dull" (*Reviews* 331). Chief among critical voices in what one scholar (Douglas Robillard) calls "the demonic school" of O'Connor criticism is O'Connor's fellow novelist and friend John Hawkes, whom she greatly admired as a writer of the avant-garde and with whom she frequently corresponded. Hawkes's still influential 1962 article published in *Sewanee Review* entitled "Flannery O'Connor's Devil" presents her fictional world and authorial presence as ultimately diabolical. In his brief essay, Hawkes examines passages in *The Violent Bear It Away* and in two stories from O'Connor's first collection, "A Good Man Is Hard to Find" and "The Life You Save May Be Your Own," and finds that O'Connor's authorial voice converges with that of her bedevilled characters, whom he suggests are projections of her "demonic" imagination (16). Hawkes concludes that "her central fictional allegiance" is toward the dark side more than focused on the kingdom of light (17). Whether this view of O'Connor as a diabolist merits further critical attention, as Robert Donahoo argues favorably in a recent essay (245), is for future scholars to exorcise further from her fictions. (O'Connor is unequivocal in asserting that the subject of her fiction is "*the action of grace* in territory held largely by the devil," a territory about which she is evidently quite familiar (*MM* 117-18, emphasis added). But Flannery O'Connor held an unholy regard and no sympathy for the Devil.

There are, however, critics who find O'Connor's religious vision and beliefs offensive or affrontingly unconvincing and who have written book-length nay-saying critical assessments of her fiction. One of O'Connor's earliest detractors is Josephine Hendin in *The World of Flannery O'Connor* (1970), who remarkably finds resemblance between O'Connor's fiction and the writings of William Seward Burroughs, what she calls "the literature of disgust." Hendin dismisses O'Connor's Catholic worldview as irrelevant to reading her fiction and describes her characters as soulless and her fictional world as one-dimensional, summing up her work as "art of raw power without depth" (155). Martha Stephens's *The Question of Flannery O'Connor* (1973) is likewise a protracted scholarly attack on O'Connor's Catholic view of life, which in a modern, post-Christian age Stephens find undeserving of serious critical attention. While she admires O'Connor's "technical brilliance" as a writer of short fiction, Stephens finds O'Connor's view of life "repugnant" and her fiction devoid of any significant meaning (3). O'Connor's perceived "contempt for ordinary human life" (10) is met with Stephens's own critical contempt for what she terms the objectionable "tonal dimension" of her art. In *Flannery O'Connor's Dark Comedies: The Limits of Inference* (1980) Carol Shloss offers the first reader-response approach to O'Connor's fiction. Shloss explores the difficulty experienced by the nonreligious reader in finding the mystery entwined in the manners of O'Connor's stories. O'Connor "manipulates" readers toward accepting her religious viewpoint, Shloss argues, and fails to show the workings of grace in the lives of her characters. For Shloss, there is "nothing" in O'Connor's stories that "compels a theological reading" (8), and the tattoo of Christ on O. E. Parker's back is "just a picture" (126). The majority of O'Connor scholarship holds opposing views to these three notable critical voices that loudly resist O'Connor's religious worldview. Like the characters in her fiction, as given in the epigraph to her most famous story "A Good Man Is Hard to Find," O'Connor's journey through the critics has meant having "to pass by the dragon" of disbelievers.

Essay Collections

Friedman and Lawson's *The Added Dimension: The Art and Mind of Flannery O'Connor* (1966; 2d rev ed, 1977), the first gathering of scholarly essays on the author, offers a sampling of early critical responses to O'Connor's fiction and to her identity as a writer. Essays by esteemed postwar literary critics Frederick Hoffman, Louis D. Rubin, Jr., and Irving Malin and others offer broad critical assessments of O'Connor in light of Southern literary traditions and the literature of the grotesque. Included as well are early religious readings of her fiction and samplings from her letters, essays, and interviews, edited by O'Connor's friend and correspondent William Sessions, along with the first substantial scholarly bibliography. Robert Reiter's *Flannery O'Connor* (1968) collects previously published essays that emphasize Christian readings of O'Connor by largely Catholic scholars. An anomaly is the inclusion of John Hawkes's famously contentious essay, "Flannery O'Connor's Devil."

Other significant collections include *Critical Essays on Flannery O'Connor* (1985), edited by Melvin Friedman and Beverly Clark, a generous offering of twenty-eight reviews and critical essays related to O'Connor's life and work. Changing directions in O'Connor scholarship are signalled in essays by poststructuralist French critics André Bleikasten and Michel Gresset. Also reprinted are Thomas Merton's "Prose Elegy" to O'Connor, famously quoted on the dust jacket to *The Complete Stories*, in which he compares her to the Greek tragedian Sophocles, and Alice Walker's biographical, early feminist assessment, "Beyond the Peacock: The Reconstruction of Flannery O'Connor."

Harold Bloom's collection of O'Connor criticism, *Flannery O'Con-*

nor: Modern Critical Views (1986) gathers together, in Bloom's view, "the best criticism available" on O'Connor's fiction from leading O' Connor scholars and a number of literary luminaries—John Hawkes, Robert Fitzgerald, Joyce Carol Oates, Ralph C. Wood, and Frederick Asals. Bloom also has edited a volume for Chelsea House's Bloom's Major Short Story Writers series, *Flannery O'Connor: Comprehensive Research and Study Guide* (1999), which offers background materials and excerpts from a wealth of published scholarship on the four O'Connor stories that most often appear in college anthologies of literature: "A Good Man Is Hard to Find," "Good Country People," "Everything That Rises Must Converge," and "Revelation."

Two collections of essays edited by Scandinavian scholars Jan Gretlund and Karl-Heinz Westarp provide an eclectic range of O'Connor scholarship. The twenty essays collected in *Realist of Distances: Flannery O'Connor Revisited* (1987) were originally presented at an international O'Connor symposium held in Sønderborg, Denmark in 1984, which drew O'Connor scholars from seven countries. Their more important collection, *Flannery O'Connor's Radical Reality* (2006), features fourteen previously unpublished essays, a number by leading O'Connor scholars, which explore literary, intellectual, and theological influences on O'Connor's thought and art.

Douglas Robillard Jr.'s *The Critical Response to Flannery O'Connor* (number 43 in the Praeger *Critical Response* series) (2004) collects excerpts from many influential critical responses to O'Connor, spanning a period of fifty years, from her contemporary reviewers and critics to recent feminist and postmodern theoretical approaches. Robillard's gleaning and editing from a large field of scholarship on O'Connor serves as a kind of critical history of O'Connor studies, valuable for both literary scholars and student newcomers to her fiction.

New Essays on "Wise Blood" (1995), edited by Michael Kreyling, collects some of the early revisionist voices in O'Connor scholarship. Reviewing the four essays in the collection for the *Flannery O'Connor*

Bulletin, Ralph C. Wood avers that they "celebrate the death of God in Flannery O'Connor's work" ("Review" 200). The critical theories applied to O'Connor's first novel are new historicist (Bacon), Lacanian (Mellard), and feminist (Yaeger). Likewise theoretical, but with more investment in O'Connor's vision and intentions, is *Flannery O'Connor: New Critical Perspectives* (1996), edited by Sura Rath and Mary Neff Shaw, which includes ten original essays by leading O'Connor scholars who apply a variety of postmodern critical theories to enable insightful new readings. Of particular interest are essays by Gentry, Giannone, and Reesman that discuss gender issues in O'Connor's fiction.

Both "True Believers" and "Apostates" can be found sitting in the pews (of) *Inside the Church of Flannery O'Connor: Sacrament, Sacramental, and the Sacred in Her Fiction* (2007), a unique collection of ten original essays edited by Joanne McMullen and Jon Peede. This collection provocatively juxtaposes essays by established O'Connor scholars who explore the Catholic dimensions of O'Connor's fiction with dissenting critical voices who regard O'Connor from various positions within current cultural studies perspectives. Particularly enlightening essays by Desmond, May, McMullen, and Wood explore and debate the Catholicness of O'Connor's fiction, and a provocative essay by Timothy Caron on the issue of race in O'Connor argues that her fiction is plagued by a "theological whiteness" (139).

Flannery O'Connor in the Age of Terrorism (2010), edited by Avis Hewitt and Robert Donahoo, collects fifteen critical essays that discuss the issue of violence in O'Connor's fiction from a number of current theoretical perspectives. Most interesting is Jon Lance Bacon's new historicist analysis of how the national angst during the Cold War is translated into horror comics of the 1950s, with parallels to O'Connor's own grotesque images and violent plots. A long-needed collection of essays focused exclusively on *The Violent Bear It Away* is soon forthcoming from University of Notre Dame Press. Titled *Dark Faith: New Essays on Flannery O'Connor's "The Violent Bear It Away,"* and edited by Susan Srigley, the collection will feature essays by established and emerging scholars that relate the violence in O'Connor's fiction to her theological thought.

O'Connor et al.

Books that examine O'Connor's connections with other writers appear to be increasing as scholars explore both the intersections of O'Connor's art and vision with that of other writers and her abiding legacy in both postmodern literary and popular culture. Her friend John Hawkes compared her with Nathanael West in his celebrated 1962 essay published in the *Sewanee Review*, "Flannery O'Connor's Devil." In his introductions to the Chelsea House *Flannery O'Connor: Modern Critical Views* (1986) and later *Flannery O'Connor: Comprehensive Research and Study Guide* (1999), Harold Bloom suggests that O'Connor was greatly influenced by West's *Miss Lonelyhearts* as well as Faulkner's *As I Lay Dying*. Neil Scott's *Annotated Reference Guide* lists over 30 books, articles, and theses in which O'Connor is linked to West. The best articles comparing O'Connor and West are by Laura Zaidman and O'Connor's friend and literary executor Sally Fitzgerald, both focused on West's influence on *Wise Blood* and both published in the *Flannery O'Connor Review*. Fitzgerald also suggests the influence of T. S. Eliot's *The Waste Land* on O'Connor's fiction.

Of the lionized Southern writer William Faulkner, O'Connor remarked in one of her talks, "Nobody wants his mule and wagon stalled on the same track as the Dixie Limited is roaring down" (*MM* 45). While her contemporary book reviewers readily compare O'Connor with Faulkner, and the shadow his influence cast on her work as a Southern writer is certainly a critical commonplace, O'Connor is not, as a number of reviewers state, "a female William Faulkner": neither in vision, scope, nor in her achievements in fictional form. Later critics appear to have respected O'Connor's sense of her accomplishments against Faulkner's overwhelming presence in Southern literature. Indeed, there is no full-fledged literary critical monograph that compares the two great Southern writers. Scott's *Annotated Reference Guide* lists only a handful of articles that engage in extended critical comparisons of O'Connor and Faulkner. And Faulkner figures only slightly in the early criticism described in Robert Golden's *A Reference Guide*. This is perhaps in accord with Caroline Gordon's pronouncement in her 1968 article "Heresy in Dixie" for the *Sewanee Review* that comparisons of O'Connor with Faulkner, Eudora Welty, or Truman Capote are "profitless" since her stories explore "*depths*" of "the human spirit" beyond the work of her contemporaries (269 original italics). A recent Special Feature section of the *Flannery O'Connor Review* 8 (2010) offers a collection of essays that compare the respective accomplishments of O'Connor and Faulkner in the short story form, gleaned from papers presented at a conference hosted at Georgia College and State University in 2008 entitled "The Stories of Flannery and Faulkner: A Conference and Celebration."

Several recent monographs explore the connections between O'Connor and her fellow Catholic southerner and friend Walker Percy, most notably Farrell O'Gorman's *Peculiar Cross Roads: Flannery O'Connor, Walker Percy, and Catholic Vision in Postwar Southern Fiction* (2004), which traces biographical similarities between the two writers and notes like theological and philosophical influences; John D. Sykes Jr.'s *Flannery O'Connor, Walker Percy, and the Aesthetic of Revelation* (2007) explores similar themes in the two writers and their common Christian existentialist concerns. Percy scholar Gary Ciuba's groundbreaking study *Desire, Violence, and Divinity in Modern Southern Fiction: Katherine Anne Porter, Flannery O'Connor, Cormac McCarthy, Walker Percy* (2007) explores the relationship between violence and the sacred in the titled writers based on the influential theories of French cultural critic René Girard and briefly notes O'Connor's influence on Percy's novel *The Thanatos Syndrome*. Here Ciuba offers "the most astute and compelling" reading of *The Violent Bear It Away* in published criticism, according to Sarah Gordon ("Review" 115). Further recent criticism in this vein has more deeply explored connections between visions of violence in O'Connor and contemporary American novelist Cormac McCarthy.

Critics have seen evidence of O'Connor's influence on the fictions of a number of notable contemporary American writers, including Joyce Carol Oates, Larry Brown, Bobbie Ann Mason, Barry Hannah, and Anne Tyler. Canadian O'Connor scholar Frederick Asals has identified her influence on a number of contemporary Canadian writers, including Leon Rooke, Jack Hodgins, Hugh Hood, and, most professedly, acclaimed short story writer and 2009 Booker Prize winner Alice Munro ("Glimpses"). A number of articles linking O'Connor and Munro have appeared in literary journals. To a list of Canadian writers who acknowledge their debt to O'Connor must be added Rudy Wiebe and W. P. Kinsella. Kinsella has published a parody of an O'Connor story titled "Red Wolf, Red Wolf" narrated by her *Wise Blood* character Enoch Emory.

Psychoanalytical Criticism

Freudian analysis of O'Connor's fiction is not new, and O'Connor was wary that psychoanalytical critics would have a heyday with her stories, particularly *The Violent Bear It Away*. She remarks in a letter to Betty Hester, "a Freudian could read this novel and explain it all on the basis of Freud" (*HB* 343). As psychoanalytical criticism of her works emerged, O'Connor lamented in a letter to Cecil Dawkins in September 1962, "Freud is dogging my tracks all the way" (*HB* 491). While O'Connor studies has attracted a number of responses from psychoanalytic critics, the most doggedly Freudian study of O'Connor's fiction is found in Part I of Suzanne Morrow Paulson's *Flannery O'Connor: A Study of the Short Fiction* (1988), a volume for the Twayne Studies in Short Fiction series. Whereas O'Connor contends that the meaning of her stories "does not begin except at a depth where adequate motivation and adequate psychology and the various determinations have been exhausted" (*MM* 41-42), Paulson asserts that "psychoanalytic approaches are essential to any basic understanding of Flannery O'Connor's stories" (5). The Freudian notion of "the divided self" is particularly employed in Paulson's analyses of the characters in O'Connor's short fiction. Freudian readings of O'Connor via the theories of postmodern French philosopher and psychoanalyst Jacques Lacan have found a place in a couple of essay collections, notably André Bleikasten's "The Heresy of Flannery O'Connor," collected in Friedman and Clark's *Critical Essays on Flannery O'Connor* (1985) and James Mellard's Lacanian reading of Hazel Motes in "Framed in the Gaze: Haze, *Wise Blood*, and Lacanian Reading," collected in *New Essays on "Wise Blood"* (1995). Other interesting Lacanian readings of O'Connor's short fiction include Bleikasten's "Writing on the Flesh: Tattoos and Taboos in 'Parker's Back'" (1982) and Mellard's reading of O'Connor's story "A View of the Woods" in a 1989 essay published in the journal *American Literature* entitled "Flannery O'Connor's *Others*: Freud, Lacan, and the Unconscious."

O'Connor and Postmodern Critical Theory

With the seeming exhaustion of religious readings of O'Connor's fiction, announced by Frederick Crews in *The Critics Bear It Away* (1992) and again of late by Robert Donahoo ("Everything"), scholars have found fruitful approaches to O'Connor's fiction from a number of new critical theoretical perspectives, most productively through Bakhtinian, new historicist, and revisionist feminist readings.

Robert Brinkmeyer's study of O'Connor's "dialogic imagination" in his 1989 book *The Art and Vision of Flannery O'Connor* adds to Gentry's Bakhtinian analysis of her work. Brinkmeyer examines the role of O'Connor's narrators in creating tension between her Catholic vision and her rendering of fictional truth. The perspective of O'Connor's often fundamentalist narrators is frequently undercut in the action and character transformations in her stories, he argues.

Thomas Hill Schaub includes a chapter on O'Connor's first story collection, *A Good Man Is Hard to Find*, in his well-reviewed book *American Fiction in the Cold War* (1991). Schaub reads her stories as fictional critiques of changing liberal values in Cold War America. Similarly focused, *Flannery O'Connor and Cold War Culture* (1993) by Jon Lance Bacon ranks as one of the most original works of scholarship on O'Connor. Bacon's new historicist analysis places O'Connor's fiction and ideas against the social and political milieu of the times in which she lived.

Bacon relates O'Connor's fiction to the popular culture, advertising, editorial cartoons, political rhetoric, and pop sociology to which she would have been exposed, and argues convincingly that O'Connor's work can be regarded as a direct response to the Cold War rhetoric and ethos of the 1950s. *Return to Good and Evil: Flannery O'Connor's Response to Nihilism* (2002), by Henry T. Edmondson III, a professor of political philosophy at O'Connor's alma mater, Georgia College and State University, might be considered a work of philosophical history. Edmondson attempts to define O'Connor's art as a response to the nihilistic and Nietzschean philosophies that prevailed in the age in which she lived. Discussions of modern philosophy in this book are solid, as are Edmondson's engaged readings of O'Connor's stories.

O'Connor and "The Feminist Business"

The first wave of feminist critics responded with ire toward or had little interest in O'Connor, given the perceived powerlessness and repeated victimization of female characters in her stories. One of the earliest feminist responses to O'Connor's work is Louise Westling's *Sacred Groves and Ravaged Gardens: The Fiction of Eudora Welty, Carson McCullers, and Flannery O'Connor* (1985). Westling discusses the ways in which patriarchal Southern notions of the feminine self affected the fictions of these three writers. She sees O'Connor's female characters as sexually repressed and ultimately punished for transgressing against an earthly patriarchal authority that is guarded by and grounded in the God of O'Connor's patriarchal religion. Fifteen years later this feminist position on O'Connor is both reinforced and somewhat revised by Sarah Gordon in *Flannery O'Connor: The Obedient Imagination* (2000). Gordon observes that O'Connor's education and religious convictions "caused her to ally herself with the very masculinist modern tradition," while granting that "some rebellion against the patriarchal view of women in clearly evident" within her fiction (16). In her highly-praised feminist study, *Revising Flannery O'Connor: Southern Literary Culture and the Problem of Female Authorship* (2001), Katherine Hemple Prown stands in agreement with those feminist scholars who regard O'Connor as subscribing to the traditions and beliefs of Southern patriarchy. From careful examination of the manuscripts for *Wise Blood* and *The Violent Bear It Away*, Prown reveals that O'Connor suppressed her feminine voice as a writer and instead chose to "bury her female self beneath layers of masculinist forms and conventions," as Prown concludes, in order to succeed in a male-dominated literary world (161).

Given O'Connor's oppressed and often victimized woman, and her dismissal of what she referred to as "the subject of the feminist business" (*HB* 176), pro-feminist readings of O'Connor have been few. But there is a growing body of criticism favorably reevaluating Flannery O'Connor from feminist perspectives that counter feminist responses like those of Westling, Gordon, and Prown that judge her as largely complicit with the definitions of femaleness under Southern patriarchy. Recent feminist criticism has come to regard O'Connor as more subversive in her representations of female oppression and identity than earlier granted. For example, Cynthia L. Seel in *Ritual Performance in the Fiction of Flannery O'Connor* (2001) views O'Connor's fiction, through a largely Jungian and loosely New Age lens, as animated by an "archetypal feminine principle" that can be seen as "holistic, creative, and redemptive" (50). *"On the Subject of the Feminist*

Business": Re-reading Flannery O'Connor (2004), edited by Teresa Caruso, offers ten original essays, including several by established O'Connor scholars, which examine O'Connor's fictions from affirming points of view using mainstream feminist approaches that produce what the editor calls "resisting" readings. The O'Connor that emerges from these essays is seen as more in travail against than complicit with the Southern patriarchy of the 1950-1960s. Further scholarship on "the subject of the feminist business" in O'Connor's works is needed.

Conclusion

Flannery O'Connor once remarked to an interviewer that she could wait fifty to one hundred years to have her fiction understood (Magee 87). Since critical responses to O'Connor's art and vision began in book reviews of *Wise Blood* and *A Good Man Is Hard to Find* in the early to mid-1950s, and O'Connor studies began in earnest in the early 1960s during her lifetime, readers of her fiction have indeed been trying to understand her work for over fifty years now. If the current pace of O'Connor scholarship and her increasing presence in popular culture are any indication of future interest in her work, perhaps the next fifty years will bring us closer to understanding the depth of O'Connor's vision and the wisdom incarnate in her fiction. The kind of fiction that interested her was that which "push[ed] its own limits outward toward the limits of mystery" (*MM* 41). The considerable critical response to O'Connor's work so far has not reached either of these limits—nor will it ever. In an early letter to Eileen Hall, then editor of the local diocesan newsletter, *The Bulletin*, to which O'Connor regularly contributed book reviews, O'Connor defines fiction as "the concrete expression of mystery—mystery that is lived" (*HB* 144). At the end of all our exploring and enquiring of her art and life, there will still be that quality of mystery in her work which for Flannery O'Connor was at the heart of all of her stories, essential to the "deeper kinds of realism" that inform all of her writing.

Works Cited

Asals, Frederick. *Flannery O'Connor: The Imagination of Extremity*. Athens: U of Georgia P, 1982.

___________. "Some Glimpses of Flannery O'Connor in the Canadian Landscape." *Flannery O'Connor Bulletin* 23 (1994-1995): 83-90.

Bacon, Jon Lance. *Flannery O'Connor and Cold War Culture*. New York: Cambridge UP, 1993.

Baumgaertner, Jill P. *Flannery O'Connor: A Proper Scaring*. Wheaton, IL: Harold Shaw, 1988.

Bleikasten, André. "The Heresy of Flannery O'Connor." *Critical Essays on Flannery O'Connor*. Ed. Melvin J. Friedman and Beverly Lyon Clark. Boston: G. K. Hall, 1985. 138-58.

___________. "Writing on the Flesh: Tattoos and Taboos in 'Parker's Back.'" *Southern Literary Journal* 14.2 (1982): 8-18.

Bloom, Harold, ed. *Flannery O'Connor: Comprehensive Research and Study Guide*. Bloom's Major Short Story Writers Series. Broomall, PA: Chelsea House, 1999.

___________, ed. *Flannery O'Connor: Modern Critical Views*. New York: Chelsea House, 1986.

Brinkmeyer, Robert H. *The Art and Vision of Flannery O'Connor*. Baton Rouge: Louisiana State UP, 1989.

Browning, Preston M. *Flannery O'Connor*. Carbondale: Southern Illinois UP, 1974.

Burns, Stuart. "Freaks in a Circus Tent: Flannery O'Connor's Christ-Haunted Characters." *Flannery O'Connor Bulletin* 1 (1972): 3-18.

Butler, Rebecca Roxburgh. "Review of Jill Baumgaertner's *Flannery O'Connor: A Proper Scaring*." *Flannery O'Connor Bulletin* 17 (1988): 101-04.

Caron, Timothy Paul. "'The Bottom Rail Is on the Top': Race and 'Theological Whiteness' in Flannery O'Connor's Short Fiction." *Inside the Church of Flannery O'Connor*. Ed. Joanne Halleran McMullen and Jon Parrish Peede. Macon, GA: Mercer UP, 2007. 138-64.

Caruso, Teresa, ed. *"On the Subject of the Feminist Business": Re-reading Flannery O'Connor*. New York: Peter Lang, 2004

Ciuba, Gary. *Desire, Violence, and Divinity in Modern Southern Fiction: Katherine Anne Porter, Flannery O'Connor, Cormac McCarthy, Walker Percy*. Baton Rouge: Louisiana State UP, 2007.

Coles, Robert. "Flannery O'Connor: Letters Larger Than Life." *Flannery O'Connor Bulletin* 8 (1979): 6.

___________. *Flannery O'Connor's South*. Baton Rouge: Louisiana State UP, 1980.

Desmond, John. *Risen Sons: Flannery O'Connor's Vision of History*. Athens: U of Georgia P, 1987.

Di Renzo, Anthony. *American Gargoyles: Flannery O'Connor and the Medieval Grotesque*. Carbondale: Southern Illinois UP, 1993.

Donahoo, Robert. "Everything That Rises Does Not Converge: The State of O'Connor Studies." *Flannery O'Connor in the Age of Terrorism*. Ed. Avis Hewitt and Robert Donahoo. Knoxville: U of Tennessee P, 2010. 241-58.

Drake, Robert. *Flannery O'Connor: A Critical Essay*. Grand Rapids, MI: William B. Eerdmans, 1966

Driskell, Leon V., and Joan T. Brittain, eds. *The Eternal Crossroads: The Art of Flannery O'Connor*. Lexington: UP of Kentucky, 1971.

Edmondson, Henry T., III. *Return to Good and Evil: Flannery O'Connor's Response to Nihilism*. Lanham, MD: Lexington Books, 2002.

Feeley, Kathleen. *Flannery O'Connor: Voice of the Peacock*. New Brunswick, NJ: Rutgers UP, 1972.

Fitzgerald, Sally. "The Owl and the Nightingale." *Flannery O'Connor Bulletin* 13 (1984): 44-58.

Friedman, Melvin J., and Beverly Lyon Clark, eds. *Critical Essays on Flannery O'Connor*. Boston: G. K. Hall, 1985.

Friedman, Melvin J., and Lewis A. Lawson, eds. *The Added Dimension: The Art and Mind of Flannery O'Connor*. New York: Fordham UP, 1966.

Gentry, Marshall Bruce. *Flannery O'Connor's Religion of the Grotesque*. Jackson: UP of Mississippi, 1986.

Giannone, Richard. Flannery O'Connor and the Mystery of Love. Urbana: U of Illinois P, 1989.

____________. *Flannery O'Connor, Hermit Novelist*. Urbana: U of Illinois P, 2000.

Golden, Robert E., and Mary C. Sullivan. *Flannery O'Connor and Caroline Gordon: A Reference Guide*. Boston: G. K. Hall, 1977.

Gordon, Caroline. "Heresy in Dixie." *Sewanee Review* 76 (1968): 263-97.

Gordon, Sarah. *Flannery O'Connor: The Obedient Imagination*. Athens: U of Georgia P, 2000.

____________. "Review of Gary M. Ciuba's *Desire, Violence, and Divinity in Modern Southern Fiction: Katherine Anne Porter, Flannery O'Connor, Cormac McCarthy, Walker Percy*." *Flannery O'Connor Review* 7 (2009): 115-24.

Gretlund, Jan Nordby, and Karl-Heinz Westarp, eds. *Flannery O'Connor's Radical Reality*. Columbia: U of South Carolina P, 2006.

Hawkes, John. "Flannery O'Connor's Devil." *Flannery O'Connor: Modern Critical Views*. Ed. Harold Bloom. New York: Chelsea House, 1986. 9-17.

Hendin, Josephine. *The World of Flannery O'Connor*. Bloomington: Indiana UP, 1970.

Hewitt, Avis, and Robert Donahoo, eds. *Flannery O'Connor in the Age of Terrorism*. Knoxville: U of Tennessee P, 2010.

Hyman, Stanley Edgar. *Flannery O'Connor*. University of Minnesota Pamphlets on American Writers No. 54. Minneapolis: U of Minnesota P, 1966.

Kilcourse, George. *Flannery O'Connor's Religious Imagination: A World with Everything Off Balance*. New York: Paulist Press, 2001.

Kreyling, Michael, ed. *New Essays on Wise Blood*. New York: Cambridge UP, 1995.

Lake, Christina Bieber. *The Incarnational Art of Flannery O'Connor*. Macon, GA: Mercer UP, 2005.

McMullen, Joanne Halleran, and Jon Parrish Peede, eds. *Inside the Church of Flannery O'Connor: Sacrament, Sacramental, and the Sacred in Her Fiction*. Macon, GA: Mercer UP, 2007.

Magee, Rosemary, ed. *Conversations with Flannery O'Connor*. Jackson: UP of Mississippi, 1987.

Malin, Irving. "Flannery O'Connor and the Grotesque." *The Added Dimension*. Ed. Melvin J. Friedman and Lewis A. Lawson. New York: Fordham UP, 1966. 108-22.

Martin, Carter W. *The True Country: Themes in the Fiction of Flannery O'Connor*. Nashville, TN: Vanderbilt UP, 1968.

May, John R. *The Pruning Word: The Parables of Flannery O'Connor*. Notre Dame, IN: U of Notre Dame P, 1976.

Mellard, James. "Flannery O'Connor's *Others*: Freud, Lacan, and the Unconscious." *American Literature* 61.4 (1989): 625-43.

____________. "Framed in the Gaze: Haze, *Wise Blood*, and Lacanian Reading." *New Essays on Wise Blood*. Ed. Michael Kreyling. New York: Cambridge UP, 1995. 51-69.

Montgomery, Marion. *Hillbilly Thomist: Flannery O'Connor, St. Thomas, and the Limits of Art*. 2 vols. Jefferson, NC: McFarland, 2006.

Muller, Gilbert H. *Nightmares and Visions: Flannery O'Connor and the Catholic Grotesque*. Athens: U of Georgia P, 1972.

O'Connor, Flannery. *Collected Works*. Ed. Sally Fitzgerald. New York: Library of America, 1988.

____________. *The Habit of Being: Letters of Flannery O'Connor*. Ed. Sally Fitzgerald. New York: Farrar, Straus and Giroux, 1979. (Cited in the text as *HB*).

____________. *Mystery and Manners: Occasional Prose*. Eds. Sally Fitzgerald and Robert Fitzgerald. New York: Farrar, Straus and Giroux, 1969. (Cited in the text as *MM*).

____________. *Wise Blood*. 2d ed. New York: Farrar, Straus and Giroux, 1962. (Cited in the text as *WB*).

O'Gorman, Farrell. *Peculiar Crossroads: Flannery O'Connor, Walker Percy, and Catholic Vision in Postwar Southern Fiction*. Baton Rouge: Louisiana State UP, 2004.

Orvell, Miles. *Invisible Parade: The Fiction of Flannery O'Connor*. Philadelphia: Temple UP, 1972.

Paulson, Suzanne Morrow. *Flannery O'Connor: A Study of the Short Fiction*. Boston: Twayne, 1988.

Prown, Katherine Hemple. *Revising Flannery O'Connor: Southern Literary Culture and the Problem of Female Authorship*. Charlottesville: UP of Virginia, 2001.

Rath, Sura P., and Mary Neff Shaw, eds. *Flannery O'Connor: New Perspectives*. Athens: U of Georgia P, 1996.

Reiter, Robert E., ed. *Flannery O'Connor*. The Christian Critic Series. St. Louis, MO: B. Herder, 1968.

Robillard, Douglas, Jr., ed. *The Critical Response to Flannery O'Connor*. Troy, MO: Greenwood Publishing, 2004.

Schaub, Thomas Hill. *American Fiction in the Cold War*. Madison: U of Wisconsin P, 1991.

Scott, R. Neil. *Flannery O'Connor: An Annotated Reference Guide to Criticism*. Milledgeville, GA: Timberlane Books, 2002.

Scott, R. Neil, and Irwin Streight, eds. *Flannery O'Connor: The Contemporary Reviews*. New York: Cambridge UP, 2009.

Seel, Cynthia. *Ritual Performance in the Fiction of Flannery O'Connor*. Rochester, NY: Camden House, 2001.

Shloss, Carol. *Flannery O'Connor's Dark Comedies: The Limits of Inference*. Baton Rouge: Louisiana State UP, 1980.

"Special Feature." *Flannery O'Connor Review*. 8 (2010): 1-47.

Srigley, Susan. *Flannery O'Connor's Sacramental Art*. Notre Dame, IN: U of Notre Dame P, 2004.

Stephens, Martha. *The Question of Flannery O'Connor*. Baton Rouge: Louisiana State UP, 1973.

Sykes, John D., Jr. *Flannery O'Connor, Walker Percy, and the Aesthetic of Revelation*. Columbia: U of Missouri P, 2007.

Walters, Dorothy. *Flannery O'Connor*. New York: Twayne, 1973.

Westarp, Karl-Heinz, and Jan Nordby Gretlund, eds. *Realist of Distances: Flannery O'Connor Revisited*. Aarhus, Denmark: Aarhus UP, 1987.

Westling, Louise. *Sacred Groves and Ravaged Gardens: The Fiction of Eudora Welty, Carson McCullers, and Flannery O'Connor*. Athens: U of Georgia P, 1985.

Wood, Ralph C. *The Comedy of Redemption: Christian Faith and Comic Vision in Four American Novelists*. Notre Dame, IN: U of Notre Dame P, 1988.

____________. *Flannery O'Connor and the Christ-Haunted South*. Grand Rapids, MI: William B. Eerdmans, 2004

____________. "Review of Margaret Early Whitt's *Understanding Flannery O'Connor*, Ted R. Spivey's *Flannery O'Connor: The Woman, the Thinker, the Visionary*, and *New Essays on "Wise Blood"*." *Flannery O'Connor Bulletin* 23 (1994-95): 195-206.

Zaidman, Laura M. "Varieties of Religious Experience in O'Connor and West." *Flannery O'Connor Bulletin* 7 (1978): 26-46.

CRITICAL READINGS

Flannery O'Connor and the Art of the Holy

Arthur F. Kinney

For Dorothy Tuck McFarland

Flannery O'Connor was an extraordinary person, an extraordinary thinker and writer—and she knew it. Once a student in Texas asked her why she wrote. She later told John Hawkes her reply: "'because I'm good at it,' says I." She had meant to display disgust at shallowness and impertinence, but it also shows her quick and ready wit—and her abiding attitude. "Every serious novelist," she wrote, "is trying to portray reality as it manifests itself in our concrete, sensual life, and he can't do this unless he has been given the initial instrument, the talent, and unless he respects the talent, as such." For herself, she had no doubts.

She had her reasons, of course, and, as a Catholic, a firm sense of duty and responsibility that imposed additional demands. "The poet is traditionally a blind man," she remarked, thinking of such bards as Homer and the singer of *Beowulf*, "but the Christian poet, and storyteller as well, is like the blind man whom Christ touched, who looked then and saw men as if they were trees, but walking. This is the beginning of vision, and it is an invitation to deeper and stranger visions that we shall have to learn to accept if we want to realize a truly Christian literature." So she gave us Mr. Fortune's vision in turn in "A View of the Woods" ("On both sides of him he saw that the gaunt trees had thickened into mysterious dark files that were marching across the water and away into the distance") and the vision of Mrs. Turpin in, appropriately enough, a late story called "Revelation" ("She saw the streak [of light] as a vast swinging bridge extending upward from the earth through a field of living fire. Upon it a vast horde of souls were rumbling toward heaven").

And such unshakable beliefs led her to write imperishable works. From the beginning, she was sure of her talent, confident of her ideas. Her "gravest concern," she stated at the outset—again to John

Hawkes—"is always the conflict between an attraction for the Holy and the disbelief in it that we breathe in with the air of the times." "I have found, in short, from reading my own writing, that my subject in fiction is the action of grace in territory largely held by the devil." It is this persistent need and concern that reverberates throughout the canon, that lies just beneath the exterior of each moment of her stories, the need to

> suggest both the world and eternity. The action or gesture I'm talking about would have to be on the anagogical level, that is, the level which has to do with the Divine Life and our participation in it. It would be a gesture that transcended any neat allegory that might have been intended or any pat moral categories a reader could make. It would be a gesture which somehow made contact with mystery.

She knew her talent was secure, that is, because it dominated a principled art.

She seems always to have dominated the existence of her own fictions, too, and to be able to characterize them, when called upon, with an astonishing acuity, a dazzling candor.

> The novelist with Christian concerns will find in modern life distortions which are repugnant to him, and his problem will be to make these appear as distortions to an audience which is used to seeing them as natural; and he may well be forced to take ever more violent means to get his vision across to this hostile audience. When you can assume that your audience holds the same beliefs you do, you can relax a little and use more normal means of talking to it; when you have to assume that it does not, then you have to make your vision apparent by shock—to the hard of hearing you shout, and for the almost-blind you draw large and startling figures.

So she consciously developed, too, a conscious aesthetic for grotesquerie, creating an art of distortion, eccentric characters, even freaks, hoping to show how malformed the "normal" among us who sin must appear violent and deformed from the perspective of Christ. She drew on Poe and Hawthorne for models; her reading (and her library) show us too that she learned, from the start, from Gogol. Her sense of humor, once larklike and satiric, turned grim and mordant. The urgency she felt to draw boldly the queerness that marked souls deliberately turned from Christianity despite their conventional allegiances—mere mockeries, those—meant an increasingly queer art, too, one that, to her surprise, failed to communicate. Still she held firm. Her faith, in her religion and in her art, remained rocklike and hard. "When I sit down to write, a monstrous reader looms up who sits down beside me and continually mutters, 'I don't get it, I don't see it, I don't want it,'" she remarked in 1960 in an address at Georgia College, her alma mater. "Some writers can ignore this presence, but I have never learned how. I know that I must never let him affect my vision, must never let him gain control over my thinking, must never listen to his demands unless they accord with my conscience; yet I feel I must make him see what I have to show, even if my means of making him see have to be extreme." Yet for all her faith in her beliefs and her fiction, the monstrous readers were too numerous for her, and her letters, filled with a stubborn disappointment at the misinterpretations, the denigrations, and the trivializations her work suffered at their hands, led to a kind of benign resignation. "I can wait fifty years, a hundred years for it to be understood. . . . It will take a while . . . for people to see what I mean."

II

What she meant was conveyed—and with a fine transparency—through images whose power and significance she read about in her library. Her naturally searching, naturally syncretic mind joined theology and literature, her chief interests, as her reading now documents, in the words she marked by Aquinas and by Conrad. For her St.

Thomas's call for "the accurate naming of the things of God" allowed her to follow Conrad's advice, in his preface to *The Nigger of the 'Narcissus,'* to "render the highest possible justice to the visible universe." For her, then, the secular and sensual world contains—and also requires—perceptual transpositions. Objects and events demand metamorphosis into higher apprehensions of Reality. The burning tree which appears like Moses' burning bush ("Parker's Back"), the stained ceiling that descends irrevocably in the shape of the Pentecostal dove ("The Enduring Chill"), or Atlanta envisioned as an Inferno which can be transformed into Purgatory ("The Artificial Nigger") are all, in O'Connor's chemistry, alive with the power of the miraculous which embattles a more rational world of statistics and probabilities. And our leap of faith invites a reciprocal leap of grace. Although O'Connor views this technique of her fiction as prophetic, drawing on the events of the Bible and the acts of Old Testament prophecy, her method ironically reverses them: she starts with phenomena and only hints at the noumena which give them what power and significance, what form and function, her stories realize.

So we constantly find in her fiction, discovering in her country our own, strange juxtapositions of events, intrusions of the divine, and the effronteries of grace (not to mention its apparent gratuity) clearly designed (in imitating the ways of the Lord) to "upset the balance" of life. Mrs. McIntyre says as much in "The Displaced Person," claiming the Christ-like Mr. Guizac upsets the stable and self-sufficient farm the judge has left her. Such arrangements of characters and events—in "The Displaced Person" a Polish refugee displaces a peacock and both are displaced for Mrs. McIntyre who may, in turn, be the most displaced of them all in this world—are strange amalgamations, as discordant as Hazel Motes and Enoch Emery in the early novel *Wise Blood*, or as Tarwater and his uncle Rayber in the late novel *The Violent Bear It Away*. But these novels, too, the one a comic flight toward salvation, the other a tragic struggle toward it, both display Thomistic incarnations of truth despite the fact that the first was a Georgian's synthesis of

The Waste Land and *Oedipus Tyrannos*—like so much of her work, a book built on books—while the second transformed the revelation of St. Matthew—"From the days of John the Baptist until now, the kingdom of heaven suffereth violence, and the violent bear it away"—into a second apocalypse.

Such ironies of juxtaposition and transformation—where everything signifies something larger and deeper, something sacred—abound in O'Connor's fiction. We find it in characters, such as fat Alonzo Myers and the freakish hermaphrodite who image holy incarnation to a girl just entering puberty in "A Temple of the Holy Ghost." We find it in encounters such as that between a hypocritical Bible salesman and a feigned atheist in "Good Country People." We find it also in events such as the fire set by the three boys who destroy God's woods to prove they do not belong to Mrs. Cope, in "A Circle in the Fire." And we find it in images such as Rufus Johnson eating pages of the Bible at the dinnertable ("The Lame Shall Enter First"). Often O'Connor intimates her ideas through implied analogies—as the arson alludes to Daniel 3:91 and the Bible-eating to Apocalypse 10:10—but some significations, such as the homosexual rapist in *The Violent Bear It Away* or the criminal Misfit in "A Good Man Is Hard to Find" or the drifter Mr. Shiftlet in "The Life You Save May Be Your Own," draw surprisingly large figures while others, such as the bull that gores Mrs. May ("Greenleaf") or the tattoo of a Byzantine Christ on Parker's back in which the Word is literally made flesh, in which God actually gets beneath the skin of the sinner, seem downright blasphemous. For O'Connor they are all of a glorious similarity, revealing "a peculiar crossroads where time and place and eternity somehow meet."

And that governing idea, too, stems from her reading, from the work of Mircea Eliade which she owned and admired. "It is impossible to overemphasize the paradox represented by every hierophany, even the most elementary," Eliade writes in *The Sacred and Profane* (which she owned).

> By manifesting the sacred, any object becomes *something else*, yet it continues to remain *itself*, for it continues to participate in its surrounding cosmic milieu. A *sacred* stone remains a *stone*; apparently (or, more precisely, from the profane point of view), nothing distinguishes it from all other stones. But for those to whom a stone reveals itself as sacred, its immediate reality is transmuted into a supernatural reality. In other words, for those who have a religious experience all nature is capable of revealing itself as cosmic sacrality. The cosmos in its entirety can become a hierophany.

For O'Connor, Eliade is at one with Aquinas (and Conrad); her crossroads were not so much the interruption of opposed lines of traffic as meeting places of the concrete and the eternal. Hazel Motes' self-blinding is meant to relate him to Oedipus but also to Tiresias—and to Asa Hawks whom he would expose and to Christ's story of a man who was blind but (*because* he was blind) could see; the Greenleaf bull takes us toward Zeus and Dionysus—and also toward the Greenleafs; and Mrs. May's stricken look in that story recalls the agonized ecstasy on Bernini's statue of St. Teresa. "The Life You Save May Be Your Own" is a commonplace highway sign (even in the story); it is also an echo of the gospel according to Matthew: "He that findeth his life, shall lose it; and he that shall lose his life for me, shall find it" (Matthew 10:39). Like Christ, O'Connor found in paradox the *drama* of reality as well as the truth of it. In such a world, it is natural that a peacock reify the Transfiguration ("The Displaced Person") and the setting sun should become a blood-drenched Host ("A Temple of the Holy Ghost"). Nor can we any longer be astonished that what Melvin J. Friedman calls her "chaste, unimposing sentences" can survive such burdens. For the pressures of perceptual transformation causes her to witness to the world as, essentially, opportunities and acts for inward and outward conversion of mind and soul.

III

But to an incarnational writer like Flannery O'Connor, the greatest possibility of art, its greatest appeal and its greatest mystery, was the reification of the prototypical Incarnation: the awareness that all of us are, actually or potentially, temples of the Holy Ghost. It is ourselves, stout bulwarks of pride and passion, that must withstand the assaults of grace, the daily wars with mercy which serve, insistently, as telling exposures of our inadequacies. The city of Taulkinham—its streets and moviehouses, boardinghouses, zoos, and filling stations, its Frosty Bottle, Paris Diner, and Slade's Used Car Lot—is not only ugly and empty of meaning, a dusty reminder of living death like the mummy disintegrating in its case, but it is also ridiculous. Its hollowness is telling. Indeed, such a sight can even lead the steadfastly unregenerate Hazel Motes to his first sense of loss, informing his patched-up, urgent initial response in *Wise Blood*: a street gospel that proclaims "'there was no Fall because there was nothing to fall from and no Redemption because there was no Fall and no judgment because there wasn't the first two.'" Pilgrim souls become moral derelicts in Taulkinham not because they lack the capacity to believe but because they see, rightly, only a city of ashes. The waste land of Eliot—whose books O'Connor collected over the years, one by one—epitomizes the landscapes of many of her characters, forcing them to a total, evangelical commitment to the Lord or to a total repudiation of Him and all He represents. The harsh self-sufficiency of her people, their rigidity of spirit and their willingness to suffer for a sense of glory, born of strict propriety of the self, leads them inexorably to a sense of painful alienation, a radical sense of estrangement.

"Almost everywhere in her fiction," Friedman contends, some person is trying to fulfill a mission in unfamiliar surroundings." But her maimed souls and mutilated consciousnesses, turned self-styled prophets, are mirrors of the ragged figures that pass between ominous silences in her work, fallen counterparts of the tattered alter-ego that lurks behind every tree Hazel Motes seems to pass. Their ancestors are the Old Testament prophets who speak to someone like young Hazel

Motes, whose wise blood is not so easily beckoned as Enoch Emery's but instead struggles to surface. Their oracular pronouncements are divided between the threats of Ecclesiasticus—

> They that forsake God shall fall into [hell], and it shall burn in them, and shall not be quenched, and it shall be sent upon them as a lion, and as a leopard it shall tear them— (28:27)

and the commands of Isaias—

> Wash yourselves, be clean, take away the evil of your devices from my eyes: cease to do perversely. (1:16)

It is a tradition of fear and trembling, with ancient pedigree, that threatens Hazel Motes and his successors, the great-uncle and great-nephew Tarwater, while it hurtles them toward some awful, perhaps final confrontation with God. Their biographies bear witness to life as an endless field of struggle, seemingly without armistice.

For O'Connor, Hazel and the Tarwaters are souls *in extremis* but not, for all that, misrepresentative. On a subtler level, Julian ("Everything That Rises Must Converge") and Joy/Hulga ("Good Country People"), the grandmother ("A Good Man Is Hard to Find") and the boy Harry Ashfield/Bevel ("The River") also face life as dissatisfying and unfulfilling and come to realize, in studied alterations of circumstances, the contingencies of the human condition which create a perpetually endangered species. What many of O'Connor's story protagonists share, in more commonplace guises than the protagonists of the novels, is an estrangement from God's plenitude, and thus a false, deluded sense of freedom which is in fact, O'Connor warns us, a desperate state of self-bondage. Liberty and captivity are central issues as her "more normal" characters fashion their roads of life as misconceived pathways to salvation. It takes, instead, something considerably less easy and pleasant than passive acquiescence to arrive at atonement in our dark and bloody land, to respond to the violence by which the grace of God can seize us. O'Connor owned the Douay translation of the Holy Scriptures, which, upon occasion, she marked; she also owned Ronald Knox's translation, which she did not. Knox may have mistranslated the verse from Matthew that serves as the title of her late novel: "Ever since John the Baptist's time," Knox has it, "the kingdom of heaven has opened to force; and the forceful are even now making it their prize." Either way, force and destruction or else prolonged alienation and suffering are the means—we can *break* the seven seals of our fates—and Julian's mother suffers a stroke, Joy/Hulga has her leg removed and stolen; the grandmother is shot, the boy drowned. The road to glory is not merely awesome but painful and dangerous. The intensification of conflict which John the Baptist, Christ, and Matthew envision at the arrival of the Messianic kingdom is shadowed forth in the visions, actions, and deaths in O'Connor's fictional kingdom. They, too, then, are deliberately conceived as incarnational acts.

These ideas are what many books in Flannery O'Connor's personal library—her theological works, her lives of the saints—taught her. "There are long periods in the lives of all of us, and of the saints," she writes to her anonymous friend "A.," "when the truth as revealed by faith is hideous, emotionally disturbing, downright repulsive." "Remember the wrath that shall be at the last day, and the time of repaying when he shall turn away his face," she adds, recalling Ecclesiasticus again (18:24). This sense of the apocalyptic is what O'Connor transfers into the more commonplace continuum of our humdrum lives. For while those lives could lurch her into the comic and the farcical (Hazel Motes' glare blue suit with the price tag of $11.98 still stapled to it; Mrs. Wally Bee Hitchcock heavy and pink, in a pink wrapper with her knobs of hair resembling toadstools; characters named Hoover Shoats and Red Sammy Butts, Leora Watts and Sally Poker Sash), her fiction was really designed to lead *away* from the conventional, to show, in fact, how *grotesque* conventionality itself is, in a fiction of extraordinary moments, those far more precious, far more revelatory moments that record the death of complacency. In the end, this time through radio rather than through books, she was drawn to the shouting, berating indefatigable *Protestant* preachers whose messages of Doomsday characterized the Bible Belt where her long illness caused her to reside all her adult life. Like her, they recognized hard realities; and they saw life, as she did, as transient, vulnerable, inescapably subject to the heaven or hellfire that awaited in an existence beyond. Indeed, the itinerant Baptist preacher's most reiterated cry (as it was Scripture on most billboards populating her countryside, both then and now) was that "The wages of sin is death. But the grace of God, life everlasting, [is] in Christ Jesus our Lord" (Romans 6:23)—an absolute and final choice which is terrifying *because* it is absolute and final: *everything* is in jeopardy.

Such a warning, laundered for most of us into a harmless cliché, remained for O'Connor a dreadful and violent truth which informed her Bible, her faith, and her library even as it informs her fiction. "I came not to send peace, but the sword," Matthew announces (10:34). Isaias sees the wrongdoing of Judah and Jerusalem as a violence which insures violence in turn: "Woe to the sinful nation, a people laden with iniquity, a wicked seed, ungracious children: they have forsaken the Lord, they have blasphemed the Holy One of Israel, they are gone away backwards" (1:4). Amos speaks of God's denunciation of Israel: "in every street there shall be wailing. . . . I will turn your feasts into mourning, and all your songs into lamentation" (5:16, 8:10). Jeremias has the same message for the Jews: "Thy own wickedness shall reprove thee, and thy apostasy shall rebuke thee. Know thou, and see that it is an evil and a bitter thing for thee, to have left the Lord thy God" (2:19). Even the prophet Micheas, speaking of Samaria, carries the identical message: "I will make Samaria as a heap of stones in the field when a vineyard is planted: and I will bring down the stones thereof into the valley, and will lay her foundations bare" (1:6). Such threats, so O'Connor must have reasoned, were delivered to God's *chosen* people: what, then, would be the fate of her own? Suffering and blessing as indivisible experiences were a direct consequence of the intrusion of God into the consciousness of men. Such intrusions disturb Hazel Motes and Francis Marion Tarwater, who insist they do not need God; such an intrusion leads to the deformed, ugly, and painful thoughts of Hulga and to the disturbingly sweet innocent love of God by Bevel. And self-crucifixions like Hulga's or self-redemptions like Bevel's (who is *escaping* Mr. *Paradise*!) lead us, with our own habits of being, into what Julian senses as a world of guilt and sorrow. His story ("Everything That Rises Must Converge"), like all their stories, is one of a suffering human being as a potential *alter Christus* for the rest of us, if not for himself.

IV

So, wondrously like grace, there is imbedded in the heart of her violence not only the frustration that grotesque fallen souls embody but the fact of conversion: there is theological point and purpose even to her use of the sinning, the deformed, and the damned as subjects fleeing or searching for redemption. "It seems to me," Jacques Maritain wrote Maurice Coindreau, the French translator of O'Connor's novel *Wise Blood*,

> It seems to me that the critics have a poor understanding of her. Yes, doubtless she hated these wild prophets, but they fascinated her. Am I wrong in thinking that to her they were like saints of the devil stripped of everything by him, as real saints are stripped by God, and really poor miserable men in whom she saw a certain greatness? It was the devil she hated. As for them, she pitied them and I think that deep down she loved them.

Precisely. For O'Connor, this was a holy kind of horror which aroused and earned her compassion because *she* was *their* prophet, realizing the ignored truths they themselves faltered in communicating to a world larger than their own backwoods congregations. She shared with them a sense of vocation, a calling from and to God.

For the other side of fear is love, and the other side of violence is peace. Her basic theme, first and always, is the separation of nature and grace, the curving arc of her fictions, the convergence and divergence of the two. Her displaced persons are displaced, as her mentor Caroline Gordon knew and said, because they choose to live in spheres outside the state of grace; but in Flannery O'Connor's traditional and persistent taxonomy this, too, can be promising: "The fear of the Lord is the beginning of wisdom" (Ecclesiasticus 1:16). Her characters' stumbling spiritual growth, their faltering or mistaken gestures, give her fiction its sense of pain, her characters' rigid refusal of spiritual growth its contour of violence. But "With the serious writer," she said, "violence is never an end in itself. It is the extreme situation that best reveals what we are essentially, and I believe these are times when writers are more interested in what we are essentially than in the tenor of our daily lives." So spiritually moribund did she find her monstrous readers, suffering interminably in losses unawares, that only a radical view of human suffering and a dark reading of the human soul could invade their vulgar present and startle them into an awareness sufficient to cleanse and purify their intentions and acts. Her endless parade of needy souls, her Christian (or proto-Christian) wayfarers marching, trudging, struggling, or slouching toward Bethlehem to be reborn led to portraits pained by the intensities of beliefs. "And I saw, when he had opened the sixth seal, and behold there was a great earthquake, and the sun became black as sackcloth of hair: and the whole moon became as blood" (Apocalypse 6:12). This revelation, which the adolescent protagonist of "A Temple of the Holy Ghost" shares with St. John, is the work of a modern-day prophet laboring for our cognition. "Truth—the living God—is a terrifying vision, to be faced only by the stout of heart," Father Leonard Mayhew, an Atlanta priest, wrote of her in *Commonweal* by way of eulogy; "Flannery O'Connor was [herself] such a seer, of stout heart and hope." She shared this vision, too, with Francis Marion Tarwater, who learned its weight of terror, responsibility, and fear of the Lord in *The Violent Bear It Away*: "Go warn the children of God of the terrible speed of mercy," as she tells us, for she had set for herself an identical purpose: she, too, set her face "toward the dark city, where the children of God lay sleeping."

V

Yet what moves us still so intensely in her work is not merely the fear and trembling which, sharing, she writes of so feelingly; it is the awesome uncertainty, the insecurity of human life that is the corollary. Her fiction, which can simultaneously be howlingly funny and awesomely close to the bone, finds further reinforcement in her sense of the fragility of life, of her own life, in fact. Her father died when she was 16 of a rare, nonhereditary disease, then always fatal, lupus erythematosus; suddenly, when she was 25, she had it too. The last 14 years of her life—she died just short of her 40th birthday—she fought a losing battle of passion, body, and even spirit against it. Near the end she told C. Ross Mullins in an interview that "I'm a born Catholic and death has always been brother to my imagination." She had attended daily Mass whenever she could, receiving the sacraments, watching in the Eucharist the daily death of the Lord Himself, Christ crucified, and so "I can't imagine a story that doesn't properly end in it or in its foreshadowings." Five years earlier, in somewhat better health, the idea of death and its significance was still at the center of her thought. Having finished a novel by Boris Pasternak that was once part of her library, she wrote with unaccustomed enthusiasm to Dr. T. R. Spivey, a professor of English at Georgia College, that *Dr. Zhivago* "is a great book. At one point [Pasternak] has Dr. Zhivago say: 'Art has two constants, two unending concerns: it always meditates on death and thus creates life.' All great, genuine art resembles and continues the Revelation of St. John."

This clear eye she fixed on her own condition matched the clear vision she had about what she attempted in her fiction. An autodidact, she disciplined her writing as consciously and carefully as she understood the discipline of the liturgical hours, turning her cramped bed-sitting room at the dairy farm outside Milledgeville, Andalusia, into a convent of one. It had taken her 2,000 pages of trial and error to produce 150 pages of *Wise Blood* over five years; it took her now seven more to write her second novel. And still neither one satisfied her. "Our souls are restless till they find rest in Thee," Augustine says in his *Confessions* (she owned a 1952 paperback edition), but through her searching, she heard, as Tarwater hears in the end, a voice that speaks with no human sound or syntax yet tells what one must stay and do. She surrendered no sense of the horror of sin nor the grotesquerie of those whose lives are tattered or in shambles, although in the end, it seems, Pierre Teilhard de Chardin replaced Augustine in her consciousness; she collected his work, praised it in letters; and gathered commentary on it for review. To Augustine's sense of dissatisfaction, Teilhard added a sense of amelioration that now evidently also appealed to her. "Remain true to yourselves, but move ever upward toward greater consciousness and greater love!" Teilhard advocates in *The Phenomenon of Man* (also in her library). "At the summit you will find yourselves united with all those who, from every direction, have made the same ascent. For everything that rises must converge." Grace as a condition which is not in time but which unites all time is behind Mr. Fortune's vision of walking trees, behind Mrs. Turpin's vision of a classless society, and behind Flannery O'Connor's final missionary sense of fiction. "The type of mind that can understand good fiction is not necessarily the educated mind," she pronounced, "but it is at all times the kind of mind that is willing to have its sense of mystery deepened by contact with reality, and its sense of reality deepened by contact with mystery."

The integrity of this vision, realized through all the stages of her work, is what grows out of her reading, her library and her theology, her faith. The "encounter with Him" which, says Robert Drake, "is the one story she keeps telling over and over again," pursued her, as it pursues us, as relentlessly as the hound of heaven. "There is nothing sweet or sentimental about Him," Drake adds, "and He terrifies before He can bless." Yet not until her final years do O'Connor's tales of God's Kingdom and man's kingdoms suggest Teilhard's Omega point of universal convergence; and, even then, convergence is redefined as collision. "The other day I ran up on a wonderful quotation," she writes her close anonymous friend "A." in January 1956.

> The other day I ran up on a wonderful quotation. "The dragon is at the side of the road watching those who pass. Take care lest he devour you! You are going to the Father of souls, but it is necessary to pass by the dragon." That is Cyril of Jerusalem instructing catechumen.

The idea of life and of faith as apparently antagonistic, of existence as a kind of *coincidentia oppositorium* was, says Robert Coles (who knew her slightly), an idea that haunted her. "She would never tell a story, write a novel, without tapping her readers forcefully on the shoulder with that message [of Cyril], worked into country talk, country description, country manners." For all its horror, the journey by the dragon, however, would always lead directly to the Father of souls; and Kierkegaard's sense of religion (which she studied) as infinite passion and Tillich's more cerebral sense of it (which she knew too) as an ultimate concern were at one for her, as her fiction was at one with them as both a secular ritual *and* a sacred revelation. Her final rage then was to undistort, to make whole and perfect the deformed man reformed in Christ. Her art was in terror and pain and rage, but *a rage for the holy.* In this way, her habit of art became her habit of being (in the Thomistic sense of habit). And like them the mystery of being—of mystery *and* being—made the Satanic avenger (Rufus, the Misfit, Julian) and the prophetic savior, in the end, indistinguishable. Thus she, like the letter writer St. Paul, would see through the glass, if darkly, her letters, her fictions serving as works of imperishable illumination—now dim, now dazzling in their brightness—in which the holy in art and the art of the holy convert and become one.

Flannery O'Connor's "Spoiled Prophet"

T. W. Hendricks

Writing in 1961 to a teacher who had sent her an interpretation of "A Good Man is Hard to Find" that she found especially misguided, Flannery O'Connor described that story as "a duel of sorts between the Grandmother and her superficial beliefs and the Misfit's more profoundly felt involvement in Christ's action which set the world off balance for him."[1] In general, critics have directed their efforts to explaining how the grandmother attains her "moment of grace" when she reaches out to touch the Misfit's shoulder.[2] Few critics have tried to explain the Misfit's part in the duel or how he is involved in Christ's action. The Misfit is in fact a fully developed character with intelligible motives. He is also a prophet, albeit a misguided one, like Hazel Motes in *Wise Blood* and the two Tarwaters in *The Violent Bear It Away*. If we consider the Misfit in the light of O'Connor's view of the role of the prophet, we see that he is not a monster, but a tragic figure, the victim of what O'Connor regarded as a profound misunderstanding of the relation between humanity and God.

In another letter, O'Connor called the Misfit a "spoiled prophet" who "could go on to great things."[3] Although O'Connor did not elaborate on that claim, it is significant because she was deeply interested in the role of the prophet. Karl Martin has shown that O'Connor read and reviewed contemporary books on the social role of prophets and revelation and that her fiction is "closely related to, and informed by, her systematic study of the role of the prophet in culture."[4] O'Connor was committed to what Martin calls a "prophetic vision of history," the view that human history is the story of humanity's relation to God. Consequently the role of the prophet is to maintain the purity of the nation's spiritual life, especially to keep the nation from being overwhelmed by materialism. O'Connor described this effort in the case of old Tarwater:

> The old man is very obviously not a Southern Baptist, but an independent, a prophet in the true sense. The true prophet is inspired by the Holy Ghost, not necessarily by the dominant religion of his region. Further, the traditional Protestant bodies of the South are evaporating into secularism and respectability and are being replaced on the grass roots level by all sorts of strange sects that bear not much resemblance to traditional Protestantism—Jehovah's Witnesses, snake-handlers, Free Thinking Christians, Independent Prophets, the swindlers, the mad, and sometimes the genuinely inspired.[5]

If the dominant religion has lost its spiritual urgency and become secular and respectable, the modern prophet is implicitly its critic.

In the first half of "A Good Man Is Hard to Find," O'Connor portrays two modern families who are far gone in spiritual exile, the families of Bailey and Red Sammy. Bailey and his wife and children are completely indifferent to their roots in the old South; they are going to the artificial world of Florida for their vacation. The structure of the family is in disarray. Bailey is crippled by his resentment of his domineering mother; the only part he can take in family life is to exercise his uncertain authority. Rather than deal with his mother's objections to the trip, he pretends to be absorbed in the sports pages. The prospect of leading the family on this expedition makes Bailey so anxious that he won't let his mother bring her cat, and he drives in silence, his jaw "rigid as a horseshoe." Bailey curtly refuses to make the detour to see the plantation house, and then yields with bad grace when the children scream and kick the back of his seat. Faced with the Misfit and his gang, Bailey insists that he is in charge, but he is helpless to act.

Bailey's wife is as mute and passive as a rabbit. Throughout the story she is preoccupied with the baby, so preoccupied that she doesn't bother to change her clothes for the trip. The two older children are spoiled and insolent, and neither parent makes any effort to teach or discipline them. John Wesley, whose name suggests that his parents had high hopes for him, is rude to his grandmother and scornful of his family's history. Nevertheless he thinks of himself as a young Superman; he announces he will strike the Misfit in the face if they encounter him. John's sister, June Star, has some skill at tap dancing, which gets her the praise and attention of adults. She bears an entertainer's name, and she already has the temperament of a child star.

Red Sammy Butts, the proprietor of the Tower roadhouse, and his wife are similarly demoralized. Although his roadside signs call him "THE FAT BOY WITH THE HAPPY LAUGH," Sammy is discouraged and bitter. His signs claim that his barbecue is famous, but the restaurant is deserted when the family arrives. Sammy is past caring what impression he makes on customers; when Bailey pulls up, Sammy is working out front underneath a truck. He is not plump with good spirits but simply obese. His stomach hangs over his belt "like a sack of meal swaying under his shirt." Sammy complains to his customers and orders his wife around as if she were an employee. He has been unfaithful to her, and she resents it enough to hint about it to the family. Childless herself, Sammy's wife invites June Star to come and be her "little girl"; she doesn't know how to praise June Star's dancing except by patronizing her.

Compared to the other characters, the grandmother is a figure of grace and dignity. She dresses carefully for the trip because she is a lady, polite to strangers and sympathetic to the poor. The children giggle when they see a half-dressed black child, but the grandmother reminds them that black children in the country "don't have the things we do." She is proud of the history and geography of the region and tries to interest the children in their heritage. The grandmother keeps the children from throwing their sandwich wrappers out the car windows, plays games with them, breaks up their squabbles, and tries to improve their manners.

These efforts, however, are largely wasted. John Wesley declares that Tennessee is "a hillbilly dumping ground . . . and Georgia is a lousy state too." June Star scornfully tells Red Sammy's wife that she "wouldn't live in a broken-down place" such as the Tower "for a million bucks." (A million bucks is evidently June Star's standard of value.) Even the grandmother acknowledges to herself that no one will know she is a lady unless they are involved in an accident and she is killed.

The grandmother's good qualities are, however, compromised by her delusions about her background and social status. She expresses concern for the plight of the rural poor but still regards them as part of the picturesque landscape. Her ideas of Southern history and culture come from works of romantic fiction such as *Gone With the Wind*. Her suitor, Edgar Atkins Teagarden, may have had charming manners, but he became wealthy by a lucky investment in Coca-Cola. The grandmother probably used her pretensions to dominate Bailey, and they irritate the rest of the family.

In fact, the grandmother's notions are the source of her most serious shortcoming—her firm, and eventually fatal, conviction of her own rightness. At the opening of the story, the grandmother goes behind Bailey's back to get him to change their vacation destination. She smuggles the cat along in the car against Bailey's wishes. After lunch, she again undermines Bailey by exciting the children with the false story about hidden silver. Their crying and whining persuade Bailey to leave the highway for a deserted dirt road, where the cat distracts him and makes him send the car over the embankment.

The grandmother seals the family's fate when she foolishly blurts out the Misfit's identity. If the Misfit had any doubts about killing the family, the grandmother made up his mind. The Misfit has Hiram and Bobby Lee dispatch Bailey and John Wesley first—they are potentially the most troublesome. As it happens, father and son make no trouble at all. Bailey's pretense of self-assurance and his son's bravado have evaporated. A few minutes later, the mother, carrying the baby, meekly goes to the woods with Hiram and Bobby Lee. June Star grumbles at taking Bobby Lee's hand, but complies.

The family members enter the fatal woods without resisting because for all of the noisy self-assertion that Bailey, John Wesley, and June

Star make, they are accustomed to doing what is expected of them: Bailey takes the family to Florida for vacation, even though no one seems to want to go. John Wesley likes to think of himself as a comic strip hero; June Star pictures herself as another Shirley Temple. None of them is an autonomous being. None can act in his own interest because he has no idea who he really is.

The grandmother is the exception. She is the only one who tries to talk the Misfit into sparing her. While Hiram and Bobby Lee are killing the other members of the family, the grandmother offers four appeals for her life. She is unsuccessful; the Misfit rejects all of them. In doing so, he demonstrates the superficiality of the beliefs on which they are grounded. The "duel" that O'Connor considered the main point of the story emerges in the dialogue between the grandmother and the Misfit while five murders are taking place.

The grandmother first appeals to the Misfit's decency. She suggests that he's too good a man to shoot a lady. (She doesn't seem to consider her daughter-in-law a lady.) The Misfit replies noncommittally, so the grandmother presses the point, nearly screaming, as if the Misfit doesn't understand: "I know you're a good man. You don't look a bit like you have common blood. I know you must come from nice people." The Misfit agrees that his parents were nice people—"finest people in the world"—but he does not concede that he himself is a good man.

In fact, the Misfit states after a pause that he is not a good man, although not "the worst in the world neither." His problem is not that he is a bad man but that he is an exceptional one, "a different breed of dog," a skeptic, as his father recognized:

> [I]t's some that can live their whole life out without asking about it and it's others has to know why it is, and this boy is one of the latters. He's going to be into everything!

The Misfit routinely questioned conventions and institutions. Unfortunately he grew up in a society that equated goodness with accepting conventions and institutions. Consequently he was not a good man in the eyes of the people around him. The Misfit's father, by contrast, was by no means an upright man, but he was canny enough to stay out of trouble with the "Authorities"—evidently the Misfit lacked his father's tact.

The grandmother concludes that the Misfit's problem is that he has not tried hard enough to reconcile himself to the demands of the "Authorities." Accordingly, she tries another appeal. She tries to convince him that a conventional life is not only within his reach, but it is better than the life he is leading: "Think how wonderful it would be to settle down and live a comfortable life and not have to think about somebody chasing you all the time." The grandmother is, of course, unrealistic. If the Misfit were ever capable of leading a conventional life, that possibility has ended by now. He and his boys are running for their lives.

The grandmother thinks the Misfit agrees with her when he replies. "Yes'm," he says, "somebody is always after you." She assumes that he means that he is overwhelmed by his troubles. In her view, what he needs to do then is to pray. She asks him if he ever does. The Misfit shakes his head and replies, "Nome." At this point there are two pistol shots from the woods, underscoring the finality of the Misfit's answer.

The Misfit does not react to the shots. He gives her a summary of his life. It has been full of variety, danger, even horror. The grandmother assumes that he is taking the first step to salvation, admitting his sinfulness. She begins repeating, "Pray, pray," as if she were a congregation of one urging a sinner to repent. Prayer, however, won't help the Misfit because he doesn't consider himself a sinner. He was never a bad boy, but he did something wrong. He does not, however, know what it was. The Misfit admits he wasn't sentenced by mistake; the authorities "had the papers" on him. He didn't kill his father, as he thought the prison psychiatrist reported, and he hadn't stolen anything, as the grandmother suggests. Nevertheless, he was sent to a penitentiary. He found life in prison intolerable: he was "buried alive." What the experience taught him is that it doesn't matter whether you've committed a serious crime or a trifle—killing a man or taking a tire off his car—you're going to be punished for something, no matter what.

The Misfit sends Hiram and Bobby Lee back to the woods with June Star, the mother, and the baby. The grandmother again tries to persuade the Misfit that all will be well, if he will only pray. Now, knowing that her son and grandson are dead, her daughter-in-law and other grandchildren are about to die, and that she is next, the grandmother cannot find her voice. When she does, she realizes she is saying "Jesus, Jesus," "as if she might be cursing."

The Misfit seems to agree that Jesus should be cursed. He states that Jesus "thown everything off balance." Jesus's case was the same as his own. Jesus hadn't committed any crime, yet He'd been punished. Jesus at least knew what He was being punished for; the Misfit has no idea. Consequently he calls himself "The Misfit" because, he says, "I can't make what all I done wrong fit what all I gone through in punishment."

From the Christian point of view, what the Misfit is saying about himself is true of all humanity. We are all being punished for Adam's disobedience—the Misfit is Everyman. Furthermore we are all being punished out of proportion to our crime. Did Adam and Eve deserve to lose Eden for that single act of disobedience? Does every descendant of Adam deserve to suffer for it? Even John Milton had trouble with those questions. The grandmother offers the standard Christian reply: those questions are no longer important because Jesus atoned for the sins of Adam and everyone else. Through Him any of us can be saved.

The Misfit, however, rejects the grandmother's plea that he appeal to Jesus. He doesn't believe he is guilty of a felony, to say nothing of original sin. Nevertheless, in the penitentiary, he was being punished for a felony, and everywhere else he is treated as an unregenerate sinner. Like Bailey's family he is in a "predicament"; he can't call on Jesus unless he is prepared to acknowledge his sins and ask for forgiveness. However, the Misfit truly believes he has no sins to acknowledge. But if he believes he has no sins, he is at odds with the fundamental proposition of Christianity that all humans are born in a state of sin.

Therefore, by insisting on his own innocence, the Misfit is actually committing a graver sin than whatever got him into the penitentiary: he is in fact a heretic.

The Misfit claims that Jesus himself put humanity in this dilemma. By raising Lazarus from the dead, Jesus upset the balance between belief and skepticism. Jesus upped the ante, so to speak: if you believe he raised Lazarus, the Misfit reasons, you have no excuse not to forsake all and follow Him. But if you do not believe that Jesus raised Lazarus, you can hardly believe in His own resurrection. Therefore you are clearly beyond salvation. You have no hope of a good life in this world or bliss in the next. In that case, "it's nothing for you to do but enjoy the few minutes you got left the best way you can—by killing somebody or burning down his house or doing some other meanness to him."

This is exactly where the Misfit finds himself. He is one of the unregenerate, the lost. It's not because of any wrong he's done—that would have been easy enough to atone for. He's damned because he is a "different breed of dog." He is different because he can't accept what people tell him; he wants to know everything for himself. He tells the grandmother he wishes he had been present when Jesus raised Lazarus: "It ain't right I wasn't there because if I had of been there I would of known . . . if I had of been there I would of known and I wouldn't be like I am now." What "ain't right" was for Jesus to have placed such a demand on his credence. If the Misfit had been able to see the miracle of Lazarus for himself, he would have believed that Jesus was the Son of God, and he would have been able to live a conventional Christian life. Since he wasn't there, however, the Misfit remained unsure. Consequently he was never able to make a full and honest profession of faith.

Since the Misfit was unable to make a profession of faith, the people around him considered him a lost soul and treated him accordingly. As the Misfit grew up he found himself shut out of the inner life of his community. Positions of leadership and responsibility never seemed to come his way. He moved from place to place, from job to job, never establishing a home or a career. When anything went wrong he was the one who got the blame and bore the punishment. Finally he was sentenced to prison, although he didn't understand why. Since his punishment didn't fit any crime he was aware of having committed, he called himself "the Misfit."

In fact, the Misfit was a misfit long before he was sent to the penitentiary. All his life he suffered from a skepticism that left him an outsider among the faithful. The Misfit's neighbors believed that he was sinful because he was "into everything." Under those circumstances the Misfit was not likely to hear Jesus's call; he probably wasn't encouraged to listen for it. Furthermore, the Misfit's skepticism probably wasn't limited to the divinity of Jesus. We can guess that he was the one to ask the awkward questions about everything else around him, including the honesty of those who professed their faith most dramatically. The reaction of people to his questions was predictable: people regarded him as an outsider wherever he went. Unsurprisingly, the Misfit felt there was something wrong with him; it would take remarkable strength of character not to think so. Consequently he came to the bitter conclusion that there is "no pleasure but meanness," nothing for him to do but enjoy his "few minutes" on earth by hurting others.

This speech brings the Misfit to an emotional pitch. The Misfit's voice seems to the grandmother about to break; in a moment of clarity she concludes that he is open to a final, emotional appeal. She murmurs, "Why you're one of my babies. You're one of my own children," and touches him on the shoulder. She believes that he is one of the saved after all. He has only strayed, like a lost sheep. She even feels she may be the instrument of his salvation. All she has to do is touch his shoulder; his hard heart will melt, and he will be filled with grace. But instead of breaking down, the Misfit recoils in horror at the grandmother's touch and fires three rounds into her chest.

O'Connor makes it clear in letters to Betty Hester ("A."), Andrew Lytle, and John Hawkes that she intended the grandmother, in her final moments, to have been led by grace to be personally concerned about the Misfit: "[T]he grandmother is not in the least concerned with God but reaches out to touch the Misfit."[6] "[T]he grandmother recognizes the Misfit as one of her own children and reaches out to touch him. It's the moment of grace for her anyway—."[7] She reaches out because "she has been touched by the Grace that comes through him in his particular suffering."[8]

The Misfit, however, tragically misunderstands the grandmother's gesture. According to O'Connor the Misfit considers her "a silly old woman"; she is a hypocrite, and she reflects "the banalities of the society" in which the story takes place.[9] In killing her, the Misfit believes he is demolishing her most presumptuous belief, the idea that he is any child of hers. After all, he has been told all his life that to enter the kingdom of heaven he would have to become as a little child. To the Misfit, however, being a little child means accepting everything without questioning. All of his life he has been told to act like a little child and accept the authority of parents, employers, officers, and ministers. Up to the moment when she touched his shoulder, he believed that the grandmother was trying to understand him, that she was sympathetic to his dilemma. However, when she calls him one of her "babies" he concludes that she is speaking for the society that had rejected him all along. He feels betrayed; he had opened himself up to her only to hear the same sermon all over again.

Hiram and Bobby Lee come back from the woods, and the Misfit tells them to take the grandmother's body where they "thown the others." Bobby Lee observes cheerfully that the old lady was "a talker, wasn't she?" He's right: it was her loose tongue that brought about all the trouble in the first place. The Misfit replies that she'd have been a "good woman . . . if it had been somebody there to shoot her every minute of her life." O'Connor comments to Hawkes that the Misfit "pronounces his judgment: she would have been a good woman if *he* had been there every moment of her life."[10]

O'Connor's restatement of the line, with the emphasis on *he*, shows that she intended the Misfit to think of himself as a prophet. He believes he could have been the grandmother's sentinel. If he had been around, he would have warned her to give up her banal and hypocritical version of Christianity and seek a deeper involvement with Christ. In this respect the Misfit is following the example of Ezekiel, who urged the Jewish exiles to stop thinking of the Temple as the home of Yahweh and seek Him in their own hearts instead (cf. Ezekiel 24:21). However, the Misfit was not around to sound the trumpet every moment of the grandmother's life; he was in jail. When he did appear, she wouldn't stop talking long enough to hear him.

Bobby Lee considers the whole incident—six murders—"Some fun!" There is no question that Bobby Lee is unregenerate: his idea of pleasure is meanness. The Misfit corrects Bobby; "It's no pleasure in life," he tells him, echoing Ezekiel 33:11:

> As I live, saith the Lord GOD, I have no pleasure in the death of the wicked; but that the wicked turn from his way and live: turn ye, turn ye from your evil ways; for why will ye die, O house of Israel?

The Misfit is not killing the family out of "meanness" or despair, as he had suggested earlier, but fulfilling a grim duty in which there is no pleasure. He is now, in effect, both prophet and Yahweh. The people, such as the grandmother, have failed to respond to the sentinel's warning, so he has himself brought the sword upon the land by killing the grandmother and her family.

The Misfit, however, is delusional to think of himself as God's agent. O'Connor told Hawkes that she meant the grandmother to be the medium of grace:

> More than in the Devil I am interested in the indication of Grace, the moment when you know that Grace has been offered and accepted—such as the moment when the Grandmother realizes the Misfit is one of her own children.[11]

In a letter to Betty Hester, O'Connor claims that grace, properly experienced, changes one's personal qualities:

> The action of grace changes a character. Grace can't be experienced in itself.
>
> An example: when you go to Communion, you receive grace but you experience nothing; or if you do experience something, what you experience is not the grace but an emotion caused by it.[12]

In O'Connor's view, any physical sensations associated with worship are secondary to the real action of grace on one's moral outlook.

O'Connor maintains in her letters that all of her stories "are about the action of grace on a character that is not very willing to support it."[13] All too frequently individuals fail to accept the action of grace: "There is a moment of grace in most of the stories, or a moment where it is offered, and is usually rejected."[14] O'Connor's characters are unwilling to accept the action of grace because they expect the medium of grace to be as pure as grace itself. O'Connor maintains, however, that grace can come by means of an imperfect medium: "Grace, to the Catholic way of thinking, can and does use as its medium the imperfect, purely human, and even hypocritical." In fact, the Catholic writer is distinguished by the ability to understand that grace can act on and by means of ordinary, sinful people.[15]

The Misfit is spoiled as a prophet because he fails to understand that grace is actually at work in the grandmother's banal touch of his shoulder. He assumes that "because of her hypocrisy and humanness and banality" the grandmother cannot "be a medium for Grace."[16] In fact, he can't believe that grace can come through humanity at all. As O'Connor observed to John Hawkes, the Misfit should be able to appeal to Jesus, but Jesus has been presented to him not as a mediator but an existential challenge:

> Haze [Hazel Motes] knows what the choice is and the Misfit knows what the choice is—either throw away everything and follow Him or enjoy yourself by doing some meanness to somebody, and in the end there's no real pleasure in life, not even in meanness.[17]

But the Misfit can't throw away everything and follow Him because he wasn't there when Jesus raised the dead. As much as he would like to believe Jesus did, the Misfit cannot, so he believes he might as well "do meanness."

In letters to T. R. Spivey and John Hawkes, O'Connor states that the inability to see that grace can act through imperfect people is a consequence of what she regards as the "Protestant temper—approaching the spiritual directly instead of through matter."[18] The Catholic position, according to O'Connor, is that "[e]verything has to operate first on the literal level."[19] Any awareness of the spiritual, that is, originates in material objects, such as the sacramental bread and wine or other human beings. The tragedy of the Misfit is that he knows of no means to advance beyond the literal level to the level of the spirit except the immediate intervention of God, as demonstrated by such phenomena as "wise blood."

> Wise blood has to be these people's means of grace—they have no sacraments. The religion of the South is a do-it-yourself religion, something which I as a Catholic find painful and touching and grimly comic. It's full of unconscious pride that lands them in all sorts of ridiculous religious predicaments.[20]

The Catholic Church, in O'Connor's view, could have solved the Misfit's religious predicament by means of the sacraments: "Christ gave us the sacraments in order that we might better keep the two great commandments": love God and love your neighbor.[21] The sacraments help us keep the commandments by serving as the link between matter and spirit. If the Misfit had had access to the sacraments, he would not have had to depend on a conviction he didn't feel or a revelation he hadn't experienced.

In O'Connor's view, the Misfit's skepticism made him a potential prophet. Ezekiel, for example, was skeptical of the importance of the destruction of Jerusalem and the Temple. He insisted that that catastrophe did not mean that Yahweh had abandoned Israel. By letting the Babylonians sack Jerusalem, Yahweh was warning the people all the more urgently to give up their preoccupation with the Temple, which led them to idolatry. Similarly, the Misfit is skeptical of what people like the grandmother considered the evidence of salvation: good family, good manners, respect for one's heritage. To the extent that he can see through such "superficial beliefs," the Misfit has the "prophetic vision" that O'Connor ascribed to the creative writer.

The real tragedy of the Misfit, in O'Connor's view, is that he lives in a community that has stopped believing that matter can be a means of grace. If matter cannot be a means of grace, grace cannot act through ordinary human beings, such as a silly old woman. Consequently the Misfit cannot appreciate the grandmother's "humanness." As the world has become polarized between spirit and matter, or grace and nature, according to O'Connor, human values have become polarized as well. The Misfit can either leave everything and follow Jesus or get what amusement he can from abusing others.

O'Connor believed that the Misfit feels he faces such a stark choice because he despairs of believing on his own. Christ's raising Lazarus becomes an obstacle to the Misfit because he concludes that no one could believe such a story without the aid of grace. As a Catholic, however, O'Connor believed that grace pervades and sustains all creation. In "Novelist and Believer," O'Connor points out that Catholic theology has always maintained that God is the "divine source" of the material world:

> St. Augustine wrote that the things of the world pour forth from God in a double way: intellectually into the minds of the angels and physically into

> the world of things. To the person who believes this—as the western world did until a few centuries ago—this physical, sensible world is good because it proceeds from a divine source.[22]

The word *source* is literal; the "things of the world" flow continuously from God as streams flow from their heads. The creation of the world was not a one-time event; the world is re-created by grace every moment. Grace, then, is what brought the world about and what keeps it going. It follows that God and creation are not separate but connected by grace. The person of Jesus makes that connection for humans. The sacraments, in this view, sum up the action of grace in creation. The sacraments remind us that grace is always at hand, and their availability makes it possible for us to grow in belief. The tragedy of the Misfit, like that of so many of O'Connor's characters, is that he is expecting grace to come to him in glory. Consequently he fails to recognize it when it does appear.

From *Modern Age* 51.3-4 (Summer/Fall 2009): 202-210.

Notes

1. *Flannery O'Connor: Collected Works* (New York: Literary Classics of the United States, 1988), 1148-49. All the quotations from "A Good Man is Hard to Find" are from this volume.
2. Ibid., 1121.
3. Flannery O'Connor, *The Habit of Being*, ed. Sally Fitzgerald (New York: Vintage, 1979), 465.
4. Karl Martin, "Flannery O'Connor's Prophetic Imagination," *Religion and Literature* 26, No. 3 (1994), 34.
5. *Collected Works*, 1131.
6. Ibid., 1124.
7. Ibid., 1121.
8. Ibid., 1125.
9. Ibid., 1121, 1125.
10. Ibid., 1125.
11. Ibid., 1119.

12. *Habit of Being*, 275.
13. *Collected Works*, 1067.
14. Ibid., 1121.
15. Ibid., 1125-26.
16. Ibid., 1125-26.
17. Ibid., 1108.
18. Ibid., 1080.
19. Ibid., 1076.
20. Ibid., 1107.
21. Ibid., 1102-3.
22. Flannery O'Connor, *Mystery and Manners*, ed. Sally and Robert Fitzgerald (New York: Farrar, Straus and Giroux, 1969) 157.

Flannery O'Connor's Misfit and the Mystery of Evil

John Desmond

It is not difficult to label the agent of evil in Flannery O'Connor's signature story, "A Good Man is Hard to Find." An escaped convict, self-named the Misfit, dispassionately orders the murder of a Georgia family—everyone from grandmother to baby—after coming upon them when their car overturns along a dusty country road. The Misfit orders the murders because the Grandmother has, foolishly, recognized and named him, and also to steal the family's car. But as in all of O'Connor's stories, the violent surface action only begins to suggest the depths and complexities of meaning embedded in the story. This is especially true when considering the mystery of evil and its relation to the action of grace.

On one level the story's title refers to the words of a popular song—"A good man is hard to find/ You always get the other kind." But on another level it also suggests Christ's rebuke to Peter when Peter tried to call him good, and Jesus responded that no one should be called good (Mark 10:18)—a mistake the Grandmother makes repeatedly in her encounter with the Misfit. At the same time, it is also true to say that, excepting Satan, no one should be called totally evil, certainly not in any absolute sense. Good and evil, as potentialities and as actualities, are inextricably intertwined in human beings, and this is true for both the Grandmother and the Misfit. It is more accurate to speak of gradations of human good and evil, and of the drama of choice in the face of competing moral options. O'Connor's story explores a range of these options and their consequences, as well as suggesting the mysterious invisible forces beyond personality and circumstance that help to shape human destiny.

A central principle of O'Connor's Catholic theology, expressed by St. Thomas Aquinas and other theologians, is that evil has no being, and that evil always appears as a good to the one who commits it, i.e., as something good for him. Granted this principle, one can see that the Misfit's murderous actions are committed under the delusion that somehow they will reap some good for him, and somehow answer to his need. But stealing the family's battered car, while important, is only the immediate goal of the Misfit; it is not the locus of his inner energy and desire. His conversation with the Grandmother reveals many things about his deeper desires, the most important of which is that the Misfit wants some rationale and justification for his spiritual predicament. He wants an understanding of what he sees as the disproportion between the personal suffering he feels afflicted with and the actions he has committed. As he tells the Grandmother: "I call myself 'The Misfit' . . . because I can't make what all I done wrong fit what all I gone through in punishment."[1] The Misfit feels the mystery of evil in his bones, and he finds it incomprehensible. While there are surely elements of self-pity and self-justification in his statement, his mental suffering, his sense of guilt, and his questioning cannot be ignored or dismissed, because it reflects a spiritual condition that is both fundamentally human and conspicuously modern in temper. Though he commits evil deeds, the Misfit is also a seeker who wants some answers to the mystery of evil he feels both in himself and witnesses in the world. His keen sense of evil suggests implicitly that he also has an appreciation of the good, however distorted or misguided it may be.

The Misfit openly acknowledges his own evil. When the Grandmother tries to type him as a "good" man, i.e. a gentleman, he answers: "Nome, I ain't a good man . . . ," and then adds: "but I ain't the worst in the world neither" (148). He admits that "somewhere along the line" he has "done something wrong" and been sent to prison. Subsequently, he has "forgotten" what he has done wrong, yet he feels the weight of some indefinable original sin. He also acknowledges that the punishment was "no mistake." The punishment is justified, he recognizes, but he still finds it incommensurate with his life. So now his rational solution is to sign for everything he does and get a copy of it. That way, he says, "you'll know what you done and hold up the crime to the punishment and see do they match and in the end you'll have something to prove you ain't been treated right" (151). But of course this does not explain the original sense of sin and injustice he feels. The strict logic of his proposal is impotent before the mystery of evil his life embodies.

The Misfit, then, wants not only to understand the mystery of evil he feels, but also, somehow, to be justified in the face of it. He wants justice as well as knowledge, and also to be liberated from his predicament. The desire itself is good; the Psalms exalt the human longing for a world of justice and constancy (Psalm 96). However, the Misfit seems more interested in personal vindication rather than communal justice. Yet better than anyone else in the story, the Misfit recognizes the ultimate stakes in the drama—personal salvation. His sense of the absolute significance of individual actions is profound. Yet supreme rationalist that he is, the Misfit cannot admit the need of a power beyond logic and human justice that is, one can believe, more than commensurate to the mystery and power of evil. For O'Connor, such a power is divine grace, made available through Christ's death and resurrection. The Misfit acknowledges this, yet refuses to submit his will to God's. "I don't want no hep," he tells the Grandmother. "I'm doing all right by myself" (150).

His refusal casts him into a posture of moral self-sufficiency and isolation, signified in part by his act of naming himself the Misfit. In this act of naming he resembles another of O'Connor's proud self-namers, Hulga Hopewell in "Good Country People," whose chosen ugly name "Hulga" serves as her defense against admitting her ordinary human frailty and need, as well as being a badge of her pride. Naming, as Walker Percy has pointed out, is being.[2] So also, false naming reveals non-being, a refusal to speak truly of who or what one is. The Misfit says that his name signifies his awareness of the disproportion between his actions and their punishment (151). On the one hand this disproportion confounds him. But on the other hand he uses it to claim his difference from the general run of society. The Misfit's father, he explains, said he was a "different breed of dog" and added:

"it's some that can live their whole life without asking about it and it's some has to know why it is, and this boy is one of the latters. He's going to be into everything!" (148). The Misfit certainly claims his difference from people like the Grandmother and her family, who seem to accommodate themselves to the mystery of evil by ignoring it or glossing it over with platitudes. If so, then on this level the Misfit can be seen as O'Connor's scourge, a prophetic figure who raises the question of evil and redemption by Christ to a largely unbelieving audience in a stark and violent fashion. Seen in this way, O'Connor's challenge to her audience gives the Grandmother's bland assessment of the Misfit—that he is "not common"—an ironic ring of truth. He appears as a man suffering deep anguish over his predicament of doubt, as one oppressed by a sense of entrapment in a world of unrelieved guilt, yet also as one willing to acknowledge the profound mystery of his predicament.

The Misfit's desire for a rational system of human justice in which actions and consequences can be meaningfully "balanced out" is good, as I have said, but it is inadequate to explain the mysterious human condition. It cannot comprehend or meliorate the mystery of evil. The Misfit is caught between absurdity and faith. He rejects belief in Christ yet he recognizes that a world in which actions and consequences cannot be made sense of leads ultimately to a world in which logical distinctions between good and evil collapse. As he says, it becomes a world in which there is "no pleasure but meanness." Still, the fact that he perceives his dilemma reveals a man keenly attuned to the mystery of good and evil; in fact, one can say, a man of deeply religious sensibility like that O'Connor saw in Albert Camus.[3]

The stumbling block to faith for the Misfit, as he tells the Grandmother, is the mystery of Jesus's resurrection from the dead:

> "Jesus was the only One that ever raised the dead . . . and He shouldn't have done it. He thown everything off balance. If He did what He said, then it's nothing for you to do but thow everything away and follow Him, and if

> He didn't, then it's nothing for you to do but enjoy the few minutes you got left the best way you can—by killing somebody or burning down his house or doing some other meanness to him. No pleasure but meanness. . . ." (152)

The Misfit is well aware of the demands of faith, just as he is aware that good actions in and of themselves are insufficient for salvation. It is important to note that the Misfit first states emphatically that Jesus *did* raise the dead, implying that he believes Jesus's claim to be the savior. Yet he argues that Jesus should not have done it. Why? Denial of the resurrection would make life much simpler for the Misfit. He has heard the Gospel message, and it gnaws at his mind. Moreover, the Misfit resents Jesus's resurrection, because it upsets the human code of justice he wishes to base his life upon. Jesus's raising of the dead, with all that it demands, and all that it implies about the supernatural power of grace, knocks the Misfit's rational system of moral coherence down like a house of cards. O'Connor reports that he ends his speech on the resurrection with "almost a snarl." The Misfit is angry, angry at the inexplicable mystery of evil in which he finds himself enmeshed. Still, the depth of his anguish must be given value. At least he has a clear sense of the dimensions of the problem.

After his initial statement that Jesus is the only one who raised the dead, the Misfit is tempted to disbelief when the dazed Grandmother says: "Maybe he didn't raise the dead . . . " (154). In his answer to this tempting remark, O'Connor likens him to the apostle Thomas when he encountered the resurrected Christ: "I wasn't there so I can't say he didn't," the Misfit says. "I wish I had of been there . . . It ain't right I wasn't there because if I had of been there I would of known. Listen, lady . . . if I had of been there I would of known and I wouldn't be like I am now" (152). Thus the Misfit lives as neither believer nor unbeliever in the grey world of uncertainty, of desire for truth, and of longing for some transcendent meaning. Such is O'Connor's portrait of the modern agnostic-seeker. But the Misfit cannot accept this cloud of unknowing. In his mind, the name "Misfit" is a badge of distinction, a proud assertion of his uniqueness and superiority. Thus when the Grandmother reaches out and touches him and declares that he is one of her own children, he reacts instantly by shooting her three times in the chest.

* * *

One way to understand the Misfit's brutal reaction, and indeed his whole paradoxical identity, is through the lens of a writer who deeply interested Flannery O'Connor—the French philosopher Simone Weil. Although she did not begin to read Weil's writings until 1955, O'Connor acknowledged having read "a good bit" about Weil as early as 1952.[4] In her discussion of evil in *Gravity and Grace*, Weil says that a "hurtful act is the transference to others of the degradation we bear in ourselves. That is why we are inclined to commit such acts as a way of deliverance" (65). Shooting the Grandmother can be seen, in part, as the Misfit's spontaneous attempt to transfer his own felt degradation to another as a means of liberation. As he said earlier: "No pleasure but meanness." But as Weil also remarks: "When there is a transference of evil, the evil is not diminished but increased in him from whom it proceeds. This is a phenomenon of multiplication" (65). The Misfit's killings do not liberate him from his felt degradation. Rather, they intensify his pain, a fact O'Connor points to when the Misfit says at the end: "It's no real pleasure in life" (153).

But if the Misfit's predicament dramatizes the mystery of evil, it is not the whole story for O'Connor. There are still the actions of the Grandmother to consider, actions which allowed O'Connor to explore the mystery of evil *and* good. Again, Simone Weil's observations are helpful. She said: "Evil is to love, what mystery is to the intelligence. As mystery compels the virtue of faith to be supernatural, so does evil the virtue of charity" (*Gravity and Grace* 68). The Grandmother's faith, such as it is, is surely tested in her encounter with the criminals.

The label "good" she tries to pin on the Misfit is, of course, a shallow-minded social concept that reduces the virtue of goodness to distinctions of class, breeding and manners. The Grandmother considers herself a good Christian woman, i.e., a lady of fine manners and disposition, and a believer in Jesus to boot. But the Misfit rejects her attempts to flatter him on the basis of class and manners. This so-called gentleman will not allow such trivializing of the good; in answer to it he murders women and children in cold blood.

As the drama of their encounter unfolds, the Grandmother's sentimental self-image is shattered. Her nostalgia for a look at the old plantation is shown to be rooted in false memory and deceit: the house she begged to visit is in Tennessee, not Georgia, and she has had to lie about a "secret panel" to maneuver her son Bailey into searching for the house. Her lying and selfishness lead directly to the accident and the subsequent murder of her family. Her self-image as a "good" woman is stripped from her.

But beyond this self-discovery, the Grandmother's encounter with the Misfit tests her religious beliefs, and in so doing, unfolds the mystery of good and evil. As Simone Weil also observed, evil exposes the true good. In this case, the Misfit's evil and the Grandmother's suffering mysteriously trigger in her a gesture of charity. The Misfit not only rejects the Grandmother's facile attempts to make him a good gentleman; he also rejects her appeal to him to pray for Jesus's help. His cold refusals, sounded against the background of the murders of the family in the woods, reduce the Grandmother to confusion and doubt. "Maybe He [Jesus] didn't raise the dead," she mumbles as she slumps in the ditch. But when the Misfit starts to rail angrily because he was not there to see the resurrection, the Grandmother summons her wits to see him in a new, and truer, light—the light of charity. O'Connor writes:

> His voice seemed about to crack and the grandmother's head cleared for an instant. She saw the man's face twisted close to her own as if he were going to cry and she murmured, "Why you're one of my own babies. You're one

of my own children!" She reached out and touched him on the shoulder. The Misfit sprang back as if a snake had bitten him and shot her three times through the chest. (152)

* * *

This climactic scene, full of ambiguity, has occasioned a wealth of critical comment. O'Connor herself argued that the grandmother's final words and actions represent the mysterious action of grace.[5] Some readers have viewed it more skeptically, even arguing that the grandmother's gesture may be a final desperate attempt to save her own life. Other critics have argued a middle ground, granting O'Connor's right to her theological view, while judging the scene as satisfactory or not on the basis of strictly literary criteria. My focus here is on what this climactic scene suggests about the mysterious interpenetration of good and evil.

What initially strikes the reader about the scene is the enormous gap or lacuna between the grandmother's statement of doubt—"Maybe He didn't raise the dead . . . "—and her reaching out fatally to touch the Misfit and embrace him as "one of my babies . . . ," one of "my own children." O'Connor explains nothing of what happens in the grandmother's mind and heart to bring her to this touch of kinship with the criminal, except to say that "her head cleared for an instant." The gap is mysterious, perhaps supernatural, yet also exactly right in the human sense. Such acts of *metanoia*, while inexplicable, are totally within the range of human behavior. What is significant about her calling him "one of my babies . . . ," one of "my own children," and "touching him" is that her actions threaten to undermine his self-designation of himself as the Misfit, the name he chose to signify his difference from ordinary humanity. The Misfit rejects the communal world, just as his sense of "justice" is individualistic rather than communal. Significantly, he remarked earlier in that story that "children make me nervous." The Grandmother's claim of kinship rejects his solitary identity, and instead places him within the community as a child of man, like any other. So also, her touching him threatens his proud, isolated self-created role as the Misfit, a threat he cannot tolerate. After all, if he is not the Misfit, what is he? An ordinary frail, suffering creature. So what we view from the grandmother's perspective as a good act—her recognition of her own bond with an evil man, her complicity, yet also her compassion for his suffering—is viewed by the Misfit as evil: he springs back from her touch "as if a snake had bitten him. . . ."

Why does the Misfit regard the touch as evil, and then answer it with evil? We recall Simone Weil's maxim: "Evil is to love, what mystery is to the intelligence." The grandmother's touch brings the Misfit into direct contact with the good of charity. The touch of charity measures the gap between him and the good. He cannot abide such threatening contact because it would mean opening himself to an admission of failure, and more importantly, to the possibility of good within the human community. Instead, he chooses the "hell" of isolation and despair. The truth of compassion, and being named a child of the human community, is for the Misfit an "evil" he must escape. Once again, Weil's comments are insightful:

> The sin against the Spirit consists of knowing a thing to be good, and hating it because it is good. We experience the equivalent of it in the form of resistance every time we set our faces in the direction of good. For every contact with good leads to a knowledge of the distance between good and evil and the commencement of a painful effort of assimilation. It is something which hurts and we are afraid. This fear is perhaps the sign of the reality of the contact. The corresponding sin cannot come about unless a lack of hope makes the consciousness of the distance intolerable and changes the pain into hatred. (*Gravity and Grace* 67)

The Misfit's pain at the Grandmother's touch is instantly transformed into a hatred of the gratuitous act of charity, which he then answers with a brutal execution. What the Misfit fears is the mystery of love, the demands of love which the grandmother mysteriously responded to when faced with the criminal's suffering, and her own impending death. In her case, evil issued finally in good, or as Weil expressed it, evil exposed the good. But if the encounter with evil exposed the good in the grandmother, the final predicament of the Misfit is more complicated, more mysterious.

As I noted earlier, the Misfit acts under the delusion that his actions are somehow good, i.e., good for him. Since he cannot make sense of his spiritual condition, he now tries to reduce ethical mystery to a perverse pleasure-pain principle. Initially he told the Grandmother: "No pleasure but meanness." Yet his encounter with her touch has exposed his need, his human vulnerability. In his crucial final remark, he shifts from the earlier "No pleasure but meanness" to "It's no real pleasure in life." He has again failed to liberate himself from his predicament through violence, failed to "balance out" his deeds and find the meaning of his life. He himself is his own deepest mystery, a profoundly human condition which he can neither fathom nor abide. His last statement, that there is no "real pleasure" in life, shows that what he thought might bring pleasure, i.e., acts of meanness, has also proven to be bankrupt, a hollow illusion.

In the end, the Misfit's spiritual and mental suffering continues and intensifies, for with the failure of his code, his awareness of the gap between good and evil has widened. His violence is projected back onto himself as self-hatred. Perhaps at some future time his knowledge of this interior chasm will bring about the collapse of his self-begotten identity as a "Misfit," and an acceptance of his broken humanity. O'Connor suggested the possibility that he might ultimately be brought to such a conversion. She called the Misfit a "prophet gone wrong," and referred to the grandmother's touching him as "like the mustard-seed," which "will grow to be a great crow-filled tree in the Misfit's heart, and will be enough of a pain to him there to turn him into the prophet he was meant to become" (*Mystery and Manners* 110, 112-13). The Grandmother's touch may bring him to the point where the mystery of good and evil is finally subsumed in the mystery of love. For the Misfit, evil may, in the end, through the grace of charity, bring about his ultimate good.[6]

Notes

1. Flannery O'Connor, "A Good Man Is Hard to Find," *Collected Works*, 151.
2. Walker Percy, "Naming and Being," *Signposts in a Strange Land*, 130-39.
3. Sally and Robert Fitzgerald, eds., *Mystery and Manners*, 160.
4. Flannery O'Connor, *The Habit of Being*, 40.
5. Simone Weil, *Gravity and Grace*, 65.
6. *Mystery and Manners*, 109-113.

Works Cited

O'Connor, Flannery. "A Good Man Is Hard to Find." *Collected Works*. New York: Library of America, 1988.

____________. *The Habit of Being*. Ed. Sally Fitzgerald. New York: Farrar, Straus and Giroux, 1979.

____________. *Mystery and Manners: Occasional Prose*. Ed. Sally and Robert Fitzgerald. New York: Farrar, Straus and Giroux, 1969.

Percy, Walker. "Naming and Being." *Signposts in a Strange Land*. Ed. Patrick Samway, SJ. New York: Farrar, Straus and Giroux, 1991. 130-39.

Weil, Simone. *Gravity and Grace*. London: Routledge & Kegan Paul, 1963.

"Wingless Chickens": "Good Country People" and the Seduction of Nihilism

Henry T. Edmondson III

In a 20 July 1955 letter to Betty Hester ("A"), Flannery O'Connor once recalled news from the poultry industry involving the experimental breeding of chickens without wings so as to increase the yield of select chicken meat. She then drew a droll but arresting analogy, noting, "[T]he moral sense has been bred out of certain sections of the population, like the wings have been bred off certain chickens to produce more white meat on them. This is a generation of wingless chickens, which I suppose is what Nietzsche meant when he said God was dead" (*HB* 90)[1]. O'Connor's opposition to the philosophy of nihilism explains, in part, the dark tone of many of her stories. "With such a current to write against, the result almost has to be negative," she told Betty Hester on 29 Aug. 1955 (*HB* 97). As O'Connor saw it, nihilism had infected the very act of writing fiction itself, but her aim was to turn fiction against nihilism. She noted in a 17 Mar. 1956 letter to Shirley Abbot, "It is popular to believe that in order to see clearly one must believe nothing," but she argued, "For the fiction writer, to believe nothing is to see nothing. . . . [T]he message I find in the life I see is a moral message" (*HB* 147). Of all modern philosophies, nihilism may be the one it is most urgent to understand. Nihilism builds upon the Enlightenment hope in the infinite progress of the human race and teaches that if we are to evolve into an advanced race, traditional values and sentiments must be swept away.

In her short story "Good Country People," O'Connor gives the fable of the farmer's daughter an acutely philosophical and sinister turn. In doing so, she offers her most concise response to the threat of nihilism, making two distinct and important points about the nature of that philosophy. She suggests, as did her literary compatriot Walker Percy, that its roots are to be found in the ground made fertile by the French philosopher René Descartes; and she reiterates her warning in *Wise Blood*, but this time more emphatically, that nihilism is malevolently seductive and is likely to consume those naive enough to think they can embrace and contain it.[2]

O'Connor seemed to realize that, upon completing "Good Country People," she had written something especially important, a story unique for its significance even among her other stories. She wrote on 26 Feb. 1955 to her publisher Robert Giroux, "I have just written a story called 'Good Country People' that [my friends] Allen and Caroline both say is the best thing I have written" (*HB* 75). She allowed herself a bit of bragging in writing on 1 Apr. 1955 to her intimates, the Fitzgeralds, "I trust Giroux will be sending you a copy of the book soon. I wrote a very hot story at the last minute called 'Good Country People'" (*HB* 76). Although she occasionally suffered criticism from fellow Christians who were scandalized by her subject matter and style, she predicted that those offended by this story might be nonbelievers. With this prediction, O'Connor indicates the theologically apologetic nature of the story. She suggests to Alice Morris on 10 June 1955, "If I could be of any assistance in providing an answer to any complaints you might get about 'Good Country People,' I'll be glad to; but perhaps the complaints this time will be from pious atheists and not from irate Catholics" (*HB* 86). Whereas O'Connor usually wrote at a snail's pace, she reported that she wrote "Good Country People" very quickly—"in about four days"—suggesting she enjoyed an uncommon inspiration in the task: "[I] just sat down and wrote it," she told Betty Hester on 1 June 1956 (*HB* 160). Even at that quick pace, she was barely able to include it in her first collection of short stories. The publisher, though, was impressed enough to undertake the difficulty of incorporating it at the last minute.

The protagonist of this story is a young woman named Hulga, whose artificial leg is the consequence of a hunting accident when she was ten. Her name originally had been "Joy," but she changed it to Hulga, a change that invokes the idea of the Nietzschean imperative to create in the crucible of suffering. Ever present in Mrs. Hopewell's kitchen is her hired help, Mrs. Freeman. Mrs. Hopewell and Mrs. Freeman are, in O'Connor's phrase, "good country people" (*CW* 264). Mrs. Hopewell especially admires such people, and it is on the basis of this appreciation that she will admit into her home a devious Bible salesman. Hulga holds "good country people" in contempt; more accurately, she holds such people in disdain until she needs them, and she will need them when the Bible salesman humiliates and subjugates her.

Manley Pointer

Pointer's uncanny knack for identifying himself with little known and intimate family secrets implies that he possesses an unearthly nature and, by this and other characterizations, O'Connor suggests that Manley Pointer is something more than human. Indeed, whereas Hulga is a self-fashioned nihilist, Pointer represents the essence of nihilism itself, a concentrated and rarefied sample of the philosophy made incarnate. It is as if Hulga's persistent flirtation with nihilism, by word and behavior, has conjured up the spirit of nihilism itself and it has come to claim its own. This situation implies a parallel with Dr. Faustus and Mephistopheles, who comes at last to claim what is rightfully his, namely Faust's soul. In Hulga's case, her commitment to nihilism is not so absolute as to give Pointer such an unqualified claim, though, as the story demonstrates, she has flirted with a force she does not understand and which is competent to violate her soul in a most obscene manner, thus exposing its emptiness.

After Hulga agrees to a meeting with Manley, as she lies in bed half the night thinking about it, "she had begun to see profound implications in it" as she imagined conversations between the two of them that could reach "below to depths that no Bible salesman would be aware of" (*CW* 275). Hulga begins to anticipate their tryst as a kind of philosophical project in which she imagines that she will seduce and later master him by condescending mercifully to help her hapless victim deal with his remorse. In so doing, she will replace his backwoods religiosity with an enlightened view of existence. She knows that "[t]rue genius can get an idea across even to an inferior mind" (276). She will take "his remorse in hand" and "change it into a deeper understanding of life" (276). What Hulga does not know is that it is she who will be seduced by the shrewd Pointer.

The Loss of Hulga's Presumption

The remainder of the story is a study in manipulation, seduction, and subjugation, with Pointer as the teacher. Hulga will prove vulnerable because of the empty and wounded state of her psyche. In commentary on "Good Country People," O'Connor herself observes that Hulga "is spiritually as well as physically crippled" as there is "a wooden part of her soul that corresponds to her wooden leg" (*MM* 99). On the morning following her initial meeting with Pointer, Hulga is unsettled, finding herself alone at their designated meeting place on the highway—"She had the furious feeling that she had been tricked" (*CW* 277). Pointer suddenly stands up from behind the bush where he had been hiding and says, "I knew you'd come!" The narrator adds, "The girl wondered acidly how he had known this." He has the valise he uses to carry his Bibles, but it "did not seem to be heavy today; he even swung it." Pointer upsets her equilibrium again when "he asks softly, 'Where does your wooden leg join on?'" to which "she turn[s] an ugly red" (277). He surprises her yet again with a heavy kiss, and as they walk across the pasture, she works to maintain her equanimity.

When Pointer asks if they might sit down somewhere, Hulga suggests the barn. In response to his doubtful look that she could ascend to the loft, she "gave him a contemptuous look, and putting both hands on the ladder, . . . pulled herself expertly through the opening" (*CW* 279). Pointer feigns admiration, though his attitude is of mockery more than esteem. Once in the hayloft, Hulga lies back, and through the opening of the barn she can see outdoors: she turns her head and gazes at the “two pink-speckled hillsides” that “lay back against a dark ridge of woods. The sky was cloudless and cold blue” (279).

Manley Pointer continues setting the pace of their encounter by insisting that Hulga express her love for him. The narrator ironically interjects that Hulga “was always careful how she committed herself” (*CW* 280), but Hulga has no idea how vulnerable she has become. Hulga responds with adolescent self-assurance, employing the jargon of the nihilist: “‘In a sense,’ she began, ‘if you use the word [love] loosely, you might say that. But it’s not a word I use. I don’t have illusions. I’m one of those people who see *through* to nothing’” (280). “‘We are all damned,’ she teaches Pointer, ‘but some of us have taken off our blindfolds and see that there’s nothing to see. It’s a kind of salvation.’” Responding to more insistence from Pointer, Hulga casually offers that she “loves” him, “in a sense,” treating him, though, with condescension and reminding him, “I have a number of degrees” (280).

Pointer has been playing along, letting Hulga enjoy her false confidence, but at this point things take an unexpected turn, a turn in a direction in which her control slips away, slowly at first, and then all at once. In response to Hulga’s emotionless admission of love, Pointer demands, “Prove it” (*CW* 280). Hulga, thinking she understands, smiles and looks “dreamily out on the *shifty* landscape” (280, emphasis added). O’Connor’s use of the unusual adjective “shifty” for a line of trees and sky is undoubtedly a reference both to Pointer’s character as well as to the unstable philosophical grounding on which Hulga has based her life and which now Pointer is about to upset. Hulga concludes that she “had seduced him without even making up her mind to try.” He shocks her, though, when, as a proof of her “love” he whispers a request: “Show me where your wooden leg joins on.” Hulga is unnerved. She utters “a sharp little cry and her face instantly drained of color,” as the increasingly sinister Pointer expertly exposes the locus of her vulnerability (280).

The leg, in a perverse sort of way, is the source of Hulga’s hubristic self-confidence as well as a commentary on the wounded state of her soul. The narrator explains "she was as sensitive about the artificial leg as a peacock about his tail. No one ever touched it but her. She took care of it as someone else would his soul, in private and almost with her own eyes turned away" (*CW* 281). Still, Hulga retains an illusion of self-control, but by this time, she has fallen completely under Manley's domination. In so doing, a Ph.D. in philosophy quickly and completely falls under the control of a barely literate and uncultured itinerant salesman. As Pointer practices taking off and re-attaching the leg with a child's delight, the seduction continues, and Hulga has by now wholly lost her intellectual and psychological bearings. She is "thinking that she would run away with him and that every night he would take the leg off and every morning put it back on again" (281). But when she asks him to replace it, he murmurs, "Not yet. . . . Leave it off for a while. You got me instead" (282). Hulga gives a "little cry of alarm but he pushed her down and began to kiss her again. Without the leg she felt entirely dependent on him. Her brain seemed to have stopped thinking altogether and to be about some other function that it was not very good at." Hulga is now in danger not only of losing her leg to Pointer, but also of symbolically losing her soul to the dangerous philosophy with which she has so perilously toyed. As she often does, O'Connor now uses a description of the human eye, in this instance to indicate the nature of Hulga's captivity: "Every now and then the boy, his eyes like two steel spikes, would glance behind him where the leg stood" (282).

Pointer refuses another plea from Hulga to restore her leg and instead opens his suitcase to reveal a "flask of whiskey, a pack of cards" with "obscene" pictures, "and a small blue box with printing on it." It reads "THIS PRODUCT TO BE USED ONLY FOR THE PREVENTION OF DISEASE." Pointer "laid these out in front of her one at a time in an evenly-spaced row, like one presenting offerings at the shrine of a goddess. He put the blue box in her hand" (*CW* 282). Hulga sits as if "mesmerized." "'Aren't you,' she murmured, 'aren't you just good country people?'" (*CW* 282). This pathetic query indicates just how hypocritical has been Hulga's contempt for common, everyday life. It only takes the distress of her predicament to expose her need for that which formerly only disgusted her. This crisis further suggests that she is no more superior to ordinary folk than her mother and Mrs. Freeman, who accept the limitations of their mortality and can, in contrast to Hulga, live with a salutary everyday hope, as her mother's name implies, and enjoy the dignity of being a "free man," even though Hulga has mocked them as pitiful prisoners to their parochial attitudes and preferences. Heretofore, Hulga has only shown disdain for "good country people," but now she appeals to the reliability inherent in those who can enjoy the predictability and safety of ordinary life. So far from being Nietzsche's *Übermensch*, she is reduced to the status of a helpless little girl.

Like a fly caught in the web of a spider but not yet devoured, Hulga suddenly understands her conquest. "'Give me my leg!' she screamed and tried to lunge for it but he pushed her down easily" (*CW* 282). Pointer mocks her, "You just a while ago said you didn't believe in nothing. I thought you was some girl!" (283). Hulga vainly tries to save herself by appealing to a religion in which she does not believe: "'You're a fine Christian!' she hissed. 'You're a Christian! You're just like them all—say one thing and do another'" (283). Pointer disarms her with his angry reply: "'I hope you don't think . . . that I believe in that crap! I may sell Bibles but I know which end is up and I wasn't born yesterday and I know where I'm going!'" (283). She grows more desperate: "'Give me my leg!' she screeched." But she watches in horror as "[h]e jumped up so quickly that she barely saw him sweep the cards and the blue box back into the . . . valise." Helplessly, she "saw him grab the leg and then she saw it for an instant slanted forlornly across the inside of the suitcase with a Bible at either side of its opposite ends. He slammed the lid shut and snatched up the valise and swung it down the hole and then stepped through himself." Before his head disappears down the ladder, he turns back to Hulga and says, "You ain't so smart. I been believing in nothing ever since I was born!" (283).

Hulga's Seduction

In *Wise Blood*, O'Connor uses Sabbath Hawks to illustrate the seductive nature of the nihilism that Hazel Motes pursues; "Good Country People" reintroduces her argument. Two Old Testament proverbs are helpful in following her reasoning. The first warns, "Can a man hide fire in his bosom, and his garments not burn?" (Prov. 6:27). In typically Semitic style the second proverb affirms the meaning of its predecessor: "Or can he walk upon hot coals, and his feet not be burnt?" (Prov. 6:28). He who would pursue the modern spirit of nihilism will most likely find that what he has pursued will turn back to devour him. This calamity occurs more easily because of the naïveté by which one presumes to be capable of playing with such fire.

Compared with Manley Pointer, Hulga is a dilettante in nihilism, an amateur in "nothingness." She knows and believes just enough about nihilism to get herself in serious trouble. Pointer, by contrast, is an expert. But for O'Connor he is more than an expert: he represents something extra human, the spirit of nihilism himself, a force that no man or woman can master, a power only safely dealt with by its avoidance. Indicative of Hulga's comparatively childish philosophical dabbling is Pointer's contemptuous use of her name, the proud symbol of her own nihilistic creativity. O'Connor explains that he speaks "the name as if he didn't think much of it" (*CW* 283). Thus, her nihilism is a playful diversion compared with Pointer's lethal implementation of the same.

Whereas O'Connor was disturbed over nihilism, the Russian novelist Fyodor Dostoyevsky agonized over it in his novels. In *The Brothers Karamazov* he, like O'Connor, exposes nihilism's seductive character. Walker Percy once admitted that Dostoyevsky "is nearly always my model" and added, "I think maybe the greatest novel of all time is *The Brothers Karamazov*, which, written in the latter part of the nineteenth century, almost prophesies and prefigures everything—all the bloody mess and issues of the 20th century" (Percy 224).

One of the most dramatic episodes in Dostoyevsky's great work occurs when the Devil, in the guise of a "Russian gentleman" (741), visits the distraught Ivan Fyodorovich Karamazov. The visit is possibly illusory, induced by Ivan's weakened mental state, but it reveals the truth of the philosophic enterprise in which he has been engaged. Ivan has just realized that due to his nihilistic misadventures, he may have been inadvertently complicit in his own father's murder, and his atheism leaves him groundless in this moral crisis. As the satanic visitor wittily but cruelly teases him as a cat would its prey, Ivan grows aware that by embracing nihilism he has, in a sense, "waded in over his head," not understanding the implications of his intellectual pursuit. The Devil first tells the alarmed young intellectual that he, the Devil, really does exist, even though Ivan, in keeping with his faddish ideas, resists such an outmoded notion. The Devil explains that since he and his companions have had no objective other than "to negate," they have not perceived where their destructiveness will lead (741). The Devil startles Ivan with his frightening vision:

> Oh, I love the dreams of my young and ardent friends a-tremble with the thirst for life! Those new men. . . . they think they can destroy everything. . . . In my view it is not necessary to destroy anything, all that need be destroyed in mankind is the idea of God, that is what one must proceed from! . . . Once mankind, each and individually, has repudiated God. . . . the whole of the former morality, will collapse, and all will begin anew. . . . Man will exalt himself with a spirit of divine, titanic pride, and the man-god will appear. (749)

This is all too much for the young intellectual who sat "with his hands pressed to his ears and looked at the floor, but began to tremble in all his body" (Dostoyevsky 741). He becomes even more agitated as the Devil explains that this episode of destruction and re-creation may take a thousand years. In the meantime man will become a law unto himself—he will effectively have to manage a lawless society after the death of God until a new era emerges. As Ivan sees exactly what it is that he has undertaken, he physically strikes out at his sinister visitor until his nightmare is cut short by the arrival of his brother Alyosha (749-50).

An important element in the process of seduction is the elimination of the sense of modesty and shame. O'Connor explains of Hulga, "As a child she had sometimes been subject to feelings of shame but education had removed the last traces of that as a good surgeon scrapes for cancer" (*CW* 281). In George Bernard Shaw's play *Man and Superman*, the revolutionary nihilist John Tanner explains how annoyingly pernicious the cultural sense of shame has become, and passionately argues that it must be destroyed. He employs an *argumentum ad absurdum* to trivialize the human experience of shame and thereby discredit its importance:

> We live in an atmosphere of shame. We are shamed of everything that is real about us; ashamed of ourselves, of our relatives, of our incomes, of our accents, of our opinions, of our experience, just as we are ashamed of our naked skins. Good Lord.. . . we are ashamed to walk, ashamed to ride in an omnibus, ashamed to hire a hansom instead of keeping a carriage, ashamed of keeping one horse instead of two and a groom-gardener instead of a coachman and footman. (52)

Later in this play the Devil appears, as he does in *The Brothers Karamazov*. Here the Devil proclaims, "Man measures his strength by his destructiveness" (Shaw 143). In the Appendix to Shaw's book, we find John Tanner's "Maxims for Revolutionaries" in which he explains, "Self-sacrifice enables us to sacrifice other people without blushing" (265).

Through his protagonist Zarathustra, Nietzsche himself counseled against that same moral quality that involves "blushing":

> To him who has knowledge, man himself is "the animal with red cheeks." How did this come about? Is it not because man has had to be ashamed too often? O my friends! Thus speaks he who has knowledge: shame, shame,

> shame—that is the history of man. And that is why he who is noble bids himself not to shame. (200)

St. Thomas Aquinas, an important source of O'Connor's intellectual formation, teaches that both the phenomenon of shame and the virtue of modesty are integral to upright moral behavior, giving credence to the insight of both O'Connor and Shaw that these qualities are obstacles to the Nietzschean call to destructive sexual impropriety. Closely associated with virtuous behavior, shame is a passion that causes one to recoil against what is disgraceful. It fortifies an individual in resisting improper, immodest choices. Shame can be weakened if not exterminated: if one were to immerse himself or herself repeatedly in wrongful behavior, shame would lose its force. Shame employs the emotion of fear, specifically "the fear of something base, namely of that which is disgraceful" (Aquinas III, 1770). It is the "fear of doing a disgraceful deed or of a disgraceful deed" (Aquinas II-II, qu. 144, art. 1-2). Hulga, having lost her sense of shame at the university, is all the more vulnerable to Manley Pointer, whose name is redolent of the sexual methods he so expertly uses.

Aquinas also teaches that a habit of modesty is a virtue that supports moderate behavior. It has to do with both an inner attitude and the outward behavior that flows from that internal disposition. Modesty restrains a person from capitulating to impulsive, excessive behavior and is reflected in one's action, speech, and attire (Aquinas II-II, qu. 160, art. 1-2). Modesty involves humility that provides further help in avoiding arrogance and immodesty. As the scholastic philosopher notes, modesty is related to the Greek *metrioteis*, the word etymologically related to terms of measurement. Modesty thus denotes a "measured" attitude and behavior, an idea repulsive to Nietzsche, who associated such restraint with weakness and lack of vision; indeed, the whole of Nietzsche's system embodies the pride that St. Thomas emphatically condemns (Aquinas II-II, qu. 160, art. 1, 2; qu. 161, art. 4; qu. 162). Without modesty, Hulga is the more easily victimized by unrestrained sexual indulgence. O'Connor owned a copy of C. S. Lewis's *The Problem of Pain* in which he notes that "... even Pagan society has usually recognized 'shamelessness' as the nadir of the soul" (57). For that reason, Lewis maintains, "In trying to extirpate shame we have broken down one of the ramparts of the human spirit, madly exulting in the work as the Trojans exulted when they broke their walls and pulled the Horse into Troy" (57). In her personal copy of Eric Voegelin's *The World of the Polis*, O'Connor marked the author's discussion of Aristotle's classic work of moral philosophy, the Nicomachean Ethics. In that passage, Voegelin explains that for the ancient Greeks, *aidos*, alternately translated as shame or modesty, is "the condition of a good society" (157-58).

O'Connor's Concern with Cartesianism

Sometimes, Mrs. Hopewell finds Hulga's behavior inscrutable. The handicapped girl once stood up in the middle of a meal with "her mouth half full" and exclaimed:

> "Woman! Do you ever look inside? Do you ever look inside and see what you are *not*? God!" she had cried sinking down again and staring at her plate, "Malebranche was right: we are not our own light. We are not our own light!" (*CW* 268)

The reference to Malebranche, the seventeenth-century Cartesian philosopher and theologian, may appear to be no more than a rhetorical flourish, but O'Connor's choice of philosophers is strategic. It reveals her opinion that the troubles of the modern world find their origin in the philosophical revolution introduced by the mathematician and philosopher René Descartes. Although Descartes was not as hostile to tradition as later philosophers of the Enlightenment would be, for O'Connor, his method of doubting and ascertaining "truth," the Cartesian method, is the spring from which nihilism eventually flowed centuries later. She shared this opinion with the novelist Walker Percy, who attributed to Descartes "many of the troubles of the modern world" (160).[3] O'Connor's college philosophy textbook, *The Making of the Modern Mind: A Study of the Intellectual Background of the Present Age* by John Herman Randall, Jr., explains that the Cartesian revolution introduced a world view conspicuous for the absence of religion's mystery and notable for its reduction of not just science but moral philosophy to mechanics. Descartes was the "great formulator of the new world view," and beginning with his *Discourse on Method* (1637), he sought to take the enthusiasm for science and mathematics and apply its methodology to all experience (Randall 224). He hoped to unlock not only the conundrums of mathematics but also the mysteries of human existence by applying quantitative measurement and analysis to life itself. As Descartes explains,

> I took especially great pleasure in mathematics because of the certainty and the evidence of its arguments. But I did not yet notice its true usefulness and, thinking that it seemed useful only to the mechanical arts, I was astonished that, because its foundations were so solid and firm, no one had built anything more noble upon them. (4)

And so Descartes decided that "I could not do better than to try once and for all to get all the beliefs I had accepted from birth out of my mind, so that once I have reconciled them with reason I might again set up either other, better ones or even the same ones" (7). Accordingly, he adopted the attitude that he would only accept that which could be held with absolute certainty: "I took to be virtually false everything that was merely probable" (5).

As Randall explains, since Descartes conceived of the world entirely in material terms, amenable to scientific investigation, the entire universe, with all its mystery, was nothing more than a giant physics problem resolvable by the disciplined use of the scientific method (Randall 224, 220):

> To Descartes . . . space or extension became the fundamental reality in the world, motion the source of all change, and mathematics the only relation between its parts. . . . He had made of nature a machine and nothing but a machine; purposes and spiritual significance had alike been banished. . . . Intoxicated by his vision and his success, he boasted, "Give me extension and motion, and I will construct the universe." (Randall 241-42)

Unfortunately, as Randall observes, "The Cartesian world had exempted two things from its all-embracing mechanical sweep, God the creator, and the soul of man" (244). As O'Connor would have argued to Descartes, both the concept of God and the concept of man's soul will always remain in the shadow of mystery; this means that they will always be shaded by doubt. For Descartes to assume the rigid position that, "I reject as absolutely false everything in which I could imagine the least doubt" (17), then he would necessarily have to reject anything obscured by mystery. As O'Connor saw it, Descartes set a tone for modern philosophy in which the most important things with which philosophers should be concerned must all be rejected peremptorily before they might be probed.

O'Connor may also have learned from her textbook that there were two responses to Descartes's method in France; one camp was "primarily interested in natural science," and the other camp, which included Malebranche, was interested in "establishing tottering religious ideas upon the firm Cartesian foundation of the method of reason" (286). Malebranche "particularly attempted to prove by reason the truth of the religious tradition" (286). There was then, for O'Connor, a fundamental contradiction in Malebranche's endeavor because he sought to use Descartes to remedy the damage Descartes had already inflicted on the Classical Judeo-Christian heritage. Malebranche was opposed by Pascal, among others, who realized that much of the mystery of human nature was simply not amenable to rational resolution in the manner by which a problem of physics might yield to analysis. Thus, under Malebranche's stewardship, faith would be stripped of much of its meaning. Randall writes, "Malebranche's attempt might just as easily have established Mohammedanism or Judaism;—might better have done so, in fact, since they contained fewer 'mysteries' than orthodox Christianity" (286).

Malebranche advocated that which O'Connor most opposed: the unlawful divorce of theory from actual experience. Malebranche maintained that sensation and even imagination are produced, not by the everyday objects with which we have contact, but directly by God himself. He argued, just as Descartes had, that ideas are the only genuine substance of the world. Malebranche promoted Descartes's divorce of mind and matter, and though he did so under the cover of religion, he was still fundamentally at odds with the Aristotelian-Thomistic system that never allows theory to ignore common experience. O'Connor found Malebranche's rationalization of religion at the expense of its mystery an unacceptable transaction.

But O'Connor's concern over forcing life and religion to be "reasonable" was no depreciation of reason itself. In Randall's, Jacques Maritain's, and O'Connor's view, it was the impossible role that Descartes assigned to reason that spawned the utopian promise of curing life of all misery, an impossibility that in turn deteriorated into a loss of confidence in reason itself. When Descartes announced that "what pleased me the most" about his new methodology was that he "was assured of using [his] reason in everything," he failed to appreciate the naïveté of his endeavor and failed to realize that he was assigning a role to reason that would prove its undoing because of the impossibility of its demands (12).

O'Connor learned from Maritain's *The Range of Reason* that to recover the essential but balanced use of reason, it must be put "in the proper perspective, where it serves and not substitutes for revelation." In her review of his work, O'Connor also notes,

> The age of the Enlightenment substituted reason for revelation, with the result that confidence in reason has gradually decayed until in the present

> age, which doubts also fact and value, reason finds few supporters outside of Neo-Thomist philosophy. (*PG* 124)

She was attracted to Maritain's writing because he "has been one of the major voices in modern philosophy to reassert the primacy of reason" (*PG* 124) when it is applied in a balanced way.

When confidence is lost in reason, as has happened in recent decades, an overreliance is placed upon "feeling." As T. S. Eliot has suggested, though our heads may be stuffed with "straw," we are "trembling with tenderness" (58).[4] In the absence of faith and reason, all that is left is unstructured emotion, and because of its isolation, "compassion" is prone to become ugly and abusive. Though the path may be paved with good intentions, the modern virtue of "tenderness," when "detached from the source of tenderness" and deprived of the guiding hand of reason, will end logically in "terror" in the Nietzschean-inspired "forced labor camps and in the fumes of the gas chamber" (*CW* 830-31).

The Cartesian revolution has also opened a doorway to "scientism," the unauthorized dominance of science in all human affairs that has introduced the unquestioned reign of "the experts": the credentialed elite who exercise a dubious rule over all human activity, not merely the properly narrow sphere of their expertise. O'Connor's opinion of these technical mandarins is like Mrs. Hopewell's opinion of her daughter, who is "brilliant," but doesn't "have a grain of sense" (*CW* 268).

One can carry this analysis a step further and expose its link to Nietzsche. Confusion over the source and exercise of authority is a prelude to the emergence of the undemocratic rule of Nietzsche's "overman," especially since ordinary common sense is scorned as ignorant and irrelevant. In the "Revolutionary's Handbook," George Bernard Shaw's Tanner urges the rise of the "Superman" who is essential to man's improvement and without whom progress will be no more than a broken promise. If the Superman is to emerge, however, the average citizen who is too shortsighted or cowardly to permit his preeminence must not limit him: “We must eliminate the Yahoo, or his vote will wreck the commonwealth” (Shaw 245).

On one occasion, Mrs. Hopewell picks up one of Hulga’s books and finds the following underlined passage:

> Science, on the other hand, has to assert its soberness and seriousness afresh and declare that it is concerned solely with what-is. Nothing—how can it be for science anything but a horror and a phantasm? If science is right, then one thing stands firm: science wishes to know nothing of nothing. Such is after all the strictly scientific approach to Nothing. We know it by wishing to know nothing of Nothing. (*CW* 269)

Although Mrs. Hopewell doesn’t understand what she has read, the words work on her “like some evil incantation in gibberish.” She subsequently “shut the book quickly and went out of the room as if she were having a chill” (269).

O’Connor’s quote from the existentialist philosopher Heidegger surely is meant to demonstrate the bankruptcy of reason to which Descartes led philosophy. Even in science, where reason rightly should dominate, Heidegger introduced an irrational nihilistic impulse, as he was preoccupied, not with science, but with the “nothingness” that lay behind it. More specifically, the reference is from Heidegger’s essay “What is Metaphysics?” in which the author proposes that metaphysics, the concern with “being” itself and with the first principles of existence, ought not to exclude the study of “nothing,” the opposite of being (359). He asks, “Why is there any Being at all—why not far rather Nothing?” (361). Heidegger argues that we should not limit ourselves to rational inquiry but pay closer attention to our “feelings” and “moods,” and specifically to the vague emotion of “dread.” Dread, by its very ambiguity and fear of the unknown, is an indication of, and a possible channel to, “nothing” (361). In other words, in response to Heidegger’s question, “Where will we find nothing?” he himself answers, "Dread reveals Nothing" (Heidegger 366). Taking this route constitutes a kind of "leap" that involves "letting ourselves go into Nothing, that is to say, freeing oneself from the idols we have and to which we are wont to go cringing." Reason, if it is to support such a proposition, must be redefined, as must logic itself. Heidegger argues, "If this thesis is correct then the very possibility of negation as an act of reason, and consequently reason itself, are somehow dependent on Nothing" (361).

Heidegger proposes a pursuit of Nothing through dread by redefining reason. For O'Connor, Heidegger's proposal may represent the nadir of the deterioration of rationality begun with Descartes. In contrast to Heidegger, O'Connor believes that the recovery and right use of reason as traditionally understood are vital for man's well-being. As St. Thomas explains in the "Treatise on Happiness," because one's happiness is ultimately a *rational activity*, happiness is most fundamentally a function of the intellect. It is the apprehension of truth and of God (Aquinas II, 583-618). Accordingly, and again as O'Connor had learned from St. Thomas and Maritain, reason's proper function is crucial to one's ability to live an ethical and contented life. As Aquinas would explain, if reason does not occupy a place of dominion over one's "emotions," "feelings," and "moods," and if life is not lived logically with respect to the principles and assumption upon which good behavior is based, then men and women cannot possibly be happy and free (Aquinas I-II, qus. 1-5).

Conclusion

The story of Hulga suggests a problem centuries in the making. It began with a demand for certitude that asked of science and reason the impossible—to cure all human misery—and to do so by means of a method that discredited or denied the transcendent. The result has been the diminished authority of reason itself, in favor of an irrational pursuit of "nothingness." And whereas the persistence of human suffering in a technological age should temper Cartesian hubris, for some it becomes an excuse for cynicism; for others, it provides the pretext for radical Nietzschean pretension expressed in the kind of moral "creativity" that Hulga pursued in her Vulcan's forge. The name "Hulga" is an anagram of the word "laugh"; if O'Connor wants us to notice the anagram, then O'Connor is cleverly telling us that the last laugh will be on those who deny man's need for the divine and put their faith instead in their own self-created "nothingness." This in turn reminds us of the striking passage in Psalm 2:4, "He that dwelleth in heaven shall laugh at them; and the Lord shall deride them."

"Good Country People" also teaches that a belief in nihilism is something less than a clear, rational choice; it is more likely an example of seduction. And contrary to what one may believe, those who choose the moral void of "nothingness" will not so much exercise their freedom as they will suffer a victim's fate. Whatever decision they make, the message of "Good Country People" seems clear: roll in the hay with nihilism and you'll be left without a leg to stand on.

Notes

This article is a revised version of a chapter from Edmondson's book *Return to Good and Evil: Flannery O'Connor's Response to Nihilism*.

1. Nietzsche's infamous statement may be found in his *The Gay Science* (167, 181) and in *Thus Spake Zarathustra* in *The Portable Nietzsche* (124).

2. Also see Wood.

3. Also see Rosen, who argues the progression from Descartes to Nietzsche thoroughly. William Sessions told me that he once lent O'Connor his copy of *The Dream of Descartes* by Maritain, the thesis of which is consistent with the argument made here.

4. T. S. Eliot, "The Hollow Men." In respect to O'Connor's interest in Eliot, she wrote her former classmate Betty Boyd Love, on 23 Dec. 1950, from the hospital, "I have been reading *Murder in the Cathedral* and the nurses thus conclude I am a mystery fan. It's a marvelous play if you don't know it, better if you do" (*HB* 23).

Works Cited

Aquinas, St. Thomas. *Summa Theologica*. Westminster, MD: Christian Classics, 1981.

Descartes, René. *Discourse on the Method for Rightly Conducting One's Reason and for Seeking Truth in the Sciences*. Trans. Donald A. Cress. Indianapolis: Hackett, 1980.

Dostoyevsky, Fyodor. *The Brothers Karamazov*. Trans. David McDuff. London: Penguin, 1993.

Eliot, T. S. *The Complete Poems and Plays, 1909-1950*. New York: Harcourt, 1971.

Heidegger, Martin. *Existence and Being*. Trans. R. F. C. Hull and Alan Crick. Chicago: Regnery, 1949.

Lewis, C. S. *The Problem of Pain*. New York: MacMillan, 1962.

Maritain, Jacques. *The Dream of Descartes*. Trans. Mabelle L. Andison. New York: Philosophical Library, 1944.

Nietzsche, Friedrich. *The Gay Science*. New York: Vintage, 1974.

____________. *Thus Spake Zarathustra*. *The Portable Nietzsche*. Trans. Walter Kaufmann. Middlesex, Eng.: Penguin, 1954. 103-439.

O'Connor, Flannery. *Flannery O'Connor: Collected Works*. Ed. Sally Fitzgerald. New York: Library of America, 1988.

____________. *The Habit of Being*. Ed. Sally Fitzgerald. New York: Farrar, Straus and Giroux, 1979.

____________. *Mystery and Manners, Occasional Prose*. Ed. Sally Fitzgerald and Robert Fitzgerald. New York: Farrar, Straus and Giroux, 1969.

____________. *The Presence of Grace and Other Book Reviews*. Comp. Leo J. Zuber. Ed. Carter W. Martin. Athens: U of Georgia P, 1983.

Percy, Walker. *More Conversations with Walker Percy*. Ed. Lewis A. Lawson and Victor A. Kramer. Jackson: UP of Mississippi, 1993.

Randall, John Herman, Jr. *The Making of the Modern Mind: A Survey of the Intellectual Background of the Present Age*. Boston: Houghton, 1926.

Rosen, Stanley. *Nihilism: A Philosophical Essay*. New Haven: Yale UP, 1969.

Shaw, George Bernard. *Man and Superman: A Comedy and a Philosophy*. London: Penguin, 2000.

Voegelin, Eric. *The World of the Polis: Order and History*. Vol. 2. Baton Rouge: Louisiana State UP, 1957.

Wood, Ralph C. "Flannery O'Connor, Martin Heidegger, and Modern Nihilism: A Reading of 'Good Country People.'" *The Flannery O'Connor Bulletin* 21 (1993): 100-18.

"Through Our Laughter We Are Involved": Bergsonian Humor in Flannery O'Connor's Fiction

J. P. Steed

In his film *Manhattan* (1979), Woody Allen's character, Isaac Davis, complains about the poor quality of the TV sitcom that he writes, exclaiming, "It's worse than not insightful: it's not funny!" The implication here, of course, is that being funny is better and more important than being insightful. This sentiment may seem to run counter to conventional wisdom (and indeed it is this incongruity that lends the exclamation its touch of humor), but upon further examination it seems to have merit—after all, to be funny requires insight, and that which is funny often provides insight; thus, being funny encompasses and surpasses being merely insightful. Moreover, according to Jewish proverbial wisdom, the presence of humor means the presence of understanding and self-criticism. And this seems to be a primary function of humor: to provide and provoke self-examination, self-understanding, self-criticism. Don't we laugh hardest at—and appreciate most—those books, movies, and comedians that are able to most deftly, most *insightfully* expose our faults, foibles, and failures? Recognizing this, then, the question becomes one of direction. Once humor has exposed our faults and we are faced with examining and criticizing them, what do we do? Where do we go? And does the humor itself, after exposing these faults, suggest any solutions?

Flannery O'Connor is an author whose use of humor has attracted a great deal of scholarly attention. In her study of O'Connor's fiction, for example, Dorothy Walters notes that the "thrust of tragic intention against comic implication is of major importance." Walters observes that O'Connor asks, perhaps even forces, the reader to "recognize that the world is peopled by figures essentially laughable in their basic makeup and ludicrous in their typical life response." "Our initial reaction," Walters continues, "may be a superior grin at the spectacle of a world teeming with inanity. But, through our laughter, we are involved; and we are led to reflect upon the most serious questions touching the human experience" (25). In other words, O'Connor's humor is insightful, and provokes self-examination and self-criticism.

Walters's succinct and astute assessment aligns the source and function of O'Connor's humor squarely with the philosophy of Henri Bergson; and indeed, Walters mentions Bergson twice in her study, though only briefly and somewhat superficially. Bergson's theories of laughter and humor have much in common with a long tradition of superiority theories—theories of humor that state, in essence, that laughter is condescending, we laugh at what is beneath us. But what sets Bergson's theory apart is his insistence that laughter serves a distinctly social function as a potential *remedy* for undesirable human traits. That is to say, while superiority theories of humor generally see laughter's function as primarily derisive—the response of a "superior" subject to an object's perceived inferiority—Bergson insists that the function is, more properly, *corrective* in nature. The distinction here is subtle but crucial: the former sees laughter as essentially alienating, while the latter sees it as essentially assimilating. As Walker attests, when O'Connor makes us laugh at a character's stubborn and foolish pride, "we are involved." Our laughter is turned inward, so that we are not merely deriding that pride, alienating it as something outside and away from ourselves; rather, we are shifting in our seats, making internal adjustments that, in effect, are assimilating. And perhaps this is why so many of those who write about O'Connor's humor have a tendency to characterize it as satirical—because satire has as its essential quality the provocation of uneasiness in the reader, urging some sort of reform.

In this essay I will expand on this interpretation of Bergson's philosophy of humor and demonstrate more thoroughly its relevance to O'Connor's fiction, focusing on two of her stories in particular: "Good Country People" and "A Good Man Is Hard to Find." Miles Orvell claims that "what is most difficult to define" in O'Connor's fiction is her "peculiar blend of comic violence and mysterious shock" (54), and indeed most of those who have written on O'Connor's fiction have commented on this "peculiar blend" of violence and humor. It is, at least in part, the goal of this essay to examine this mixture and to define it, finally, as a result of O'Connor's distinctively Bergsonian humor.

I

The principal trait of the Bergsonian comic figure is inflexibility, a certain "mechanical inelasticity" that surfaces "just when one would expect to find the wide-awake adaptability and the living pliableness of a human being" (Bergson, 120-21). According to Bergson, life is a continuous process of becoming. But the rational mind divides this process into discrete states of being, treating new objects and experiences as repetitions of familiar concepts, so that life is transformed into a succession of these states of being rather than a fluid, continuous, and irreversible flow. This approach is helpful in many respects: for example, I am thankful that I do not have to treat every encounter with a locked door as a new experience—I can rely on the familiar concept of unlocking the door with a key, to gain access to what is behind it. But, for Bergson, a sensitiveness to the uniqueness of objects and experiences, a certain flexibility or contextual awareness, is essential to free, well-adapted human behavior. And the comic figure is the figure that displays a lack of this flexibility. Thus, if I approach a door while holding a key in my hand, only to discover that the door has no lock, it will be my frantic search for a place to insert the unnecessary key, and my inability to gain access without completing the ritual, that will transform me into the observer's object of laughter.

But this example, it must be made clear, though it may fit within a broad interpretation of Bergson's theory, is not properly what I am referring to when I speak of Bergsonian humor. Where Bergson's philosophy distinguishes itself from traditional superiority theories is not only in its specificity of the source of the laughter as the presence of inflexibility, but also in its insistence on the essentially social function of that laughter. In Bergsonian humor, "the comic demands something like a momentary anesthesia of the heart. Its appeal is to the intelligence, pure and simple" (Bergson, 118). For Bergson, laughter, or humor, is not a feeling or an emotion; it is an intellectual response. More pointedly—and perhaps more significantly—it is a social, contextual response. The intelligence which responds to the comic

> must always remain in touch with other intelligences. . . . You would hardly appreciate the comic if you felt yourself isolated from others. Laughter appears to stand in need of an echo. . . . Our laughter is always the laughter of a group. . . . However spontaneous it seems, laughter always implies a kind of secret freemasonry, or even complicity, with other laughers, real or imaginary. How often has it been said that the fuller the theatre, the more uncontrolled the laughter of the audience! On the other hand, how often has the remark been made that many comic effects are incapable of translation from one language to another, because they refer to the customs and ideas of a particular social group! (119)

This complicity with other laughers constitutes the social nature of humor, but while this assertion, concerning the social *nature* of humor, might hold true in any (even every) philosophy of humor, Bergson continues: "To understand laughter, we must put it back into its natural environment, which is society, and above all must we determine the utility of its function, which is a social one" (119). This social *function* of laughter, concludes Bergson, is to remove the inflexibility which is its object, through humiliation and ridicule. That is, its function is to promote freedom and adaptability—a sense of the process of becoming—over the too-rational and too-inflexible insistence on a state or states of being.

"There are vices," writes Bergson, "into which the soul plunges deeply with all its pregnant potency." "The vice," he continues, "capable of making us comic is . . . that which . . . lends us its own rigidity instead of borrowing from us our flexibility" (123). In other words, if a character in a story exhibits a vice, such as greed, which elicits the extension of our flexibility—that is, if the character's flaws draw out our sympathies then that character becomes to some degree a tragic figure. But the character that imposes his or her rigidity on us, that elicits an intellectual rather than an emotional response, is the comic figure. And our response to the imposition of that rigidity, signified by derisive laughter (there is, presumably, no other kind), is an attempt to throw it off—and attempt to avoid or to *correct* it.

My example of the door without a lock, then, might be said to fit within a broad interpretation of this philosophy, as my rigidity in looking for the absent lock becomes the object of laughter and that laughter functions as a corrective to my rigidity (i.e., you laugh because you are convinced you would not behave this way; you would correct my behavior). But I submit that this is too broad and simplistic an application of Bergson's philosophy, precisely because the behavior is too easily corrected. The fact is, the observer laughs at my inflexibility, but that inflexibility makes no serious imposition on the observer; the observer feels no real threat of my inflexibility being or becoming his or her own. Thus, the behavior I am exhibiting is in no real need of correction, and the laughter it elicits can have no real social function.

True Bergsonian humor, then—that which does have a real social function—is that humor which has as its source or object a certain inflexibility, and which also has as its purpose and its function the correction of that inflexibility. This corrective function necessitates the recognition of the presence, or at least the real threat of the presence, of inflexibility within the individual observer, or at least within the group of laughers with which the individual is complicit. Otherwise there is nothing to correct. As a result, true Bergsonian humor will most likely produce a sense of uneasiness in the observer, as it attempts to provoke the observer into correcting his or her behavior. Moreover, because Bergsonian humor has society as its natural environment; because the laughter associated with it is the laughter of a perceived or real group of intelligences; and because the function of the group's laughter is to correct an inflexibility that is perceived as present within its ranks, effecting a sort of conformity in behavior, we might say that Bergsonian humor—unlike other forms, modes and theories of superiority humor—is assimilating in nature, rather than alienating. The missing door lock scenario, because it provokes no real change in the observer, is in fact an instance of a more traditional superiority humor because it alienates the object (me and my absurd inflexibility) rather than provoking assimilationist changes within the group of laughers.

If we modify the example, however, it can easily become Bergsonian. A ready-made modification is Gary Larson's *The Far Side* cartoon wherein a student at a school for the gifted is depicted as leaning heavily on a door that is clearly marked with the word "pull." Like my example of the door with the missing lock, this scenario also has inflexibility as its source of laughter. But Larson's scenario is far more capable of provoking the recognition of inflexibility within the observer. Few of us will entertain the notion that we are stupid enough to look for a lock when there isn't one, but most of us are capable of recognizing that, despite our sometimes even exceptional intelligence, we often, through a certain inflexibility, fail to apply that intelligence. (We've all pushed on the 'pull' door.) Bergsonian humor has as its purpose the correction of that inflexibility; it is, at its essence, socially persuasive; which is to say, finally, that it is essentially satirical. This is not to say that satire is, conversely, essentially Bergsonian, however. Satire and Bergsonian humor share the same general purpose—to be socially persuasive—but satire does not limit its sources or objects of humor to manifestations of inflexibility, nor does it limit its primary function to the correction of that inflexibility. In other words, Bergsonian humor is essentially satirical, but it is merely a branch, or a particular mode, of satire.

II

It is this satirical bent, this intent to persuade, that is the fundamental link between Flannery O'Connor's use of humor and Bergson's philosophy. O'Connor, after all, "displays a remarkable unity of purpose and consistency of theme" in her fiction (Walters, 35), and that purpose is founded in her Catholic convictions, so that "her aim is persuasion concerning religious matters" (Burt, 138). O'Connor's work is principally about redemption and its various forms, and O'Connor herself attests to this, and to the fact that persuasion toward redemption of the reader and of society is her aim. She asserts that "[r]edemption is meaningless unless there is cause for it in the actual life we live." And she continues:

> The novelist with Christian concerns will find in modern life distortions which are repugnant to him, and his problem will be to make these appear as distortions to an audience which is used to seeing them as natural; and he may well be forced to take ever more violent means to get his vision across to this hostile audience. (*Mystery*, 33-34)

This focused effort to persuade, to enact some social reform, permeates O'Connor's fiction and explains why so many readers have identified it as, in some way or another, satirical; for its humor elicits from the reader a distinctly uncomfortable laugh (i.e., "we are involved"?). What distinguishes her humor as Bergsonian, however, is this, coupled with the fact that the object of the reader's laughter can so often be identified as inflexibility. For O'Connor, the Christian writer who is promoting and provoking redemption, inflexibility is anathema. Christian redemption can only occur with a change of heart, and change can only occur within a flexible process of becoming. Moreover, Bergson notes that inflexibility results in "a mind always thinking of what it has just done and never of that it is doing," creating a certain absentmindedness (ergo, "a comic character is generally comic in proportion to his ignorance of himself") (122-23), and this lack of self-awareness is likewise antithetical to the epiphany or the revelation that is needed for redemption. Thus, the butt of O'Connor's corrective humor is the inflexible, the self-unaware. As Frederick Asals observes, "O'Connor's people are among the least introspective in modern fiction, with minds at once so unaware and so absurdly assured that they have refused to acknowledge any deeper self"—and in words remarkably in tune with the present argument, Asals continues to note that "her protagonists are incapable of the flexibility of development" (93). O'Connor herself, again, attests to this presence of inflexibility in her fiction, and in fact claims it as essential to any story. "When you write stories," she says, "you have to . . . start exactly there—showing how some specific folks *will* do, *will* do in spite of everything" (*Mystery*, 90, emphasis O'Connor's).

In "Good Country People," for example, it is primarily Hulga who *will* do in spite of everything, whose inflexibility and lack of self-awareness are the object of our laughter. Convinced unswervingly of her intellectual superiority, she stomps around the house like a toddler in a perpetual pout; and though she is thirty-two years old and hardly condescends to speak to her mother, everything she does is calculated to get her mother's attention. Furthermore, Hulga is fixated on the belief that "everything is nothing," that evil doesn't exist, and she sets out to educate a Bible salesman in that regard. Then, along the way, she decides to seduce him. This she will do, in spite of her extreme unattractiveness, in spite of the fact that the man, Manley Pointer, is a Bible salesman and supposedly religiously devoted—in short, in spite of everything. Clearly, Hulga is possessed of the most common of vices explored in O'Connor's fiction—namely, an excessive, inflexible, ignorant, and foolish pride. And as the object of our uneasy laughter, this pride, this inflexibility and its spawned lack of self-awareness, is corrected and a redemption of some kind is finally achieved.

Inflexibility as a theme in the story, and as a primary source of humor, is introduced in the story's opening sentence: "Besides the neutral expression that she wore when she was alone, Mrs. Freeman had two others, forward and reverse, that she used for all her human dealings"; and only a few lines later we are told that "Mrs. Freeman could never be brought to admit herself wrong on any point" (*Good Man*, 169). Mrs. Hopewell's inflexibility is then introduced, through her loyal use of and reliance on cliches, and as we learn that she still thinks of her daughter, Joy/Hulga, "as a child though she was thirty-two years old and highly educated" (170). Thus it only takes a few sentences to establish the women as comic figures, and the rigidity of their daily routine as a comic situation.

Significantly, it is the break in this daily routine—the introduction of variance into this mechanical life—that is the heart of the story, as Manley Pointer knocks on the Hopewells' door one afternoon. Mrs. Hopewell's inflexibility is highlighted, during the exchange, as she assesses Manley not with the contextual sensitivity of an individual aware of life as a continuous flow of new experience, but with a rigid insistence on some previously decided upon state of being: despite the salesman's interruption of her dinner, and despite his transparent flattery and "aw shucks" demeanor, and despite the fact that "Mrs. Hopewell never liked to be taken for a fool" (178), she welcomes him, trusts him, even admires him. In spite of everything, she displays an alarming lack of awareness by buying in to Manley's salesmanship: "'Why!' she cried, 'good country people are the salt of the earth!'" (179).

Manley's appearance, then, at once provides the opportunity for the portrayal of inflexibility, in Mrs. Hopewell and later in Hulga, as well as the potential remedy for it, as he disrupts the women's daily routine and, later, reveals to Hulga her unanticipated ignorance. The latter, occurring in the barn during Manley and Hulga's "picnic," is an example of, as Walters puts it, "the archetypal encounter of innocence with experience" (64), only, in a reversal of expectations, it is the supposedly intellectually superior Hulga who, despite her plans to educate and seduce, is revealed to be the ignorant, foolish innocent who is seduced. Manley reveals himself to be deceptive, mean, and worldly, and this revelation exposes Hulga's absentmindedness.

In other words, like many of O'Connor's stories, "Good Country People" is the story of foolish pride overthrown—a feat that is, in part, accomplished through the use of Bergsonian humor. It is important to note, too, that this humor is created both *in* the story and *by* the story.

Examples of the employment of Bergsonian humor *in* the story, ironically, at times involve Hulga as its employer. For instance, when Mrs. Freeman is talking about her girls, Glynese and Carramae, and specifically about Carramae's wedding, she says, "Lyman said it sure felt sacred to him. She said he said he wouldn't take five hundred dollars for being 'married by a preacher,'" and Hulga responds by asking, "'How much would he take?'" (183). Hulga's query is dry, but though no laughter is observed in the characters, it is clear that Hulga is amused by her own question, and when we laugh as readers, we are laughing *with* Hulga. Half a page later, this time talking about Glynese's marital situation, Mrs. Freeman tells the others that Glynese "said she would rather marry a man with only a '36 Plymouth who would be married by a preacher," and Hulga, this time, asks, "what if he had a '32 Plymouth" (183). Again, the reader laughs *with* Hulga. The humor is created *in* the story and has as its source the rigidity of Hulga's literal interpretations of Mrs. Freeman's statements; but its object is also Mrs. Freeman's and her daughters' inflexibility with regard to marital matters and social propriety. This inflexibility is recognized by Hulga, and she tries to correct it with her Bergsonian wisecracks, but it is only underscored by Mrs. Freeman's utter lack of self-awareness, as she fails to recognize herself as the butt of Hulga's humor and continues on with her stories unabashedly.

The irony, of course, is that Hulga recognizes this inflexibility in others but remains unaware of it in herself, and in fact we are told early on that this stubborn lack of self-awareness is self-imposed. O'Connor makes this clear when she describes how Hulga, at times, "would stare just a little to the side of her, her eyes icy blue, with the look of someone who has achieved blindness by an act of will and means to keep it" (171). Images of blindness are omnipresent in the story. And much of the humor created *by* the story has as its object not only the inflexibilities of Mrs. Freeman and Mrs. Hopewell, but also Hulga's inflexibility and lack of self-awareness, which is revealed in bits and pieces as the story progresses. The laughter created *in* the story, then, from the examples above, is the laughter of a group consisting of (at least) the reader and Hulga; she laughs at inflexibility and we laugh with her. Meanwhile, the laughter created *by* the story, which gradually zeroes in on Hulga as its primary source, and which has her inflexibilities as its primary object, is the laughter of an imagined group, *at* Hulga instead of *with* her. We, as readers, assume that other readers, or at least the author herself, will find Hulga's inflexibility as ridiculous as we do; and indeed, we rely on this group complicity for our laughter. In this way, our laughter is assimilationist in nature: Hulga's willful ignorance, her foolish pride, are deemed undesirable traits, recognized as vices, and we attempt to correct them with our laughter as a united (albeit imagined) group of laughers.

What makes this humor Bergsonian in nature is, in part, the gradual revelation of Manley's deception. As Manley slowly reveals Hulga's folly, he also reveals our own—as we, as readers, have been likewise taken in by Manley's con. In other words, we are involved. The inflexibility and lack of self-awareness that we perceive in Hulga, we also perceive in ourselves, or at least within our imagined group. Thus, as our laughter increases, so does our uneasiness, and the Bergsonian effect of the humor crescendos. The culmination of our discomfort comes at the end of the story, when Mrs. Freeman and Mrs. Hopewell watch Manley running off and they comment on how "simple" he is (195-96), and we realize as we laugh that the blindness, the inflexibility, has not yet been corrected but persists, so that our laughter is overshadowed by our uneasiness.

And it is this last revelation which finally gives O'Connor's humor its distinctly Bergsonian cast—for the revelation is, in effect, created *by* the story and not *in* the story itself. That is to say, while Hulga does receive a kind of revelation *in* the story, as her blindness is revealed to her, it is the revelation that is created *by* the story, *for the reader*, that is the focus of the fiction, and of the humor it employs. In effect, O'Connor reveals to us, as readers, the real presence, or at least the real threat of the presence, of inflexibility, of blindness or a lack of self-awareness in ourselves, or at least within our group of laughers; thus our laughter is uncomfortable and we are, as O'Connor hopes and intends for us to be, provoked or persuaded toward reform—in effect, toward an assimilation of and to O'Connor's sense of morality or reality. Through her use of Bergsonian humor, O'Connor strives to move society toward her version, or her vision, of redemption.

This reader-revelation is replicated in what is arguably O'Connor's finest, and certainly her most famous, story, "A Good Man Is Hard to Find." Like Hulga, the grandmother becomes the comic figure, whose inflexibility is exhibited in her selfishness, here self-absorption, and, again, in a lack of self-awareness. And, as in the previous story, a crescendo builds. The severity and extent of the grandmother's ignorance and rigidity is gradually revealed, until at last it is revealed fully in the story, to the grandmother herself—this time not by a small-time swindler like Manley Pointer, but by a serial killer who calls himself "the Misfit."

As with "Good Country People," the presence of inflexibility in "A Good Man Is Hard to Find" is introduced in the opening sentences: "The grandmother didn't want to go to Florida. She wanted to visit some of her connections in east Tennessee and she was seizing at every chance to change Bailey's mind" (9). And again, in the end the laughter that is provoked by this inflexibility is overshadowed by uneasiness. This time, however, the revelation that occurs *in* the story coincides with the revelation created *by* the story, for the reader. That is, the reader shares the revelatory experience with the grandmother, whose inflexibility is recognized in an epiphany. The grandmother exclaims, "Why you're one of my babies. You're one of my own children!" and this exclamation follows on the heels of the Misfit's own confession of rigidity: he cannot believe in Jesus because he wasn't there to witness his miracles (29). The grandmother may not be capable of articulating this moment as a recognition of her inflexibility, but as readers we have a wider perspective. We have seen the grandmother's stubbornness and we recognize the Misfit's rigidity; thus, when the grandmother makes her exclamation, what is, for her, perhaps an emotional or spiritual recognition of that which connects them is, for us, a connection that we can articulate intellectually. It is the reflection of rigidity—as though the grandmother were looking into a mirror as she looks into "the man's face twisted close to her own" (29)—that triggers the unarticulated recognition, in the grandmother, that the Misfit's rigidity is the natural offspring of her own. And this revelation is simultaneous for the reader, who recognizes the presence, or the real threat of the presence, of his or her own inflexibilities, and thus experiences a climax of uneasiness.

With this revelation, then, comes a cessation of self-unawareness, and suddenly the grandmother is transformed, according to Bergson's definitions, from comic figure to tragic figure, as she no longer imposes her inflexibility onto us, but now demands our sympathies. But that this change, this correction, has been accomplished in part through humor and laughter is reasserted by the Misfit's comment that the grandmother "would have been a good woman . . . if it had been somebody there to shoot her every minute of her life" (29). There is no single passage in all of O'Connor's fiction more exemplary of Bergsonian humor than this, as our shock and uneasiness are at their peak, yet we are still moved to laughter. Here, we share our laughter with two groups: first, with the Misfit himself (as we shared laughter, previously, with Hulga), the object of our laughter being the stubbornness of the grandmother, who refused to achieve any flexibility or self-awareness save on the point of death. And second, we return to our imagined camaraderie with other readers or the author, as we laugh at the Misfit's own rigidity—his own inability to turn from evil, for there he stands, quipping cleverly about the grandmother's failures, when he himself has failed to change, to modify or to correct his behavior, and he is utterly unaware of it. Thus we, as readers who are aware, laugh at his absentmindedness while still shaken with unease over the consequences of it, and the very real threat that such potential for rigidity exists in us all.

This recognition of inflexibility, and the reform that O'Connor hopes it will provoke, are, again, the redemption of society that O'Connor is after. And she pursues this redemption by any means necessary. She writes:

> St. Cyril of Jerusalem . . . wrote: "The dragon sits by the side of the road, watching those who pass. Beware lest he devour you. We go to the Father of Souls, but it is necessary to pass by the dragon." No matter what form the dragon may take, it is of this mysterious passage past him, or into his jaws, that stories of any depth will always be concerned to tell. . . . (*Mystery*, 35)

For O'Connor, clearly, the dragon is often represented by a confrontation with evil—in these stories, men like Manley Pointer and the Misfit. And violence often accompanies this confrontation. But humor can also be violent, and can be one of the forms this dragon takes, a refiner's fire through which the individual must pass, the laughter that is produced functioning as a corrective to the flaws and vices that are deemed undesirable. The "peculiar blend of comic violence and mysterious shock" in O'Connor's fiction, as described by Orvell, then, can be successfully defined as Bergsonian humor—which is to say that, by recognizing the humor in O'Connor's fiction as chiefly Bergsonian, we are able to reconcile and explain the coexistence of humor and horror. The "comic violence" that takes place *in* the story is combined with the "mysterious shock" created *by* the story, which we experience as readers, as we recognize the presence, or the real threat of the presence, of those flaws and vices within ourselves. In this way, through the use of a specifically Bergsonian humor, O'Connor pursues the correction of societal rigidity, promoting and provoking reform and a sense of becoming. She *involves* us, as, in effect, she pursues the assimilation of society into her distinctly Christian world.

Bibliography

Asals, Frederick. "The Double." *Flannery O'Connor*. Ed. Harold Bloom. New York: Chelsea House, 1986. 93-109.

Bergson, Henri. "Laughter: An Essay on the Meaning of the Comic." Tr. Cloudesley Brereton and Fred Bothwell. *The Philosophy of Laughter and Humor*. Ed. John Morreall. Albany: State University of New York Press, 1987. 117-26.

Burt, John. "What You Can't Talk About." *Flannery O'Connor*. Ed. Harold Bloom. 125-43.

O'Connor, Flannery. *A Good Man Is Hard to Find*. New York: Harcourt, Brace & World, 1955.

____________. *Mystery and Manners*. Eds. Sally and Robert Fitzgerald. New York: Farrar, Straus and Giroux, 1969.

Orvell, Miles. *Invisible Parade: The Fiction of Flannery O'Connor*. Philadelphia: Temple University Press, 1972.

Spacks, Patricia Meyer. "Some Reflections on Satire." *Genre*, 1 (1968), 13-20.

Walters, Dorothy. *Flannery O'Connor*. Boston: Twayne, 1973.

Carnival in the "Temple": Flannery O'Connor's Dialogic Parable of Artistic Vocation

Denise T. Askin

Faced with a dreaded pilgrimage to Lourdes in 1958, Flannery O'Connor consoled herself by gleefully anticipating the conversations of her fellow pilgrims. They could not fail to be, as she put it, "professionally rewarding" (*The Habit of Being* 264). She considered her comedic art to be her vocation, and she tamed neither her tongue nor her wild imagination in pursuing it. She dismissed edifying fiction like Cardinal Spellman's *The Foundling* for "tidy[ing] up reality" (*HB* 177). Self-consciously religious fiction she called a "smoothing-down" (*Collected Works* 830) that distorted reality and violated the demands of art. "Stories of pious children tend to be false," she wrote in her preface to "A Memoir of Mary Ann" (*CW* [*Collected Works*] 822), and she peopled her fiction with impudent, even vicious, brats typically locked in mortal combat with domineering elders. O'Connor intended for her outrageous art to shock, perhaps even to scandalize her readers, but she repeatedly defended the comic mode as a fitting vehicle for prophetic vision. She went so far as to claim that she looked for the "will of God through the laws and limitations" of her own art (*CW* 812). What God seems to have willed for O'Connor was an acid-tongued species of comic-prophetic writing that operates by unveiling human malice in unlikely characters, especially children.

Readers familiar with O'Connor's letters know the pleasure she took in portraying herself as a socially challenged curmudgeon known for her vernacular reductions of academic cant and her delight in the ludicrous aspects of her fellow humans. Her sole function at her mother's social gatherings, she said, was to cover the stain on the couch. In her letters she spoofed her significant theological learning by calling herself a "hillbilly Thomist" (*HB* 81), and she memorialized her social awkwardness among the artsy set at Mary McCarthy's sophisticated New York dinner party by telling the story of how gracelessly she blurted out her belief in transubstantiation: "Well, if it [the Eucharist]'s a symbol, to hell with it" (*HB* 125). The staunchly Catholic persona of the letters is nowhere to be found in her fiction, of course, but in the 1954 story, "A Temple of the Holy Ghost," O'Connor makes a rare departure from custom. In the unnamed adolescent protagonist she traces, not very obliquely, the lineaments of the O'Connor of the letters. The story can be read, in fact, as a wry (if cartoon-like) portrait of the artist.

In "A Temple of the Holy Ghost," O'Connor presents a twelve-year-old "born Catholic" protagonist who is as acid-tongued and socially awkward as the O'Connor of the letters. O'Connor takes the artistic risk of creating a Catholic child protagonist (the only one in her canon) in a Catholic setting. The child can be read as a projection of O'Connor herself. The author admitted to Betty Hester that in some ways she was a perpetual twelve-year old: "the things you have said about my being surprised to be over twelve, etc., have struck me as being quite comically accurate. When I was twelve I made up my mind absolutely that I would not get any older. I don't remember how I planned to stop it" (*CW* 985). The child of the story is isolated from society, uninitiated into the mysteries of sexuality, smug (if immature) in her Catholicism, and proud of her (sophomoric) intellect. She replicates O'Connor's gaucherie in McCarthy's living room when she gracelessly blurts out a defense of the Eucharistic hymn, *Tantum Ergo*. "You dumb Church of God ox," (*CW* 202) she shouts to the farm boy who cannot understand it. The prepubescent child has a precociously developed imagination that she uses to satirize the (supposed) fools around her. Surprisingly, by the end of the story, without suffering the scourge of O'Connor's signature ironic twists and violent epiphanies, the child is initiated—in a church setting—into the traditional Catholic mysteries of the Trinity and the Eucharist. While these biographical parallels are worth noting, what is significant from a literary perspective is that the protagonist—a prototype of the Catholic comedic artist—struggles with the edifying language of saints until she discovers the validity of her own comic voice. She is redeemed at last from the path of cynicism and bitterness, not by abandoning her laughter (a conventionally sappy ending that O'Connor would have scorned) but rather by uniting her comic perception to her apprehension of mystery.

Critics as perceptive as Richard Giannone have read "A Temple of the Holy Ghost" as a conventional humbling of the proud protagonist in the spirit of the desert fathers, when the child "prayerfully reflects . . . 'hep me not to talk like I do'" (Giannone 102). Christina Bieber Lake claims, more plausibly, that the child's imaginative experience with the "grotesque" hermaphrodite puts her in "a position of exceptional spiritual openness and potential fecundity" (137). O'Connor herself argued in 1955 that the conclusion reveals "the acceptance of what God wills for us, an acceptance of our individual circumstances" (*HB* 124). However, what O'Connor saw as God's will is neither a Hollywood plaster saint for her protagonist nor a parochial aesthetic for herself as writer. Through a complex interplay of contending voices, O'Connor allows the child's own comic discourse to emerge validated despite the efforts of authoritative language to suppress it. Rather than blunting the sharp edge of comic satire in the name of piety, O'Connor appropriates it as an unconventional weapon in the arsenal of grace. I will argue that the last laugh, in a story pervaded by laughter, is O'Connor's own sly endorsement of herself as comic-prophetic artist, the artist whose vocation is predicated on the inherent connection between the comic and the holy, between the carnival and the temple.

"A Temple of the Holy Ghost" can be a stumbling block even for experienced O'Connor readers because it has neither her paradigmatic plot nor her signature ironic ending.[1] Although there is relentless laughter in the first part of the narrative, the story stands out in O'Connor's corpus as singularly *un*comic. It seems rather to be a meditation on the springs (and pitfalls) of comedic vision. Further, the story is filled with pre-Vatican II Catholic "insider" references and allusions: Benediction; the monstrance; St. Scholastica, the brilliant sister of St.

Benedict; St. Perpetua, the beautiful martyr in the arena with wild animals (who also had a prophetic vision of a kind of androgyny); St. Thomas, the "dumb-ox" Scholastic; the Stations of the Cross; the legendary medieval miracle of the bloody host; and the Latin office of Corpus Christi. In this story, a vintage nun tells her charges how to handle fresh boys; the child's convent-school cousins sing the *Tantum Ergo* in Latin; and the protagonist herself winds up in the convent chapel kneeling next to a nun and recognizing that she is in the "presence of God" (*CW* 208). This is a rare and risky excursion for O'Connor into Catholic territory, and the precocious child with a sharp eye (and tongue) for the ridiculous bears a strong family resemblance to Mary Flannery herself. Moving from the protagonist's childish derision to her transcendent epiphany, the story traces the child's initiation into sacramental vision and O'Connor's vocation as a Catholic comedic artist.

The Jesuit scholar William Lynch, one of the formative influences on O'Connor's aesthetic, makes a forceful case for comedy as a fitting mode for the divine. He argues that comic vision is the enemy of rigid ideology, or as he calls it, the "univocal mind" (107). Comedy dispatches demonic abstract thinking that substitutes "phony faith for faith in the power of the vulgar and limited finite" (97). Comedy's descent into the concrete, with all its interstices and smells (95), makes it a genre well suited to the "scandal" of the Incarnation. Lynch argues that comedy serves as an antidote to angelism, the dualistic thinking that divorces the material from the spiritual. It combats pure intellectualism by depicting ludicrous human duality, insisting on images of "ugly human actuality" (98) as a path to God. The comic writer celebrates the mysterious union between the earth and Christ "with all the logic removed" (109). Lynch writes "[t]he mud in man . . . is nothing to be ashamed of. It can produce [. . .] the face of God" (109).

O'Connor appropriated Lynch's terminology in her letters and essays. In "The Nature and Aim of Fiction," she speaks of the "concrete details of life that make actual the mystery of our position on earth" (*Mystery and Manners* 68), and near the end of her life she wrote approvingly, “I agree with W. Lynch’s general theory . . . in good fiction and drama you need to go through the concrete situation to some experience of mystery” (*HB* 520). She added, however, “I am no good at theory” (*HB* 520). The parade of freaks and marginal trash (to Ruby Turpin’s eyes) that scandalizes Ruby in that raucous vision of heaven; the tattooed back of O. E. Parker that scandalizes his “Straight Gospel” wife; and the rogues’ gallery of characters that scandalizes readers looking for recognizable expressions of religious faith are the fruit of O’Connor’s vocation as a comic-prophetic writer. She makes Mrs. Greenleaf wallow in the mud shouting “Stab me in the heart, Jesus!” and Hazel Motes blind himself with lime and walk on penitential glass, and young Tarwater drown a “dim-witted child” named “Bishop” while murmuring the words of baptism. So outrageous are her inventions that John Hawkes saw her as a closet nihilist (as cited in Wood, *Comedy of Redemption* 97). But O’Connor challenges the reader to see beyond the surface to the prophetic dimension of her art. In O’Connor’s lexicon, the word “prophetic” means “‘seeing through’ reality” (Magee 89), to extend the gaze “beyond the surface” (*CW* 818) to the realm of divine life. To be true to this vocation, “[t]he prophet in [her] has to see the freak” (*MM* 82), and the artist must accept the validity of her own voice.

While Lynch provides a theoretical framework for O’Connor’s literary vocation, Mikhail Bakhtin provides a technical framework that helps to reveal the intricacy of her art. The work of the Russian dialogic critic bears striking similarities to that of the American Jesuit Lynch. What Lynch calls the univocal mind, Bakhtin calls monologic discourse. While Lynch finds *univocal* or abstract, rigid thinking to be demonic in its exclusion of the finite, sacramental dimension of reality, Bakhtin finds *monologic* discourse, an expression of repressive authority (be it Soviet or other forms), to be tyrannical in its exclusion of the multiple voices of humanity. Both of these critics, approaching fiction from their different perspectives, find an antidote in similar literary forms. For Lynch it is comedy; for Bakhtin, it is the “carnivalesque." These forms give voice to the bodily, limited, phenomenological human condition. Lynch finds comic expression redemptive in its incarnational vision; Bakhtin finds in the carnivalesque a defense against and liberation from authoritative oppression.

Incarnation is central to the work of both Bakhtin and Lynch. Bakhtin saw all language as incarnate, the utterance of concrete persons. Further, Bakhtin's preference for "heteroglossia," a style that brings together "two 'languages,' two semantic and axiological belief systems" within a single syntactic unit (*Dialogic Imagination* 304) can be traced to his orthodox roots. Bakhtin defines, according to Charles Lock, a "Chalcedonian, two-voiced, double-natured discourse" (98) that dispenses with clear markers between self-contained and singular voices, and especially in free indirect discourse, insists on "the incarnation of language" (111). Christ, he argues, is the paradigm for Bakhtin's *Dialogic Imagination*: "two natures, divine and human, in the one hypostasis of Christ . . . becomes the paradigm for the dialogical: two voices in the hypostasis of one word" (98).

Both Lynch and Bakhtin define the need for literary devices that can explode monologic discourse and revive sacred discourse through parody. Lynch argues that it is "ridiculous, in a Catholic world, to be afraid of the irreverent in so many secret places" (110). Bakhtin argues in the same vein that only through the "carnival spark" of "cheerful abuse" can calcified sacred language be liberated from "narrow-minded seriousness" and revived. The fiction writer, he says, is free to import discourses from other contexts and genres—such as poetry, song, newspaper articles, and prayer—and thereby activate a dialogue across social and ideological boundaries. This "incorporation of genres," and particularly the carnivalesque and parodic treatment of this imported discourse, serves an almost therapeutic role. It can bring language (often sacred discourse) back to life. The very "degradation" and "uncrowning" of the word, Bakhtin writes, bring about its renewal (*Rabelais and His World* 309).

What we see in "A Temple of the Holy Ghost" is not theory dressed in fiction, but rather a fictional exploration of the role of the comic artist in service of the divine mystery. The child protagonist's precocious imaginative life, rendered in free indirect discourse, outdistances the very limited lines allowed to her by polite society. For example, in response to the direct question, "how does a child like you know so much about these men [the Wilkins boys]?" she develops a rich Walter Mitty-esque fantasy about saving the Wilkins boys from Japanese suicide divers in the war. Her actual spoken response is limited to: "I've seen them around is all" (*CW* 201). The story elevates the child's artistic/imaginative discourse above the diminished possibilities of ordinary discourse with the "morons" around her.

Above all, the child protagonist in "A Temple of the Holy Ghost" is endowed with a keen eye for the "mud" or freak in others. She is on the verge of becoming one of O'Connor's gallery of "curdled" intellectuals (Wood, *Flannery O'Connor and the Christ-Haunted South* 200). The child, whose outrageous laughter, sharp tongue, and fertile imagination seem to be in need of reform or suppression, penetrates mysteries no less daunting than the hypostatic union and a sacramental universe, and she does so by employing the very qualities she believes to be at odds with the holy.

The child lives in a world of freaks: "Cheat," the goofy farmer whose face is the color of the red clay roads he travels; Alonzo the odoriferous and obese taxi driver; the Wilkins boys, who sit "like monkeys" (*CW* 201) on the porch fence. The child equates them with the dancing monkeys, the fat man, and the midget at the fair. The hermaphrodite is the freak that defies categorization, the one that activates the girl's hungry imagination. The child's eye for the freak, like O'Connor's grotesque art, is disconcerting. But if we consider the medieval folk tradition of the carnival, its licensed travesty of liturgy, its parody of sacred discourse, and its temporary replacement of the bishop by a boy/clown, we can situate O'Connor in a tradition that served, by its very excesses, to balance the church's formality and, as Bakhtin says, to renew its sacred discourse.

Both Lynch and Bakhtin identify the medieval Feast of Fools as the paradigm for the dialectic between the comic/carnivalesque and the sacred. As Lynch describes it, the "comic intrusion into the liturgy began with the singing of the Magnificat at vespers, with the words 'He hath put down the mighty from their seat and hath exalted the humble and the meek'" (108). With scripture intoning this ultimate comedic reversal, the carnival begins. Among the carnival travesties were mock sermons, reversals of class and gender roles, and clerics dressing in the clothing of women (Burke 182-89).

O'Connor develops the Feast of Fools motif from the outset: the visiting cousins doff their brown convent-school uniforms and don what can be seen as their "carnival" finery (red skirts, loud blouses, and lipstick). As brashly as carnival revelers, they perform an almost parodic rendition of the *Tantum Ergo* in the sacred language of Latin.

In a carnivalesque gesture, they literalize the trope of the "Temple." Sr. Perpetua has instructed them to fend off ungentlemanly behavior in an automobile by saying "Stop sir! I am a Temple of the Holy Ghost!" Calling themselves "Temple One" and "Temple Two," laughing uncontrollably with each utterance, the teenagers make sport of the sacred trope. Their parody reveals how diminished and calcified the sacred trope has become in the "official" discourse of the convent school.

But carnivalesque laughter, argues Bakhtin, uncrowns and debases the sacred language only to renew it. Because the child detests the mockery she witnesses, she is motivated to explore the trope of the "Temple of the Holy Ghost" that she accepts as a "present." The resulting transformation of the words "Temple of the Holy Ghost" closely conforms to a phenomenon described by Bakhtin in "Discourse in the Novel." He discusses the rare occurrence of unity between "authoritative discourse" and "internally persuasive discourse." Authoritative discourse "cannot be represented—it is only transmitted" and demands "unconditional allegiance" (*DI* 344). It is semantically inert, a relic, monologic. "Internally persuasive discourse—as opposed to one that is externally authoritative—is, as it is affirmed through assimilation, tightly interwoven with 'one's own word'" (345). In the sequence the child goes through in responding to the Temple trope, O'Connor portrays the process by which authoritative words become internally persuasive and restored to life. The phrase, "A Temple of the Holy Ghost" is, as Bakhtin writes about sacred discourse, "not so much interpreted . . . as it is further . . . developed, applied to new material, new conditions. . . . [I]n each of the new contexts that dialogize it, this discourse is able to reveal ever newer *ways to mean*" (*DI* 346, emphasis in original.) The child begins by appropriating the trope imaginatively, first for herself "I am a Temple of the Holy Ghost" (*CW* 199), then for the pathetic Miss Kirby ("and she's a Temple of the Holy Ghost, too" (200), then for all humanity by having the hermaphrodite preach: "You are God's temple, don't you know?" (207). Finally, she sees the temple in the freak. The hermaphrodite in her dream-fantasy rejoices, "I am a temple of the Holy Ghost" (207). Her imagination endows the trope with "new ways to mean."

By means of carnivalesque travesty and materialization in the figure of the hermaphrodite, the trope is transformed from the static, diminished, official injunction against sexual misconduct. Authoritative discourse becomes internally persuasive, and the phrase emerges pregnant with meaning. Calling to mind the carnivalesque Feast of Fools, O'Connor introduces the language of the sacred, subjects it to parody, and finally reclaims the trope of the Temple of the Holy Ghost through an incongruous union of profane and sacred. The cousins, having fulfilled their carnivalesque roles, end their saturnalia, return to their brown uniforms, and disappear into the anonymous convent school choir singing the *Tantum Ergo* at Benediction. Order is restored, and the sacred discourse is renewed.

Just as the girls intrude into the child's world with their carnivalesque irreverence, so the hermaphrodite takes up the carnivalesque role in the child's imagination. As Susan Srigley reminds us in *Flannery O'Connor's Sacramental Art*, Thomas Aquinas viewed the imagination to be "the main receptor of the revelatory experience" (146).

The carnival freak is a character made of words, never seen by the child, but given a voice by her imagination, nonetheless. Like a transdressing carnival participant giving a mock sermon, the hermaphrodite wears a blue dress and preaches like a revivalist in the circus tent. The hermaphrodite resides in her imagination, an "answer to a riddle that was more puzzling than the riddle itself" (*CW* 206). The physical mystery of the two-gendered freak is the gateway to the true mystery of the Temple of the Holy Ghost, a mystery that must be grasped by the imagination. The freak's speech becomes, through the child's interpolation, a version of the *Magnificat*. She assigns new words to him: "God done this to me and I praise Him. . . . A temple of God is a holy thing. . . . I am a temple of the Holy Ghost" (207). Like the medieval Lord of Misrule who intrudes into Vespers during the *Magnificat*, the carnival freak intrudes into the ceremony of Benediction. At the elevation of the monstrance, it is this discourse of the freak that the child "hears."

In order to understand the power of this unifying epiphany, we need to consider the duality or "doubleness" that constitutes the story's structure. O'Connor employs binary opposition and comedic doubling as the pathway for the child's encounter with mystery. The entire story is contrapuntal. There are two Catholic girl cousins (Temple One and Temple Two), dressed identically, and matched with two Protestant farm boy brothers; these two character pairs engage in an antiphonal duel between two religious musical traditions ("I've Got a Friend in Jesus" and "The Old Rugged Cross" versus the *Tantum Ergo*). There are two sexes in the hermaphrodite, a creature the child at first imagines having two heads, like the androgyne in Plato's *Symposium* (his mythic image of the whole human). There are two warnings that God will strike the mocker by two marginal characters: the Negro cook and the carnival freak. There are two expositions (in carnival tent and convent chapel), two ivory circles (sun and host), two narrative versions of the hermaphrodite (the cousins' story and the child's dreamlike reverie), two "Amens" (the cousins' parodic ending of the *Tantum Ergo* and the carnival audience's reverent response to the hermaphrodite in the tent). The story pulsates with *two-ness*.

Enter the child with the comedic mean streak. From the first paragraph in the story, this two-ness affects her role: "[i]f only one of them [the cousins] had come, that one would have played with her, but since there were two of them, she was out of it, and watched them suspiciously from a distance" (*CW* 197). The doubling forces the child to become a spectator, fostering both her derisive laughter and her creative imagination. As Lake remarks, the cousins are content "to live in a world of binaries defined by sexual desire" (136), but the child's ability to "see beyond the gender roles" leads her to "grasp profound spiritual concepts the girls only mock" (135).

Just as the hermaphrodite physically joins binary opposites, so the solitary child-as-artist brings together opposites throughout the story. She links the old farmer Cheat and the 250-pound Alonzo with the boy-crazy cousins, convulsing herself with laughter at the resulting incongruity. She matches the Catholic girls with the Protestant boys. She imagines martyrs wearing circus tights, and she imagines circus performers to be martyrs waiting for their tongues to be cut out. She unites the Temple of the Holy Ghost trope with the body of the hermaphrodite, seeing the *sacred* in the freak with "all the logic removed" (Lynch 109). Her quickened imagination introduces the words of the hermaphrodite at the elevation of the monstrance at Benediction, uniting profane and sacred. Finally, the child conflates the natural image of the sun, "like an elevated Host" (*CW* 209) with the supernatural presence of God in the Eucharist.

Comedic doubling and binary opposition, then, become for the child a kind of bipolar, dialogic pathway to an overarching unity—an encounter with mystery. The mysterious joining of two sexes in one body is a parodic reflection of the hypostatic union defined by the Council of Chalcedon, a mystery of the true union of two full natures with neither of them compromised—the scandal of the God-made man. O'Connor's protagonist is mystified by the concrete reality of the hermaphrodite's body, complete with a double set of genitalia. Ironically, it is this bodily manifestation of mystery that leads the child to encounter (using Lynch's phrase) "the face of God." All these connections conspire at the end to reveal the sacramental, or as Bakhtin would call it, the tropic nature of creation in the child's epiphanic vision of the sun. The intractable two-ness of the world reveals an underlying oneness. The incongruous realities of existence, then, become resolved in a new perception of congruence. Reality becomes eloquent of the sacred.

If the comic artist enjoys a double *vision*, O'Connor matches it with a *double-voiced style* in this story. O'Connor wages the battle for the comedic artist's vocation most definitively through language. As noted above, Bakhtin argues that dialogic narrative defends against the rigid reductionism of "authoritative" or monologic language. Three aspects of O'Connor's dialogic technique in this story—incorporated genres, the forging of a hybrid narrative discourse, and the contest with authoritative language—bring about the validation of the child's comedic voice.

O'Connor incorporates the genre of hymnody—both Catholic and Protestant—in a way that suggests Bakhtin's theory of uncrowning and renewing. Like Bakhtin's rebellion against the "official speech" of communism, O'Connor's parody suggests that for a secularized, desacralized discourse, the carnivalesque response can be renewing. When the "Church of God" Wilkins boys and the Catholic convent cousins engage in their musical duel, it would be a mistake to dismiss this exchange as a bit of vaudeville humor in the story. The scene "dialogizes" the narrative by introducing voices from vastly different discourses. In the process it mystifies those from other discourse traditions and excludes those who do not take pains to appropriate the discourse. "That must be Jew singing" (*CW* 202) says the farm boy when he hears the Latin hymn. By placing the Latin words into the story with neither translation nor footnote, however, O'Connor also makes the words inaccessible even to the Catholic schoolgirls and presumably to much of O'Connor's pre-Vatican II Catholic readership who knew the hymn only by rote. In similar fashion, although she provides a couple of verses of "I've Got a Friend in Jesus," the narrator merely alludes to "The Old Rugged Cross" without providing the text, thereby excluding those unfamiliar with the Gospel tradition. By alienating or hiding these discourses, O'Connor continues the "in-joke" mode she established through her allusions. Only when the reader reclaims these incorporated genres, translating or supplying the texts, will the words reveal their web of connections with the central symbolism of the text.

Just as the cousins caricatured the phrase "Temple of the Holy Ghost," they also make entertainment out of the words of the *Tantum Ergo*. Ironically, it is through their parody that the voice of Thomas Aquinas enters the dialogue, in the hymn commissioned by Pope Urban IV in 1264 for the newly-founded feast of Corpus Christi (Body of Christ). Thomas's hymn introduces references to the Eucharist (mysterious union of God and Man united mysteriously in the host) and to the equally mysterious union of three persons in the Trinity. In a different way, the narrator's allusion to "The Old Rugged Cross" taxes the reader to supply the missing discourse. Only then can its connections with the imagery of the child's inner life materialize. For example, the child is described as sometimes "think[ing] of Christ on the long journey to Calvary, crushed three times under the rough cross" (*CW* 205). Here O'Connor mixes the discourses of Protestant and Catholic traditions, because this is a distinctly "Catholic" meditation, based on the practice of the Stations of the Cross, not on Gospel accounts which make no mention of Christ's three falls.

The cross of the gospel song is "despised by the world," but also holds a "wondrous attraction"—language that can easily be applied to the child's meditation on the hermaphrodite. The cross of the gospel song is "stained with blood so divine" like the sun-host "drenched in blood" (*CW* 209) at the end of the story. In the gospel song, the cross itself will be "exchanged some day" for a "crown"—echoing the crown of martyrdom to which the child aspires, but which she hopes to achieve without the tedious journey of the cross. The gospel hymn points to the child's task in the story: to trade her romanticized fantasy of quick martyrdom for the slow way of the rugged/rough cross.

The hidden discourses of both the *Tantum Ergo* and "The Old Rugged Cross," therefore, point to the mystery the child will encounter. These incorporated genres create a multi-voiced narrative, a chorus of voices all echoing the same mystery, and reaching a crescendo when, at the second singing of the *Tantum Ergo*, the mystery of the "Temple of the Holy Ghost" comes alive to the child in the words of the carnival freak.

The two key images of the story—the hermaphrodite (half man and half woman) and the host (Christ's body under the appearance of bread)—are supported by a series of subordinate hybrid forms that surround and amplify the mysterious unions of incarnation, Trinity, and Eucharist. The images include the gospel song that is "half like a love song and half like a hymn" (*CW* 201), the child's dream of sainthood—half Hollywood and half hagiography,[2] and the hybrid discourse of the carnival freak—half *Magnificat* and half tent revival. Most significantly, O'Connor's hybrid narrative discourse works particularly well in this story to adumbrate the central theme.

The smooth discourse of the narrator is readily distinguished from the child's. Narrator: "the revolving searchlight . . . widened and shortened and wheeled in its arc" (*CW* 204). The narrator's voice tends to be objective, "[t]he sound of the calliope coming from the window kept her awake and she remembered that she hadn't said her prayers and got up and knelt down and began them" (205). The child's own direct discourse, in stark contrast to the narrator's, is laced with childish epithets and colloquial grammar: "You big dumb Church of God ox!" (202), "I ain't eating with them" (202), "Those stupid idiots" (203).

While these two idioms are readily distinguished from one another, O'Connor introduces a strategic hybrid discourse. This form of "heteroglossia," according to Bakhtin, brings together two utterances, two speech manners, in a "double-accented, double-styled" construction

(*DI* 304).[3] From the very first page, the child's "character zone," or field of action for a character's voice (*DI* 316), infiltrates the narrator's discourse, blurring the distinction between the two. O'Connor develops double-voiced sentences that shift from narrator to child within one syntactic unit: "The child decided, after observing them for a few hours, that they were *practically morons and she was glad to think that they were only second cousins and she couldn't have inherited any of their stupidity*" (*CW* 197, emphasis added). The sentence begins with the narrator's voice reporting the child's thoughts, but it ends by shifting to the child's language (italicized) through free indirect discourse. Throughout the story, the telltale idiom of the child erupts into the narrative, jostling the narrator's, and making the source of such claims as "the girls giggled *idiotically*" (202) ambiguous at best.

This extension of the child's character zone into the narrator's territory also leads to a struggle with "calcified" official language in the story. Just as Huck Finn's "conscience" (which speaks in the monologic, official language of society) nearly overrides the voice of his instinctive morality when he tries to pray, so, too, the child's authentic voice in "Temple" ["A Temple of the Holy Ghost"] struggles for survival. Huck and the "Temple" child have much in common. Both are at a threshold age, innocent of sexual awakening, exempted from polite decorum, free to follow their wits (or wit), free to be ill-mannered, to "lie" creatively or to tell the truth crassly, to see through the falsified language of the grown-up world and properly name it as "flapdoodle" and "talky-talk" (Twain, 180, 187) or "twaddle" ("Temple," *CW* 208). But Huck's voice—the triumph of Twain's work—is almost drowned out by the socially approved discourse of prayer. The problem is a real one for O'Connor, too, as she reveals in a 1956 letter to "A" regarding the language of novenas. "I hate to say most of these prayers written by saints-in-an-emotional-state. You feel you are wearing somebody else's finery and I can never describe my heart as 'burning' to the Lord (who knows better) without snickering" (*HB*, 145). By referring to the language of saints as "somebody else's finery," O'Connor points facetiously to the conflict between the discourse of others and authentic discourse in prayer. For the child in "Temple," this struggle with authorized language leads at last to the validation of her own voice.

Two crucial moments in the story, the child's meditation on sainthood and her prayer in the chapel during Benediction, often serve as proof-texts for critical judgments about the nature of her development in the story. Looking at them from a dialogic perspective, we see an internal struggle between two kinds of discourse. When the child reflects on sainthood, she concludes that her "ugly" mode of speech disqualifies her from being a saint:

> she did not *steal* or *murder* but she was a born *liar* and *slothful* and she sassed her mother and was *deliberately* ugly, to almost everybody. She was eaten up also *with the sin of Pride, the worst one*. She made fun of the Baptist preacher who came to the school at commencement to give the devotional. She would pull down her mouth and hold her forehead as if she were in agony and groan, "Fawther, we thank Thee," exactly the way he did and *she had been told many times not to do it*. She could never be a saint, but she thought she could be a martyr if they killed her quick. (*CW* 204, emphasis added)

The child's language of self-knowledge becomes self-accusation, rendered in free indirect discourse. The passage mixes the child's own idiom with the (italicized) language spoken in the confessional box, signaled by the use of a capital "P" for pride. This authoritative voice condemns the child's fertile inventiveness as "lies," labels her contempt for stupidity as "Pride," and ranks her sin at the top of the hierarchy. It requires that she suppress her outrageous language. The child "has been told many times" not to do her comic parody of the minister, a send-up in the classic carnivalesque mode (and, interestingly, precisely the sort of mimicry that O'Connor herself delighted in throughout her life, as her letters attest). From the monologic perspective, the child's sassy, comic discourse is the enemy of sanctity, but this judgment smacks of angelism, the dualistic thinking that divorces the "vulgar concrete" from the holy. The only route to sainthood in the world of monologic discourse, the child concludes, is to leapfrog over concrete reality and its slow and often ludicrous journey, and to get herself killed "quick." Comical as the wording is, the passage reveals the child's voice to be in combat with a life-denying discourse. She must be liberated if she is to fulfill her comic vocation, and, more importantly, if she is to enter into an authentic dialogue with God.

The second passage deals precisely with that dialogue with God. It is easy to hear conventional piety in the child's prayer at Benediction: "hep me not to be so mean . . . [h]ep me not to talk like I do" (*CW* 208). But we must remember that O'Connor believes that stories of pious children are usually "false." If we place the child's prayer in its linguistic context, we get a different result. Earlier in the story, the narrator had mocked the child's mechanical night prayers: "[s]he took a running start and went through to the other side of the Apostle's Creed" (205). Similarly, the narrator comments that her prayer at Benediction begins "mechanically" (208). Her rote recitation echoes the monologic catalogue of self-accusations. On the verge of renouncing her comedic role—"hep me not to talk like I do" (208)—the child is rescued by the unbidden voice of her imagination. The hermaphrodite intrudes as if in answer to her prayer: "I don't dispute hit. This is the way He wanted me to be" (209). Audaciously, O'Connor provides a vehicle for God's "voice" in the child's awakened imagination, turning her monologue into a dialogue. O'Connor described a similar dialogical process in her essay, "Catholic Novelists and Their Readers": "The Lord doesn't speak to the novelist as he did to his servant Moses, mouth to mouth. He speaks to him as he did to those two complainers, Aaron and Aaron's sister, Mary: through dreams and visions, [. . .] and by all the lesser and limited ways of the imagination" (*MM* 181). The child's acceptance of God's will, then, comes not from abstract angelism, but from its shocking opposite—from the discourse of the freak. Marshall

B. Gentry reads the scene as a validation of the child's meanness (66), and Joanne McMullen sees it as evidence of her "non-redemption" (106), but it can be more convincingly read as the validation of her comic/satiric voice and vocation.

O'Connor provides a richly dialogic ending to the story, governing the exit scene by hybrid discourse: "[a]s they were leaving the convent door, the *big nun* swooped down on her mischievously and *nearly smothered her in the black habit, mashing the side of her face into the crucifix hitched onto her belt*" (*CW* 209, emphasis added). The cheeky idiom of the child in "mashed" and "hitched" takes the hex off the potentially maudlin tableau. One could also argue that in this passage O'Connor cannot resist embedding the pun that the cross "makes an impression" on her. On the drive home, the child, like O'Connor on her pilgrimage to Lourdes, gathers professional (comic) material in the backseat of the taxi. Looking at Alonzo's ears, she sees them "pointed almost like a pig's" (209). After the epiphany, the comedic voice endures. No "pious" ending here.

Conclusion

In "A Temple of the Holy Ghost" O'Connor sets in motion a complex series of reverberations, a dialogic echo chamber that reenacts the tropic/sacramental nature of reality into which the child is initiated. Like a hall of mirrors at a country carnival, images of mysterious incarnation and containment correspond to this verbal echoing. The host of the Eucharist is God; God is three persons; the incarnate Christ unites God and humanity; the "temple" houses the Holy Ghost and therefore all three divine persons; the hermaphrodite is both male and female and is a temple of the Holy Ghost; the sun mirrors the host, and the host embodies the divine mysteries (Trinity, Incarnation); the "sign of the cross" signifies the God-made man's suffering, naming all three persons of the Trinity. The concluding epiphany points to the metaphoric way of the cross that the child and the hermaphrodite (and by implication, all human beings) must travel. Waves of refracted and resonating meaning overtake the child; the world becomes eloquent of mystery—a mystery she can participate in without being a "saint." This dazzling array of reverberations can be read as O'Connor's approximation of sacramental vision, the spiritual illumination and liberation which the child—as uniter/artist—experiences at the end of the story.

As Bakhtin claims, carnivalesque laughter and dialogic narratives are liberating. Lynch, too, argues that the comic medium reminds us that "a thing need not step out of the human . . . to achieve the liberty of the children of God. The mud in man, the lowermost point in the subway, is nothing to be ashamed of" (109). The child in "A Temple of the Holy Ghost" is liberated to see the freak in herself as well as in Alonzo and the hermaphrodite, to see the freak as the temple of God, and even to see the freak in Christ in the Eucharist, Christ who was willing, as St. Paul tells the Philippians, "to assume the condition of a slave" (i.e., a freak) for our salvation. The child is liberated, as well, to see her own outrageous voice as God's calling. The child's unifying vision can be seen as a gateway to what Susan Srigley calls O'Connor's "ethic of responsibility," the possibility of moving beyond "a life ordered solely by love of the self" (5). The isolated spectator-child with her "ugly" mean streak and sense of superiority becomes a creative unifier. She gives voice to a freak that is both mocked and mysterious, investing this "grotesque" character with prophetic utterance.

At the end of the story, the officials (preachers and police) with their univocal minds make an attempt to suppress the carnivalesque by shutting down the fair. The child is indeed silent in the last scene, but she is temporarily "shut up" more than permanently "shut down." The carnivalesque is alive in the child's comedic imagination, populated by the freaks and fat men, monkeys, farmers, and pigs she has the gift to see as both ludicrous and holy. O'Connor makes sure that the artistically risky sacramental image of the blood-drenched host in the sky[4] is followed by a vision of "a red clay road" (*CW* 209), the very road on which travel old farmer Cheatam and his Negroes, not plaster saints.

The child's comic imagination and voice are placed at last into the necessary dialogue with the sacred, and the comic artist is born.

Notes

1. The relationship between the mother and child in this story also departs from the O'Connor formula. The mother is neither domineering nor smugly complacent. Rather, she laughs (guardedly) at her daughter's rude jokes, speaks kindly to correct the child's insolent humor, and confides in the child about the horrors of the teenage visitors. This mother is so far from speaking in the clichéd discourse typically assigned to O'Connor's mother characters that she rescues the trope of the "Temple of the Holy Ghost" from the clutches of the cousins, validates it as true, and gifts her daughter with this metaphoric and mysterious "present."

2. There are striking parallels between the child's reveries about the hermaphrodite and the account of Perpetua's visions before her martyrdom. While awaiting death in the arena, Perpetua records a vision in which "all those who stood around said: Amen!" From this dream she learns, as does O'Connor's protagonist, that she "must suffer" (Musurillo, *Acts of the Christian Fathers*). In a later vision, Perpetua is called into an arena, surrounded by an "enormous crowd who watched in astonishment. . . . My clothes were stripped off, and suddenly I was a man." Perpetua becomes a woman (referred to as "her," and "daughter") in a man's body. When she dispatches her adversary in the dream, Perpetua writes "I began to walk in triumph towards the Gate of Life. Then I awoke." Her actual martyrdom proves difficult to accomplish, "as though . . . feared as she was by the unclean spirit, [she] could not be dispatched unless she herself were willing." At last she helps the gladiator to cut her throat. O'Connor's depiction of the child's martyrdom fantasy makes an interesting comparison: the lions will not maul her, and the Romans do not succeed in burning her, so "finding she was so hard to kill, they finally cut her throat." It seems to be hagiography more than Hollywood that informs the child's fantasies.

3. This dialogic form most closely approximates Bakhtin's understanding of the hypostatic union in Christ, according to Charles Lock in "Bakhtin and the Tropes of Orthodoxy."

4. McMullen argues that O'Connor gives the "commonly understood symbol" of the sun's "uncharacteristic couplings" that disorient the reader. She cites the blood-drenched sun/host as a case in point (33). Other critics have seen the bloody host image as a symbol of martyrdom, of the cross, or even of the impending onset of the menses for the prepubescent protagonist. In fact, O'Connor is more likely alluding to a story that would have been familiar to pre-Vatican II Catholic schoolchildren: the story of Peter of Prague, the thirteenth-century priest whose doubts about transubstantiation were mirac-

ulously dispelled at Mass when, at the moment of the consecration, the host began to drip with blood. Partly in response to this miracle, Pope Urban IV instituted the Feast of Corpus Christi soon thereafter to honor Christ's presence in the Eucharist. Here we see another of O'Connor's "insider" allusions to the mystery celebrated by the *Tantum Ergo*.

Works Cited

Bakhtin, Mikhail. *The Dialogic Imagination: Four Essays*. Trans. Caryl Emerson and Michael Holmquist. Ed. Michael Holmquist. Austin: U of Texas P, 1981.

____________. *Rabelais and His World*. Trans. Helene Iswolsky. Bloomington: Indiana UP, 1984.

Burke, Peter. *Popular Culture in Early Modern Europe*. New York: Harper & Row, 1978.

Gentry, Marshall Bruce. *Flannery O'Connor's Religion of the Grotesque*. Jackson: UP of Mississippi, 1986.

Giannone, Richard. *Flannery O'Connor: Hermit Novelist*. Urbana: U of Illinois P, 2000.

Lake, Christina Bieber. *The Incarnational Art of Flannery O'Connor*. Macon, GA: Mercer UP, 2005.

Lock, Charles. "Bakhtin and the Tropes of Orthodoxy." *Bakhtin and Religion: A Feeling for Faith*. Eds. Susan M. Felch and Paul J. Contino. Evanston, IL: Northwestern UP, 2001. 97-119.

Lynch, William F. "Comedy." *Christ and Apollo: The Dimensions of the Literary Imagination*. New York: Sheed & Ward, 1960. 91-113.

McMullen, Joanne Halleran. *Writing Against God: Language as Message in the Literature of Flannery O'Connor*. Macon, GA: Mercer UP, 1996.

Magee, Rosemary M., ed. *Conversations with Flannery O'Connor*. Jackson: UP of Mississippi, 1987.

Musurillo, Herbert, ed. *The Acts of the Christian Fathers*. New York: Oxford UP, 1972.

O'Connor, Flannery. *Collected Works*. Ed. Sally Fitzgerald. New York: Library of America, 1988.

____________. *The Habit of Being*. Ed. Sally Fitzgerald. New York: Farrar, Straus and Giroux, 1979.

____________. *Mystery and Manners: Occasional Prose*. Eds. Sally Fitzgerald and Robert Fitzgerald. New York: Farrar, Straus and Giroux, 1969.

Srigley, Susan. *Flannery O'Connor's Sacramental Art*. Notre Dame, IN: U of Notre Dame P, 2004.

Twain, Mark. *The Adventures of Huckleberry Finn*. 1884. Ed. John Seelye. New York: Penguin, 1985.

Wood, Ralph C. *The Comedy of Redemption: Christian Faith and Comic Vision in Four American Novelists*. Notre Dame, IN: U of Notre Dame P, 1988.

____________. *Flannery O'Connor and the Christ-Haunted South*. Grand Rapids, MI: William B. Eerdmans, 2004.

Flannery O'Connor's Empowered Women

Peter A. Smith

In a Jungian analysis of three key works of short fiction by Flannery O'Connor, "A Circle in the Fire," "The Displaced Person," and "Greenleaf," Mary L. Morton claims that these stories "dramatize the ludicrosity of women who have denied the spirit of femininity, the *anima*" and that the sympathy that O'Connor generates for the protagonists of these stories is a "trick on some readers" (57). In fact, these characters, as well as other O'Connor characters in similar positions, do not really deny their femininity, they exploit it, sometimes to the point that they seem to be parodying it. And they *should* arouse in most readers not only sympathy but also a grudging respect. Unlikable as these women may appear, all deserve credit for employing a clever strategy in attempting to survive in a man's world while essentially manless, and all deserve sympathy because they are faced with an impossible task in having to synthesize aspects of both gender roles in order to maintain their livelihoods.

While these "managerial types," as Morton terms them (58), or "assertive widows," as Suzanne Morrow Paulson refers to them (39), are all overly demanding of their hired hands, all are justified in their aggressiveness by their common economic situation. As Louise Westling has observed, O'Connor's South of the fifties is nearly as hostile to the plight of widows managing farms as the South of the immediate post-Civil War period had been, when "widows who attempted to manage their own affairs were regarded as arrogant" (146). While these women may have "consciously adopted a masculine ethic" (Morton 58), thereby denying an essential part of their own femininity, there is really little choice involved; O'Connor's empowered women all sincerely believe that typically masculine, aggressive behavior is the only way to overcome the misogyny inherent in the lower class male workers they must control in order to keep their farms operating. Each woman is forced by necessity to channel whatever nurturing instinct she has into assuring the survival of her "place," a significant term used by each.

In fact, the women from the above stories display a rather admirable adeptness at manipulating the myth of the "Southern lady" to help them survive in a patriarchal society. These women firmly maintain that, as "ladies" in the traditional Southern sense of the term, they are entitled to the respect, protection and labor of those around them, particularly those of a lower caste. They lay claim to all of the privileges due a "Southern lady" while also having assumed all of the economic power of an absent male. This proves to be an effective combination for a time, allowing this character to feel that she can—and must—be as "iron-handed" as any male property owner while still feeling perfectly entitled to sympathy for having to debase herself by running things. Her stature as a "lady" entitles her to complain about being abused and disrespected by her subordinates because she is "only a woman," yet this complaint serves as a weapon to encourage others to be far more tolerant than they would otherwise be toward a male superior.

The basic situation in these stories is the same: all of these characters are, presumably, widows who have inherited farms—but little money—from their departed husbands and are left to manage on their own, quite in conflict with what their upbringings have told them is the proper place for a "lady." The economic support traditionally provided by the husband is gone, and all three of these women are left to fill the power vacuum; they are forced to take on the completely unladylike position of manager/employer. It is a role that each woman is actually quite adept at, and each is able to keep her "place" running well for a time, despite uncooperative employees. The farms that these women inherit provide unique venues for them, since these farms constitute a confluence of the private, domestic sphere in which female empowerment is unquestioned, with the public, economic sphere in which Southern ladies traditionally have had no role. Thus each woman is able to view and run her "place" as an extension of her home.

In "A Circle in the Fire" this attempt to combine both feminine and masculine authority can be seen in Mrs. Cope's attempts to make her three uninvited visitors both "act like gentlemen" (185) and display the same amount of obedience that she has come to expect from her employees. Unfortunately for Mrs. Cope, she initially misjudges the boys and tries to control them in a purely maternal fashion, in contrast to the managerial tone she adopts with her workers. Expecting the boys to be polite and deferential around a lady who is also a social superior, Mrs. Cope is shocked when the three refugees from an Atlanta housing development refuse to respond to her insincere maternal solicitude. As Margaret Whitt has noted, "the stern, businesslike woman farmer is nowhere to be found in Mrs. Cope's handling of the boy intruders. She speaks to them as a Southern lady would" (44). Even after being informed of Powell's dismal home life, Mrs. Cope still attempts to control his behavior by reminding him of his defiance of accepted social standards: "I'm sure your mother would be ashamed of you" (188). Mrs. Cope's language here makes clear that she is still viewing her empowerment as owner of the farm in domestic terms, with herself acting as a surrogate "mother" trying to discipline unruly children. If Sally Virginia's unruly behavior is any indicator, though, Mrs. Cope is ineffective as a controlling parent—as are most of O'Connor's single mothers.

What puzzles Mrs. Cope about the boys is that they are not only ungrateful to her for her attempt to be domestically gracious to them by offering food, but they also flatly reject her economic authority, refusing even to acknowledge her ownership of the land. The boys are clearly responding to the lack of a legitimate male authority figure, as they express disgust at the presence of a female "ruling class" on the farm. As one of the boys says to Mr. Pritchard, "I never seen a place with so many damn women on it, how do you stand it here?" (186).

Mrs. Cope has every reason to believe that her tactics will work on the boys. After all, Powell's mother had once been an employee of Mrs. Cope's, and, presumably, she was able to control her as she controls her successor, Mrs. Pritchard. Although Mrs. Cope initially believes that she can control all of the "destructive and impersonal" forces on her farm, such as her black workers and the nut grass (177), this is only because none of these "forces" can question her authority. We can recognize in her paranoia about fire her awareness of how tenuous her control really is. Once she encounters a "force" that clearly challenges her feminine authority, she can only resort to the ineffective threat of summoning male authority, the sheriff, to regain control.

In donning male clothes and strapping on pistols to chase off the boys, Sally Virginia reveals that she, like Mrs. Pritchard, understands what her mother cannot: that the boys have no use for the Southern code of behavior by which a lady is owed deference, that their broken homes give them little experience in knuckling under to domestic authority, and that they will respond only to pure masculine power. Unfortunately, the only form of masculine power on the farm is in the destructiveness of the boys themselves. In fact, Powell's arson touches off a rebellion on the part of the male workers, as they refuse Mrs. Cope's final order to "hurry" to put out the fire. The male force triumphs and Mrs. Cope ultimately finds herself without any sort of authority at the most crucial time.

In a similar fashion, Mrs. McIntyre of "The Displaced Person" eventually loses control of her workers and ends up, like Mrs. Cope, losing her farm. Initially, though, Mrs. McIntryre's control grows to previously unknown levels thanks to the presence of another who, like herself prior to her marriage, had been without a "place." Irked by the same perception of disrespectful incompetence on the part of her workers that Mrs. Cope complains about, Mrs. McIntyre begins to gain a sense of strength and power once she finally hires a truly hard working, honest and knowledgeable hand. She holds the example of Mr. Guizac up to her other workers in order to create a kind of sibling rivalry among her employees to spur productivity: one can clearly hear a why-can't-you-be-like-your-brother admonition to Mr. Shortley when she compares him to Guizac. When she adds to this the substantial economic threat of firing the entire Shortley family, it is easy to see how the atmosphere of paranoia on the farm comes to exist. Mrs. McIntyre reaches the apex of her economic empowerment and comes to exploit her newfound authority with her workers. Finally, she has found a worker "who *has* to work" (215), that is, one who has to knuckle under to her dubious authority, and she proclaims that the long line of "white trash" families who have parasitized her and then left is now over. But she finds that her visions of freedom from worthless "poor white trash and niggers" who have "drained [her] dry" (202) are short-lived, as she must engage in a silent conspiracy with males of both of those groups to rid herself of Mr. Guizac.

Just as Mrs. Cope has her paranoia of losing all through fire, so does Mrs. McIntyre fear the loss of the social order which empowers her, hence the unlikely conspiracy to rid herself of her "favorite son." Because Mrs. McIntyre lacks any true maternal authority, since she is merely the childless young widow of a much older man, the social basis of her authority is of paramount importance to her. While Mr. Guizac continues to be a fine worker, his attempt to marry his cousin to Sulk, the younger black on the farm, is an affront to the social system that she just can't bear. While she herself had married in order to gain social and economic advancement, her union did not involve miscegenation, thus she cannot perceive a parallel. She had been willing to endure the laziness of the "white trash" and the stealing of the "niggers" because, in her view, these traits were to be expected of these classes; these acts merely reinforce the established order which puts the blacks on the bottom of the social scale, the poor whites in the middle and herself firmly on top. She admits her dependence on this order when she tells Guizac, "I will not have my niggers upset. I cannot run this place without my niggers" (223). To her mind, her black workers are the equivalent of weak-willed children who can always be counted on to recognize her authority as a white woman.

Mrs. McIntyre is not alone in this belief, either, as all of O'Connor's empowered women rely absolutely on their black workers' recognizing whites as their superiors—even if these women complain that blacks don't grant this recognition as readily as they once did, as Mrs. Turpin claims in "Revelation," for instance. "The Enduring Chill" provides an interesting view of the consequences of the erosion of the social division that all of O'Connor's empowered women claim *should* exist between blacks and whites. The basic situation in this story is identical to that of the above stories, with a widowed landowner, Mrs. Fox, relying upon her black workers, Randall and Morgan, to keep her dairy farm running and wanting her son to keep the social barrier in place. But Asbury, as defiant as any child of any of O'Connor's single mothers, succeeds in breaking down the barrier by enjoying a forbidden smoke with the black workers in the milking barn; the act results in "one of those moments of communion when the difference between black and white is absorbed into nothing" (368). But when he tries to push the "communion" further by drinking unpasteurized milk over Randall's objections that Mrs. Fox has strictly forbidden it, he is struck down with undulant fever and eventually pushed even further away from the black workers when his attempt to communicate with them while on his sickbed fails utterly and he must look to his mother to be "saved" from them. Asbury's attempt to defy the social hierarchy results in disaster; it leaves him ill for life and accomplishes nothing beyond what he intended all along—to annoy his mother.

We can see in Mrs. Fox's frustration with Asbury's strange desires the same emotion that is behind Mrs. McIntyre's exasperation with Guizac's failure to comprehend and bow to the accepted standards of her society and Mrs. Cope's frustration at the unwillingness of the boys to act like "gentlemen" after she has been "nice" to them. Mrs. McIntyre's words to Mr. Guizac even echo Mrs. Cope's reminder to the boys: "This is my place. . . . I say who will come here and who won't" (223). In the paranoia displayed by these women over seemingly harmless plans we can see that they realize the more profound implications of the disruption of the social order which supports their tenuous claims of authority. Without this order and the accompanying rules of conduct which restrain their workers, none of O'Connor's empowered women could function effectively as "bosses."

These characters are among a number of empowered female protagonists from O'Connor's short fiction who rigorously defend what they perceive to be the hierarchy of social classes in the South, primarily because of their own relatively lofty positions in this hierarchy. Perhaps the most obvious example is Mrs. Turpin of "Revelation," whose hobby of "naming the classes of people" (491) who exist in her perception of the world is reinforced by the high status of the home- and land-owner class, to which she and many of O'Connor's other female protagonists belong. Although Mrs. Turpin has a husband, Claud is characterized throughout the story by his meekness and compliance with his wife's wishes, so Mrs. Turpin's life on her farm involves the same sort of pride in ownership and exasperation at having to deal with non-compliant help as the lives of the empowered widows. This she makes clear in her waiting-room conversation, where she brags about her crops and livestock and bemoans her inability to find good help: "You can't get the white folks to pick [cotton] and now you can't get the niggers—because they got to be right up there with the white folks" (493). Although she readily admits to herself that her envisioning of a hierarchy based upon race, class and money is flawed, as it fails to account for richer people who are morally or racially inferior to herself, she still insists upon defending it and envisioning it—and her own position in it—even in the face of Mary Grace's "revelation" of Mrs. Turpin's true moral status.

Similarly, while having fallen from the landowner class, Julian's mother in "Everything That Rises Must Converge" also remains preoccupied with defending the social hierarchy against all of its enemies—including both Julian and the "misguided" blacks who don't agree with her pronouncement that they should be "rising" only "on their own side of the fence" (408). Once again, the defense of this hierarchy is clearly a defense of the protagonist's own sense of "place" in it. While Julian is all too aware that his mother's life has been "a struggle to act like a Chestny without the Chestny goods" (411), he doesn't seem to understand that her racist beliefs are an integral part of "knowing who she is." Without the inherited home and land, all Julian's mother has left of her former sense of empowerment is her breeding—particularly her ability to be gracious to those she believes to be social inferiors. To Julian's mother's mind, her ability to engage in conversation with those whites on the bus who are clearly "not our kind of people" (407) and to be patronizingly kind to black children is her badge of social superiority; her sense of identity enables her to be "gracious to anybody" (407).

In Julian's mother's firm belief in her own elevated position in the hierarchy, evidenced by her ability to graciously interact with her inferiors in the manner of a true Southern lady, we can hear the echoes of the voices of several of O'Connor's empowered women who point to their relationships with the families of their tenant farmers as proof of their magnanimity. For instance, we are told of Mrs. Hopewell, the farm owner in "Good Country People," that she "had no bad qualities of her own but she was able to use other people's in such a constructive way that she never felt the lack" (272). This attitude of condescending charity can be seen in what Mrs. Hopewell regards as her masterful handling of Mrs. Freeman's intrusive personality by allowing her to be "into everything" (272), and in her defending of the Freemans' worth despite her evident belief in their inferiority to herself: "they were not trash. They were good country people" (272). This is a term that Mrs. Cope might apply to the Pritchards and Mrs. McIntyre might apply to the Guizacs, both of whom rate above the "white trash" employees of their past experience but below themselves.

It is in the defending of her vision of the hierarchy that both Mrs. Hopewell and her daughter experience their downfall. Just as both Mrs. Cope and Mrs. McIntyre contribute to their own defeats by their constant assertions about the social hierarchy, so does Mrs. Hopewell open the door to calamity by enthusiastically defending her opinion of the relative worth of "good country people." Because of their belief in the hierarchy, both mother and daughter are equally duped by Manley Pointer, the travelling Bible salesman, who metaphorically keeps his foot in Mrs. Hopewell's door by claiming that Mrs. Hopewell is the type of person who doesn't "like to fool with country people like me!" (278), relying upon Mrs. Hopewell's condescending denial. Even Joy-Hulga, who seems opposed to all of her mother's ratings of the worth of fellow human beings, has bought into the idea of the hierarchy, as she sets out to seduce the salesman because she perceives him as ignorant (and thus inferior to herself), and becomes convinced that she "was face to face with real innocence" (289).

For all of these women, it is the persistent belief in their own superiority that entitles them to denigrate their fellow human beings that constitutes a spiritual defect as apparent as Joy-Hulga's physical defect. Manley Pointer is mocking the notion of his conforming to the Hopewells' stereotypical view of the "good country person," as he tells Joy-Hulga that he belongs to that class. He maintains, however, that "it ain't held me back none. I'm as good as you any day in the week" (290), pointing out how the belief in any social hierarchy always carries with it a belief in one's own superiority to others. His retort also belies the built-in assumption of superiority on the part of both of the Hopewells. He's not as "good" in the moral sense, of course, but in the social sense; he makes his living from exploiting the patronizing, superior attitude of the "upper" class, who imagine themselves to be superior in every way. And belief in a social hierarchy characterizes nearly all of O'Connor's female characters, regardless of rank. Even "white trash" women such as the one in the waiting room in "Revelation" and the one on the bus in "Everything That Rises" agree with the protagonists that the blacks' struggle for equality is a sure sign that the world has gone terribly awry (after all, it is a threat to their own status as at least one step up from the bottom of the scale). In stealing Joy-Hulga's artificial leg and strolling off under the unsuspecting eye of Mrs. Hopewell, who is convinced that he has been trying to sell Bibles to "the Negroes back in there" (291)—the implication being that such a "simple" boy could only be an effective salesperson among social inferiors—Pointer is pointing to how inane the belief in such stereotypes can be. Mrs. Freeman's sarcastic retort, "some can't be that simple . . . I know I never could" (291), also reflects the fact that it is the Hopewells who are simple and who see the world in black-and-white terms. The hoodwinking of both members of the Hopewell family (the upper class in the hierarchy) proves how silly the notion of a hierarchy is: if "good country people" can be defined by their "simplicity," then it is surely the Hopewells who are "country people."

Another flaw in the proposition that these upper caste Southern ladies are superior, as they all seem to claim, concerns their common belief in their own graciousness and politeness toward others. Even if we can grant that graciousness is a sign of proper breeding, as many of O'Connor's protagonists claim, we have to question just how a "gracious" person can irritate virtually everyone she interacts with—including her own offspring. Mrs. Hopewell is typical in this respect, since she has divorced a husband, cannot get along with her own daughter, and has apparently been through a succession of tenant workers: "Before the Freemans she had averaged one tenant family a year" (273). The latter is apparently a trait of Mrs. Cope and Mrs. McIntyre as well, as both have had problems with retaining employees—we know that at least one family preceded the Pritchards on Mrs. Cope's farm, and Mrs. McIntyre and Astor mention three families that preceded the Shortleys on her farm. This common attribute indicates a basic inability on the part of these women to deal with the needs and concerns of workers, a lack of true maternal solicitude.

Mrs. May of "Greenleaf" not only shares with other O'Connor characters an inability to get along with her own offspring and workers but also assigns the same amount of importance to the established social order as O'Connor's other empowered women. Noting the unnatural rise of the "white trash" Greenleaf boys in the world, she bemoans the possibility of the Greenleafs becoming "society," thus being beyond her control. But unlike most of the other female landowners, Mrs. May does have men on her farm who are capable of helping her run things; unfortunately, Scofield and Wesley have no interest whatsoever either in keeping the farm up or in helping to perpetuate their family. Although Mrs. May defensively refuses to admit them as such, her sons represent more of a threat to the established order than the Greenleafs do. Both are openly rude and contemptuous of their mother, and both refuse to marry and become "respectable," as O. T. and E. T. Greenleaf have done. Mrs. May complains as much as Mrs. Cope, Mrs. McIntyre and Mrs. Fox about her shiftless, lazy and parasitic tenant workers; however, Mrs. May is also burdened with two sons who are even worse than the workers. In Mrs. May's failure to get her sons to help with the farm by trying to wield domestic authority alone, we can see how these other women would be likely to fare if they lacked the additional weapon of economic authority. We can recognize that the admonishing tone used by Mrs. May when addressing her sons is identical to the tone used by the other ladies in addressing their workers, but Scofield and Wesley do not rely upon their mother for their livelihoods: each has a job which is entirely independent of the farm. The result is that they have the freedom to reject maternal authority without fear of economic consequences.

Because she is essentially left "manless" by her sons' apathy, Mrs. May, like Mrs. Cope and Mrs. McIntyre, views the survival of the farm as the product of her hard work alone. The three women virtually echo each other in this respect: Mrs. Cope asserts that she has "the best kept place in the county and do you know why? Because I work. I've had to work to save this place and work to keep it" (178); Mrs. McIntyre likens her efforts to run her farm to Mr. Guizac's "struggle" to survive his displacement, since "she had had a hard time herself. She knew what it was to struggle" (219); Mrs. May believes that "before any kind of judgement seat she would be able to say: I've worked, I have not wallowed" (332). All three women classify their efforts to keep their farms afloat as "work," yet none do any real physical labor—as befits a "lady." While they may "constantly mouth shallow beliefs in the Puritan work ethic" (Morton 58), they surely do not adhere to this ethic themselves. To them, "work" means wielding masculine authority by continually issuing orders and admonitions. Even Mrs. Cope's physical attack on the nut grass is not the act of a "worker," as O'Connor points out with the symbol of the sunhats, introduced in the first paragraph of the story: Mrs. Pritchard's is "faded and out of shape while Mrs. Cope's [is] still stiff and bright and green" (175), indicating that Mrs. Cope is the one who need not wear out her sunhat because she is the one in charge.

As with many of O'Connor's empowered women who speak as if their workers are more of a challenge and an affront than essential to economic survival, Mrs. May discounts the role played by her hired help, viewing the Greenleafs as a trial of her ability to assume the domineering role of the male required to keep her "white trash" workers in line. Mrs. May correctly senses that Mr. Greenleaf hesitates to recognize her authority, though she cannot see that this is partly because he has witnessed the complete breakdown of her maternal authority over her disrespectful sons, who are a stark contrast to his own respectful twins. Furthermore, the May farm lacks an underclass of black workers whose automatic deference to a white employer might serve to establish Mrs. May as an authority figure.

While Mrs. May bemoans the lack of a "man running this place" (329) and claims that the Greenleaf brothers ignore her demands for the removal of the bull because of her gender, it is clear that the treatment she receives is only partly due to her status as a member of the "weaker sex." Mrs. May is ignored simply because she tries too hard to compensate for the lack of a strong male figure by being overly demanding and critical. As is the case with many of O'Connor's empowered women, Mrs. May's relationship with her workers consists of little more than constant demands and complaints of non-compliance. Having been raised on a steady diet of Mrs. May's whining and now being free from their economic dependence upon her, the Greenleaf twins are glad to be able to turn even more of a deaf ear to her than their father does. Although Mrs. May imagines that she is an effective authority figure because of her ability to rule the farm with “an iron hand” (321), Scofield’s mocking of this notion by holding up his mother’s hand, which resembles a “broken lily” (322), demonstrates how weak her authority actually is.

Like Mrs. Cope and Mrs. McIntyre, Mrs. May mistakes hurling verbal abuse for strength and giving commands for struggle. This is the respect in which O’Connor’s empowered women are ultimately failures. While they are temporarily successful at using the power which comes as the result of landownership and the ability to employ workers, all cross the line that separates managing workers from abusing them. If the Southern lady is to be characterized by her ability to charm and delight others, as the stereotype would seem to indicate, then these ladies fall short of the mark. In their efforts to be effective in a traditionally male role, they sacrifice an essential part of the traditional female role for people of their stature and social class. Similarly, these women are just as ineffective in translating maternal authority into managerial authority: their employees come to resent being scolded and regarded as children and come to ignore their orders. Even if this transfer of domestic power to the workplace were possible, the fact remains that Mrs. McIntyre had never established her domestic authority in the Judge’s household, and Mrs. Cope, Mrs. Fox, Mrs. Hopewell and Mrs. May are all weak as maternal authority figures, as all fail to control the actions of their own children.

As is the case with Mrs. Cope and Mrs. McIntyre, Mrs. May also finds herself abandoned by her worker at a crucial time: Mr. Greenleaf is wandering off, ignoring her demand for the bull’s death (just as all other males, both May and Greenleaf, ignore her incessant demands) when the bull charges her. As Paulson has noted, Greenleaf’s inattention to the bull constitutes revenge upon the “castrating woman [who has] emasculated him” (44). As is the case in the other stories, true male power ultimately wins out. As she warns her sons repeatedly, her demise means the demise of the farm as well.

In the end, Mrs. Cope, Mrs. McIntyre and Mrs. May wind up losing their hold on the "places" they had managed to grab from the patriarchy because they ultimately fail to fully synthesize the necessary aspects of both traditional gender roles. All three end up, in essence, "displaced persons." They are, in Westling's terms, "rendered passive by punishment" (145). But while Westling asserts that "O'Connor seems to be demonstrating that independent female authority is unnatural and must be crushed by male force" (158), the fact is that these women's authority was never fully independent due to their absolute reliance upon a thin veneer of social propriety. Despite our distaste for these women, there is something undeniably pathetic about their fate: there is no sense of a "natural" order being restored, only a sense of destruction and loss.

While these women may seem unsympathetic in their handling of power, it should be noted that O'Connor has her disempowered women fare no better than her empowered characters—as illustrated by the fate that befalls Julian's mother at the end of "Everything That Rises," after she has her belief in the social order that elevated her literally knocked out of her. Another helpful text to look at to illustrate the plight of the widow who owns land but is completely lacking in power is "The Life You Save May Be Your Own," in which Mrs. Crater lacks the economic ability to hire workers or have repairs made. O'Connor symbolizes her disempowerment by having her show Shiftlet that she literally has no teeth (i.e., no authority) and that she and her daughter are going nowhere, as her automobile had "quit running" the day her husband died (146). Mrs. Crater is forced by poverty to barter her own daughter in order to get someone to work for her; she must give Shiftlet a share in the farm in order to get him to stay.

Her willingness to make any deal to secure a son-in-law who will agree to stay on the place is seen in her willingness to deal with Shiftlet, even though he openly admits he could be lying to her about his identity because "nowadays, people'll do anything anyways" (147), and though she knows nothing about him other than his declaration,

"I'm a man" (148). But a man is exactly what Mrs. Crater feels she needs to keep her farm running. O'Connor signals this by having her "wonder if a one-armed man could put up a new roof on her garden house" from the outset (148) and by having her offer Shiftlet as "bait" (152) the means to flee (the automobile) as part of the "package" for her daughter—despite her demand that he remain on the farm. Her ordering of items in this package deal also reveals what she knows is truly important to Shiftlet: "you'd be getting a permanent house and a deep well and the most innocent girl in the world" (152). But once Shiftlet assumes the power of her late husband by fixing the car, Mrs. Crater has no way to hold him to the bargain, and her innocent daughter ultimately pays the price for her lack of power. Unlike O'Connor's empowered women, who have the means to shelter and provide for their ungrateful children even well into their adult years, Mrs. Crater can't protect a daughter who is even more vulnerable than she. Disempowerment hardly seems an attractive alternative.

Perhaps O'Connor's stories should be taken as commentaries upon the impossibility of a woman of this society successfully negotiating her way through a patriarchal power structure, since no amount of "masculine" behavior can compensate for the fact that these empowered women are still inferior in the eyes of those they must control in order to survive. As women, their claims upon authority are dubious at best, and the males who destroy them recognize this. If O'Connor is satirizing these characters, it is only because they are too blind to realize that any attempt to mix masculine and feminine roles is destined to fail. Because they can obtain only toleration, but no true respect, from the males upon whom they must depend as a matter of economic necessity, these characters wind up being successful neither as "ladies" nor as bosses. In trying to act both gender roles, these women fail to completely fill the requirements of either. Flannery O'Connor's empowered women are eventually foiled by the representatives of a society unwilling to embrace the paradox they represent.

Works Cited

Morton, Mary L. "Doubling in Flannery O'Connor's Female Characters: Animus and Anima." *The Southern Quarterly* 23.4 (1985): 57-63.

O'Connor, Flannery. *The Complete Stories*. New York: Farrar, Straus and Giroux, 1982.

Paulson, Suzanne Morrow. *Flannery O'Connor: A Study of the Short Fiction*. Boston: G. K. Hall, 1988.

Westling, Louise. *Sacred Groves and Ravaged Gardens: The Fiction of Eudora Welty, Carson McCullers, and Flannery O'Connor*. Athens: U of Georgia P, 1985.

Whitt, Margaret. "Flannery O'Connor's Ladies." *The Flannery O'Connor Bulletin* 15 (1986): 42-50.

The Domestic Dynamics of Flannery O'Connor: *Everything That Rises Must Converge*

Bryant N. Wyatt

By her own avowal, Flannery O'Connor writes from a fixed perspective of Christian orthodoxy. "I write the way I do," she insists, "because (not though) I am a Catholic" and adds that all her stories "are about the action of grace on a character who is not very willing to accept it."[1]

Her view that her stories are all of a piece clearly is not shared by many of her readers and critics, especially those outside her faith who have interpreted her works in ways that she would consider severe distortions of her materials and aims. For example, a variety of O'Connor's critics have expressed reservations ranging from doubt as to whether *any* religious intent is realized in her writings to the suspicion that her artistry is in fact not theological but demonic.[2]

If O'Connor's fiction fails to resonate sufficiently her spiritual theme, part of the reason may lie in her approach to writing. Discussing this approach, she emphasizes her greater attention to the technical demands of the stories than to other criteria affecting the formation and portrayal of her characters. Similarly, to the charge that, morally considered, her characters are typically too ambiguous to serve as either heroes or villains, she offers the defense of her affinity for Henry James's concept of felt life, holding that the writer's moral sense and dramatic sense must coincide (*HB* 124) and that in the best fiction the moral sense will thus emerge intact.

Related to this orientation, in its effect of moderating the religious theme in her works, is the very catholicity, the encompassing embrace, of her outlook. Her protagonists may not be able to support the grace that befalls them, but she loves them nonetheless. Compounding the problem is the fact that she loves the *an*tagonists too and loves them just as much—understandably so, since these are modified into the protagonists of other works and thereby become the objects of the searching grace that finds them lacking. O'Connor confronts a drastically fallen world in which even the remnants of religious belief are vanishing and the instruments and recipients of grace themselves may be as sordid as the damned. She explains:

> I am a Catholic peculiarly possessed of the modern consciousness, that thing Jung describes as unhistorical, solitary, and guilty. To possess this *within* the Church is to bear a burden, the necessary burden for the conscious Catholic. It's to feel the contemporary situation at the ultimate level. I think that the Church is the only thing that is going to make the terrible world we are coming to endurable; the only thing that makes the Church endurable is that it is somehow the body of Christ and that on this we are fed. It seems a fact that you have to suffer as much from the Church as for it but if you believe in the divinity of Christ, you have to cherish the world at the same time that you struggle to endure it. This may explain the lack of bitterness in [my] stories. (*HB* 90)

To feel *ultimately* the contemporary world, though it is inexorably devolving to an unbearable state, as nonetheless the sole precinct and medium for the teleological realization of mankind's salvation through Christ's redemption is, perhaps inevitably, to possess a concomitant ethos riven with ambivalence—constraining love for the thing despised, cherishing of a world beyond endurance, a world of the spiritually blind, the degenerate, the odious. O'Connor's writings belie neither such an ethos nor her embracing of such a world, the world her fiction limns, one whose future inhabitants, she fears, "will know nothing of mystery or manners" (*HB* 92).

This paraphrase of the Henry James speculation on the young woman of the future charts the principal dimensions of her fiction, the nonreceptivity toward the mystery of grace by a society ever less mindful of manners (as codified *caritas*), ever less observant of the gestures and rites nourishing social interaction. At the level of realism O'Connor's fiction dramatizes the clashes among her defective characters in the domain of manners, baring their frailties—selfishness, bigotry, pride—and their dubiousness as vessels of grace. It is no wonder that the supernatural action of grace, since it is unrecognized by those it touches, is also too often scarcely detected by her readers, unless O'Connor employs some seemingly obtrusive authorial device to underscore it, thereby accenting the allegorical component of her work, but, more often than not, weakening its artistry. Both her novels are obviously "marred" by this alleged disjunction, as are several of the pieces in her first short-story collection, *A Good Man Is Hard to Find*,[3] including the title story and, to some extent, what well may have been O'Connor's favorite of all her writings, "The Artificial Nigger."

In the last-written and most realistic of her books, *Everything That Rises Must Converge*, the disjunction is present but not so pronounced, the supernatural impress not so stark, as in the earlier works. The general domestication of the supernal, its attenuation to an appropriate blend with the "manners" component signaling social decay, is indeed one measure of the greater realism of this posthumous collection. And the central locus for this interplay of mystery and manners, the arena wherein the social skirmishes erupt and find resolution, is unremittingly the *domestic* one: the home, the family.

We may say, parenthetically and with due qualification, that the cohesive and nurturing tendency suggested by the centrality of the domestic theme in her stories is one clear index of the feminine consciousness in O'Connor's canon. Another is her deference to females as protagonists, and if not protagonists, at least stabilizers of the domestic realm, keepers of the house. Feministically viewed, an arguable axiom of O'Connor's works is that a male can appear as protagonist or focal character only if he (1) is not the functional (though perhaps titular) family leader or head of household and (2) if head, has no wife alive or physically present.

With a woman, then, established principally as monarch of the domicile (a woman typically bereft, betrayed, despised), the domestic theme in O'Connor's last original collection may be examined, with attention to its sundry functions as medium and catalyst for her characteristic concerns.

* * *

The title story, "Everything That Rises Must Converge," is in its consuming secularity the most uniformly realistic of the volume, and as such provides a useful paradigm. Initially there is the conspicuous paradox of *rising descent*, the rising and convergence of a suppressed group (blacks) in society, while at the same time the society itself is devolving toward *the terrible world we are coming to*—a spiritual decay signified metaphorically by the themes of physical sordidness, displacement, hostility. This complex of degeneration marks a world "too much with us" today, presaging the irresonant, faithless world of tomorrow. The domestic arena becomes in effect a synecdoche of this transfiguration while providing a resistance to it, a tension affording possibilities for desirable modes of human interaction.

Julian's mother (note how O'Connor's women are typically designated by their *familial* roles—*Mrs.* May, his mother, Parker's *wife*, etc.), displaced from the elegant world of her childhood, suffers for attempting to practice her class-conscious mannerisms in a world that is "in a mess everywhere," where social convergence has blurred class distinctions, where "the bottom rail is on the top." Her displacement is heightened by her present status of living with her son Julian in a modest apartment in a neighborhood once fashionable but now deteriorated and dingy, as contrasted with her sense of her real home, the haven of her childhood, her grandfather's "mansion," toward which she reverts in the confusion of her fatal stroke at the story's end.

It has been said that for O'Connor home is always heaven. This is no doubt true in the light of her ultimate view of present society, but this story conveys no palpable awareness of the celestial home (as does, say, the later "Judgement Day"). Here it is only the lost mansion, not heaven, that the mother appears in the end to seek, her heritage—sold, ruined, possessed by Negroes. Significantly, Julian has an obsessive attachment to the house, regularly dreaming about it, assuring himself that only he, not his mother, could have appreciated it, and finally thinking "bitterly of the house that had been lost for him" (13).

Lost *for* him: the symbolic import of the house is enlarged. Of the mother's many sacrifices for Julian, which he rationalizes as demanded in compensation for her ineptness, that of the ancestral home is primal and encompassing. One surmises that the house was lost for Julian's *sake*, that whatever legacy there was to his mother from its sale went to augment the funds scraped together by her in the struggle to better her son's welfare, as her own was largely neglected ("her teeth had gone unfilled so that his could be straightened"). In any case, at another level the house was Julian's link to his mother's world and worldview, her manners and values; though decayed when he saw it as a child, "it remained in his mind as his mother had known it."

Clearly her vision determines and controls his own, here as in other respects, despite his professing that he is "not dominated by his mother." His very being, in fact, seems little more than a reaction to his perception of hers. "Everything that gave her pleasure," we are led to believe, "was small and depressed him," and

> in spite of her, he had turned out so well. In spite of going to a third-rate college, he had, on his own initiative, come out with a first-rate education; in spite of growing up dominated by a small mind, he had ended up with a large one; in spite of all her foolish views, he was free of prejudice and unafraid to face facts. Most miraculous of all, instead of being blinded by love for her as she was for him, he had cut himself emotionally free of her and could see her with complete objectivity. (35-36)

A judicious reading of the story would mitigate these assumptions of Julian's. Consider, for instance, the "miraculous" one that he has severed himself emotionally from his mother and does not return the "blinding" love she has for him. O'Connor is not frivolous in her use of the word *love*; it occurs with startling infrequency in her stories. She asserts,

> I don't think . . . that to be a true Christian you believe that mutual interdependence is a conceit. This is far from Catholic doctrine; in fact it strikes me as highly Protestant, a sort of justification by faith. God became not only a man, but Man. This is the mystery of Redemption and our salvation is worked out on earth according as we love one another, see Christ in one another, etc., by works. This is one reason I am chary of using the word, love, loosely. I prefer to use it in its practical forms, such as prayer, almsgiving, visiting the sick and burying the dead and so forth. (*HB* 102)

Within the family paradigm, the practical acts that issue from parental bonding, acts of caretaking, sacrificial acts, may be added to O'Connor's list, since those performing such acts (usually mothers who receive no gratitude from the children on whom their parental duties are discharged) are among the characters treated most sympathetically in her scheme of extenuation. Here Julian is correct in concluding that his mother loves him but excessive in contending that she is blinded by such love; and his cultivated ability to see her with complete objectivity looms as one of his severest frailties.

In the end what blinds her to him, beyond any recognition, is his rejection of her (evinced through various gestures, notably his viewing her as a *stranger* and contemplating abandoning her when they reach their bus stop, and culminating symbolically in his rationalized complicity with the contemporary forces that erupt in the black woman's assault on her). Ultimately this rejection is recognized for the evil that it was, and Julian tries to (re)establish genuine familial ties, discarding his conception of her as a child ironically after she has reverted psychically to her childhood, as he cries, "Mamma, Mamma." But it is too late. He has succeeded utterly in his sundering denial, succeeded in making them strangers to each other. Looking gropingly at him in the end, she finds "nothing familiar" about him, finds "nothing." She has returned to *her* world, the matrix of her identity, a world that antedates and excludes him.

Earlier Julian ridicules her contention that "he hadn't even entered the real world." It is true; if her sense of herself is unsuited to the modern temper, his premature world-weariness and arrogant misanthropy insulate him from any genuine relationship, even with his mother. It is his rejection of her, his figurative killing of her, that projects the "real world" that he must enter after her death—"the world of guilt and sorrow."

* * *

"Greenleaf" presents another struggling mother with ungrateful offspring, another who is beleaguered and victimized by the changing times. The external antagonists are again placed on the domestic stage, and again the home (homestead) is in danger of being lost. Mrs. May, through industry and perseverance, has succeeded in turning the run-down country property left her by her husband into a viable dairy farm, where she is able to rear and educate her two sons. The Greenleafs, the family of the hired tenant, epitomize for her the inferior order that threatens to supplant the "decent" class of people she represents. Like Julian's mother, she is assured of her social status and character—knows "who she is"—and like Julian, her bachelor sons are peculiarly dependent on her, while mocking her in their cavalier acceptance of, and complicity in, the social change that menaces her. The older, Scofield, takes pride in being "the best nigger-insurance salesman in the county" and taunts her with the professed intent of marrying, after her death, some farm girl to take over the place, someone like Mrs. Greenleaf.

For Mrs. May, Mrs. Greenleaf epitomizes the very dregs of the unsavory Greenleaf clan, a woman who neglects her duties toward her children (e.g., by failing to keep them clean), no mother at all, who directs her attention and energies into a particularly disgusting form of "prayer healing" involving praying and moaning while sprawling on the ground. Of course, for O'Connor Mrs. Greenleaf is a grotesque near-saint, engaged in one of those practical acts—prayer—that manifest Christian love. The prospect of having the place taken over by the likes of *her* repulses Mrs. May, affording an avenue for her son's fiendishly sadistic torment of her.

It is through the Greenleafs that the central themes of the story are realized. In the case of O'Connor's supernatural emphasis, Mrs. Greenleaf and the bull (freighted with symbolism) that finally kills Mrs. May are the principal agents. With respect to the ubiquitous theme of class displacement, the spotlight shifts to the Greenleaf sons, with their foreign wives and progeny. As usual, however, these larger concerns are viewed through the domestic lens, through their impact on the home and family.

The shiftless Greenleafs have managed to produce two sons who, through (in Mrs. May's estimation) their fool's luck, their cunning application of whatever mother wit they possessed, and the largesse of the federal government, have begun to rise in the world. Now situated nearby in their own dairy business, with equipment more modern than hers, they seem poised, in their "international" families, for social climbing and likely to become eventually what she calls "Society." In essence, they will be the inheritors. They have been variously successful where her own sons have failed, a fact kept before her by Mr. Greenleaf's harping upon the superior virtues of *his* sons, especially those involving family obligations: "If hit was my boys they would never have allowed their maw to go out after hired help in the middle of the night. They would have did it theirself." Unlike her sons, who are drastically different and forever squabbling, the Greenleaf twins are practically indistinguishable in name, appearance, family constituency, domicile, and disposition. Further, it is *their* bull that threatens to ruin her herd, which represents her sons' future, while the sons seem not at all to care what happens on or to the place. Her conviction that they will marry "trash" after her death and pass her bequest into the lineage of “scrub humans” leads her to entail the property, preventing their leaving it to their wives. The future and her legacy are reified in the homestead, which promises to be lost, ruined, as Julian’s was.

The crushing domestic blow in O’Connor is familial rejection or denial. Her much-favored story “The Artificial Nigger” reaches its peak of intensity when Mr. Head denies his grandson Nelson, who is reaching out to him for protection in a moment of crisis, by saying to the child’s persecutors, “I never seen him before.” Perhaps it is because, in the theological tradition, the archetypal denial is yoked to the archetypal betrayal in the primal Christian family group of Christ and his disciples that the willful severing of kinship is so crucial for O’Connor. Clearly in the earlier story the episode of denial is heightened, as the estranged boy refuses thereafter to come near his grandfather; and it reaches resolution, resulting in communion, only through the symbolic influence of the Negro statue, a figure for divine grace and a type of crucifix.

In “Greenleaf” there is an arresting involuntary rejection by Mrs. May of her sons when she exclaims that the Greenleaf twins should have been her sons and that *her* boys should have “belonged to that woman!”—Mrs. Greenleaf. (Significantly, this outburst occurs only after one of them declares that he would not milk a cow even to save his mother’s soul from hell.) Once uttered, Mrs. May’s denial is so horrible to her that she is blinded by tears. Again, we see the larger, external theme of class conflict, of chauvinism, being subsumed by the more tangible, internal, and affective one of family loyalty.

The rejection of Mrs. May by her sons, especially by the younger Wesley, is cumulative, reiterative, and complete. Complete, at least, within the confines of the story, since in O’Connor’s panorama there is no *earthly* closure. If her camera were to continue running after Mrs. May’s death on the horn of the bull, for instance, we might see in the sons, as intimated in the case of Julian, an embracing of her as they wake to “the world of guilt and sorrow.” But their rejection here progresses through the ghoulish anticipation of her death to Wesley’s taunting contention that they are not really her sons. This rejection is heightened by an ensuing outburst between them that ends in a fight. The rebuff wounds Mrs. May, who wheezes "like an old horse lashed unexpectedly" and runs from the room. Marking the ultimacy of the rejection is the fact that this is the last time the boys appear in the story, the last time they are together. Again the domestic dynamics inform and adumbrate O'Connor's social and religious themes.

* * *

"A View of the Woods" at its core presents an internecine clash of family loyalties configuring O'Connor's larger socio-theistic concerns. Thematically, the ecological interests implicit in the destruction of nature for the sake of "progress" merge with the spiritual ones involving the symbolic violation of the divine through the proposed sacrificing of the woods and the concomitant destruction of family unity. Tilman, the up-and-coming businessman to whom the lot fronting the woods is sold, is presented as a palpably Luciferian character who is even a little *ahead* of progress, a representative of The Future. The woods, as described and employed, and as O'Connor herself confirms, are associated with Christ. Old man Fortune allies himself with the new class, with destructive secularism, when he champions Tilman and what he stands for. Tilman's anticipated business enterprises will bring the world's conveniences and travelers of all types from across the nation to the family's door. The sale of the lot in front of their house for the construction of Tilman's gas station will initiate this new era. The sale, in Fortune's estimation, will be a supremely beneficent act, redolent of the highest ideals of patriotism, democracy, egalitarianism:

> If his daughter thought she was better than Tilman, it would be well to take her down a little. All men were created free and equal. When this phrase sounded in his head, his patriotic sense triumphed and he realized that it was his duty to sell the lot, that he must insure the future. He looked out the

> window at the moon shining over the woods across the road and listened for a while to the hum of the crickets and treefrogs, and beneath their racket, he could hear the throb of the future town of Fortune. (79-80)

Of course Mary Fortune Pitts, his granddaughter, knows nothing of these larger significances; *her* responses are domestic, familial: a gas station there would obliterate her family's view of the woods and would replace the "lawn" where her daddy, Pitts, grazes his calves. Daughter of Fortune's daughter who married the despised Pitts, the child becomes a hostage in the battle of wills between Fortune and the Pitts nuclear family. That she is like Fortune—his namesake and a replica in appearance and disposition—makes her his, the only Pitts he has any use for, the designated beneficiary of his total estate. At the same time, her parents suspect that since she is favored by her grandfather (because of her resemblance to him), she is the source of his hostility to *them*. So just as he punishes them through his partiality to her at their expense, they retaliate against him by chastising her for assumed complicity with the old man, for serving as a wedge against her own immediate family. Most remarkably, she is accused of putting him up to selling the lot to Tilman, for which suspected act she is beaten by Pitts.

The periodic beatings given Mary Fortune by Pitts remain rather mysterious and problematical throughout the story. Only within the domestic context, with respect to the issue of family integrity, do they become sufficiently meaningful. At first there is some question of whether they actually occur or are merely imagined by Fortune. When it becomes obvious that they are real, they may be assessed as a kind of bugaboo of Fortune's, enraging him by reason of the girl's acceptance of them, her displaying even "something very like cooperation." What remains baffling is that the child continues to fiercely deny them, proclaiming "Nobody's ever beat me in my life and if anybody did, I'd kill him."

A plausible explanation is that for O'Connor the beatings have a far larger symbolic than literal import, that they are received by the child not as punishment for particular wrongdoing (since from all indication she has done no particular wrong) but as acts of familial bonding, acknowledgment by her father and family that she is indeed one of theirs—a Pitts. They become expressions of acceptance denoting a parental prerogative that Fortune cannot proscribe and that, to his dismay, the child embraces.

It follows then that when Fortune attempts to usurp Pitts's authority and beat her himself for the first time (becoming the *nobody* who has ever beaten her, the *anybody* who ever might beat her), the beating becomes a literal one; and she makes good her pledge by, effectively, killing him.

The most conclusive blow in this homicide is not physical but psychological, and again domestic. Once more it is the ultimate terrestrial rejection: the denial of kin. After the girl pounds the old man to the ground in their mortal combat at the end of the story, she looks down into his eyes and says, "You been whipped by me, and I'm PURE Pitts." There are layers of implications here. Fortune, looking up into her eyes, sees his own image as she announces his vanquishment by pure Pitts. Apart from the evident symbolism of the Pitts clan's finally defeating and supplanting him is the less distinct form betokening his ultimate *self*-defeat. The pride resulting in his rejection of his daughter's family, except for the member he appropriates as his own, is incarnated in Mary Fortune; so that pride is the cause of his final overthrow, at the same time that he is inadvertently extinguishing it, as he slays the granddaughter who has spiritually betrayed and abandoned him in identifying with her father, the detested Pitts.

Fortune, of course, has rejected *her* earlier, in another instance of heightened familial denial. Significantly, it occurs when he belittles her for accepting the beatings from her father:

> "Are you a Fortune," he said, "or are you a Pitts? Make up your mind."
>
> Her voice was loud and positive and belligerent. "I'm Mary—Fortune—Pitts," she said.

> "Well I," he shouted, "am PURE Fortune!"
>
> There was nothing she could say to this and she showed it. For an instant she looked completely defeated, and the old man saw with a disturbing clearness that this was the Pitts look. What he saw was the Pitts look, pure and simple, and he felt personally stained by it, as if it had been found on his own face. (82)

The impact of this rejection on the child is telling, and the defeat she suffers associates her thereafter with her father and against Fortune. From this point on in the story, she is deeply morose, glumly unresponsive to all Fortune's efforts to revive their previously communicative banter; "for all the answer he got," "he might have been chauffeuring a small dead body," we are told at one point. She will indeed soon be a small dead body, but already she is dead to him.

Not ignored by O'Connor in her complex of domestic concerns is the dutiful homemaker, Mrs. Pitts, who discharges what she deems her familial obligations to her father in taking care of Fortune in his old age. If her motivation is to be accepted as genuine, against Fortune's conviction of her ulterior motives, she is performing a sacrificial act, being regarded by her father as no more than a tenant while she, apparently against her family's persuasions and with no expectation of reward, stays to care for him. Fortune virtually rejects her when she marries Pitts, concluding that in so doing she has shown that she "preferred Pitts to home"; and a true home is what he has denied her ever since.

* * *

"The Enduring Chill" is the first story in the volume that does not end with an actual or imminent death, though Asbury's conviction of his impending demise suffuses the work. Asbury, the intellectual and would-be artist, has renounced his provincial home and family, seeing his mother as the culprit in the utter failure of his life; but, of necessity, it is to *home* that he returns to die.

Though Asbury is the story's protagonist, the one to be touched by O'Connor's "action of grace," as manifested in the conspicuous descent of the symbolized Holy Ghost upon him at the end, it is his mother who is the domestic focus. He blames her for his expected death; she dismisses the notion that she would *allow* him to die under her parental care, and it is through her efforts—deflecting his verbal attacks and stripping away his illusions at every turn—that his life is dispensed to him and he may begin to become a New Man. Mrs. Fox contends to him that he has a home, something his admired Northern associates would wish they had, and forces upon him the services of the local physician he despises, who, she is aware, will take a personal interest in him. The priest she secures for him expects that he will pray—with his family—and, if they do not pray, will pray *for* them. The mother's black dairy workers, with whom Asbury tries to establish an egalitarian rapport, wonder why he disparages his mother and speculate that the reason is her failure to "whup" him enough when he was little. His efforts to have "communion" with them by inducing them to drink with him unpasteurized milk—against his mother's rules, in defiance of the social and racial taboo, but in this instance also a medical taboo—results in his true disease. He drinks the milk (though the workers do not) and contracts undulant fever, which the country doctor, Block, eventually diagnoses, concluding that Asbury must have drunk some unpasteurized milk "up there."

Essentially it is Asbury's assumed realization that his woes have, in the main, resulted not from his mother's values, the values of home, but from his rejection of them that signals the final peeling away of his illusions. His spiritual deficiencies, exposed by the priest, may be most immediately tied to the religious climax at the end, but the realization of his *domestic* failures undergirds it.

* * *

"The Comforts of Home," as the title suggests, is anchored in the domestic, and in domestic disruption, since the loss of such comforts eventuates for the story's reflector, Thomas. While treating moral concerns, this work is less recognizably religious than "The Enduring Chill." O'Connor's dogma is well insulated by her domestic drama.

What is accentuated in the dramatization is the social theme. Sarah Ham, the "little slut" that Thomas's mother all but adopts and that she obtrudes upon their domain, brings with her the taint of ineffective, perhaps misdirected, institutionalized social services. The mother avers that what she truly needs is a home, though in providing her one she is displacing and alienating her son. A dissembling nymphomaniac who calls herself Star Drake, even Sarah dismisses the woman's do-goodism by labeling her "about seventy-five years behind the times," providing another instance of the ingratitude that frequently greets altruistic efforts in O'Connor's works.

The story illustrates some of the difficulties encountered in O'Connor that inevitably lead to interpretations she would find objectionable. In this regard it is instructive to view it alongside the next story in the collection, "The Lame Shall Enter First." Here, too, out of the impurely good intentions of the homeowner, a disruptive force is brought into the home. Sheppard, seeing the potential in the clubfooted Rufus, attempts to rescue the boy from the stultifying and corruptive effects of his sordid background and the ineptness of related welfarism and to "reform" the boy himself by providing him a real home, even telling himself also that Rufus's presence will have a salutary, charity-building influence on Norton, Sheppard's young son.

Other parallels abound. Like Sarah Ham, Rufus feels no gratitude for the efforts directed toward his betterment and continues to pursue his usual antisocial, even criminal behavior while in the home of his benefactor, in some sense treacherously desecrating its sanctity. Neither has had a genuine home before, but each seems remarkably indifferent to the one generously provided. Thomas informs his mother that Sarah is "nothing but a slut. She makes fun of you behind your back.

She means to get everything she can out of you and you are nothing to her" (119). His mother concedes as much, saying, "I know I'm nothing but an old bag of wind to her." Likewise, when Norton tries to protest to his father about Rufus's breach of domestic ethics—sullying the sanctum of his dead mother's room and her personal effects, dancing, in her corset, with the black cook—Sheppard condemns him for tattling and will brook no denigration of Rufus, who mocks his reform attempts and disparages him for thinking himself Jesus Christ. The "congenital liar" Sarah, having been analyzed and instructed by psychiatrists, "knows" that she is incorrigible, that there is "no hope for her." Rufus flaunts *his* resistance to (Sheppard's) do-goodism, bragging that he persists in committing crimes because he's good at it and that he is in the power of Satan. The similarities go on and on.

A crucial difference is in intended impact; one gathers that O'Connor sanctions the charitable efforts of Thomas's mother. She has written that in "The Comforts of Home" "nobody is redeemed" but she explains that

> the old lady is the character whose position is right and the one who is right is usually the victim. If there is any question of a symbolic redemption, it would be through the old lady who brings Thomas face to face with his own evil—which is that of putting his own comfort before charity (however foolish). His doing that destroys the one person his comfort depended on, his mother. (*HB* 434)

Her opinion of Sheppard's efforts, however, is clarified when she labels him "a man who thought he was good and thought he was doing good when he wasn't" (*HB* 490).

It may be asked to what extent these contrasting assessments are supported by O'Connor's fictional treatment and realized through her dramatization. Her tenet that the one who is right is usually the victim may be illuminating, but questions are raised concerning her definition of victimization. Does the victim have to die, for example, as Thomas's mother does and O'Connor's characters so often do? If a necessary determinant, is death a *sufficient* determinant of victimization? A case can be made in Thomas's behalf, defending him against the charge of "evil" that O'Connor makes. His analysis of his mother's behavior seems sound enough:

> There was an observable tendency in all her actions. This was, with the best of intentions in the world, to make a mockery of virtue, to pursue it with such mindless intensity that everyone involved was made a fool of and virtue itself became ridiculous. . . . Had she been in any degree intellectual, he could have proved to her from early Christian history that no excess of virtue is justified. . . . His own life was made bearable by the fruits of his mother's saner virtues—by the well-regulated house she kept and the excellent meals she served. But when virtue got out of hand with her, as now, a sense of devils grew upon him. (114)

Likewise, Walter Sullivan sees the mother's generosity as representing a "kind of sentimental, self-serving charity" resulting "from a misunderstanding of ultimate truth" (10). Furthermore, Thomas's perception of Sarah's incorrigibility, her being beyond their help and better off in an institution, appears plausible.

The key to his culpability in O'Connor's scheme seems to lie in her rather deterministic revelation that Thomas "had inherited his father's reason without his ruthlessness and his mother's love of good without her tendency to pursue it." In other words, his problem is his very makeup as a family constituent. But in the context of the story this is far from obvious as a problem of culpability. Sarah is such an utterly repulsive character that his stance toward her has merit, and he does wonder, at least, what the attitude of God was to the "moral moron" Sarah—"meaning if possible to adopt it." Moreover, the voice of his dead father impugning the mother's impulsive violation of their home seems a defensible complement to Thomas's own outrage. Additionally, Thomas's mother virtually rejects him, ostensibly a grievous offense in O'Connor's moral scheme. He gives his mother an ultimatum—she must choose between him and Sarah, and she obviously chooses "the little slut" by bringing her back to the house. And on another occasion she allows the girl to stay there longer than just the one night she assures him of; so her credibility as a character is further reduced vis-à-vis his.

The voice of the dead father warrants further consideration. It is one of several components suggesting a mildly feminist strain in the story, wherein the inferior status of female characters is tacitly criticized through the mere highlighting of selected features illustrating their secondary condition. The man, we learn, was ruthless and a hypocrite, a dissembler who, in making the country men regard him as one of them, had "lived his lie" without ever having to tell one. Clearly, while alive he had been at odds with his wife over her "mindless charity" but apparently knew how to "handle her," how to "put his foot down." Thomas lacks his father's attributes in this respect, and to the old man this indicates that Thomas's masculinity is questionable. He belittles Thomas for letting a woman dominate him, proclaiming that she had never driven *him* from his own table. "Show her who's boss," his voice goads Thomas; "[you] let her run over you. You ain't like me. Not enough to be a man" (120).

Extending this strain is Farebrother, the sheriff that Thomas finally goes to see for help, who has known the father and who apparently shares his temperament and tendencies. Farebrother reminds Thomas that the old man would never truckle to a woman and, after agreeing to come to the house and investigate Sarah's taking of the gun, orders him to "keep out of my way—yourself and them two women too."

There are hints of the feminist concern in other stories, e.g., "Greenleaf," where the Greenleaf females seem to be slighted in deference to the male children and to diminish in importance as the action progresses, and where Mrs. May laments that she is the victim, has always been because she is a woman. In "The Comforts of Home," though, as has been suggested, the voice of the dead father may well be taken not merely as a continuation of the battle of wills between the man and his widow but as the force sent to correct the disgraced status of the house resulting from her disruption of its domestic harmony through her "mindless" charity.

The word "mindless" is pertinent, since it fits into the mind-heart dichotomy so prominent in O'Connor's works. (The argument in the title story over the seat of genuine culture—the mind versus the heart—exemplifies the pattern of hyperrational, unfeeling characters scattered through her fiction.) Here the dichotomy operates most intensely within Thomas himself. Arguably, he may possess the better, or at least less extreme, qualities of both his respective parents—his father's reason, his mother's love of good—without their "worse" ones—ruthlessness and the (excessive) tendency to pursue good. But it is the ruthlessness of the dead father that invades Thomas in the end, signified by the gun (inherited from the old man) and her dead husband's voice that the mother hears issuing from the lips of her son before the trigger is pulled to end her life. The old man evidently triumphs.

Perhaps the strongest feature of the mother's altruism, making it a thing of the heart and therefore blessed for O'Connor, is again domestically based; it is seeing others as her own children. The protagonist of the title story in O'Connor's first volume evinces the action of grace when she recognizes the Misfit as one of her children before he kills her. Thomas's mother demonstrates the radical Christian virtue of loving thy neighbor as thyself, of holding even strangers in no less esteem than one's own kin. This is driven home to us by the reiterated explanation for her avid concern with Sarah's welfare: "I keep thinking it might be you," she repeatedly tells her son. The familial dimension of "The Comforts of Home" is vital. In no other of O'Connor's stories is it more deeply based or more multifunctional.

The altruism of Sheppard in "The Lame Shall Enter First" is of a different order. His attitude toward his son Norton falls somewhere between condescension and contempt. Hence his benevolence concerning Rufus is hollow—vain, mind-driven, absent of heart. His actions are dictated by self-regard, cold theory, social scientism, as opposed to sincere personal engagement. Rufus succinctly sizes up Sheppard by remarking that he may be good but he "ain't *right*."

Symbolically, because of the emptiness of his motivation, Sheppard is unable to create the family he attempts by positioning Rufus as a prospective brother to (actually a replacement of) his real son, and (the father rationalizes) deflecting Norton's obsessive attachment to his dead mother.

Sheppard stresses the "selfishness" in the child's fixation, but at least the attachment is concrete—to a real person whose death Norton cannot comprehend or accept, which cannot be mitigated (but rather is enhanced) by Sheppard's materialistic denial of a hereafter. And Norton's devotion is necessarily filial, born of a relationship with an integral member of the family and home he has known. Ironically, just as Rufus supplants Norton as Sheppard's son, he also replaces Sheppard as Norton's parent.[4] The latter act is prepared for by Sheppard's rejection of Norton—as usual in highly intensified scenes. After desecrating the dead mother's room, Rufus is given her bed to sleep in; Norton becomes so incensed that his father whips him. Then the utter denial occurs when Sheppard refuses to entertain the thought that Rufus, despite the certainty of the police concerning his guilt, could have left the movie he attended with Norton and broken into a house, as alleged. The captivation is so complete that he misconstrues the words expressing Rufus's enthrallment of him as *thanks* and responds by calling Rufus "son." Immediately thereafter, as he sees Norton beckoning him from across the hall, he decides he cannot go to him without violating Rufus's presumed trust. Norton, of course, would have told him that Rufus *did* leave the theater to commit the break-in, but Sheppard willfully ignores the child's call. He denies his son. We are told that, in response, the child "sat for some time looking at the spot where his father had stood. Finally his gaze became aimless and he lay back down" (153).

After this, we may conclude, the forsaken Norton's central objective is to establish contact with his *one* parent—who resides, according to Rufus, in the sky. Rufus plants the seed of suicide in the child's consciousness through teaching him the Bible, and finally triumphs over Sheppard in their struggle for the boy's soul when Norton hangs himself to join his mother in heaven.

The story shows that rationalized "good works" fail and that human (i.e., familial) sentiment is genuine, *right*, as the ground of altruism. But O'Connor becomes uncharacteristically didactic at the end and restates what has been portrayed, that Sheppard had tried to stuff "his own emptiness with good works" and "had ignored his own child to feed his vision of himself" (164). He at long last feels a rush of love for Norton, vows never to let him suffer again; but the child is gone. With this culmination the religious and domestic themes converge, and, as the story's action illustrates, the domestic configuration is once again a sounding board for the spiritual voice.

* * *

In "Revelation" the domestic theme is rendered essentially in interfamilial terms. O'Connor again brings to the fore class-consciousness and apprehension regarding the changing times, the new age, connecting the two with her religious component and giving them all about equal emphasis. The most comic of these stories, "Revelation" presents the unlikely phenomenon in O'Connor of a female protagonist with a living spouse, a more than incidental feature.

Through Mrs. Turpin's consciousness the gallery of characters is introduced in the doctor's waiting room; the descriptive details individualize each, yet place them all neatly in her pattern of class stratification, as outlined in her pastime of "naming the classes of people":

> On the bottom of the heap were most colored people . . . then next to them . . . were the white trash; then above them were the home-owners, and above them the home-and-land-owners, to which she and Claud belonged. Above

> she and Claud were people with a lot of money and much bigger houses and much more land. But here the complexity of it would begin to bear in on her, for some of the people with a lot of money were common and ought to be below she and Claud and some of the people who had good blood had lost their money and had to rent and then there were colored people who owned their homes and land as well. . . . Usually by the time she had fallen asleep all the classes of people were moiling and roiling around in her head, and she would dream they were all crammed in together in a box car, being ridden off to be put in a gas oven. (170)

Those in the waiting room are delineated by their words, dress, and demeanor, but it is important to note that *domestic* connections form the axis on which the class distinctions revolve and are a principle of character evaluation. Being "white-trashy," for instance, does not inhere simply in lack of possessions or education; it is revealed in the failure to keep one's child clean or teach it proper behavior. Also, the familial focus can serve as a means of *dis*junction. Mary Grace, the ugly girl whose pivotal act of assaulting Mrs. Turpin forms the story's climax, is viewed as an ungrateful family aberration, almost incomprehensible to her mother. A friendly and "stylish" lady, the mother criticizes the girl's thanklessness and failure to appreciate her advantages, i.e., her supportive, loving, sacrificing family and all it has provided for her. In this way the familial theme is dispersed in the story, serving as a generalized elastic device of coherence and emphasis. It is the abstract concept of family that serves functionally as a kind of meta-setting, as opposed to the conventional O'Connor application of the literal and immediate family.

But the immediate familial relationship is not completely neglected. Just before Mary Grace attacks her, Mrs. Turpin is rhapsodically expressing gratitude for her blessings:

> "If it's one thing I am," Mrs. Turpin said with feeling, "it's grateful. When I think who all I could have been besides myself and what all I got, a little of

> everything, and a good disposition besides, I just feel like shouting, 'Thank you, Jesus, for making everything the way it is!' It could have been different!" For one thing, somebody else would have got Claud. At the thought of this, she was flooded with gratitude and a terrible pang of joy ran through her. "Oh thank you Jesus, Jesus, thank you!" she cried aloud. (177)

It is worthy of note that the possibility of someone else's getting her husband Claud is not part of what she says, but something she thinks, realizes—and the realization of her husband as a gift fills her with joy and impels her to shout her thanks; which in turn causes the ugly Mary Grace to hurl the book at her face. Aside from whatever O'Connor's intent may be in having the assault occur on this note, the fact remains that what is set in pointed relief here is the primary domestic relationship—husband and wife.

At this point, with the girl's attack, the dispersed domesticism of the waiting room ends, and the reader is prepared for the Turpins' return to their actual domicile and family context. Emphasis here appears in the fact that Mrs. Turpin cherishes the reality that their home is still there ("she would not have been startled to see a burnt wound between two blackened chimneys"). More appears in the rather peculiar exchange between the spouses later, in bed, when instead of discussing the girl's indictment of her (an "old wart hog" from hell), Mrs. Turpin solicitously asks her husband how his injured leg feels, and later, when he is about to leave to take their workers home, impulsively says, "Kiss me." And, finally, before she has her revelation—of all the classes of people ultimately marching into heaven—there is a signal occurrence. She has just vocally confronted Christ, charging that even if he decrees that the class divisions be erased and the "bottom rail" put on top, there will still be a class system, a hierarchy, "a top and a bottom." Then she sees in the distance Claud's departing truck and realizes that "at any moment a bigger truck might smash into it and scatter Claud's and the niggers' brains all over the road" (185). She remains fixed and anxious until she sees Claud's truck returning, sees it turn into their own road, to safety; only then does the spiritual revelation occur to her. In short, "Revelation" stresses social class-consciousness, minimizes *starkly* moral concerns, and follows the expected pattern of rendering the spiritual message in a domestic context.

* * *

"Parker's Back" is the least verisimilar, the most biblically allegorical, of all the stories in the collection. It has the least coherence and substance in the mimetic sense, and its characters are seemingly the most manipulated by O'Connor's religious thrust. The religious theme is paramount, even to the extent that it distorts and vitiates the realistic tenor of O'Connor's presentation. Despite all this, however, the domestic theme is discernible in several respects relating to significant events in the title character's life: (1) Parker's *mother* took him to revival, though he ran away and joined the navy; (2) his mother is responsible—paid—for the notable tattoo of his, but insisted that it include her name; (3) against his will Parker gets married, but marriage makes him gloomier than ever; (4) he feels the need for a tattoo on his back, but wants only one his wife would like; (5) he is surprised to be capable of staying with a woman who is pregnant; (6) he is driven to get a strange tattoo on his back (he says) *because* he married a woman who is pregnant; (7) it seems that all along his real desire was to please her (his wife); and so on.

Further, though relatively muted, a pattern of O'Connor's larger domestic concerns is detectable. For example, one senses the theme of displacement when Parker is in the city getting his transforming tattoo. He feels isolated and longs to be home with his wife, Sarah Ruth. And of course there is the theme of rejection—by Parker's cohorts, his "society," when he is thrown out of the pool hall,[5] and by his wife. He has in a sense betrayed her through dissimulation regarding his female employer's attitude toward him and the like. Sarah Ruth rejects him, at least the secular him that has attempted to deceive her, by not responding at last to his preferred name but only to the Testamentary one—Obadiah Elihue.[6]

In this story the domestic theme resonates in other subtle ways. When Parker comes home with his ultimate tattoo and his wife will not admit him until he submits to identifying himself with the name he despises, she has symbolically *named* him. After chastening him for his deception, aware now of the truth of his status with the female employer, she whips him with a broom. At one level of implication, she has become his mother, dominating him as she might a child. Here, earlier strains assume related significance—the fact that she had to marry before having children, that he has been repulsed by her pregnancy, that he from all appearances has never known his own motivations, his identity. The story ends with him beaten, standing outside, "crying like a baby." Metaphorically, he is a baby, i.e., "born again"—the symbolic fruition of her pregnancy; and whatever implication this episode may carry thematically, it is steeped in domesticity.

* * *

The closing story, "Judgement Day," fittingly recapitulates a number of themes sounded in the earlier selections. Not the least of these is that of domestic displacement. As in the title story, the family holdings have been lost, along with the social status they signified. Old Tanner, a former landowner who raised four children, "was somebody when he was somebody," his daughter contends, but now he is decrepit and dispossessed, feebly seeking his Georgia homeland to serve as his final resting place. He, like Julian's mother, is spiritually rebuffed by his offspring and suffers a stroke after being accosted by a Negro who takes offense at a racially insensitive act.

Again the racial encounters illustrate the social phenomenon of rising descent that O'Connor projects. The blacks, as they advance—demonstrating for some the government's inexorable effort to turn society "upside-down," to put "the bottom rail on top"—grow ever more assertive and testy, consequently engaging in confrontations with those Southern whites continuing to exhibit traditional racial mores. Sometimes, as in the cases of Julian's mother and Tanner, these confrontations prove deadly.

But the roles of the blacks in "Judgement Day" are just as vital to O'Connor's treatment of the story's domestic theme. Coleman, whom Tanner has mentally vanquished with the symbolic aid of the "spectacles" he absently fashions from bark and hay wire, becomes Tanner's domestic servant in their "home"—the shack they construct together as squatters on a plot of vacated land later purchased by a local Negro (only part black, also Indian and white), Doctor Foley. Tanner realizes, as does Foley, that his white skin, with "the government" against him, is no longer a badge of superiority; and Foley gives him the option of becoming *his* servant or being evicted.

Rather than accept such a humiliating role, Tanner goes to live with his daughter in her apartment in New York—which he finds a hellish new world, an impersonal "no-place," inhabited by "all stripes of foreigner, all of them twisted in the tongue." Desmond summarizes its racial and social dynamics:

> The New York world of Tanner's daughter is one ostensibly marked by social progress, at least to the extent that a relative equality exists between whites and Negroes. But underlying this superficial advance is the deeper fact of spiritual alienation, signified by the estrangement from others that characterizes urban life there, the people of each race guardedly "minding their own business." In short, it is a mock community, a perversion of the idea of mystical community, a society which has lost the long view of history because it has turned away from the spiritual roots of such a mystical vision. (78)

Here even Tanner's daughter is a stranger to him, one whose philosophy, too, is non-engagement ("Live and let live"), who shuts him out by conversing with herself, who ridicules his religious beliefs as "Baptist hooey," and who intends to renege on her promise to have him buried at home, in Georgia. This familial betrayal is the unkindest cut of all, and Tanner concludes that he made a colossal mistake in coming to live with her, that Coleman and he constituted a more genuine family, and that now he would gladly be Foley's lackey, his "white nigger," if it meant he could live again in the departed shack that used to be his home.

From this ungodly no-place, symptomatic of that terrible world we are coming to, Tanner must escape. His attempts to do so bring O'Connor's social and theistic themes into panoptic integration with their domestic vehicle. The black actor, whom Tanner has refused to except from his racially stereotypical views, tellingly asserts his difference by proclaiming that he is not any "coal man" before his violent disposal of Tanner as the story draws to a close. The irony in his apparently mistaking Tanner's confused tentative greeting—"Coleman?"—as merely a vocational label, instead of in effect a compounded racial typing, is pronounced. Even more so is the irony suffusing the fatal attack itself on Tanner, in response to the old man's plea for help to get home, an act of hostility that results in sending him not at once to the geographical home, which the old man immediately seeks, but to the otherworldly, eternal one for which he secretly longs.[7] The homicidal act by "Preacher" becomes underhandedly a benevolent rite.

It remains only for the daughter to complete the domestic resolution of the work. She betrays her pledge to Tanner and buries his body there in New York City. But afterward, though herself a professed nonbeliever like the black Northern actor, she is unable to sleep well until she has her father raised and sent home as she had promised—after which her peace and good looks return. We may well see this corrective adjustment in the daughter's attitude as yet another instance of O'Connor's "action of grace." Nonetheless, its resulting gesture, the final and consummating act of the book, is firmly positioned on the clearly *domestic* fulcrum of filial obligation, familial duty.

Notes

1. *The Habit of Being* (hereafter cited as *HB*) 275.

2. See Gentry, ch. 8.

3. Reprinted, along with the two novels, in *Three*.

4. Gentry validly sees Sheppard taking Rufus to replace the dead wife and cites as evidence Rufus's putting on her corset, being given her room, insinuating vague "immoral suggestions" on Sheppard's part, etc. (155-59).

5. For commentary on the virtual absence of society in O'Connor and its implications, see Kessler ch. 11 (esp. 71-73).

6. Useful remarks on the biblical significance of the name are provided by Driskell and Brittain (116 ff.).

7. O'Connor's frequent ambiguity regarding death with respect to her characters has led critics to disagree over how, and sometimes even whether, they die (Tanner, Mr. Fortune, Julian's mother, etc.). The question here is not whether Tanner dies but the nature and extent of involvement by the black actor in the death. Walker, for example, observes that "he stuffs [Tanner's] head, arms, and legs through the banisters of the stairway 'as if in a stockade,' and leaves him to die" (54). Whether Tanner's actual death occurs after, before, or during the stuffing, the actor's assault(s) must be taken as its major literal cause. The figurative causes (typically precipitating the literal), in this story and other pertinent ones, have to do with character deficiencies in the victims themselves.

Works Cited

Desmond, John F. *Risen Sons: Flannery O'Connor's Vision of History*. Athens: U of Georgia P, 1987.

Driskell, Leon V., and Joan T. Brittain. *The Eternal Crossroads: The Art of Flannery O'Connor*. Lexington: UP of Kentucky, 1971.

Gentry, Marshall Bruce. *Flannery O'Connor's Religion of the Grotesque*. Jackson: UP of Mississippi, 1986.

Kessler, Edward. *Flannery O'Connor and the Language of Apocalypse*. Princeton: Princeton UP, 1986.

O'Connor, Flannery. *Everything That Rises Must Converge*. 1965. New York: Signet, 1967.

____________. *The Habit of Being*. Ed. Sally Fitzgerald. New York: Farrar, Straus and Giroux, 1979.

____________. *Three: Wise Blood (1952), A Good Man Is Hard to Find (1955), The Violent Bear It Away (1960)*. New York: Signet, 1964.

Sullivan, Walter. "Flannery O'Connor, Sin, and Grace: *Everything That Rises Must Converge*." *The Hollins Critic* 2.4 (1965): 1-10.

Walker, Alice. "Beyond the Peacock: The Reconstruction of Flannery O'Connor." *Ms*. Dec. 1975. Rpt. in *In Search of Our Mothers' Gardens*. New York: Harcourt, 1984. 42-59.

"The Artificial Nigger" and the Redemptive Quality of Suffering

Richard Giannone

> . . . suffering produces endurance, and endurance produces character, and character produces hope. . . .
>
> —Romans 5:3

"The Artificial Nigger" occupies a special place among the ten stories comprising *A Good Man Is Hard To Find*. "I suppose," Flannery O'Connor writes to her friend "A," "'The Artificial Nigger' is my favorite."[1] Since 1955, when it was published, "The Artificial Nigger" has come to rank just as high in its appeal to readers. It is a staple of anthologies and a source of continual analysis. But the fascination that "The Artificial Nigger" holds for readers runs counter to O'Connor's enthusiasm. In fact, the history of its popularity is a history of discontent, especially over the way in which the action ends.

At the center of the controversy lies a simple tale. Mr. Head takes his grandson to Atlanta for the day. Nelson was born in Atlanta and uses his place of birth to boast of his importance. The boy's impudence rankles Mr. Head, so he plans the trip to teach the boy a few things about authority. Once in Atlanta, they get lost. Exhausted and terrified, Nelson accidently knocks down a woman, who screams for justice by threatening Mr. Head. Frightened himself, Mr. Head says that he does not know the boy. The denial estranges grandson from grandfather. As they walk back single file for the train, they see a battered lawn statue of a Negro. This plaster figure unites them, and they return to their rural home.

This one-day excursion has called forth multiple readings. Critics have provided the expected glosses on Nelson's rite of passage,[2] Mr. Head's bigotry,[3] their joint reenactment of original sin,[4] and the descent they make into hell.[5] O'Connor herself widens the interpretive horizon by citing "Peter's denial" (*Letters*, p. 101), "the Christ-Child"

(*Letters*, p. 78), and "what the South has done to itself" (*Letters*, p. 140). She complicates matters further by sweeping aside speculation to say that "The Artificial Nigger" is "a story in which there is an apparent action of grace" (*Letters*, p. 160). "What I had in mind to suggest with the artificial nigger," she avows to Ben Griffith, "was the redemptive quality of the Negro's suffering for all of us" (*Letters*, p. 78).

The intrusion of God's favor through the statue has been anything but apparent to most readers. Critical consensus translates the statue back into its opposite, finding it a means of punishment. James Napier cites O'Connor's remarks on the story to show how far astray the assertions of imprisonment and ironic salvation have taken us from O'Connor's clear intention.[6] However, such quarrels are instructive. They tell us something about the assumptions O'Connor's art contends with, and they invite us to consider just what signals in the story are evident to O'Connor but equivocal to her audience.

Since the ending of the story does not bring the reader to the barricades of civil protest, the social activist will be disappointed with this version of the South's tragedy. Even the reader with larger moral interests is left pondering how the statue acquires its saving purpose when all we have is a quiet homecoming to an all-white backwoods. Were the story political, the question would be superfluous, since the urgency of reform would be built into the stereotyped figure. O'Connor is not, of course, one for ready-made liberalism. Meaning for her comes through what is shown, and she then goes after a significance beyond the sociological and psychological. Frederick Asals is sensitive to that felt meaning and still has reservations about the outcome of the story. "What after all have the Heads really learned by the end of 'The Artificial Nigger'? How have their attitudes toward blacks been altered?"[7]

If we require a political answer, the story will frustrate us. Moreover, we will miss the story's depth. Even the word *radical* in its sharpest political denotation will not touch the root of Mr. Head's transformation. The old man learns the lesson of the cross. That recognition of his share in the suffering of another person for him alters more than his attitude toward blacks. It changes his attitude toward himself, toward everyone, and toward God. The result is that Mr. Head and Nelson and the artificial nigger become one in an invisible body. But in using such a Pauline phrase as "invisible body" so soon, the argument is running ahead of itself. The essential point to be made now concerns how a writer with a theological habit of mind works. The spiritual writer not only takes shortcuts through social history but reverses the direction of analysis. To the historian, injustice and bigotry and war and anguish all cause human psychological disorder. To O'Connor, however, racism is not the cause but the result of an inner disruption. Human exploitation is another manifestation of the spirit's refusal to know itself and to accept its own suffering. Racism, seen by this light, is a disease of the soul which spreads out into human relationships and to the body politic. What would seem to have gratified O'Connor was how "The Artificial Nigger" forced her special kind of spiritual inquiry through a burning political surface into the fallen center of the human condition.

The sore point between the sixty-year-old Mr. Head and the ten-year-old Nelson is their need for each other. After his wife dies, and after his daughter runs away only to return with Nelson before she herself dies, Mr. Head becomes the sole parent of the one-year-old boy. He raises Nelson to be independent and strong-willed, strengths that would make the hard job of raising a grandson easier. Mr. Head succeeds so well at parenthood that he makes Nelson into a feisty competitor. They clash to preserve their cherished independence. Atlanta is a ruse. The distant city allows them to assert their authority without upsetting the balance of domestic caretaking both strike with each other. They can argue about Atlanta and still be vulnerable in the everyday ways that count. They take for granted their shared male life in the hills. On the day they see the real Atlanta, old man and young boy also see the rare gift of love they enjoy.

O'Connor gives us hints of the journey's importance. She compares Mr. Head to Vergil going to Dante, "or better, Raphael, awakened by a blast of God's light to fly to the side of Tobias."[8] Raphael, whose name means "God heals" in Hebrew, is Mr. Head's image of his moral guidance of Nelson through the strange city. But as it turns out, the angel of healing comes to remove the white film of self-sufficiency from the eyes of both. Angelic intervention comes none too soon. Rivalry is wearing them down into reflections of each other's willfulness; "they looked enough alike to be brothers and brothers not too far apart in age . . ." (105). They do battle from the moment they wake up. Nelson has corn pone cooking and meat fried before his grandfather rises. As they eat breakfast, each stares at "a fiercely expressionless face" (105) that resists owning up to their nine years of dependency.

Racism arises not out of any direct contact with blacks but rather out of this condition of unexpressed feeling. Since the boy has a headstart on the day by preparing breakfast, the man recovers his place by asserting the one bit of knowledge he has about their destination. Atlanta will not please Nelson, Mr. Head declares, because "'It'll be full of niggers'" (105). Nelson has never seen a black person; they were run out of his grandfather's county twelve years ago. "Nigger" for the ten-year-old means the power Mr. Head holds over him which he must overcome. What Nelson hates is his own weakness. He calls that shadow of himself *nigger*. In hating the shadow, he can avoid facing the actual peril and obligation of susceptibility. Racism works the same way for the old man. The boy's ingratitude, heightened by the self-doubt a rural man feels about the big city, can be put aside by having a "nigger" on whom to heap all the fear and denial. The very word "nigger" becomes a talismanic justification for a meanness which Mr. Head would ordinarily find inconsistent with "that calm understanding of life that makes him a suitable guide for the young" (102).

On the train, Mr. Head manages to allay his apprehension about Atlanta. He projects onto Nelson his fear of being exposed as inadequate in the same way that he used the shadow of the black person. "'He's never seen anything before,'" Mr. Head announces across the train aisle to a bleary-eyed stranger, "'Ignorant as the day he was born, but I mean for him to get his fill once and for all'" (108). Mr. Head basks in confidence. Soon a black man escorting two black women comes down the aisle, and Mr. Head can show off. Vergil quizzes Dante on the new sight. "'What was that?'" (110). Nelson describes the man as the man he is, apart from Mr. Head's projected image. The boy fails to see a "nigger," "'his first nigger'" (111), Mr. Head informs the weary stranger across the aisle. Mr. Head alleviates his fear of appearing a bumpkin by humiliating Nelson through a stranger. Nelson's humiliation solidifies his racism. The boy cannot admit his vulnerability with his grandfather and finds an object [outside himself] to make his pain and rage concrete. "He felt that the Negro had deliberately walked down the aisle in order to make a fool of him and he hated him with a fierce raw fresh hate; and also, he understood now why his grandfather disliked them" (110-111). Hatred curtains responsibility. The guilt Nelson incurs from ill-will dissolves in the accusation of the innocent black passerby. Now the black man owes Nelson the expiation of the boy's inhibited guilt feeling.

The formal aura of the dining car brings out the intimidation which Nelson tries to mask through racist projection. Mr. Head decides to show Nelson the kitchen, but a black waiter stops him. To save face before the black man's rebuff, Mr. Head shouts an accusation about cockroaches in the kitchen. However feeble it may seem to other passengers, such quick wit before sudden rebuke impresses Nelson. The boy takes pride in the verbal finesse with which his grandfather handles threats to his dignity. The boy senses that he will need that protection against the unknown terrors of Atlanta. As they approach the wicked city, Nelson appreciates that he "would be entirely alone in the world if he were ever lost from his grandfather" (112). Here is the part of Nelson that will not be lied to; it speaks to him now about his need and love for Mr. Head. From this honest place rushes an impulse to seize the man's coat. But Nelson holds back. The price Nelson pays for not expressing the truth "that his grandfather was indispensable to him" (113) is the loss of comfort he needs.

In town the fear bedeviling both comes true. They get lost. The psychological effect is strong. But *lost* is in this story more than a hillbilly's paralysis amid a department-store maze, more than his forfeiting a lifelong reputation of competence in the backwoods. A fundamental security is at stake. Direction involves the heart's inclination toward the bond between grandparent and grandchild. The reference to Dante suggests how we are to take their being lost in Atlanta. Those who leave the straight path "walk in the ways of darkness," we read in Proverbs 2:13-14, and they "rejoice in doing evil and delight in the perverseness of evil." So goes the scriptural source for Dante's awakening before his infernal journey. There are many allusive signposts alerting the reader that Mr. Head and Nelson are moving in Dante's footsteps. The dome, like Dante's sun in Purgatory, is the geographical center of the journey. It points homeward. O'Connor's Vergil strays from the guiding center. Mr. Head turns "to the left" (115). Left and left again, this suitable guide for the young misguides his charge. They head into Dante's sinister (*sinistra*) way. The landscape grows treacherous. The strange woman indigenous to the underworld presses the evil allurements of the region on the innocent young visitor. As Dante negotiates hell in circles, so O'Connor's travelers proceed through Atlanta in circles. For them the circular passage traces a vicious repetition of their old feud. As they go lower, their power-play intensifies, until they live out the dire prediction of Wisdom in Proverbs that those who stray from the commandment to love will take pleasure in evil. Mr. Head and Nelson enjoy malice. Each strikes at the other's weakness with satanic precision. "'This is where I come from!'" (115) taunts Nelson. With a cruelty equal to the assault on his authority, Mr. Head shoves the boy's head into the sewer. Again the old codger transfers his fear of the city to the boy, now in vivid images of rats and of overwhelming pitch-black tunnels. The boy who has learned quickly how to overcome his genuine terror with accusation, shifts blame back onto his guide. "'I don't believe you know where you're at!'" (116) The boy's newfound racism allows him to brag of a security he does not feel. And racism allows Mr. Head a momentary upper hand. "'Anybody wants to be from this nigger heaven can be from it!'" (118)

Their delight in can-you-bottom-this culminates when a crowd of women gathers around Nelson. In a daze the boy runs down an elderly woman. Other women are milling around "to see justice done." "'You've broken my ankle,'" screams the old woman on the pavement, "'and your daddy'll pay for it!'" (122). At the shout of "'Police! Police!'" Mr. Head reluctantly edges forward from his hiding place, from which he startled Nelson into running in the first place. Terror triggers in the boy the basic instinct to grasp secure warmth. When Nelson sees Mr. Head, the child clings to his grandfather's hips. But the old man's inner demon has a tighter grip on him. He is afraid of the city police, so he shirks from paying what he owes and he succumbs to his dread. "'This is not my boy,' he said. 'I never seen him before'" (123).

When panic strikes, Wisdom cautions, "calamity comes like a whirlwind" (Proverbs 1:27). The tumult bears retribution, for "they shall eat the fruit of their way" (Proverbs 1:31). The arrogant must swallow their pride and taste humility. O'Connor's narrative turn stays close to her scriptural source. The vainglorious Mr. Head becomes abased; the stubborn Nelson, shattered. Having plunged headstrong at each other for so long, they receive what they have given. Nelson repays Mr. Head's denial by staring through him, disdaining an offer of water to ease his thirst. The whirlwind buffets them in the gnawing cold generated by their pride. Nelson's mind freezes "around his grandfather's treachery" (125). The Atlanta landscape becomes the adventurers' mindscape. They wander into a grand suburb where mansion after mansion appears "like partially submerged icebergs" (126) and where the sidewalks disappear. For guidance, they have only driveways which wind around "in endless ridiculous circles" (126). The dome cannot be seen. They have drifted into the abyss.

The climate duplicates the condition in the pit of Dante's hell. Here Satan is locked in ice at the farthest remove from God's warming love.

O'Connor's language stresses her pilgrims' sinking into the origin of evil. Mr. Head begins to realize that "he [had] lost all hope" (125). His face looks "ravaged and abandoned" (125) as he absorbs the boy's eyes "piercing into his back like pitchfork prongs" (124). Not even Mr. Head's prayer of helplessness melts the boy's steely retaliation. "'Oh Gawd I'm lost! O hep me Gawd I'm lost!'" (126) Both suffer intensely; but here, where Satan reigns, pain freezes to stone in their heart. Before his guardian's humiliation, the boy's eyes remain "triumphantly cold" (126). Pride is its own punishment.

Through affliction lies the way out. By observing their physical posture, we can see how O'Connor imbeds grief and expiation in one image and condition. Their necks bend forward to nearly the same degree; their shoulders arch in identical curves. Something weighs on both Mr. Head and Nelson. That unseen burden recalls the heavy stone of self-elation pressing down on the proud in Dante's *Purgatorio* (Cantos X and XI). To pay for their pride, the shades must bow down to take in examples of the submission they lacked. The abashed state also prepares Mr. Head and Nelson to recognize humility. They spy a lawn statue about Nelson's size sitting bent over on a brick fence. Its creator meant to depict a carefree, grinning Negro savoring a watermelon slice. Now, however, the statue has a chipped eye which throws off "a wild look of misery" (127) as it hovers on the verge of toppling over. This conventional decoration, twisted into a bogeyman, puts the fear of God into the strangers. Whether vandals or weather have deformed the statue, the ruin appeals to the old man and boy for aid. They know the need. Their own tilted bodies send out the same mute cry for help. Sorrow has twisted all three bodies out of shape, chiseled away differences in race and years to form one ageless figure of hardship. Adversity forges a communal tie that contentment does not make. The chastened white man and boy see their need for rescue in the artificial version of the black man they helped to oppress. Mr. Head and Nelson must be saved from their idea of being superior, good men. The scapegoat points the way. It exposes the wounds received from their displaced suffering. Grace, in their condition, allows them to experience the guilt they have repressed. Such is the direction of retribution.

O'Connor does not end the Atlanta trip with mere hints of repentance. Mr. Head's discovery comes with Lear's intensity. Such an extension is a rare flourish in a collection that leaves to the imagination the effect of the same truth borne by the protagonists in other stories. The grandfather sees for the first time in himself the corruption he attributed to the outside world. Innocence lost in old age goes with a searing blast. The fire King Lear summons to cleanse nature of unkindness rages in Mr. Head. And the flame cracks the mold of his temperament. Back at the junction near home, Mr. Head views his safe return as an undeserved kindness. It is. He "burned with shame" that he could bring to his Maker at death so little humility. His penitent heart gives him access to the circle of healing fire. "He stood appalled, judging himself with the thoroughness of God, while the action of mercy covered his pride like a flame and consumed it" (129). Cauterized of pretense to virtue, he can bear the knowledge of his "true depravity," which vanity prevented him from receiving.

Even the postponement is a blessing. Only in dotage can Lear accept love; only at sixty can Mr. Head take to heart the gift of mercy. Mr. Head's accepting grace may arise from the basic security of being brought home, but it spreads in a startling way. Grace alters his understanding of the pain brought about in being lost. His agony, he knows, goes deeper than the city's sewer system; it goes beyond Nelson's arrogance and even his own pride. Suffering is part of the saving plan that guided him to safety. With God's aid "no sin was too monstrous for him to claim as his own." Not even the first cause of it all. Mr. Head goes so far as to acknowledge having "conceived in his own heart the sin of Adam" (129). Forgiven now, he can admit betraying his grandson. Forgiving, he can win the boy. Through the old man's quiet contact with "poor" Nelson, the mercy given to Mr. Head becomes homage rendered to God, who "from the beginning of time" (129) paid Mr. Head's debt. Taking on those monstrous crimes, Mr. Head will pay his portion by suffering for sins he did not commit. The image of sage-guide transforms into that of the submissive servant. The hell of Atlanta behind him and the purgatorial fire of the junction fortifying him, Mr. Head feels "ready at that instant to enter Paradise."

The auspicious end of this perilous journey was in the air from the start. When Mr. Head awakens at 2:00 a.m. for an early departure, moonlight fills his bedroom. Silver carpets the floorboards. Everything basks in a "dignifying light" (102) of nobility. From Mr. Head's shaving mirror, the moon seems poised "as if it were waiting for his permission to enter." For all its majestic courtesy, the lunar face is "grave." Before the old man invites the moon into his house, the moon patiently accompanies him and his grandson during the day to Atlanta. The moon, of course, illumines the night when the sun does not shine. It is the guiding influence in darkness. Night guidance is what Mr. Head needs. The influence that sees the two strangers through their moral darkness in Atlanta is not the terminal dome; nor is it the sun. It is God's will. Though providence controls with lordly forbearance, the stern aspect of the moon makes clear that the travelers will have to rise to the high occasion of His command.

When Mr. Head feels his safe return as miraculous, his gratitude grants God a way into his heart. Praise calls forth thanksgiving throughout creation. And the moon springs "from a cloud and flood[s] the clearing with light" (128). The moon rolls out the silver carpet of reunion as Mr. Head and Nelson step off the train at the junction. The moon itself is restored "to its full splendor." The full moon greets the renewal in Mr. Head. Moon, sage grass shivering in shades of silver, gigantic white clouds, all these details of nature compose a living doxology that attends the royal entry of the spirit into Mr. Head's life. The hidden—as the moon is hidden during the day—but effective control over the old man's life shines fully. The purpose of Mr. Head's exile can be seen in this light as a preparation for a return home. Home is the new temple housing the royal caller, the spirit's most welcome guest.

Before Mr. Head can reach home, he must go all the way back to where the human story begins. He and Nelson are remanded within the protecting "walls of a garden" (128) formed by the treetops at the railroad junction. The train coils past them "like a frightened serpent" and vanishes. This garden bears the marks of two opposite states of consciousness. It is Eden where sin is discovered, and it is Gethsemane where sin is overcome. A habit emerges from each habitat. Adam was the first sinful man, and he tried to repudiate guilt. Adam hides from God and covers himself up out of shame. Gethsemane reverses the impulse to escape. Jesus is the first sinless man, and he takes for his own the guilt of all sin. He is the first person to expose his spirit to the glare of God's light. At the junction, Mr. Head gains the knowledge of Eden and the promise of Gethsemane. He is brought to the garden at the time he accepts his sinfulness. The proud grandfather sees that the disobedience of the grandparent of sin is his own. Mr. Head stands exposed to himself, to Nelson, and to his maker. Uncovered, he stands in dignity "ready at that instant to enter Paradise," the ultimate garden.

In O'Connor's art the joyous aspect is the implicit one. The final tableau of "The Artificial Nigger" presages a great deal of joy. The boasting is gone from Mr. Head and Nelson. Their mouths quiver. When they were lost, both were glib. When recovered, they have but a few words, and these words are tender amends. Nelson's face brightens beneath his dark hat brim. "'I'm glad I've went once, but I'll never go back again!'" So run the final words of the story. Harangue ends in quiet. Their agony has been as acute as that of the protagonists in the other stories of *A Good Man Is Hard To Find*, but the physical maiming and death that underscore the ending of the other stories are absent here.

The mercy that touches Mr. Head also tempers the ending. Grandfather and grandson are in sorrow but not as orphans or victims. The poetry of Flannery O'Connor's ideas endows the Atlanta trip with the depth of an eternal experience, of which racism is one contemporary manifestation. In this profound moment, Mr. Head and Nelson stand very still, balanced in their momentary victory over the fleeing serpent. They share the happy conviction that they are on their way home. For O'Connor, their intimate communication in the garden is a hieroglyph of the submission that opens a way into the life of faith.

Notes

1. Flannery O'Connor, *The Habit of Being*, ed. Sally Fitzgerald (New York: Farrar, Straus and Giroux, 1979), p. 101. Hereafter pages are cited within the body of the text as *Letters*.

2. Carter W. Martin, *The True Country: Themes in the Fiction of Flannery O'Connor* (Nashville, TN: Vanderbilt University Press, 1968), pp. 112-116.

3. Frederick Asals, *Flannery O'Connor: The Imagination of Extremity* (Athens: The University of Georgia Press, 1982), pp. 79-92.

4. Kathleen Feeley, *Flannery O'Connor: Voice of the Peacock* (New Brunswick, NJ: Rutgers University Press, 1972), pp. 120-124.

5. Gilbert H. Muller, *Nightmares and Visions: Flannery O'Connor and the Catholic Grotesque* (Athens: University of Georgia Press, 1972), pp. 71-75.

6. James J. Napier, "'The Artificial Nigger' and the Authorial Intention," *The Flannery O'Connor Bulletin*, 10 (Autumn 1981), 87-92. The essay gives a good account of the recent responses to "The Artificial Nigger."

7. Asals, p. 91

8. *A Good Man Is Hard To Find* (1955, Harvest ed., New York: Harcourt Brace Jovanovich, 1977), p. 103. Hereafter pages are cited within the body of the text.

Wise Blood: O'Connor's Romance of Alienation

Ronald Emerick

Flannery O'Connor is operating in the mainstream of American romance. Both of her short novels and all of her stories participate in the genre of the American romance, a form both defined and illustrated by Nathaniel Hawthorne. She acknowledges her debt to Hawthorne in a letter to John Hawkes: "I think I would admit to writing what Hawthorne called 'romances'" (Reiter 25). In a later letter to William Sessions she reconfirms the debt: "Hawthorne said he didn't write novels, he wrote romances; I am one of his descendants" (qtd. in Friedman, *Dimension* 223). Even though O'Connor is writing one hundred years after Hawthorne, about Southerners rather than New Englanders, and in a style and language both simpler and more concrete than Hawthorne's, she follows almost exactly the principles of romance established by Hawthorne in his critical prefaces, principles reiterated by O'Connor in her own critical essays.

Nowhere is O'Connor's debt to Hawthorne more obvious than in her first novel, *Wise Blood*. O'Connor's depiction of Hazel Motes's adventures in the city of freaks, Taulkinham, may seem remote from the happenings in the gloomy woods of *The Scarlet Letter* and "Roger Malvin's Burial," the equally dark and mysterious city of "My Kinsman, Major Molineux," or the exotic garden of "Rappaccini's Daughter." But closer inspection reveals numerous similarities to Hawthorne in O'Connor's use of the cornerstones of romance: mood, setting, and character. In her emphasis on mystery, in her distortion of reality to reveal essential truths, and in her depiction of obsessed, alienated protagonists, O'Connor follows closely in Hawthorne's footsteps. Although they are primarily comic figures, Hazel Motes and Enoch Emery bear striking resemblances to Arthur Dimmesdale, Reuben Bourne ("Roger Malvin's Burial"), Roderick Elliston ("Egotism: or The Bosom Serpent"), Parson Hooper ("The Minister's Black Veil"), and numerous other obsessed and guilt-ridden seekers after peace of mind in Hawthorne's tales.

Hawthorne, in several critical prefaces, identifies important characteristics of the romance and explains why the romance rather than the novel is better suited to his purposes. In his preface to *The House of the Seven Gables* Hawthorne points out that the romance need not be a strict imitation of nature. Rather the writer of romance may rearrange nature in order to reveal essential truths, to expose "the truth of the human heart." Although the romance writer may sacrifice both probability and surface reality, he gains greater universality and deeper insights about man's essential humanity. Hawthorne also suggests that the romance writer can enrich his tales by using the supernatural in order to create a special atmosphere of ambiguity and indefiniteness. In "The Custom House," the introduction to *The Scarlet Letter*, Hawthorne elaborates upon this special atmosphere, defining romance as the meeting place of the actual and the imaginary. In his preface to *The Snow-Image and Other Twice-Told Tales* Hawthorne mentions another essential element, psychological truth. His primary concern is the exploration of character and human nature, more specifically the moral and psychological consequences of guilt and sin. In his preface to *The Marble Faun* Hawthorne cites the need for an element of ruin, of mystery, in the romance. In his treatment of nature Hawthorne creates this element of mystery; his treatment of nature is both transcendental and sacramental. He views the natural world as a symbol and embodiment of spiritual reality, thus suffusing nature with mystery and the supernatural.

Like Hawthorne, O'Connor conceives of the romance as a borderland between two worlds, the natural and the supernatural, a land suffused with truth and mystery. Also like Hawthorne, O'Connor defines extensively her theory of romance in the essays collected in *Mystery and Manners*. In "Some Aspects of the Grotesque in Southern Fiction" she refers to Hawthorne and echoes his theory that the romance offers greater freedom to a writer than the novel. She stresses that the writer must concern himself with "deeper kinds of realism." The romance genre provides for such realism because it permits the distortion of reality for the purpose of emphasizing essential truths. O'Connor refers to this distortion of reality as the grotesque, but she emphasizes that only external reality may be distorted. Internal reality, the integrity of the human soul, must not be violated and is subject to the strictest demands of realism.[1]

At the core of O'Connor's definition of romance is the concept of mystery, her term for the deeper realism and essential truths which the romance writer seeks to portray. The mysterious is that which lies beneath the surface of reality, the essential nature of reality, which cannot always be explained or understood.[2] In the essay "On Her Own Work" O'Connor describes the mysteries which she attempts to reveal as essentially spiritual ones, "the central Christian mysteries." Also in "Novelist and Believer" she defines nature in terms both transcendental and sacramental. Nature is holy, and the visible world contains also an invisible world which the romance writer aims to illuminate and make believable for her audience.[3]

Finally, in "Some Aspects of the Grotesque in Southern Fiction" O'Connor associates the role of romance writer with that of the prophet and the poet, and she associates both roles with Hawthorne:

> The Southern Writer is forced from all sides to make his gaze extend beyond the surface, beyond mere problems, until it touches that realm which is the concern of prophets and poets. When Hawthorne said that he wrote romances, he was attempting, in effect, to keep for fiction some of its freedom from social determinism, and to steer it in the direction of poetry. . . . The direction of many of us will be more toward poetry than toward the traditional novel. (45-46, 50)

Therefore, as André Bleikasten explains, although "less delicately shaded in its artistry and far less muted in its effects," O'Connor's fiction is part of the same romance tradition as Hawthorne's. In both writers "symbol, allegory, and parable are never far away," and O'Connor, like Hawthorne, employs the "rich mythology of Christian culture" and the pervasive influence of "the power of darkness" (qtd. in Friedman and Clark 138). The mythology of Christianity and the power of darkness play major roles in O'Connor's first romance, *Wise Blood*. Unlike most of Hawthorne's romances, however, *Wise Blood* is a comic romance, and its hero Hazel Motes is a caricature, distorted for comic effect. As Sister Kathleen Feeley notes, "The world he inhabits has the real-yet-unreal quality which infuses the romance" (56).

Expanding upon the unreal quality of O'Connor's world in *Wise Blood*, Lewis A. Lawson points out that much of the plot development and character motivation is absurd: "Any resemblance to the world of objective reality is certainly incidental" (51). Rather, Lawson continues, O'Connor's purpose is to convey her vision by means of paradox and illogicality. She deliberately creates a hero who is bizarre, distasteful, and ridiculous in order to force the reader not to identify with him but maintain objectivity (Friedman and Lawson, 52). And it is not just Hazel Motes but all of the major characters in *Wise Blood* who are distorted and freakish. As Irving Malin points out, characters like Enoch Emery, Asa Hawks, and Sabbath Lily are also grotesque because, like Haze, they have sacrificed their humanity by yielding to a single truth and attempting fanatically to live by it (109-10).

Most freakish is Haze himself, who is a "Christian *malgré lui*" (O'Connor's own phrase to describe Haze in her 1962 preface to *Wise Blood*). Grounded in guilt, Haze's monomania is reminiscent of that of two of Hawthorne's guilt-ridden characters, Arthur Dimmesdale and Reuben Bourne. Like Dimmesdale and Bourne, Haze suffers immeasurably for his sin, in his case the rejection of Christ; and it is only after he recognizes his sin and actively seeks to atone for it that he achieves his ultimate salvation and release from guilt.

Haze's original rejection of Christ is the result of complex and upsetting experiences during his youth. His grandfather had been "a circuit preacher, a waspish old man who had ridden over three counties with Jesus hidden in his head like a stinger" (20). Preaching from the hood of his automobile, he used to point to his grandson Haze to illustrate that even a worthless, sinful boy would be hounded endlessly by Christ in order to insure the salvation of his soul. Jesus "would chase him over the waters of sin! . . . That boy had been redeemed and Jesus wasn't going to leave him ever. Jesus would never let him forget he was redeemed. What did the sinner think there was to be gained? Jesus would have him in the end!" (22). To the impressionable youth, Jesus becomes a frightening figure: "He saw Jesus move from tree to tree in the back of his mind, a wild ragged figure motioning him to turn around and come off into the dark where he was not sure of his footing, where he might be walking on the water and not know it and then suddenly know it and drown" (22). As a result, Haze concludes that in order to avoid Jesus he must avoid sin.

But avoiding sin is not an easy task, as Haze's experience with his father at a carnival points out. After watching a naked woman performing in a coffin-like box, Haze returns home confused and feeling vaguely sinful. His mother intuitively recognizes his guilt and punishes him, beating him with a stick and, at the same time, stressing the belief that Jesus died to redeem him. This crucial experience produces in Haze a "nameless unplaced guilt" (63) for which he tries to do penance by putting rocks in his shoes and walking for a mile. As Brian Abel Regan explains, "it is the nameless unplaced guilt—the guilt of Original Sin—that the young Motes is trying to work off" by walking with stones in his shoes (170).[4] But Christ (or the guilt-ridden Haze) does not seem satisfied, and Haze begins to realize that by totally rejecting Christ he can avoid the consequences of sin and guilt feelings in the future. If Haze refuses to believe in Christ, Christ can no longer terrify him or hound him.

After a stint in the army and because of a little coaxing from his fellow soldiers, Haze becomes a confirmed sinner and adopts a philosophy of nihilism. As he proclaims to a taxi driver when he arrives in

Taulkinham, "Get this: I don't believe in anything" (32). But somehow a life of sin and nihilism doesn't satisfy Haze. He is still obsessed with redemption, accusing strangers on the train of not being redeemed; and he frequently points out to others that he has rejected Christ, as if he needs constantly to convince himself of this fact. In addition, other characters recognize his obsession with Christ and, to Haze's dismay, continually point this out to him. Enoch Emery, for example, tells Haze: "I knew when I first seen you didn't have nobody nor nothing but Jesus. I seen you and I knew it" (58). Similarly, Asa Hawks perceives that Haze's fascination with him is an attraction to the act of faith which Hawks's supposed blindness represents.

Haze's obsession with Christ and fascination with Hawks are unconscious and mysterious. Like Hawthorne's Reuben Bourne, who is drawn mysteriously to the site of Roger Malvin's "grave," Haze cannot explain his behavior. Subconsciously, both Reuben and Haze seek atonement for their sins—Reuben for abandoning his dying friend and soon-to-be father-in-law, Roger Malvin; Haze for rejecting his spiritual father, Jesus Christ. Both characters seek relief from guilt, and peace of mind and soul.

Becoming aware of his ambivalence toward Christ and his failure to dismiss the "ragged figure" from his mind, Haze desperately steps up his campaign against Christ. He buys "a high rat-colored car," a kind of dilapidated portable pulpit, and begins to actively preach the Church Without Christ. He asks for "a new Jesus" to take the place of the old one from whom he so urgently desires to escape. But even this desperate ploy ultimately breeds failure, for two symbolic epiphanies convince Haze that Christ is inescapable. When Onnie Jay Holy tries to profit from Haze's Church Without Christ by finding a double for Haze and duplicating his style of preaching, Haze follows his double, Solace Layfield, and gruesomely runs over him with the Essex. But as he murders his double, Haze symbolically murders his old self, the part of him which has preached a nihilistic philosophy that he, in reality, cannot accept because of his unconscious obsession with Christ. Ironically referring to himself, Haze accuses Layfield of not being honest about his true beliefs: "What do you get up on top of a car and say you don't believe in what you do believe in for? . . . You ain't true. . . . You believe in Jesus" (203). As if attempting to escape this epiphany, Haze then decides to leave Taulkinham and begin preaching in a new city, but an encounter with a highway patrolman produces a second epiphany. The patrolman, disturbed by Haze's arrogance and his lack of a driver's license, pushes the Essex over an embankment. The literal and symbolic destruction of Haze's pulpit, his church, is the final blow to his nihilistic philosophy. As he examines the landscape, Haze penetrates its surface and faces the mystery of Christ for the first time: "His face seemed to reflect the entire distance across the clearing and on beyond, the entire distance that extended from his eyes to the blank gray sky that went on, depth after depth, into space" (209). Realizing that his nihilism has been a sin against Christ, Haze decides to blind himself with quicklime and pursue a life of deprivation and self-imposed suffering to do penance for his sins.

Haze's penance is not unlike that which Arthur Dimmesdale imposes upon himself in *The Scarlet Letter.* When he stands on the scaffold late at night with Hester and Pearl, Dimmesdale acknowledges his guilt and his sinful link with Hester. Although his penance is neither as public nor as grotesque as Haze's, it is equally profound and sincere. Similarly grotesque, however, is the guilt which gnaws at his heart and eventually manifests itself as the letter *A* on his chest. The power of guilt to seek its own penance, almost against the conscious will of the individual, can be seen in both Dimmesdale and Haze.

In her preface to *Wise Blood* O'Connor describes the central mystery of the novel as free will, Haze's freedom to accept or reject Christ:

> That belief in Christ is to some a matter of life and death has been a stumbling block for readers who would prefer to think it a matter of no great consequence. For them Hazel Motes' integrity lies in his trying with such

> vigor to get rid of the ragged figure who moves from tree to tree in the back of his mind. For the author Hazel's integrity lies in his not being able to do so. Does one's integrity ever lie in what he is not able to do? I think that usually it does, for free will does not mean one will, but many wills conflicting in one man. Freedom cannot be conceived simply. It is a mystery and one which a novel, even a comic novel, can only be asked to deepen. (5)

Even though Haze fights desperately to rid himself of Christ, O'Connor rejoices in his ultimate acceptance of Christ and rewards him with salvation. In fact, she portrays the penitent Haze as a kind of Christ figure himself, who symbolically reveals the mystery of redemption to his practical-minded and materialistic landlady, Mrs. Flood. In an attempt to understand Haze's blindness Mrs. Flood associates it with a pinpoint of light:

> She imagined it was like you were walking in a tunnel and all you could see was a pin point of light. She had to imagine the pin point of light; she couldn't think of it at all without that. She saw it as some kind of a star, like the star on Christmas cards. She saw him going backwards to Bethlehem and she had to laugh. (218-19)

But when Haze lies dead in her rooming house, having been clubbed to death in a ditch by two policemen, Mrs. Flood gazes into his eyes and faces mystery herself. She sees Haze as the pinpoint of light, the star over Bethlehem, the symbol of Christ the Redeemer: "She sat staring with her eyes shut, into his eyes, and felt as if she had finally got to the beginning of something she couldn't begin, and she saw him moving farther and farther away, farther and farther into the darkness until he was the pin point of light" (232).[5] Thus, ironically, Haze has himself become "the new jesus" for which he had pleaded so urgently as minister of the Church Without Christ.[6]

Paralleling the career of Haze in the novel on a more comic but equally grotesque level is Enoch Emery. Like Haze, Enoch is the victim of compulsions which he cannot resist. He is a slave to his wise blood, a special intuitive knowledge which he has inherited from his daddy and which determines most of Enoch's actions in the novel. Although he is proud of his unique power, Enoch also realizes that it sometimes impels him to perform mysterious and irrational acts: "He didn't want to justify his daddy's blood, he didn't want to be always having to do something that something else wanted him to do, that he didn't know what it was and that was always dangerous" (135). Nonetheless Enoch obeys the promptings of his blood without hesitation. It leads him first to the city park, where he takes a job as guard, and then to the mystery at the heart of the park, a shriveled mummy in a glass case:

> There was something, in the center of the park, that he had discovered. It was a mystery, although it was right there in a glass case for everybody to see and there was a typewritten card over it telling all about it. But there was something the card couldn't say and what it couldn't say was inside him, a terrible knowledge without any words to it, a terrible knowledge like a big nerve growing inside him. He could not show the mystery to just anybody; but he had to show it to somebody. Who he had to show it to was a special person. This person could not be from the city but he didn't know why. He knew he would know him when he saw him and he knew that he would have to see him soon or the nerve inside him would grow so big that he would be forced to steal a car or rob a bank or jump out of a dark alley onto a woman. His blood all morning had been saying the person would come today. (81)

His wise blood leads Enoch to Hazel Motes, the special person with whom he can share the mystery of the mummy.

On the psychological level Enoch's problem is loneliness. Alone and friendless in the city, he seizes upon Haze, another outsider, as a potential friend:

> He strode along at Haze's elbow, talking in a half mumble, half whine. Once he caught at his sleeve to slow him down and Haze jerked it away. "My daddy made me come," he said in a cracked voice. Haze looked at him and saw he was crying, his face seamed and wet and a purple-pink color. "I ain't but eighteen year old," he cried, "an' he made me come and I don't know nobody, nobody here'll have nothing to do with nobody else. They ain't friendly." (57)

On the spiritual level, however, Enoch's problem is precisely the same as Haze's. He represents modern man in search of a meaningful existence. Enoch maintains a daily ritual, first hiding in the bushes and watching the swimmers at the swimming pool, next drinking a chocolate milkshake at The Frosty Bottle, then making obscene comments to the animals in the zoo, and finally visiting the mysterious mummy in the museum. Enoch thus approaches the godlike mummy each day like a worshipper in a grotesque religious rite. But the mummy is just a shriveled man, not a god, and therefore fails to satisfy Enoch's needs. Like modern man, Enoch hungers for spiritual satisfaction; failing to satisfy his hunger by turning to religion, he remains dissatisfied.

Becoming desperate in his need for both friendship and a meaningful life, Enoch turns criminal at the end of the novel. When he hears Haze ask for "a new jesus" for the Church Without Christ, Enoch realizes the purpose of his mysterious attraction to the mummy. Hoping to provide the answer to Haze's plea and at the same time seal his friendship with Haze, Enoch steals the mummy from the museum and delivers it to Haze. Although disillusioned at having risked so much for a shriveled mummy, Enoch hopes to be rewarded for his services:

> He had only a vague idea how he wanted to be rewarded, but he was not a boy without ambition: he wanted to become something. He wanted to better his condition until it was the best. He wanted to be THE young man of the future, like the ones in the insurance ads. He wanted, some day, to see a line of people waiting to shake his hand. (191)

The reward comes in the form of Gonga the gorilla. When Enoch shakes hands with Gonga, he experiences warmth and friendship for the first time. Desirous of renewing the experience, he decides to assume the role of Gonga himself, thus insuring a future of warm greetings and people waiting in line to shake his hand. Consequently Enoch assaults the current inhabitant of Gonga's costume, takes the costume, buries his own clothes, and puts on the gorilla suit.

Like Haze, Enoch has destroyed his old identity and adopted a new one. Also like Haze, he has ironically become "the new jesus," the young man of the future. Unlike Haze, however, Enoch comes to represent modern man separated from religious faith and reduced to an animalistic state. As Enoch assumes the role of Gonga, he loses his essential humanity and becomes an animal, an "it":

> Then it began to growl and beat its chest; it jumped up and down and flung its arms and thrust its head forward. The growls were thin and uncertain at first but they grew louder after a second. They became low and poisonous, louder again, low and poisonous again; they stopped altogether. The figure extended its hand, clutched nothing, and shook its arm vigorously; it withdrew the arm, extended it again, clutched nothing, and shook. It repeated this four or five times. Then it picked up the pointed stick and placed it at a cocky angle under its arm and left the woods for the highway. No gorilla in existence, whether in the jungles of Africa or California, or in New York City in the finest apartment in the world, was happier at that moment than this one, whose god had finally rewarded it. (197-98)

For Enoch, therefore, there is no salvation in *Wise Blood*. Although satisfied that his new role will produce friendship and meaning in his life, Enoch discovers that he is now even further alienated from his fellow man. When he approaches a man and woman to test his new identity, they flee in terror, leaving Enoch astounded and, again, alone: "The gorilla stood as though surprised and presently its arm fell to its side. It sat down on the rock where they had been sitting and stared over the valley at the uneven skyline of the city" (198). The mysterious free will, which for Hazel Motes has yielded renewed faith and redemption, for Enoch Emery produces only greater dissatisfaction and alienation. By not locating his freedom in Christ, O'Connor appears to be saying, man only further imprisons himself.

In their deep-seated guilt and alienation, Hazel and Enoch have much in common with Hawthorne's guilt-ridden protagonists, and they are forerunners of such later obsessed O'Connor protagonists as O. E. Parker ("Parker's Back") and Francis Marion Tarwater (*The Violent Bear It Away*). In subsequent tales such as *The Violent Bear It Away*, O'Connor will even expand her debt to Hawthorne by portraying another typical protagonist from Hawthorne's romantic gallery of grotesques: the man or woman consumed with intellectual pride. In Joy-Hulga ("Good Country People"), Asbury Fox ("The Enduring Chill"), Julian ("Everything That Rises Must Converge"), Sheppard ("The Lame Shall Enter First"), and Rayber (*The Violent Bear It Away*), O'Connor echoes the smug superiority of such Hawthorne intellectuals as Dr. Rappaccini, Aylmer ("The Birthmark"), Ethan Brand ("Ethan Brand"), and Roger Chillingworth, men who would sacrifice a fellow human being's soul for the sake of a scientific experiment or intellectual curiosity.

Both Haze and Enoch are grotesque figures, performing unrealistic and symbolic acts, and their creator is clearly a practitioner of romance in the tradition of Hawthorne. Although at first glance the differences between Arthur Dimmesdale and Hazel Motes may seem vast, and *The Scarlet Letter* and *Wise Blood* may seem miles apart, a closer examination reveals that the same principles of creation are operating in both instances. In the genre of the American romance, Flannery O'Connor is a disciple of Hawthorne in both theory and practice.

Notes

1. Brian Abel Regan agrees that both Hawthorne and O'Connor make extensive use of the grotesque. Like O'Connor, says Regan, Hawthorne is a "grotesque writer whose subject is sin and guilt" (6).

2. Edward Kessler suggests that O'Connor uses metaphor to penetrate mystery that is undefinable: "metaphor makes it possible for a poet to engage a mystery she cannot define" (76).

3. In his analysis of the sacramental quality in the fiction of Hawthorne and O'Connor, Kessler notes that in Hawthorne community is "an inescapable reality confirmed by history," while in O'Connor community is essentially a metaphor (71). O'Connor "seems to have transferred to external nature the sacramental quality Hawthorne assigned to community" (72).

4. Regan also notes a parallel with Hawthorne in O'Connor's emphasis on original sin. O'Connor, too, is an "opponent of the party of Hope, the strain in American literature that denies Original Sin and declares Man's innocence" (88).

5. Kessler notes an interesting similarity between Mrs. Flood and Hawthorne's Hester Prynne. Like Hester, says Kessler, Mrs. Flood receives just slight divine illumination at the end of *Wise Blood* (138).

6. As Jill P. Baumgaertner points out, Haze is "one of O'Connor's reluctant prophets" (122). He is constantly running from Jesus, but "in his attempt to escape from Jesus, he has not put any distance at all between them." Ironically, at the end of the novel, "he is motionless, but he moves" (125).

Works Cited

Baumgaertner, Jill P. *Flannery O'Connor: A Proper Scaring*. Wheaton, IL: Harold Shaw, 1988.

Feeley, Sister Kathleen. *Flannery O'Connor: Voice of the Peacock*. New Brunswick, NJ: Rutgers UP, 1972.

Friedman, Melvin J., and Beverly Lyon Clark, eds. *Critical Essays on Flannery O'Connor*. Boston: G. K. Hall, 1985.

Friedman, Melvin J., and Lewis A. Lawson, eds. *The Added Dimension: The Art and Mind of Flannery O'Connor*. New York: Fordham UP, 1966.

Kessler, Edward. *Flannery O'Connor and the Language of Apocalypse*. Princeton, NJ: Princeton UP, 1986.

Malin, Irving. *New American Gothic*. Carbondale: Southern Illinois UP, 1962.

O'Connor, Flannery. *Mystery and Manners*. Eds. Sally and Robert Fitzgerald. New York: Farrar, Straus and Giroux, 1970.

___________. *Wise Blood*. New York: Farrar, Straus & Cudahy, 1962.

Regan, Brian Abel. *A Wreck on the Road to Damascus*. Chicago: Loyola UP, 1989.

Reiter, Robert E., ed., *Flannery O'Connor*. St. Louis: B. Herder, 1968.

From Manners to Mystery: Flannery O'Connor's Titles[1]

Marie Lienard

It is no surprise that Flannery O'Connor chose the short story as her privileged mode of expression. The short story is characterized by a vision and an open-endedness that is very puzzling to the reader. As Terry Eagleton indicates, "the short story revolves around a moment of revolt or revelation which it is hard to totalize or sustain." The short story is thus the perfect literary tool for O'Connor, who constantly emphasized the importance of "vision" and "revelation," most notably in *Mystery and Manners* or *The Habit of Being*.[2] For her, the short story stages an epiphany or a "conversion" in an episode that would reveal the misery of man without God or his grandeur when he opens up to God's grace—a project that resembles Blaise Pascal's, whom O'Connor admired. Both of their writing combined irony, epigram and poetry, and their work never achieved completion as death claimed their lives before they reached their fortieth birthday.

The numerous interpretations offered about O'Connor's fiction testify to the difficulty of understanding her imagination. One way to approach that complexity is to think of her short stories as parables.[3] Parables traditionally propose a story that illustrates certain truths. They start from the audience's experience and concrete situations to engage with a deeper symbolic meaning. They operate on two levels: the level of the characters and the level of the message conveyed through them. Christ privileged the parable as a mode of teaching, and he often had to explain their meaning to his audience. O'Connor's writing revolves around "anagogy," that is "the kind of vision that is able to see different levels of reality in one image or one situation" as O'Connor explains in "The Nature and Aim of Fiction" (MM 72-73). The Greek term signifies "that which leads, elevates" and the Littré dictionary defines an anagogic interpretation as one which goes from the literal to the figurative.[4] Such a narrative and semiotic mode resembles the parabolic mode that combines realism and symbolism.

One element is central to the hermeneutics of her short story writing: the title. The titles often strike the reader because of their banality or, on the contrary, their cryptic resonance. They sometimes appear at odds with the story, either disclosing or confusing signification. I think that they have to be understood as dues in the move from the literal to the figurative; they are key elements in the parabolic genre as a construction of the text and a construction of meaning. Through the title, we come to understand how the literal (the manners) connects to the spiritual (the mystery). The title brings some interpretative closure to the message of the story and might be O'Connor's way of introducing the voice of the author; she indeed shared with Catholic writer François Mauriac the problem of combining her religious vision with her literary art. The title, suspended between the two levels of the analogy, reveals, like a film negative, the image that will "connect or embody two points": as O'Connor elaborates, "one is a point in the concrete, and the other is a point not visible to the naked eye, but believed in by him [the writer] firmly, just as real to him, really, as the one everybody sees" (MM 42-43). The title thus orients the reading by designating the network of metaphors. It articulates the movement between the observation of the real and some intimation of the spiritual. To use the Misfit's words, the title "throws everything off balance," throws meaning off balance by setting it in motion.

The title therefore cannot be reduced to a mere diegetical function. This article would like to propose a hermeneutics of the titles to understand the role they play in disclosing O'Connor's staging of the "mystery" she saw as the defining element in her faith and fiction, her personal and artistic credo. We would like to illustrate the poetics of O'Connor's title by offering a reading of some of her most famous short stories in both collections. From *A Good Man is Hard to Find*, we will examine "A Good Man is Hard to Find," "The Artificial Nigger," "A Late Encounter with the Enemy," and "The Displaced Person";

from *Everything that Rises Must Converge*, we will analyze "Greenleaf," "A View of the Woods," and "Parker's Back."[5]

The first collection of stories, *A Good Man is Hard to Find*, explores the definitions given to "good." The word "Man" should be understood in its universal dimension. The term "good" is not reduced to the moral arena and the mere opposition to evil. It takes on a broader meaning to include what is authentic, for example, or devoid of hypocrisy: to be good is to be true to oneself. Each story addresses the difficulty of being "good," that is of coinciding with oneself; human beings are caught in their webs of habits and ideas, be they moral or cultural, even religious. Some epiphany takes place because difficult does not mean impossible: the transforming power of God's grace creates a reversal that enables goodness to emerge, and sometimes, even prevail. The verb "to find" calls on the intellect and the senses, and encompasses the different modes of the search: difficult to see, to feel, to hear, and to touch. O'Connor's quest joins with the Augustine paradigm of starting from the flesh to reach the spiritual. Finally the title evokes the resistance of the creature to the creator; because of "free will" the creature takes liberty to reject goodness, hence the divine statement: "a good man is hard to find," echoing Christ's question: "if the Son of Man were to come back, where would he find faith?" But humanity is redeemed through the Incarnation, a mystery that O'Connor kept on exploring.

The most famous story in the collection, "A Good Man is Hard to Find," reads like a *mise en abyme* of the different motifs of goodness and their attending definitions. The term "a good man" refers to many characters, male and female. The grandmother and Red Sammy share the same social definition of good and show the same prejudices and narrow-mindedness. They see themselves as "good," law-abiding, and self-righteous people. Their goodness depends on a normative, societal definition; it is empty, and meaningless. Bailey presumably is a "good" father and spouse, but his self-absorption and aloofness undermine his real goodness as a loving, attentive person. The Misfit, because of this insecurity, and mistrust, has created a cruel persona, which has covered his "goodness." In a way, all of O'Connor's characters are "misfits," marginalized by their own limits and refusal to welcome God's grace; the capital letter calls for a general reading, like the indefinite article in "*a* good man."

The Misfit justifies the nickname that he gives himself: "I call myself the Misfit because I can't make what all I done wrong fit what all I gone through in punishment" (CS 131). He feels that some deep injustice is at work in the world and launches in a quest for meaning; John Desmond calls him "a seeker who wants some answers to the mystery of evil he feels both in himself and witnesses in the world."[6] His persona enables him to escape from his own suffering. The "goodness" in him has been covered by a skillfully staged meanness. But this meanness is "displaced" to reveal the sensitivity and vulnerability of his being, as triggered by the gesture of the grandmother that opens up a gap, a rift in the texture of the role. Like the hole in the road which causes the accident, the grandmother's move disrupts and destabilizes habits and postures to enable goodness to emerge, if only briefly. When the Misfit takes off his glasses, he drops the mask, in a way: "without his glasses, the Misfit's eyes were red-rimmed and pale and defenseless-looking" (CS 132-133). The gesture of the grandmother has stirred a humanity that he can't accept, having always forcefully claimed independence. But O'Connor invites her readers to compare this gesture to the mustard seed: the title hints at this promising resolution—this hope.

On the other hand, another accident 'happens' to the grandmother. She feels a real empathy for the Misfit that is not dictated by the "good" feelings connected to some notion of "lady" hood. She thus becomes a "good woman" as the Misfit rightly notes. The grandmother sheds off the persona of the 'lady' to coincide with her real self and to find the innocence of a child that opens the way to the kingdom of God: at the end she sits "with her legs crossed under her like a child's and her face smiling up at the cloudless sky" (CS 132).

The short story therefore stages different ways of moving away from oneself, and the "difficulty" of retrieving one's goodness. In a way, O'Connor's quest for goodness recalls, paradoxically, the Sartrean notion of good faith and authenticity; the grandmother and the Misfit, like Hugo in *Dirty Hands*, illustrate the difficulty of coinciding with oneself. The grandmother is caught in the literality of a culture which dictates certain roles: the episode of the watermelon with the inscription EAT illustrates the danger of taking the literal as the only dimension of reality. The Misfit, because he chooses to operate in a Manichaean world, trades easy answers for the complexity of choice and freedom. The reference to the blues echoed in the title sheds light on the motif of self-assertion beyond trouble and slavery—whether the enslavement is actual or symbolic.[7] The blues celebrates inner freedom and endurance, as Faulkner would say—an affirmation of the self against all forms of bondage.

"The Artificial Nigger" was one of O'Connor's favorite stories. The statue—the artificial nigger—figures the fixity and rigidity of Mr. Head's prejudices. As his name indicates, Mr. Head approaches reality in a cerebral way. Maris Fiondella thus explains: "Mr. Head lives in a world of discourse in which 'others' are personifications of projected desires or fears."[8] Therefore he is ill prepared to face the complexity of the situation in which his grandson Nelson throws him; denying Nelson's existence is the only way to cope with the difficulty of the situation. To be "good," in his case, is to recognize his humanity, and the others by overcoming the ready-made ideas he has adopted about them. He has in effect commodified the others, turning them into plaster statues—artificial creatures. The word 'artificial' also connotes the superficial aspect of his vision of the world—which falls apart when confronted with the reality of the world. He has lost all bearings; his physical wanderings mirror his inner loss. The vision of the statue resembles an epiphany: "they stood gazing at the Artificial Negro as if they were faced with some grand mystery" (CS 269). The character of the black man crystallizes an otherness that Mr. Head has refused to acknowledge. The statue therefore comes to embody a mirror image of him. As Fiondella underlines, "the statue embodies a stereotype prior to Mr. Head's and Nelson's view of it, and its trivialized use implies blindness or indifference to the fact."[9] But it also offers, as O'Connor notes, the image of redemptive suffering: "what I had in mind to suggest with the artificial nigger was the redemptive quality of the Negro's suffering for us all" (HB 78). Mr. Head understands that he is forgiven: "he felt the action of mercy touch him" (CS 269). He feels that he is called to move beyond the harshness of the plaster to discover his own sense of humility and grandeur though forgiveness; O'Connor indicates: "Mr. Head is changed by his experience" (HB 275). He might be able to see the "face" of the other, as Levinas would put it, including his own human face.

"A Late Encounter with the Enemy" is one of the most interesting stories since it combines a fine satire of the South with theology. It illustrates the juxtaposition of mystery and manners dear to the writer. O'Connor uses the themes of the Southern imaginary for her religious imagination. The obsession with glory, memory, the cult of the past, the denial of the present, and the ghosts are the ingredients that orchestrate a play on the encounter with the enemy. The enemy of the South, after the North, is time, change, and reality. The general crystallizes the artificial and delusional side of the worship of the past. He figures the vanity of commemoration, its limits and lies. The image of the hole, as in "A Good Man is Hard to Find"—here, a good general is hard to find!—causes a reversal. The enemy that the general has to face is himself: who he really is, what he has accomplished. The true self he has avoided all his life by hiding it behind social masks looms up when these masks become useless. While he mixes battle names, people's names and names of places, he starts remembering the battlefield of his private life quite vividly. His biological death coincides with a sort of personal rebirth as he dies to a life by proxy, caught as he was in the glorious and vain persona of the confederate general he had come to embody (see the pun on "late"). The irony of the final image gives an insight into the real proportions of his self-aggrandized existence: he leaves behind a corpse that has been consumed and discarded, like the empty cans of Coke of the vending machine; his final vision—his epiphany—has led him into another dimension: goodness. His agony is his final battle, as the Greek term "agon" points out, but it is a battle that belongs to a "different order" in Pascal's words.

If O'Connor's characters are "misfits," they are also "displaced." "The Displaced Person" stages a character whose geographical displacement figures the overall sense of alienation characteristic of O'Connor's world: the capital letters show the symbolic dimension of Mr. Guizac. The divine revelation displaces human beings out of the comfort of their ideas and habits into a place where they can welcome God's grace. The term displaced is as central to O'Connor's fiction as the term "stranger" in Camus's work. Mr. Guizac is displaced geographically and culturally, the Shortleys are displaced in their habits and manners, and Mrs. McIntyre is "displaced" out of her hardness and narrow-mindedness. As O'Connor notes: "the displaced person did accomplish a kind of redemption in that he destroyed the place, which was evil, and set Mrs. McIntyre on the road to a new kind of suffering" (HB 118). O'Connor actually added the last part of the story to pave the way for Mrs. McIntyre's "displacement" into the strange land of compassion and suffering. As in "A Good Man is Hard to Find," the displacement is not described in the story but articulated in the title.

In the other collection of short stories, titles play the same heuristic role. *Everything That Rises Must Converge* is inspired by Pierre Teilhard de Chardin's idea of a convergence of the whole universe—nature and human beings—toward what he called the "Omega point," some unity in the divine. O'Connor takes from *The Human Phenomenon* the phrase she used as the title of her collection and a short story. She thus writes in her report on the work: "His [T's] is a scientific expression of what the poet attempts to do: penetrate matter until spirit is revealed in it."[10] She related to the thought of the French theologian; as Harbour Winn notes, "Teilhard's vision seems to correspond with O'Connor's, for the central element of each centers around belief in a world penetrated by spirit." Winn adds: "In his evolutionary system, Teilhard sees the continuing movement of diverse species into higher and higher forms of consciousness until, ultimately, they combine or converge upon one another at what he calls the Omega point, the stage at which spirit and matter exist in equal proportion and blend together as one. According to Teilhard, the individual must grow from egoism to self-awareness and love for human history to evolve toward Omega."[11] Each story spells out this move out of egoism, the struggle out of blind selfishness and self-righteousness to reach another level of consciousness. The stories stage some convergence with the divine after some epiphanic experience. The Teilhardian resonance of the title is therefore crucial in understanding the underlying pattern of rise and union.

"Greenleaf" is one of the stories where the title can be the most misleading. Indeed, instead of referring only to the characters by the same name, the term "greenleaf" also refers to qualities that they have but that Mrs. May has lost. Her name indicates that the dimension of greenness—freshness, life—is in her, but has been stifled by the boredom and business of daily life. "Greenleaf" stands for life, the spring that she intuitively feels in the green of the pasture, the blue of the sky or the call of the birds (CS 319). The bull crystallizes the force of nature that she has forgotten. She only sees in the bull some disturbing nuisance, some annoying presence that she has to get rid of because it disrupts the orchestrated order of her property and schedule. It is in the pasture of the bull that she touches base with the 'green' life around her. Her death is described as a match between her and "some tormented lover." The horn that causes her death resembles the gesture of the grandmother in "A Good Man is Hard to Find" toward the Misfit: it performs inter-connectedness between beings in the convergence described by Teilhard. Like Teilhard's intuition and writing, such a text strikes through its pagan dimension. It helps the reader understand the place of the body in O'Connor's work. The kinship established by the term "greenleaf" between human beings and nature inscribes the link between pagan and Christian, immanent and transcendent.

"A View of the Woods" explores the dimension of nature and its convergence with humanity further. The woods symbolize an order beyond or apart from business and profit. Mr. Fortune is losing his woods to greed and pride: "He turned and looked away over the lake to the woods, and told himself that in five years, instead of woods, there would be houses and stores and parking places, and that the credit for it could go largely to him" (CS 343). By claiming his identity and his filiation with her father—"I am PURE Pitts" she says (CS 355)—his granddaughter brings him back to the dimension of the earth. The hole (another one!) dug by the excavator (also consider the pun on "Pitts") precipitates the crisis. The trees overcome Mr. Fortune, like the awareness that the other is a different, autonomous individual, and not a mere replica of himself or a puppet he can control. In the woods, which symbolize the place of otherness, he assesses his rightful place. When he ordered the disappearance of the "view of the woods," he severed his tie with his family, in particular with his granddaughter—and with nature. The ending stages the expulsion out of a lost paradise; the separation from nature proves fatal and causes the destruction that the bulldozer materializes: "he looked around desperately for someone to help him but the place was deserted except for one huge yellow monster which sat to the side, as stationary as he was, gorging itself on clay" (CS 356). Such a story reminds the reader of Faulkner's thematics of nature. Some passages of *Go Down, Moses*, in particular, present the destruction of nature as the agent and sign of the curse of the South. Faulkner shows how the destruction of nature has led to the destruction of man, which Mr. Fortune realizes in a prophetic moment: "Held there in the midst of an uncomfortable mystery that he had not apprehended before. He saw it, in his hallucination, as if someone were wounded behind the woods and the trees were bathed in blood" (CS 348).[12]

"Parker's Back" is characteristic of the way that a parable works: as the title indicates, everything revolves around a common physical element—Parker's body part—which builds a network of symbols and illustrates O'Connor's interest in the Revelation and the Incarnation. Parker can neither see God's face nor imprison Him in a representation, yet it is his back that reveals the divine to him—not in the tattoo but through the very impossibility of seeing the tattoo. It is when Parker leans against the tree that he can experience God—and therefore 'sees' Him. He indeed encounters him through his physical and emotional suffering, a suffering that God himself experienced through his Incarnation in Christ. Just as God reached humanity by taking up its bodily condition, Parker can reach the divine with his suffering human condition: the mystery of the Incarnation marks the convergence of the divine and the human. The distance between the creator and the creature is abolished, which is outrageous in other religions where the divine is conceived as separated from the human. Parker sees God and His face through his back; that is the suffering he feels in his body. The tattoo takes up an allegorical value as, according to C. S. Lewis's phrase, "allegory consists in giving an imagined body to the immaterial": the tattoo inscribed on the flesh leaves a mark and symbolizes God's presence in him. As a subject for vanity and boasting, the tattoo is invisible; Parker cannot see it. It is when he suffers because of it that it becomes visible to him, when he literally feels his back.

To the image of the dragon proposed by O'Connor, I would add the image of the Sphinx—a freak that could easily fit within her gallery of grotesque characters.[13] The Sphinx would propose enigmas like the equation between the Misfit and "a good man." But the text proposed by the Sphinx can be enjoyed as a story without imposing the heuristics of a mystery to be solved: O'Connor's "mystery" is no riddle, but it is a life and death issue, because it is a mystery that belongs to the "other order" of the Pascalian phrase. O'Connor, like Pascal, offers a gamble on meaning. For her, the meaning encoded in her stories and as revealed in her titles figures the larger meaning of a life that moves from manners to mystery, yet remains elusive. As she says, "the meaning of a story should go on expanding for the reader the more he thinks about it, but meaning cannot be captured in an interpretation" (HB 437). The title, in its simplicity and mystery, keeps the promise of a meaning that is always deferred—yet present.

Notes

1. *Heathcliff and the Great Hunger*, London, New York, Verso, 1995, p. 150.

2. References to these texts in the article are MM and HB, respectively.

3. See my article "Flannery O'Connor: la nouvelle comme parabole" in *Études*, Paris, May 2005.

4. See also HB, p. 469.

5. References to the individual short stories will be made to *The Complete Stories* (CS followed by page number).

6. In "Flannery O'Connor's Misfit and the Mystery of Evil," *Renascence* vol. LVI, No. 2, Winter 2004 (129-137), p. 130.

7. See Jacques Pothier in *Les Nouvelles de Flannery O'Connor*, Nantes, *Éditions du temps* 2004.

8. "Augustine, the 'letter' and the failure of love in Flannery O'Connor's 'The Artificial Nigger,'" *Studies in Short Fiction*, vol. 24 Spring 1987 (119-129), p. 125.

9. Id p. 128.

10. Quoted in Lorine Getz, *Flannery O'Connor, Literary Theologian: The Habits and Discipline of Being*. Lewiston, the Edwin Mellen Press, 1999, p. 180.

11. "Everything That Rises Must Converge: O'Connor's seven-story cycle" in *Studies in Short Fiction* vol. 1, no 2, Winter 1964 (187-211), p. 190.

12. The same imagery of the symbiosis between the destruction of nature and man can be found in Catholic writer Mauriac, whose work O'Connor appreciated greatly.

13. The 1963 reedition of *A Good Man is Hard to Find* contained the following epigraph by Saint Cyril of Jerusalem: "The dragon is by the side of the road, watching those pass. Beware lest he devour you. We go to the father of souls, but it is necessary to pass by the dragon." O'Connor comments on this quote in *Mystery and Manners*: "No matter what form the dragon may take, it is of this mysterious passage past him, or into his jaws, that stories of any depth will always be concerned to tell" (MM 35).

Works Cited

O'Connor, Flannery. *The Complete Stories*. London: Faber & Faber, 1990.

____________. *The Habit of Being: Letters of Flannery O'Connor*. Sally Fitzgerald (ed.), New York: Farrar, Straus & Giroux, 1979.

____________. *Mystery and Manners: Occasional Prose*. Sally and Robert Fitzgerald (eds.), New York: Farrar, Straus & Giroux, 1969.

Called to the Beautiful:
The Incarnational Art of Flannery O'Connor's *The Violent Bear It Away*

Christina Bieber

> Persecuted like the wise man and almost like the saint, the artist will perhaps recognize his brothers at last and discover his true vocation again: for in a way he is not of this world, being, from the moment that he works for beauty, on the path which leads upright souls to God and manifests to them the invisible things by the visible.
>
> —Jacques Maritain, *Art and Scholasticism*

The Flannery O'Connor we have come to know from her letters and occasional prose was a craftsman committed to the powerful possibilities of all. Fiction, she believed, could achieve the miraculous; it could communicate the ineffable to readers who are not even listening. O'Connor knew that this would be difficult: to present the spiritual reality her readers would rather ignore, she would seek new and shocking ways to use the concrete world her readers had to accept. Thus she came to describe her own work as "incarnational art," for it reenacts the word become flesh, the mystery made visible, the universal born into a particularity. And in so doing, it represents the possibility of redemption.

We have come to expect of any enduring work of art, but particularly from any work since the modern period, a certain self-reflexivity: that it would take as a primary theme the aesthetic vision of the artist. As a self-conscious artist of her time, O'Connor did not leave discussion of the writer's struggle to communicate to her occasional writings. That battle, largely a battle between what there is to be seen and those who refuse or are unable to see it, became part of the fiction she created, part of its symbolic drama. But O'Connor did not write a *künstlerroman*, and very few of the stories contain artist figures; for her, the calling of the artist was so similar to the calling of the prophet that the two stories could be told in one. *The Violent Bear It Away*, with its insistence that the prophet must violently struggle in order to be true to his vision of ineffable mystery, tells that story.

Although Tarwater's story is by no means a pure allegory of the artist's struggle, the language with which O'Connor describes Tarwater's call to be a prophet bears a striking similarity to that which she uses to describe her own vocation as an artist. When critics interpret *The Violent Bear It Away* as a conflict between the old man and Rayber over who will be able to indoctrinate young Tarwater more thoroughly, they tend to ignore what is to a large degree already present in young Tarwater's blood—a virtually indomitable sense of his calling.[1] Like the prophets of the Hebrew scriptures, particularly Jonah, Tarwater knows what he must do, but resists it. The old man Tarwater and Rayber have surprisingly limited influence as teachers—Tarwater's decision is ultimately his own.

That Tarwater is not merely a *tabula rasa* struggling against his great uncle Tarwater's indoctrination is clear from the fact that Tarwater has a different kind of vision, and in many ways a larger and deeper one, than the old man's. When the old man brings Tarwater along on a business trip into the city, Tarwater sees, without effort and in spite of himself, the spiritual reality around him. Tarwater "realized, almost without warning, that this place was evil—the ducked head, the muttered words, the hastening away. He saw in a burst of light that these people were hastening away from the Lord God Almighty. It was to the city that the prophets came and he was here in the midst of it" (346). Immediately after his vision, Tarwater realizes that his great uncle has no concern for the people in the city, and so he criticizes him for calling himself a prophet. The old man retaliates "I'm here on bidnis . . . if you been called by the Lord, then be about you own mission" (347).

Thus early in the reader's introduction to Tarwater O'Connor separates Tarwater's spiritual vision from the old man's, illustrating that Tarwater felt the call to be a prophet in his blood; and that this calling was a gift (which is, to Tarwater, more of a burden) from God.[2] Importantly, this call is to *action* within Tarwater's particular situation, action that would come as the necessary and natural result of his wider vision of the world. In the same way, O'Connor considered the ability to write fiction as a special gift that is the necessary and natural outcome of poetic vision within an artist's particular situation. Poetic vision is so important to O'Connor's theory of art that she describes art in terms of prophecy—like the prophet's, the writer's work depends upon her ability to see and say the truth, to show others what she sees in the world around her. Following Aquinas, O'Connor often called this poetic vision anagogical vision, which she said "is not a matter of seeing clearly, but of seeing what is distant, hidden" (*The Habit of Being* 365).[3] "The fiction writer should be characterized by his kind of vision. His kind of vision is prophetic vision . . . The prophet is a realist of distances, and it is this kind of realism that goes into great novels" (*Mystery and Manners* 179). It is critical to understand at this juncture that O'Connor is not talking about using fiction to promote Catholic dogma. To "see clearly" implies that the writer/prophet has all the answers and knows God with certainty; to "see prophetically" is to see spiritual depth that allows room for mystery and possibility.

In "The Nature and Aim of Fiction" O'Connor stated that "there is no excuse for anyone to write fiction for public consumption unless he has been called to do so by the presence of a gift" (*Mystery and Manners* 81). But unlike the romantic poets, who very nearly put the writer on the same plane as God, giving him a kind of ultimate freedom, O'Connor believed that this gift came with considerable responsibility and was "a mystery in itself, something gratuitous and wholly undeserved" carrying with it the need to practice a certain asceticism in order to use the gift properly (*Mystery and Manners* 81).[4]

O'Connor attributed her aesthetic ideas to St. Thomas Aquinas, especially as they came to her through Jacques Maritain, the Catholic philosopher she claimed she "cut [her] aesthetic teeth on" (*Collected Works* 1031). In *Art and Scholasticism*, Maritain describes art as a habitus of the practical intellect. Maritain defines *habitus* as "qualities a class apart . . . which are essentially stable dispositions perfecting in the line of its own nature the subject in which they exist" (10). The term carries within in it both the idea of *inhabitation* and *habit*; since the writer's talent is given as a gift, she must cultivate that gift by submitting herself to intellectual discipline. Like Prudence, art is a virtue of the practical intellect, but unlike Prudence, its sole end is for the good of the work. Because art is concerned with making the beautiful, the artist must submit himself to the mystery he is attempting to incarnate.

The fact that Tarwater is a reluctant seer—and hardly humble in the face of mystery—is what makes *The Violent Bear It Away* a picture of the struggles and pitfalls that face the modern artist. Tarwater has two teachers who respond to his vision differently; the old man who tries to get him to submit to it and Rayber, the schoolteacher uncle, who tries to get him to explain it away. The two teachers and their pushing and pulling of Tarwater is reminiscent of O'Connor's discussion of the writing teacher in "The Nature and Aim of Fiction," in which she argues that the teacher cannot teach vision, but needs to be able to identify it, cultivate it. Talent alone is not enough: "What you need is the vision to go with it," O'Connor writes, "and you do not get this from a writing class" (*Mystery and Manners* 86).

When it comes to the cultivation of Tarwater's prophetic vision, there can be no doubt which of the two teachers O'Connor stood behind. Critics struggle with the way in which the authorial consciousness in *The Violent Bear It Away* clearly favors the old man's radicalism; they fault O'Connor for her monologic vision, or try to find some other way to apologize for her acceptance of him as a teacher for the young Tarwater.[5] But in cheering for the old man O'Connor does not advocate a carte blanche acceptance of all his behavior or ideas; she only lends her approval of his teaching Tarwater that the prophet's call to mystery—like the writer's call to art—requires a violent commitment to the call and a violent separation from a world full of gainsayers.[6] In a letter, O'Connor explains: "people are depressed by the ending of *VBIA* because they think: poor Tarwater, his mind has been warped by that old man and he's off to make a fool or a martyr of himself. They forget that the old man has taught him the truth and that now he's doing what is right, however crazy" (*Collected Works* 1191).

In fact, using the old man as a necessarily faulty carrier of the truth only strengthens O'Connor's theme. Mason Tarwater, whose name D. G. Kehl found evokes a quack healing potion, is a mere earthen vessel—an image the apostle Paul uses to illustrate that mere men carry the Holy Spirit around in their bodies, and to emphasize the "light of the knowledge of the glory of God in the face of Christ . . . is from God and not from us" (New American Standard version). The gospel Mason preaches is perfect, eternal, salubrious, and stable—Mason is not. Naming the old man after a mason jar also enables O'Connor to use him to symbolize the nature of the work of art; like Wallace Stevens's jar in Tennessee, this novel plants itself in the wilderness and takes dominion everywhere. While Stevens was more concerned with the artificiality and self-consciousness of the work of art as it brings order out of chaos, O'Connor uses Mason Tarwater, as she uses the work of art, to privilege the communication of the prophet's mysterious message over its communicator. That a mason is a bricklayer adds further emphasis to the idea that human creativity, like God's original creation, builds with the stuff of earth. Young Tarwater eventually acknowledges himself as the same earthen vessel, a fragile carrier of divine mystery, when at the end of the novel he smears dirt on his forehead to signify his acceptance of his vocation and of his own eventual death.

The most essential focal point of Tarwater's struggle with his vocation is the character of Bishop. While the old man knows that Tarwater's calling will take a different form from his own, he also knows that the first task God will give him will be to baptize Bishop. "'If by the time I die,' he says to Tarwater, 'I haven't got him baptized, it'll be up to you. It'll be the first mission the Lord sends you'" (335). It is also this very thing that Rayber fights most against; he spends most of the novel trying to dislodge from Tarwater's head the idea that Bishop needs to be baptized.

Although criticism has tended to minimize Bishop's importance in the novel by treating Tarwater's call as merely the vestiges of the old man's vision, O'Connor's prose illustrates the clear centrality of the character as one that represents the divine mystery Tarwater will have to come to terms with before he can begin his ministry.[7] It is Bishop's beauty that Tarwater has to learn to see. The old man's primary mission is to separate Tarwater from Rayber's rationalism, however violently, so that he can be free to see mystery (the beauty of Bishop) and then act on it (baptism). It is important to note that while the old man does plant the seeds in Tarwater's mind, it is not the old man's voice that Tarwater hears when he makes his way back to the schoolteacher's house for the first time. Soon after Tarwater begins to explain to Rayber how he did the right thing by burning down the house to kill the old man, his vision is suddenly mysteriously drawn by Bishop. "His eyes widened and an inner door in them opened in preparation for some inevitable vision" (388). The inevitable vision is of his own relationship to Bishop, who "stood there, dim and ancient, like a child who had been a child for centuries." Tarwater knows instantly "with a certainty sunk in despair . . . that he was called to be a prophet and that the ways of his prophecy would not be remarkable" (389).

As soon as Tarwater receives his unglamorous calling and knows his course is inevitable, he fights it. Tarwater's call is to be a John the Baptist prophet for his time, one who would respect the light of the mystery that came before him and say, like John, "this was He of whom I said, 'He who comes after me has a rank higher than I, for He existed before me'" (John 1:15). Resisting his calling, Tarwater refuses to look at Bishop, and on his first encounter with the child, he precisely inverts John the Baptist's declaration, saying to Bishop with indignation "before you was here, I was here" (350). When he finally does look at Bishop, he ties the child's shoelaces—signifying his realization that the presence of the mystery of God is so much greater than he.

Tarwater humbles himself like John the Baptist: "I baptize you in water, but among you stand One whom you do not know. It is He who comes after me, the thong of whose sandal I am not worthy to untie" (John 1:26-27).

That O'Connor intended for Bishop to be the symbolic focal point of the story—the incarnation of mystery for which the artist strives with necessary humility—is clear from her repetition of the two major scenes concerning Bishop. The two scenes are dramatized both in Tarwater's vision and in Rayber's.[8] In one of these scenes, Tarwater nearly baptizes Bishop in a fountain. Because Tarwater has not completely deadened his spiritual vision (as Rayber has), he cannot avoid seeing Bishop as a transcendental mystery; although here in the flesh, he, like Christ, represents something profound and ineffable in the beyond:

> The sun, which had been tacking from cloud to cloud, emerged above the fountain. A blinding brightness fell on the lion's tangled marble head and gilded the stream of water rushing from his mouth. Then the light, falling more gently, rested like a hand on the child's white head. His face might have been a mirror where the sun had stopped to watch its reflection. (432)

Critics have discussed the Biblical significance of the lion's head and the fountain, emphasizing how the light serves as a sign for Tarwater (Gianonne 135-137). But when considering Tarwater as a reluctant John the Baptist (and remembering that we are seeing through Tarwater's eyes now) the presence of the light is more than a sign—it identifies Bishop with the incarnation. The light resting on the child's head evokes Jesus' baptism, when the Father sent a dove to "light on his head," and said from heaven "this is my beloved son, with whom I am well pleased," and is also reminiscent of the brilliant light seen at Christ's transfiguration and ascension. As a Christ type, Bishop illuminates the mysterious nexus between the visible world and the invisible one.[9] Rayber's vision of the scene has the same emphasis on light, but significantly, Rayber does not understand what he is seeing: "he felt that something was being enacted before him and that if he could understand it, he would have the key to the boy's future" (421).

Bishop's transcendental brightness makes him operate in this text as a symbol for the work of art itself—a created form whose beauty derives from its visible embodiment of the mystery of being. Following after Aquinas and Maritain, O'Connor believed that a work of art's beauty derives from, above all, its ability to capture the object's essential radiance. In the work of art, this radiance delights the intellect:

> If beauty delights the intellect, it is because it is essentially a certain excellence or perfection in the proportion of things to the intellect. Hence the three conditions Saint Thomas assigned to beauty: *integrity*, because the intellect is pleased in fullness of being; *proportion*, because the intellect is pleased in order and unity; and finally, and above all, *radiance* or *clarity*, because the intellect is pleased in light and intelligibility. (24)

It is critical to recognize that Maritain and Aquinas used the term "radiance of form" (interchangeable with "clarity") very precisely to mean the radiance of the object chosen by the artist, a radiance that does not depend upon our ability to see it (or even the artist's ability to render it). As Maritain writes:

> The words *clarity*, *intelligibility*, *light*, which we use to characterize the role of "form" at the heart of things, do not necessarily designate something clear and intelligible *for us*, but rather something clear and luminous *in itself*, intelligible *in itself*, and which often remains obscure to our eyes, either because of the matter which the form in question is buried, or because of the transcendence of the form itself in the things of the spirit. The more substantial and the more profound this secret sense is, the more hidden it is for us; so that, in truth, to say with the Schoolmen that the form is in things the proper principle of intelligibility, is to say at the same time that it is the proper principle of mystery. (There is in fact no mystery where

> there is *nothing to know*; mystery exists where there is more to be known than is given to our comprehension.) To define the beautiful by the radiance of the form is in reality to define it by the radiance of a mystery. (28)

Tarwater, like the artist, can see the radiance of form especially in Bishop, this useless idiot child who only embarrasses his unseeing parents. Bishop's physical ugliness and dim-wittedness emphasize the inexplicable propensity of the divine to take on the humblest forms. But in spite of his ability to see what Bishop represents, Tarwater still fights against the proper response to it.

Rayber is as crucial to the novel as Tarwater's other teacher—the reform minded social scientist who wants to purge Tarwater of his prophetic "delusions." O'Connor correctly predicted that many of her early readers, unable to see the truth within the old man's radicalism, would identify with Rayber and applaud his struggle to "free" Tarwater from the old man's radicalism.[10] But a careful reading of the story illustrates that this schoolteacher receives O'Connor's most vicious attacks. A kind of secondary protagonist, Rayber, too, has the prophet's blood in him; he had heard the call as a young man and then turned away. Rayber represents modern man's philosophy of life and of art that either ignores the transcendent by trying to explain it away, or tries to create its own, controllable world by ignoring reality and living out meaningless abstractions. O'Connor uses Rayber to dramatize the fate of a person and an artist if he or she does not properly respond to mystery.

I have argued that Bishop symbolizes the aim of O'Connor's incarnational art: the manifestation of the mysterious in the concrete, a repetition of the act of the word made flesh. Rayber, ironically the child's father, cannot understand the mystery that he is raising in his own household; his every act (really non-acts, since he can do nothing) operates as a kind of reverse incarnation. He is trying to turn the flesh into word, to use language with the purpose of controlling, and thereby killing, the mystery.

Rayber's effort to kill the mystery initially becomes apparent through his treatment of the old man. Not understanding the nature of Old Tarwater's call, and not being able to separate the content of his beliefs from his eccentricities, Rayber tries to explain him away with words. Rayber interviews the old man for a magazine article that labels his behavior as a psychological aberration, thereby giving Rayber the freedom to ignore everything he says. Tarwater remembers the old man's talking about it, and he reflects: "The old man had not known when he went there to live that every living thing that passed through the nephew's eyes into his head was turned by his brain into a book or a paper or a chart" (341). When Rayber sees living things with his eyes, he extinguishes the life in them; by straining the mysterious through his brain, he flattens it into a quantifiable chart, book, or set of figures. Thus Rayber treats the inexplicable in the same fashion as does the modern scientist or the analytic philosopher—as a puzzle to solve by manipulating the unknowns into answerable questions. The end result is the elimination—to Rayber's mind anyway—of mystery.[11]

Mason Tarwater intuitively understands that the words to which Rayber tries to reduce him are stillborn. While the old man had thought that Rayber's interest in him indicated a return to the faith of his childhood, he soon discovers that Rayber really intended to explain away the family madness:

> The old man had thought this interest in his forebears would bear fruit, but what it bore, what it bore, stench and shame, were dead words. What it bore was a dry and seedless fruit, incapable even of rotting, dead from the beginning. From time to time, the old man would spit out of his mouth, like gobbets of poison, some of the idiotic sentences from the schoolteacher's piece. Wrath had burned them on his memory, word for word. (141)

Christ refers to the kingdom of heaven metaphorically as a seed with great potential for growth and multiplication. Here, Rayber's words are dry and seedless, dead from the beginning. In the view of Pierre Teilhard de Chardin and Claude Tresmontant, writers O'Connor read and respected, Christ's incarnation validated the created world and encouraged people to be a part of its ongoing creation, growth, and evolution. Here, Rayber works against that life force by trying to reduce the whole of a human person into the sum of his psychological parts, parts that can be described and categorized with abstract words. Rayber's attempt to make flesh into word is so far from being life giving that it cannot even rot.

Rayber's inability to accept mystery is especially revealed in his attitude toward Bishop. He tries to contain what he does not understand by ignoring his feelings and ignoring Bishop altogether. In many ways, the very existence of Rayber's idiot child is his moment of grace, because the child serves as a constant reminder that God's ways are inexplicable. With his belief in modern science, Rayber cannot accept the possibility of an unanswerable question and uses Bishop as a focal point for his anger against God and for his attack on the old man. When the old man tries to baptize Bishop, Rayber shouts "You get away from here . . . Ask the Lord why He made him an idiot in the first place, uncle. Tell him I want to know why!" The old man responds "Yours not to ask! Yours not to question the mind of the Lord God Almighty. Yours not to grind the Lord into your head and spit out a number!" (351). Rayber tries to use the existence of the inexplicable to mock the idea of God, reducing creation to a random accident.

Rayber also represents what O'Connor and Maritain describe as the modern impulse to value every object according to its utility. Rayber cannot understand why God would create an idiot child who has no usefulness to society; he looks on Bishop with a scornful attitude, calling him "five years old for all eternity and useless forever" (351). When Tarwater first visits their house, Rayber gets excited about the possibility of molding Tarwater into the son he wanted to have: "You're going to have a chance now for the first time in your life. A chance to develop into a useful man, a chance to use your talents, to do what you want to do and not what he wanted—whatever idiocy it was" (389). But Tarwater is not listening to Rayber and his schemes to make him a useful man; his eyes are drawn to Bishop standing beyond, and his pupils dilate. Rayber's attitude is clear: "That's only Bishop," he tells Tarwater, "he's not all right . . . all the things that I would do for him—if it were any use—I'll do for you" (389).

Because Rayber cannot mold Bishop into anything "useful," he refuses to see Bishop's essential beauty, and constantly averts his eyes from him in disgust. Maritain argues that the modern world's insistence on the sovereignty of rationalism leads it to treat as useless whatever is truly beautiful; the modern man "must, if he is to be logical, treat as useless, and therefore as rejected, all that by any grounds bears the mark of the spirit" (37). If this modern spirit contaminates the artist, he will fail. He will either expect of art "the mystical fullness God alone can give" or fail to understand that the value of art lies in its merely being good in and of itself. O'Connor reflects on this latter problem in "Catholic Novelists": "St. Thomas Aquinas . . . says that a work of art is a good in and by itself. Now we want to make something that will have some utilitarian value. Yet what is good in itself glorifies God because it reflects God" (*Mystery and Manners* 171).

The Violent Bear It Away most dramatically illustrates O'Connor's aesthetic concerns through its treatment of Rayber's inexplicable love for Bishop. Accustomed to seeing love as a tool that can be used to transform psychological "cases" when nothing else works, Rayber recognizes his own love for Bishop as of another order entirely. "It was not the kind that could be used for the child's improvement or his own. It was love without reason, love for something futureless, love that appeared to exist only to be itself, imperious and all demanding, the kind that would cause him to make a fool of himself in an instant" (401).

In O'Connor's theory of art, Rayber's love for Bishop is the same love that will result in the reader if the artist properly renders the beautiful. Rayber's love scares him because it puts him in danger of coming outside of himself and into a spiritual relationship with God and creation; the love, O'Connor writes, "only began with Bishop and then like an avalanche covered everything his reason hated. He always felt with it a rush of longing to have the old man's eyes—insane, fish-coloured, violent with their impossible vision of a world transfigured—turned on him once again" (401). Bishop, as an incarnation of the mystery of being, has the power to transform vision by drawing the viewer out of himself and into his first steps toward God. Bishop thus operates in the story both as an object Rayber responds to and as a symbol for the well-written story that the reader responds to. It is this redemptive power of the beautiful that most interested O'Connor; she would agree with Maritain that "the beautiful is essentially delightful. This is why, of its very nature and precisely as beautiful, it stirs desire and produces love . . . love in its turn produces ecstasy, that is to say, it puts the lover outside of himself; ec-stasy, of which the soul experiences a diminished form when it is seized by the beauty of the work of art, and the fullness when it is absorbed, like the dew, by the beauty of God" (26-27). When Rayber feels this love for Bishop, it changes his vision; he is tempted to love the world—not for the world as if it was its own end, but with a love that will lead him to God.[12]

Rayber, of course, fights that love and all of its expansive potential. By anesthetizing himself to Bishop, he anesthetizes himself to God. Like a man trying to fortify his belief that the earth is flat by converting the undecided, he tries to get Tarwater to see Bishop, and the rite of baptism, precisely the way he does. "Just forget Bishop exists," he grits his teeth and tells Tarwater, "He's just a mistake of nature. Try not even to be aware of him" (403). Ironically, Rayber believes that if he can just get Tarwater to look at Bishop, he will see him for what Rayber thinks he is—a meaningless freak of nature—and have the power to resist baptizing him. But it is precisely when Tarwater does look at Bishop with his prophet/artist eyes that he recognizes the mystery and understands that he will have to actively fight off the urge to baptize him in order to avoid his calling. When Tarwater accidentally looks at Bishop in the Cherokee Lodge scene, the mystery expands to overtake his entire visual field: "He seemed to see the little boy and nothing else, no air around him, no room, no nothing, as if his gaze had slipped and fallen into the center of the child's eyes and was still falling down and down and down" (427).

A writer who believes in mystery, O'Connor points out, "will be interested in what we don't understand rather than in what we do. He will be interested in possibility rather than in probability" (*Collected Works* 816). In *The Violent Bear It Away*, Bishop's eyes represent that window into the world of possibility, a world that O'Connor represents metaphorically as a silent and invisible country. While Rayber is always trying to bind the mystery of life up into meaningless words, to contain it in some package, Tarwater knows that the mystery behind Bishop is ineffable and wordless. It is the silence that he feels urging him to baptize Bishop—a silence that speaks even more loudly in contrast to the sibilant and prolix voice of his "friend." Tarwater's choice is a choice between listening to this persistent voice, with its constant rationalizations, or to the silent call of mystery. In this scene, Tarwater cannot avoid seeing the silent country:

> It was a strange silence. It seemed to lie all around him like an invisible country whose border he was always on the edge of, always in danger of crossing. From time to time as they had walked in the city, he had looked to the side and seen his own form alongside him in a store window, transparent as a snakeskin. It moved beside him like some violent ghost who had already crossed over and was reproaching him from the other side. If he turned his head the opposite way, there would be the dim-witted boy, handing onto the schoolteacher's coat, watching him. His mouth hung in a lopsided smile but there was a judging sternness about his forehead. The boy never looked lower than the top of his head except by accident for the silent country appeared to be reflected again in the center of his eyes. It stretched out there, limitless and clear. (429)

O'Connor often uses the mirror image in her fiction when her characters face struggles with themselves. Mr. Head and Nelson in "The Artificial Nigger" see similar ghostly reflections in the train window. Here,

Tarwater is able to see the silent country through his transparent reflection; it is a vision of himself decreasing so that the mystery might increase. Thinking he can avoid that vision, he turns his head toward Bishop, but Bishop's eyes again reflect the silent country to which he is called. The only thing that keeps Tarwater from baptizing Bishop here, Tarwater realizes, is the "wise voice that sustained him"—the stranger that has become confidant, full of verbal reproaches to fill the silence Tarwater so wants to avoid.

I have been arguing that when Rayber tries to get Tarwater to see Bishop the way he does, he becomes O'Connor's representation of that tendency in modern man to try to eliminate, contain, or avoid mystery. The modern fiction writer, with his insistence on realism, is in the same danger of writing myopically about this present world and avoiding the one beyond. But in O'Connor's aesthetics, this is not the only danger the writer faces. The writer, particularly the Catholic novelist, is in danger of bypassing the real world in order to try to get to the transcendental world directly; he is in danger of skipping the "what-is" in order to communicate his vision. In O'Connor's view of art, the central paradox is that it is mainly due to the artist's adherence to the visible that he is able to reveal the invisible; the artist has to accept limitations in order to transcend them. "What the fiction writer will discover, if he discovers anything at all," she writes "is that he himself cannot move or mold reality in the interests of abstract truth. The writer learns, perhaps more quickly than the reader, to be humble in the face of what-is" (808).

Rayber commits the error O'Connor discusses: he tries to make reality conform to his abstractions. Rayber believes that he can re-create Tarwater into his image of a useful adult. Not surprisingly, Rayber can only believe in his own project when Tarwater is not in the room; when Tarwater is present, the "what-is" overwhelms him. "Once out of sight of the boy [Rayber] felt a pressure had been lifted from the atmosphere. He eliminated the oppressive presence from his thoughts and retained only those aspects of it that could be abstracted, clean, into the future person he envisioned" (441).

Rayber's abstract reform impulse fails for the same reason a new writer's abstractions fail: it avoids reality. In "The Nature and Aim of Fiction" O'Connor describes this pitfall. Her description of the bad novelist sounds remarkably like a description of Rayber:

> But the world of the fiction writer is full of matter, and this is what the beginning fiction writers are very loath to create. They are concerned primarily with unfleshed ideas and emotions. They are apt to be reformers and to want to write because they are possessed not by a story but by the bare bones of some abstract notion. They are conscious of problems, not of people, of questions and issues, not of the texture of existence, of case histories and of everything that has a sociological smack, instead of with all those concrete details of life that make actual the mystery of our position on earth. (68)

Like the utopian who believes he can ignore reality to engineer his fantasy, Rayber refuses to see what is around him. In *The Violent Bear It Away*, O'Connor mocks Rayber through Mason Tarwater, who spots his impotent idealism right away. When Tarwater asks his great uncle why Rayber did not come back for him, the old man says "I'll tell you exactly why. It was because he found you a heap of trouble. He wanted it all in his head. You can't change a child's pants in your head" (378). O'Connor adamantly enjoins the fiction writer not to avoid dirty diapers; they are the material of his art. She insists that "the materials of the fiction writer are the humblest. Fiction is about everything human and we are made out of dust, and if you scorn getting yourself dusty, then you shouldn't try to write fiction. It's not a grand enough job for you" (68). Rayber's subjective idealism also heightens the story's irony: while Rayber thinks the old man's calling is only in his head, he fails to realize that by ignoring the what-is, he has created his own reality—he is the true schizophrenic whose delusions come from within.

O'Connor's most vicious attack against the rational idealism Rayber represents consists in making Rayber into a character completely unable to act. Able to tolerate neither Bishop's physical grotesqueness nor the transcendental mystery he represents, Rayber decides to escape Bishop by drowning him. But Rayber finds that he cannot act against the mystery any more than he can understand it; when trying to drown Bishop, he loses courage when he realizes that his violent love would have no focus without Bishop and that he would have to face it in himself if Bishop were gone. It is not because Rayber cannot see the mystery that he does not act; it is because he knows that acting against Bishop would not kill the mystery, only complicate it, free it to take on other, unpredictable forms. Fearing what he cannot control, Rayber's modern faith renders him powerless to do anything but anesthetize himself to the mysterious. Like modern man, his very last defense against what he cannot know is not to think about it.

It is Tarwater who can act. O'Connor's most searing irony in *The Violent Bear It Away* is that Tarwater is better at being Rayber than Rayber is; in a final attempt to ignore his calling as a prophet, he drowns Bishop with little difficulty, thinking that it will mean the end of his struggles. "Now all I have to do is mind my own bidnes until I die. I don't have to baptize or prophesy" (458). But while Tarwater believes that he controls the situation by overpowering Bishop, in actuality the mystery controls him; he accidentally says the words of baptism over him, inadvertently fulfilling his first mission as a prophet, and opening him up to later visions.

This murder/baptism scene is, without doubt, the novel's center point. Like the near baptism in the fountain, it is played out once through Rayber's experience of it, and again through Tarwater's, emphasizing their different views. In Catholic theology, the sacrament of baptism is the first and most necessary, because it is the way by which individuals become children of God; therefore, in this novel, it is the focal point of the mystery of God's involvement with His creation. But O'Connor knew that for the modern reader, baptism had become a meaningless rite that had to be reinvested with significance. In an unforgettable scene, she conflates murder with baptism to shock the reader into paying attention to the sacrament of baptism and to the struggle in Tarwater between the physical and spiritual realms. In "Novelist and Believer," O'Connor explains:

> When I write a novel in which the central action is a baptism, I am very well aware that for a majority of my readers, baptism is a meaningless rite, and so in my novel I have to see that this baptism carries enough awe and mystery to jar the reader into some kind of emotional recognition of its significance. To this end I have to bend the whole novel—its language, its structure, its action. I have to make the reader feel, in his bones if nowhere else, that something is going on here that counts. Distortion in this case is an instrument; exaggeration has a purpose, and the whole structure of the story or novel has been made what it is because of belief. This is not the kind of distortion that destroys; it is the kind that reveals, or should reveal. (*Mystery and Manners* 162)

It is important to point out that O'Connor believed the kind of distortion she describes here has limits. The writer cannot invent for the character some kind of unbelievable action; Tarwater has to be capable of committing this murder, and the murder has to be capable of revealing the mystery to him in spite of his best intentions to avoid it. The murder/baptism conflation thus perfectly represents the struggle the writer faces when he wants to ground the mystery in the concrete. One way this can be seen is to imagine what the novel would be like if O'Connor went for the sentimental effect, instead: the common way to evoke sentimentality in this scenario would be to have Tarwater baptize Bishop and accidentally drown him in the process. For O'Connor this would be destructive manipulation; as Maritain writes "if [the work] aims at emotion, at affecting the appetites or arousing the passions, it falsifies itself, and thus another element of lie enters into it" (62). O'Connor's distortions, as the above quote reveals, carry the purpose of revealing the mystery to the reader, even though the reader has to work for it.

And if the reader must rigorously work her intellect in order to understand the mystery, O'Connor has her right where she wants her. O'Connor devised the murder/baptism scene to compound signification, to make the moment operate anagogically. Consider the depth of meaning in the scene. Because Bishop dies, his innocent murder makes him a Christ figure. Tarwater both baptizes him and kills him, evincing the choice all humanity makes between being a confident prophet or one of Christ's murderers.[13] Since baptism means that the believer is "buried with Christ in his death" O'Connor reminds the reader that these truths are far from merely metaphorical, and also provides links to the old man's death and Tarwater's awareness of his own mortality. O'Connor has fulfilled her prescription for a novel, that it provide a slow accretion of details that will "accumulate meaning from the story itself, and when this happens, they become symbolic in their action" (*Mystery and Manners* 70). And all this is done without resorting to the sentimentality that would cheapen the story's central action.

Ultimately the conflation of the murder—with its association of violence and struggle for the prophet, and the baptism—with its association of ineffable mystery, compounds the metaphorical depth of the scene that in O'Connor's aesthetics lends the entire work its beauty. Maritain writes that "the more things given to the intellect, the greater is the possibility of delight. This is why art as ordered to beauty refuses—at least when its object permits it—to stop at forms or colors, or sounds or words grasped in themselves as things, but it grasps them also as making known something other than themselves, that is to say, as signs . . . the more the object of art is laden with signification . . . the greater and richer and higher will be the possibility of delight and beauty" (54). O'Connor winds many of the details she had been using since the beginning of the novel into the baptism scene, lending to it the kind of beauty Maritain admires.

The reader is not the only one left pondering the scene. Try as he might, Tarwater cannot get the baptism out of his mind. He tells the truck driver who picks him up about it, and when he falls asleep in the cab, he re-envisions the entire episode. He has to "deliberately, forcefully close the inner eye" that presents the scene to him again and again (463). When he thinks of saying the words of the baptism, he must remind himself that it was an accident in order to not be affected by the mystery. He does not succeed. Because of the strange conflation of violence with the sacramental rite, the reader replays the scene as well; to make sense of the story, the reader's vision must operate anagogically, too; and so now has O'Connor tricked the reader into sharing Tarwater's participation in the depth of mystery. Tarwater baptizes Bishop in spite of himself, and we see the mystery operate in spite of ourselves.

Under the pressure of his own participation in the mystery of baptism, and in the face of increasing spiritual hunger, Tarwater has an experience of malevolent evil that finally pushes him to obey his call. The inner voice of the "stranger" who had been trying to dissuade him from his vocation is incarnated in the form of a homosexual rapist whose attack reminds him of the city to which God originally called him. "He threw himself to the ground and with his face against the dirt of the grave, he heard the command. GO WARN THE CHILDREN OF GOD OF THE TERRIBLE SPEED OF MERCY. The words were as silent as seeds opening one at a time in his blood" (478).

Just as the mystery of God's call opens up inside Tarwater's blood, the symbolic layering of the novel opens up inside the reader's mind as the story draws to a close. Dramatizing her struggle to make her fiction live by giving form to ineffable truths, O'Connor successfully follows her own dictum that "A story really isn't any good unless it successfully resists paraphrase, unless it hangs on and expands in the mind" (*Mystery and Manners* 108). And for O'Connor, this is the moment of redemption for the reader, for it is when a story expands in the mind that it makes room for mystery.

Notes

1. Stephens, for example, sees the ending as Tarwater's "yielding . . . to the vision of the old man" (102). While certainly the old man's voice represents the call Tarwater struggles against, Tarwater is also aware that the old man's voice is not the call itself. Without this distinction the novel deflates into a mere psychological battle over the formation of a young person's mind, a reading O'Connor clearly resisted.

2. It is useful to compare *The Violent Bear It Away* with *Wise Blood* to strengthen this point. Hazel Motes has no influences but the fading memory of his mother—his call comes absolutely from a given knowledge.

3. This letter is particularly useful because it separates the prophet's imaginative vision from his morality. The writer is like the prophet not because he has a moral base, but because he can see into the spiritual depth of the physical world.

4. For an essay treating the asceticism of O'Connor's art, see Brinkmeyer, "Asceticism."

5. Robert Brinkmeyer's *The Art and Vision of Flannery O'Connor*, though an excellent study, is a good example of how most critics want to apologize for the fundamentalism of the narrator in *The Violent Bear It Away*. Brinkmeyer argues that the narrator succeeds in destroying modern rationalism completely; I believe that O'Connor illustrates that Tarwater must learn how to submit his rational thought to the vision he has been given by God. This is a reversal of the modern belief.

6. In a letter to A., O'Connor wrote "there is a great deal that has to be given up or be taken away if you are going to succeed in writing a body of work" (*The Habit of Being* 176). Brinkmeyer's "Asceticism" addresses more fully the rigid disciplines O'Connor believed the artist must live by to follow his or her calling.

7. Particularly puzzling is Johansen's reading of Bishop: "Young Tarwater also resists the seeds in the blood and flees to the periphery where he confronts an idiot child" (131), and Baumgaertner's argument that Bishop is a manifestation of the metaphor of the dead word (148).

8. Asals illustrates how the repetition enables O'Connor to emphasize the tremendous similarity and dissimilarity between Tarwater's and Rayber's vision (171).

9. Not that Bishop acts like Christ, but that his existence ontologically points to Christ's embodiment as a man in this world. This distinction is important.

10. For a description of some of these early reviews, see Stephens.

11. Foster argues that "the goal towards which both scientist and philosopher are working is a state in which there will be no more mystery" (20). O'Connor would have agreed.

12. It is important to note that his experience of this love is not only through his intellect, but is more accurately an aesthetic experience, a widening of his vision via his imagination as well as his mind.

13. For a discussion of the paradoxical nature of violence in O'Connor's fiction, see Muller.

Works Cited

Asals, Frederick. *Flannery O'Connor: The Imagination of Extremity*. Athens: U of Georgia P, 1982.

Baumgaertner, Jill P. *Flannery O'Connor: A Proper Scaring*. Wheaton, IL: Harold Shaw Publishers, 1988.

Brinkmeyer, Robert H., Jr. *The Art and Vision of Flannery O'Connor*. Baton Rouge: Louisiana State UP, 1989.

____________. "Asceticism and Imaginative Vision." In *Flannery O'Connor: New Perspectives*. Athens: U of Georgia P, 1996.

Foster, Michael Bishop. *Mystery and Philosophy*. Westport, CT: Greenwood Press Publishers, 1957.

Frederic, Sister M. Catherine, O.S.F. *The Handbook of Catholic Practices*. New York: Hawthorn Books, 1964.

Gianonne, Richard. *Flannery O'Connor and the Mystery of Love*. Urbana: U of Illinois P, 1989.

Johansen, Ruthann Knechel. *The Narrative Secret of Flannery O'Connor: The Trickster as Interpreter*. Tuscaloosa: U of Alabama P, 1994.

Kehl, D. G. "Flannery O'Connor's Catholicon: The Source and Significance of the Name 'Tarwater.'" *Notes on Contemporary Literature* 15:2 (1985): 2-3.

Maritain, Jacques. *Art and Scholasticism and The Frontiers of Poetry*. Trans. Joseph W. Evans. New York: Charles Scribner's Sons, 1962.

Muller, Gilbert H. *Nightmares and Visions: Flannery O'Connor and the Catholic Grotesque*. Athens: U of Georgia P, 1972.

O'Connor, Flannery. *Collected Works*. Ed. Sally Fitzgerald. New York: Library of America, 1988.

____________. *The Habit of Being*. Ed. Sally Fitzgerald. New York: Farrar, Straus and Giroux, 1979.

____________. *Mystery and Manners: Occasional Prose*. Ed. Sally Fitzgerald and Robert Fitzgerald. New York: Farrar, Straus and Giroux, 1969.

Stephens, Martha. *The Question of Flannery O'Connor*. Baton Rouge: Louisiana State UP, 1973.

Teilhard de Chardin, Pierre. *The Divine Milieu*. New York: Harper & Row, 1960.

Tresmontant, Claude. *A Study of Hebrew Thought*. Trans. Michael Francis Gibson. New York: Desclee Company, 1960.

RESOURCES

Chronology of Flannery O'Connor's Life

1925	Flannery O'Connor is born on March 25 to Edward O'Connor, Jr., and Regina Cline O'Connor in Savannah, Georgia.
1938	O'Connor's father takes job in Atlanta with the Federal Housing Administration; O'Connor and her mother move to Milledgeville, Georgia.
1941	O'Connor's father dies of lupus.
1941	O'Connor graduates from Peabody High School.
1945	O'Connor graduates from Georgia State College for Women.
1945	O'Connor enters journalism program at University of Iowa.
1945	O'Connor enrolls in Iowa Writers' Workshop.
1946	O'Connor publishes her first short story, "The Geranium," in *Accent.*
1947	O'Connor receives her M.F.A. degree from Iowa.
1948	O'Connor goes to Yaddo, the writers' colony in Saratoga Springs, New York.
1949	O'Connor leaves Yaddo after a dispute about the center's director.
1949	O'Connor lives with Robert and Sally Fitzgerald in Connecticut.
1950	On trip to Milledgeville, O'Connor falls ill and is diagnosed with lupus.
1951	O'Connor goes with her mother to live at Andalusia, a farm outside of Milledgeville.
1952	O'Connor publishes her first novel, *Wise Blood.*

1955	O'Connor publishes her first short story collection, *A Good Man is Hard to Find, and Other Stories*.
1958	O'Connor visits Lourdes in France and has an audience with Pope Pius XII in Rome.
1960	O'Connor publishes *The Violent Bear It Away*.
1964	O'Connor dies of kidney failure on August 3 and is buried in Milledgeville next to her father in Memory Hill Cemetery.
1965	*Everything That Rises Must Converge* is published.
1969	*Mystery and Manners* is published.
1971	*The Complete Stories* is published.
1972	*The Complete Stories* wins the National Book Award.
1974	The Flannery O'Connor Memorial Room is dedicated at Georgia College and State University.
1979	*The Habit of Being: Letters* is published.
1980	John Huston's film *Wise Blood* is released.
1983	*The Presence of Grace* is published.
1986	*The Correspondence of Flannery O'Connor and the Brainard Cheneys* is published.
1987	*Conversations with Flannery O'Connor* is published.
1988	*Collected Works* is published by Library of America.
2009	*The Collected Stories* is named Best of the National Book Awards Fiction from 1950 to 2008.

Works by Flannery O'Connor

Long Fiction

Wise Blood, 1952
The Violent Bear It Away, 1960

Short Fiction

A Good Man Is Hard to Find, and Other Stories, 1955
"Good Country People," 1955
"Revelation," 1964
Everything That Rises Must Converge, 1965
The Complete Stories, 1971

Nonfiction

Mystery and Manners, 1969
The Habit of Being: Letters, 1979 (Sally Fitzgerald, editor)
The Presence of Grace, 1983
The Correspondence of Flannery O'Connor and the Brainard Cheneys, 1986

Miscellaneous

Collected Works, 1988

Bibliography

Ambrosiano, Jason. "'From the Blood of Abel to His Own': Intersubjectivity and Salvation in Flannery O'Connor's *The Violent Bear It Away*." *Flannery O'Connor Review* 5 (2007): 130-40.

Asals, Frederick. *Flannery O'Connor: The Imagination of Extremity*. Athens: University of Georgia Press, 1982.

Askin, Denise T. "Anagogical Vision and Comedic Form in Flannery O'Connor: The Reasonable Use of the Unreasonable." *Renascence* 57 (Fall 2004): 47-62.

Bacon, Jon Lance. *Flannery O'Connor and Cold War Culture*. New York: Cambridge University Press, 1993.

Balee, Susan. *Flannery O'Connor: Literary Prophet of the South*. New York: Chelsea House, 1994.

Baumgaertner, Jill P. *Flannery O'Connor: A Proper Scaring*. Wheaton, IL: Harold Shaw, 1988.

Bleikasten, André. "Beginning and Ending in Flannery O'Connor." *Mississippi Quarterly* 59 (2005-06): 177-86.

___________. "The Heresy of Flannery O'Connor." *Critical Essays on Flannery O'Connor*. Ed. Melvin J. Friedman and Beverly Lyon Clark. Boston: G. K. Hall, 1985.

Bloom, Harold, ed. *Flannery O'Connor*. New York: Chelsea House, 1986.

___________, ed. *Flannery O'Connor: Comprehensive Research and Study Guide*. Broomall, PA: Chelsea House, 1999.

Bolton, Betsy. "Placing Violence, Embodying Grace: Flannery O'Connor's 'Displaced Person'." *Studies in Short Fiction* 34 (Winter 1997): 87-104.

Brinkmeyer, Robert H. *The Art and Vision of Flannery O'Connor*. Baton Rouge: Louisiana State University Press, 1989.

___________. "Borne Away by Violence: The Reader and Flannery O'Connor." *Southern Review* 15 (1979): 313-21.

Browning, Preston M. *Flannery O'Connor*. Carbondale: Southern Illinois University Press, 1974.

Caruso, Teresa, ed. *"On the Subject of the Feminist Business": Re-reading Flannery O'Connor*. New York: Peter Lang, 2004.

Cash, Jean. *Flannery O'Connor: A Life*. Knoxville: University of Tennessee Press, 2002.

Ciuba, Gary. *Desire, Violence, and Divinity in Modern Southern Fiction: Katherine Anne Porter, Flannery O'Connor, Cormac McCarthy, Walker Percy*. Baton Rouge: Louisiana State University Press, 2007.

Coles, Robert. *Flannery O'Connor's South*. Baton Rouge: Louisiana State University Press, 1980.

Daniel, Scott. "Gender-Bending Innuendo and Mystical Theology in O'Connor's *Wise Blood*." *Flannery O'Connor Review* 4 (2006): 110-21.

Darretta, John Lawrence. *Before the Sun Has Set: Retribution in the Fiction of Flannery O'Connor*. New York: Peter Lang, 2007.

Desmond, John. "By Force of Will: Flannery O'Connor, the Broken Synthesis, and the Problem with Rayber." *Flannery O'Connor Review* 6 (2008): 135-46.

____________. "Flannery O'Connor and the Symbol." *Logos* 5 (2002): 143-56.

____________. *Risen Sons: Flannery O'Connor's Vision of History*. Athens: University of Georgia Press, 1987.

Di Renzo, Anthony. *American Gargoyles: Flannery O'Connor and the Medieval Grotesque*. Carbondale: Southern Illinois University Press, 1993.

Drake, Robert. *Flannery O'Connor: A Critical Essay*. Grand Rapids, MI: William B. Eerdmans, 1966.

Driggers, Stephen G., Robert J. Dunn, and Sarah E. Gordon. *The Manuscripts of Flannery O'Connor at Georgia College*. Athens: University of Georgia Press, 1989.

Driskell, Leon V., and Joan T. Brittain, eds. *The Eternal Crossroads: The Art of Flannery O'Connor*. Lexington: University Press of Kentucky, 1971.

Edmondson, Henry T., III. "Modernity Versus Mystery in Flannery O'Connor's short Story 'A View of the Woods.'" *Interpretation* 29 (2001): 187-204.

____________. *Return to Good and Evil: Flannery O'Connor's Response to Nihilism*. Lanham, MD: Lexington Books, 2002.

Edmunds, Susan. "Through a Glass Darkly: Visions of Integrated Community in Flannery O'Connor's *Wise Blood*." *Twentieth Century Literature* 37 (Winter 1996): 559-85.

Edwards, Bruce L., Jr. "Flannery O'Connor: Defamiliarizing the Mystery of Godliness." *Literature and Belief* 4 (1984): 69-78.

Eggenschwiler, David. *The Christian Humanism of Flannery O'Connor*. Detroit, MI: Wayne State University Press, 1972.

Enjolras, Laurence. *Flannery O'Connor's Characters*. Lanham, MD: University Presses of America, 1998.

Feeley, Kathleen. *Flannery O'Connor: Voice of the Peacock*. New Brunswick, NJ: Rutgers University Press, 1972.

Feth, Michel. "The Stained-Glass Man: Word and Icon in Flannery O'Connor's 'Parker's Back.'" *Journal of the Short Story in English* 45 (Autumn 2005): 2-11.

Fickett, Harold, and Douglas R. Gilbert. *Flannery O'Connor: Images of Grace*. Grand Rapids, MI: William B. Eerdmans, 1986.

Fowler, Doreen. "Deconstructing Racial Difference: O'Connor's 'The Artificial Nigger.'" *Flannery O'Connor Bulletin* 24 (1995-96): 22-32.

Friedman, Melvin J., and Beverly Lyon Clark, eds. *Critical Essays on Flannery O'Connor*. Boston: G. K. Hall, 1985.

Friedman, Melvin J., and Lewis A. Lawson, eds. *The Added Dimension: The Art and Mind of Flannery O'Connor*. 2d ed. New York: Fordham University Press, 1977.

Gentry, Marshall Bruce. *Flannery O'Connor's Religion of the Grotesque*. Jackson: University Press of Mississippi, 1986.

Getz, Lorine M. *Nature and Grace in Flannery O'Connor's Fiction*. New York: Edwin Mellen Press, 1982.

Giannone, Richard. *Flannery O'Connor and the Mystery of Love*. Urbana: University of Illinois Press, 1989.

____________. *Flannery O'Connor, Hermit Novelist*. Urbana: University of Illinois Press, 2000.

____________. "Making It in Darkness." *Flannery O'Connor Review* 6 (2008): 103-18.

Golden, Robert E., and Mary C. Sullivan. *Flannery O'Connor and Caroline Gordon: A Reference Guide*. Boston: G. K. Hall, 1977.

Gooch, Brad. *Flannery*. New York: Little, Brown, 2009.

Gordon, Sarah. *Flannery O'Connor: The Obedient Imagination*. Athens: University of Georgia Press, 2000.

____________, ed. *Flannery O'Connor: In Celebration of Genius*. Athens, GA: Hill Street Press, 2000.

Gretlund, Jan Nordby, and Karl-Heinz Westarp, eds. *Flannery O'Connor's Radical Reality*. Columbia: University of South Carolina Press, 2006.

Grimshaw, James A., Jr. *The Flannery O'Connor Companion*. Westport, CT: Greenwood Press, 1981.

Haddox, Thomas F. "'Something Haphazard and Botched': Flannery O'Connor's Critique of the Visual in 'Parker's Back.'" *Mississippi Quarterly* 57 (Summer 2004): 407-21.

Hardy, Donald W. *Narrating Knowledge in Flannery O'Connor's Fiction: A Linguistic Approach to the Novels and Short Stories of Flannery O'Connor*. Columbia: University of South Carolina Press, 2003.

Havird, David. "The Saving Rape: Flannery O'Connor and the Patriarchal Religion." *Mississippi Quarterly* 47 (1993): 15-26.

Hawkes, John. "Flannery O'Connor's Devil." *Flannery O'Connor*. Ed. Harold Bloom. New York: Chelsea House, 1986. 9-17.

Hawkins, Peter S. *The Language of Grace: Flannery O'Connor, Walker Percy, and Iris Murdoch*. Cambridge, MA: Cowley, 1983.

Hendin, Josephine. *The World of Flannery O'Connor*. Bloomington: Indiana University Press, 1970.

Hewitt, Avis. "'Someone to Shoot Her Every Minute of Her Life': Maternity and Violent Death in Helena Maria Viramontes and Flannery O'Connor." *Flannery O'Connor Review* 4 (2006): 12-26.

Hewitt, Avis, and Robert Donahoo, eds. *Flannery O'Connor in the Age of Terrorism*. Knoxville: University of Tennessee Press, 2010.

Humphries, Jefferson. *The Otherness Within: Gnostic Readings in Marcel Proust, Flannery O'Connor, and François Villon*. Baton Rouge: Louisiana State University Press, 1983.

Hurley, Jennifer A., ed. *Readings on Flannery O'Connor*. San Diego, CA: Greenhaven Press, 2001.

Hyman, Stanley Edgar. *Flannery O'Connor*. University of Minnesota Pamphlets on American Writers: No. 54. Minneapolis: University of Minnesota Press, 1966.

Johansen, Ruthann Knechel. *The Narrative Secret of Flannery O'Connor: The Trickster as Interpreter*. Tuscaloosa: University of Alabama Press, 1994.

Jordan, Michael M. "Flannery O'Connor's Writing: A Guide for the Perplexed." *Modern Age* 47 (Winter 2005): 48-57.

Katz, Claire. "Flannery O'Connor's Rage of Vision." *American Literature* 46 (March 1974): 54-67.

Kessler, Edward. *Flannery O'Connor and the Language of Apocalypse*. Princeton, NJ: Princeton University Press, 1986.

Kilcourse, George. *Flannery O'Connor's Religious Imagination: A World with Everything Off Balance*. New York: Paulist Press, 2001.

Kinney, Arthur F. *Flannery O'Connor's Library: Resources of Being*. Athens: University of Georgia Press, 1985.

Kreyling, Michael, ed. *New Essays on Wise Blood*. New York: Cambridge University Press, 1995.

Lake, Christina Bieber. *The Incarnational Art of Flannery O'Connor*. Macon, GA: Mercer University Press, 2005.

Logsdon, Loren, and Charles W. Mayer, eds. *Since Flannery O'Connor: Essays on the Contemporary American Short Story*. Macomb: Western Illinois University Press, 1987.

McFarland, Dorothy Tuck. *Flannery O'Connor*. New York: Frederick Ungar, 1976.

McGill, Robert. "The Life You Write May Be Your Own: Epistolary Autobiography and the Reluctant Resurrection of Flannery O'Connor." *Southern Literary Journal* 36 (Spring 2004): 31-46.

McKenzie, Barbara. *Flannery O'Connor's Georgia*. Athens: University of Georgia Press, 1980.

McMullen, Joanne Halleran, and Jon Parrish Peede, eds. *Inside the Church of Flannery O'Connor: Sacrament, Sacramental, and the Sacred in Her Fiction*. Macon, GA: Mercer University Press, 2007.

Magee, Rosemary, ed. *Conversations with Flannery O'Connor*. Jackson: University Press of Mississippi, 1987.

Martin, Carter W. "Comedy and Humor in Flannery O'Connor's Fiction." *Flannery O'Connor Review* 4 (1975): 1-12.

__________. *The True Country: Themes in the Fiction of Flannery O'Connor*. Nashville, TN: Vanderbilt University Press, 1968.

May, John R. *The Pruning Word: The Parables of Flannery O'Connor*. Notre Dame, IN: University of Notre Dame Press, 1976.

Monroe, W. F. "Flannery O'Connor's Sacramental Icon: 'The Artificial Nigger.'" *South Central Review* 1 (Winter 1984): 64-81.

Montgomery, Marion. *Hillbilly Thomist: Flannery O'Connor, St. Thomas, and the Limits of Art*. Jefferson, NC: McFarland, 2006.

Muller, Gilbert H. *Nightmares and Visions: Flannery O'Connor and the Catholic Grotesque*. Athens: University of Georgia Press, 1972.

Nielsen, Erik. "The Hidden Structure of *Wise Blood*." *The New Orleans Review* 19 (1992): 91-97.

O'Gorman, Farrell. *Peculiar Crossroads: Flannery O'Connor, Walker Percy, and Catholic Vision in Postwar Southern Fiction*. Baton Rouge: Louisiana State University Press, 2004.

Orvell, Miles. *Flannery O'Connor: An Introduction*. Jackson: University Press of Mississippi, 1991.

____________. *Invisible Parade: The Fiction of Flannery O'Connor*. Philadelphia: Temple University Press, 1972.

Paulson, Suzanne Morrow. *Flannery O'Connor: A Study of the Short Fiction*. Boston: Twayne, 1988.

Perreault, Jeanne. "The Body, The Critics, and 'The Artificial Nigger.'" *Mississippi Quarterly* 56 (Summer 2003): 389-410.

Prown, Katherine Hemple. *Revising Flannery O'Connor: Southern Literary Culture and the Problem of Female Authorship*. Charlottesville: University of Virginia Press, 2001.

Ragen, Brian Abel. *A Wreck on the Road to Damascus: Innocence, Guilt, and Conversion in Flannery O'Connor*. Chicago: Loyola University Press, 1989.

Rath, Sura P., and Mary Neff Shaw, eds. *Flannery O'Connor: New Perspectives*. Athens: University of Georgia Press, 1996.

Reiter, Robert E., ed. *Flannery O'Connor*. The Christian Critic Series. St. Louis, MO: B. Herder, 1968.

Robillard, Douglas, Jr., ed. *The Critical Response to Flannery O'Connor*. Troy, MO: Greenwood, 2004.

Scott, R. Neil. *Flannery O'Connor: An Annotated Reference Guide to Criticism*. Milledgeville, GA: Timberlane Books, 2002.

Scott, R. Neil, and Irwin Streight, eds. *Flannery O'Connor: The Contemporary Reviews*. New York: Cambridge University Press, 2009.

Seel, Cynthia. *Ritual Performance in the Fiction of Flannery O'Connor*. Rochester, NY: Camden House, 2001.

Shloss, Carol. *Flannery O'Connor's Dark Comedies: The Limits of Inference*. Baton Rouge: Louisiana State University Press, 1980.

Simpson, Melissa. *Flannery O'Connor: A Biography*. Troy, MO: Greenwood, 2005.

Spivey, Ted Ray. *Flannery O'Connor: The Woman, the Thinker, the Visionary*. Macon, GA: Mercer University Press, 1995.

Srigley, Susan. *Flannery O'Connor's Sacramental Art*. Chicago: University of Notre Dame Press, 2004.

___________. "Penance and Love in *Wise Blood*: Seeing Redemption." *Flannery O'Connor Review* 7 (2009): 91-100.

Stephens, Martha. *The Question of Flannery O'Connor*. Baton Rouge: Louisiana State University Press, 1973.

Streight, Irwin Howard. "The Ghost of Flannery O'Connor in the Songs of Bruce Springsteen." *Flannery O'Connor Review* 6 (2008): 11-29.

___________. "Is There a Text in This Man? A Semiotic Reading of 'Parker's Back.'" *Flannery O'Connor Bulletin* 22 (1993): 1-11.

Sykes, John D., Jr. *Flannery O'Connor, Walker Percy, and the Aesthetic of Revelation*. Columbia: University of Missouri Press, 2007.

Walters, Dorothy. *Flannery O'Connor*. New York: Twayne, 1973.

Weisenburger, Steven. "Style in *Wise Blood*." *Genre* 16 (1983): 75-97.

Westarp, Karl-Heinz. *Precision and Depth in Flannery O'Connor's Short Stories*. Aarhus, Denmark: Aarhus University Press, 2002.

Westarp, Karl-Heinz, and Jan Nordby Gretlund, eds. *Realist of Distances: Flannery O'Connor Revisited*. Aarhus, Denmark: Aarhus University Press, 1987.

Westling, Louise. "Flannery O'Connor's Mothers and Daughters." *Twentieth Century Literature* 24 (Winter 1978): 510-22.

___________. *Sacred Groves and Ravaged Gardens: The Fiction of Eudora Welty, Carson McCullers, and Flannery O'Connor*. Athens: University of Georgia Press, 1985.

Whitt, Margaret Earley. *Understanding Flannery O'Connor*. Columbia: University of South Carolina Press, 1995.

Wilson, Carol Y. "Family as Affliction, Family as Promise in *The Violent Bear It Away*." *Studies in the Literary Imagination* 20 (Fall 1987): 77-86.

Wood, Ralph C. *The Comedy of Redemption: Christian Faith and Comic Vision in Four American Novelists*. Notre Dame, IN: University of Notre Dame Press, 1988.

___________. *Flannery O'Connor and the Christ-Haunted South*. Grand Rapids, MI: William B. Eerdmans, 2004

Young, Thomas Daniel. "Flannery O'Connor's View of the South: God's Earth and His Universe." *Studies in Literary Imagination* 20 (Fall 1987): 5-14.

CRITICAL INSIGHTS

About the Editor

Charles E. May is Professor Emeritus at California State University, Long Beach. He is the author of *Edgar Allan Poe: A Study of the Short Fiction* and *The Short Story: The Reality of Artifice*. He is editor of *Short Story Theories*, *New Short Story Theories*, *Twentieth-Century European Short Story*, and *Fiction's Many Worlds*. He has published more than three hundred articles and reviews on the short story in various scholarly journals, literary quarterlies, reference works, and newspapers. He writes a blog titled "Reading the Short Story" at may-on-the-short-story.blogspot.com.

About *The Paris Review*

The Paris Review is America's preeminent literary quarterly, dedicated to discovering and publishing the best new voices in fiction, nonfiction, and poetry. The magazine was founded in Paris in 1953 by the young American writers Peter Matthiessen and Doc Humes, and edited there and in New York for its first fifty years by George Plimpton. Over the decades, *The Paris Review* has introduced readers to the earliest writings of Jack Kerouac, Philip Roth, T. C. Boyle, V. S. Naipaul, Ha Jin, Ann Patchett, Jay McInerney, Mona Simpson, and Edward P. Jones, and published numerous now-classic works, including Roth's *Goodbye, Columbus*, Donald Barthelme's *Alice*, Jim Carroll's *Basketball Diaries*, and selections from Samuel Beckett's *Molloy* (his first publication in English). The first chapter of Jeffrey Eugenides's *The Virgin Suicides* appeared in *The Paris Review*'s pages, as have stories by Rick Moody, David Foster Wallace, Denis Johnson, Jim Crace, Lorrie Moore, and Jeanette Winterson.

The Paris Review's renowned Writers at Work series of interviews, whose early installments include legendary conversations with E. M. Forster, William Faulkner, and Ernest Hemingway, is one of the landmarks of world literature. The interviews received a George Polk Award and were nominated for a Pulitzer Prize. Among the more than three hundred interviewees are Robert Frost, Marianne Moore, W. H. Auden, Elizabeth Bishop, Susan Sontag, and Toni Morrison. Recent issues feature conversations with Jonathan Franzen, Norman Rush, Louise Erdrich, Joan Didion, Norman Mailer, R. Crumb, Michel Houellebecq, Marilynne Robinson, David Mitchell, Annie Proulx, and Gay Talese. In November 2009, Picador published the final volume of a four-volume series of anthologies of *Paris Review* interviews. *The New York Times* called the Writers at Work series "the most remarkable and extensive interviewing project we possess."

The Paris Review is edited by Lorin Stein, who was named to the post in 2010. The editorial team has published fiction by Lydia Davis, André Aciman, Sam Lipsyte, Damon Galgut, Mohsin Hamid, Uzodinma Iweala, James Lasdun, Padgett Powell, Richard Price, and Sam Shepard. Recent poetry selections include work by Frederick

Seidel, Carol Muske-Dukes, John Ashbery, Kay Ryan, Mary Jo Bang, Sharon Olds, Charles Wright, and Mary Karr. Writing published in the magazine has been anthologized in *Best American Short Stories* (2006, 2007, and 2008), *Best American Poetry*, *Best Creative Non-Fiction*, the Pushcart Prize anthology, and *O. Henry Prize Stories*.

The magazine presents three annual awards. The Hadada Award for lifelong contribution to literature has recently been given to Joan Didion, Norman Mailer, Peter Matthiessen, John Ashbery, and, in 2010, Philip Roth. The Plimpton Prize for Fiction, awarded to a debut or emerging writer brought to national attention in the pages of *The Paris Review*, was presented in 2007 to Benjamin Percy, to Jesse Ball in 2008, and to Alistair Morgan in 2009. In 2011, the magazine inaugurated the Terry Southern Prize for Humor.

The Paris Review was a finalist for the 2008 and 2009 National Magazine Awards in fiction and won the 2007 National Magazine Award in photojournalism. *The Los Angeles Times* recently called *The Paris Review* "an American treasure with true international reach," and *The New York Times* designated it "a thing of sober beauty."

Since 1999 *The Paris Review* has been published by The Paris Review Foundation, Inc., a not-for-profit 501(c)(3) organization.

The Paris Review is available in digital form to libraries worldwide in selected academic databases exclusively from EBSCO Publishing. Libraries can contact EBSCO at 1-800-653-2726 for details. For more information on *The Paris Review* or to subscribe, please visit: www.theparisreview.org.

Contributors

Charles E. May is Professor Emeritus at California State University, Long Beach. He is the author of *Edgar Allan Poe: A Study of the Short Fiction* and *The Short Story: The Reality of Artifice*. He is editor of *Short Story Theories*, *New Short Story Theories*, *Twentieth-Century European Short Story*, and *Fiction's Many Worlds*. He has published more than three hundred articles and reviews on the short story in various scholarly journals, literary quarterlies, reference works, and newspapers. He writes a blog titled "Reading the Short Story" at may-on-the-short-story.blogspot.com.

Paul Elie is the author of *The Life You Save May Be Your Own*, a group portrait of Flannery O'Connor, Walker Percy, Dorothy Day, and Thomas Merton.

Susan Srigley's area of expertise is religious ethics and literature. Her work has focused on the interplay between ancient spiritual thinkers and traditions and their dramatic representation in modern literary texts. She is the author of *Flannery O'Connor's Sacramental Art* (University of Notre Dame Press, 2004), and the editor and one of the contributors to a forthcoming collection of essays, *Dark Faith: New Essays on Flannery O'Connor's "The Violent Bear It Away,"* to be published by the University of Notre Dame Press.

John Hayes is Visiting Assistant Professor of History at Wake Forest University. A native of Atlanta, he holds a Ph.D. in history from the University of Georgia. He is currently completing a book manuscript on folk religion in the New South. He first encountered Flannery O'Connor's fiction in college, and he has been captivated by her violent, grotesque "Christ-haunted" South ever since. He confesses to having made a very amateurish film based on "Good Country People," and to sneaking onto the grounds of Andalusia years before it was legally open to the public.

Avis Hewitt, Associate Professor of English at Grand Valley State University in Allendale, Michigan, has published essays on Mary McCarthy, Denise Levertov, John Updike, and Flannery O'Connor in *Christianity and Literature*, *Renascence*, the *Flannery O'Connor Review*, and three book collections. In 2006 she directed an O'Connor conference in Grand Rapids, and in 2010 a collection of essays that she coedited was published by University of Tennessee Press under the title *Flannery O'Connor in the Age of Terrorism*. She serves as editor of *Cheers! The Flannery O'Connor Society Newsletter.*

Irwin H. Streight is Associate Professor in the Department of English at the Royal Military College of Canada in Kingston, Ontario. He is coeditor, with R. Neil Scott, of two major reference works on Flannery O'Connor: *Flannery O'Connor: An Annotated Reference Guide to Criticism* (2002), which won a *Choice* Outstanding Academic Title award; and *Flannery O'Connor: The Contemporary Reviews* (2009), volume 16 in the Cambridge University Press American Critical Archives series. He has also coedited *Reading the Boss: Interdisciplinary Approaches to the Works of Bruce*

Springsteen (2010), which includes a chapter that explores O'Connor's influence on Springsteen's artistic vision and songcraft.

Arthur F. Kinney is Thomas W. Copeland Professor of Literary History and Director of the Massachusetts Center for Renaissance Studies at the University of Massachusetts, Amherst. He has published a catalogue of Flannery O'Connor's library in addition to essays on her and several books on Faulkner, including *Faulkner's Narrative Poetics*. He holds both the Paul Oskar Kristeller and Jean Robertson Lifetime Achievement Awards.

T. W. Hendricks teaches English and philosophy at Stevenson University in Maryland. He has spoken and published on Edwin Arlington Robinson, Robert Frost, Archibald MacLeish, and Robert Lowell. He received his doctorate from the Catholic University of America for a dissertation on Theodore Maynard, an expatriate British poet who wrote perceptively about American modernist poetry. He is presently researching Flannery O'Connor's reading of François Mauriac.

John Desmond is Professor of English Emeritus at Whitman College. He is the author of *Risen Sons: Flannery O'Connor's Vision of History* (1987), *At the Crossroads: Ethical and Religious Themes in the Writings of Walker Percy* (1997), *Walker Percy's Search for Community* (2005), and *Gravity and Grace: Seamus Heaney and the Force of Light* (2009). He also has published numerous essays on Flannery O'Connor, Walker Percy, William Faulkner, Eudora Welty, Seamus Heaney, Graham Greene, Bernard Malamud, Mark Twain and Don Delillo.

Henry (Hank) T. Edmondson III teaches in the Department of Government at Georgia College, Flannery O'Connor's alma mater, where he is the Director of the Center for Transatlantic Studies. He is the author of, among other books, *Return to Good and Evil: Flannery O'Connor's Response to Nihilism* (Lexington Books, 2002) and numerous articles on O'Connor in a variety of journals and magazines. He was the co-director of "Reason, Fiction & Faith: An International Flannery O'Connor Conference" in Rome, Italy, April 20-22, 2009.

J. P. Steed earned his M.F.A. in creative writing at the University of Idaho and his Ph.D. in American literature at the University of Nevada, Las Vegas. He taught literature and writing for several years, publishing nearly two dozen scholarly articles as well as short fiction and poetry before leaving academia to go to law school. He now practices law in Austin, Texas—and continues to read O'Connor as much as possible.

Denise T. Askin is Professor of English Emerita at Saint Anselm College, where she also served as Executive Vice President. She received her Ph.D. from the University of Notre Dame and has taught courses in American Literature, the theory of comedy, and Native American literature. Her publications include articles on Walt Whitman, T. S. Eliot, Flannery O'Connor, and the eighteenth-century Mohegan preacher Samson Occom.

Peter A. Smith holds a Ph.D. from the University of Notre Dame, specialization in American fiction. He has been teaching for more than twenty-five years and currently teaches American literature and other classes at Kentucky State University, where he is a Professor of English.

Bryant N. Wyatt is the author of articles on Mark Twain, John Steinbeck, Frank Norris, and John Updike. He taught English at Virginia State University for twenty-nine years, from which he retired as a distinguished professor emeritus. Professor Wyatt died on January 27, 2007.

Richard Giannone, professor of English at Fordham University, is the author of *Flannery O'Connor and the Mystery of Love* (1989) and *Flannery O'Connor, Hermit Novelist* (2000).

Ronald Emerick is a professor of English at Indiana University of Pennsylvania, where he teaches undergraduate American literature courses and graduate courses in contemporary American fiction, Southern witers, and realism and naturalism. Recent publications include articles on Flannery O'Connor, Gail Godwin, Amy Tan, Frank Norris, and Philip Roth.

Marie Lienard-Yeterian is Associate Professor of American Literature and Cinema at the École Polytechnique, France. Her major fields of research are Southern literature, American theater, and the American South in film. Her publications include articles on William Faulkner, Flannery O'Connor, Ernest Gaines, Tennessee Williams, J. Ray, *Deliverance*, *Midnight in the Garden of Good and Evil*, *Cold Mountain*, and *No Country for Old Men*. She also has written a book titled *Faulkner et le cinéma* (Michel Houdiard Editeur, 2010), and she has coauthored a book on the Southern Gothic and Grotesque (*Nouvelles du Sud*, Éditions École Polytechnique, 2007) and coedited *Le Sud au cinéma* and *Culture et Mémoire* (Éditions de l'École Polytechnique, 2008 and 2009).

Christina Bieber Lake is Associate Professor of English at Wheaton College, where she teaches classes in contemporary American literature, African American literature, and literary theory. Author of *The Incarnational Art of Flannery O'Connor* (Mercer University Press, 2005), she is interested in the theological importance of embracing one's limitations in a culture that explicitly denies them. She is currently at work on *Prophets of the Posthuman*, a project that examines, through fiction, motivations for human enhancement through biotechnology.

Acknowledgments

"The *Paris Review* Perspective" by Paul Elie. Copyright © 2012 by Paul Elie. Special appreciation goes to Christopher Cox, Nathaniel Rich, and David Wallace-Wells, editors at *The Paris Review.*

"Flannery O'Connor and the Art of the Holy" by Arthur F. Kinney. From *Virginia Quarterly Review* 64.2 (Spring 1988): 215-230. Copyright © 1988 by *Virginia Quarterly Review.* Reprinted with permission of *Virginia Quarterly Review.*

"Flannery O'Connor's 'Spoiled Prophet'" by T. W. Hendricks. From *Modern Age* 51.3-4 (Summer/Fall 2009): 202-210. Copyright © 2009 by Intercollegiate Studies Institute. Reprinted with permission of Intercollegiate Studies Institute.

"Flannery O'Connor's Misfit and the Mystery of Evil" by John Desmond. From *Renascence* 56.2 (Winter 2004): 129-137. Copyright © 2004 by Marquette University. Reprinted with permission of Marquette University.

"'Wingless Chickens': 'Good Country People' and the Seduction of Nihilism" by Henry T. Edmondson III. From *Flannery O'Connor Review* 2 (2003-2004): 63-73. Copyright © 2004 by *Flannery O'Connor Review.* Reprinted with permission of *Flannery O'Connor Review.*

"'Through Our Laughter We Are Involved': Bergsonian Humor in Flannery O'Connor's Fiction" by J. P. Steed. From *The Midwest Quarterly* 46.3 (Spring 2005): 299-313. Copyright © 2005 by *The Midwest Quarterly.* Reprinted with permission of *The Midwest Quarterly.*

"Carnival in the 'Temple': Flannery O'Connor's Dialogic Parable of Artistic Vocation" by Denise T. Askin. From *Christianity and Literature* 56.4 (Summer 2007): 555-572. Copyright © 2007 by *Christianity and Literature*. Reprinted with permission of *Christianity and Literature*.

"Flannery O'Connor's Empowered Women" by Peter A. Smith. From *The Southern Literary Journal* 26.2 (1994): 35-47. Copyright © 1994 by the Department of English and Comparative Literature of the University of North Carolina at Chapel Hill. Published by the University of North Carolina Press. Used by permission of the publisher. www.uncpress.unc.edu

"The Domestic Dynamics of Flannery O'Connor: *Everything That Rises Must Converge*" by Bryant N. Wyatt. From *Twentieth Century Literature* 38.1 (1992): 66-88. Copyright © 1992 by *Twentieth Century Literature*. Reprinted with permission of *Twentieth Century Literature*.

"'The Artificial Nigger' and the Redemptive Quality of Suffering" by Richard Giannone. From *Flannery O'Connor Bulletin* 12 (January 1983): 5-16. Copyright © 1983 by *Flannery O'Connor Review.* Reprinted with permission of *Flannery O'Connor Review.*

"*Wise Blood*: O'Connor's Romance of Alienation" by Ronald Emerick. From *Lit-*

erature and Belief 12 (1992): 27-38. Copyright © 1992 by Brigham Young University Press. Reprinted with permission of Brigham Young University Press.

"From Manners to Mystery: Flannery O'Connor's Titles" by Marie Lienard. From *South Atlantic Review* 71.2 (Spring 2006): 115-125. Copyright © 2006 by South Atlantic Modern Language Association. Reprinted with permission of South Atlantic Modern Language Association.

"Called to the Beautiful: The Incarnational Art of Flannery O'Connor's *The Violent Bear It Away*" by Christina Bieber. From *Xavier Review* 18.1 (January 1998): 44-62. Copyright © 1998 by Xavier Review Press. Reprinted with permission of Xavier Review Press.

Index